Annual Editions:
Health,
Thirty-Sixth Edition

Eileen L. Daniel

http://create.mheducation.com

ISBN-10: 125924315X   ISBN-13: 9781259243158

Contents

Preface

America is in the midst of a revolution that is changing the way millions of Americans view their health. Traditionally, most people delegated responsibility for their health to their physicians and hoped that medical science would be able to cure whatever ailed them. This approach to healthcare emphasized the role of medical technology and funneled billions of dollars into medical research. The net result of all this spending is the most technically advanced and expensive healthcare system in the world.

In an attempt to rein in healthcare costs, the healthcare delivery system moved from privatized healthcare coverage to what is termed "managed care." While managed care has turned the tide regarding the rising cost of healthcare, it has done so by limiting reimbursement for many cutting-edge technologies. Unfortunately, many people also feel that it has lowered the overall quality of care that is being given. Perhaps the saving grace is that we live at a time in which chronic illnesses rather than acute illnesses are our number one health threat, and many of these illnesses can be prevented or controlled by our lifestyle choices. The net result of these changes has prompted millions of individuals to assume more personal responsibility for safeguarding their own health. Evidence of this change in attitude can be seen in the growing interest in nutrition, physical fitness, dietary supplements, and stress management.

If we as a nation are to capitalize on this new health consciousness, we must devote more time and energy to educate Americans in the health sciences, so that they will be better able to make informed choices about their health. Health is a complex and dynamic subject, and it is practically impossible for anyone to stay abreast of all the current research findings. In the past, most of us have relied on books, newspapers, magazines, and television as our primary sources for medical/health information, but today it is possible to access a vast amount of health information, any time of the day, without even leaving one's home. Unfortunately, quantity and availability does not necessarily translate into quality, and this is particularly true in the area of medical/health information. Just as the Internet is a great source for reliable and timely information, it is also a vehicle for the dissemination of misleading and fraudulent information. Currently, there are no standards or regulations regarding the posting of health

content on the Internet, and this has led to a plethora of misinformation and quackery in the medical/health arena. Given this vast amount of health information, our task as health educators is twofold: (1) to provide our students with the most up-to-date and accurate information available on major health issues of our time and (2) to teach our students the skills that will enable them to sort out facts from fiction, in order to become informed consumers. *Annual Editions: Health* was designed to aid in this task. It offers a sampling of quality articles that represent the latest thinking on a variety of health issues, and it also serves as a tool for developing critical thinking skills.

The articles in this volume were carefully chosen on the basis of their quality and timeliness. Because this book is revised and updated annually, it contains information that is not generally available in any standard textbook. As such, it serves as a valuable resource for both teachers and students. This edition of *Annual Editions: Health* has been updated to reflect the latest thinking on a variety of contemporary health issues. We hope that you find this edition to be a helpful learning tool with a user-friendly presentation. The topical areas presented in this edition mirror those that are normally covered in introductory health courses: Promoting Healthy Behavior Change, Stress and Mental Health, Nutritional Health, Exercise and Weight Management, Drugs and Health, Sexuality and Relationships, Preventing and Fighting Disease, Healthcare and the Healthcare System, Consumer Health, and Contemporary Health Hazards. Because of the interdependence of the various elements that constitute health, the articles selected were written by authors with diverse educational backgrounds and expertise, including naturalists, environmentalists, psychologists, economists, sociologists, nutritionists, consumer advocates, and traditional health practitioners.

Editor
Eileen Daniel is a professor of Health Science and Associate Vice Provost for Academic Affairs at SUNY College at Brockport. She earned her doctorate in health education from the University of Oregon and a BS in Dietetics and Nutrition from the Rochester Institute of Technology. She has published over 40 articles in the scientific press and is also the author of *Taking Sides: Clashing Views on Health*.

Correlation Guide

The *Annual Editions* series provides students with convenient, inexpensive access to current, carefully selected articles from the public press. **Annual Editions: Health, 36/e** is an easy-to-use reader that presents articles on important topics such as *consumer health, exercise nutrition,* and many more. For more information on *Annual Editions* and other *McGraw-Hill Create*™ titles, visit www.mcgrawhillcreate.com.

This convenient guide matches the articles in **Annual Editions: Health, 36/e** with **Core Concepts in Health, Brief, 13/e** by Insel/Roth.

Core Concepts in Health, Brief, 13/e	Annual Editions: Health, 36/e
Chapter 1: Taking Charge of your Health	Crimes of the Heart Solve Your Energy Crisis: A Guide to Finding—and Fixing—the Cause of Your Fatigue The Perils of Higher Education
Chapter 2: Stress: The Constant Challenge	Go Forth in Anger Internet Addiction Social Withdrawal and Violence—Newtown, Connecticut Sound Mind, Sound Student Body
Chapter 3: Psychological Health	Giving ADHD a Rest: with Diagnosis Rates Exploding Wildly, Is the Disorder a Mental Health Crisis—or a Cultural One? Internet Addiction Social Withdrawal and Violence—Newtown, Connecticut
Chapter 4: Intimate Relationships and Communication	Masters of Their Domain The Marriage Paradox: Love, Lies, and the Power of Self-Deception The Mixed-Bag Buddy [and Other Friendship Conundrums] There's No Evidence Online Dating Is Threatening Commitment or Marriage
Chapter 5: Sexuality, Pregnancy, and Childbirth	Masters of Their Domain The Marriage Paradox: Love, Lies, and the Power of Self-Deception The Mixed-Bag Buddy [and Other Friendship Conundrums] There's No Evidence Online Dating Is Threatening Commitment or Marriage
Chapter 6: Contraception and Abortion	Masters of Their Domain The Marriage Paradox: Love, Lies, and the Power of Self-Deception The Mixed-Bag Buddy [and Other Friendship Conundrums] There's No Evidence Online Dating Is Threatening Commitment or Marriage
Chapter 7: Drug Abuse and Addiction	Drowned in a Stream of Prescriptions Philip Seymour Hoffman Death: a Cautionary Tale about Branded Heroin? Pot Goes Legit: What the End of Prohibition Looks Like in Colorado Rethinking Drug Policy Assumptions So Long, Lance. Next, 21st-Century Doping Sparking Controversy
Chapter 8: Alcohol and Tobacco	Drowned in a Stream of Prescriptions Rethinking Drug Policy Assumptions So Long, Lance. Next, 21st-Century Doping Sparking Controversy
Chapter 9: Nutrition Basics	Fat Facts and Fat Fiction Wonderful Wheat: Why This Ancient Staple Is Still Good for You Yes, Healthful Fast Food Is Possible. But Edible?
Chapter 10: Exercise for Health and Fitness	Eat Like a Greek Solve Your Energy Crisis: A Guide to Finding—and Fixing—the Cause of Your Fatigue
Chapter 11: Weight Management	Dieting on a Budget Eat Like a Greek The Surprising Reason Why Heavy Isn't Healthy Yes, Healthful Fast Food Is Possible. But Edible?
Chapter 12: Cardiovascular Disease and Cancer	The Broken Vaccine The High Cost of "Hooking Up" The New Sex Cancer
Chapter 13: Immunity and Infection	Antibiotics and the Meat We Eat Refusing Vaccination Puts Others at Risk The Broken Vaccine The High Cost of "Hooking Up" The Secret Life of Dirt: At the Finnish-Russian Border, Scientists Investigate a Medical Mystery

(continued)

(concluded)

Core Concepts in Health, Brief, 13/e	Annual Editions: Health, 36/e
Chapter 14: Environmental Health	Antibiotics and the Meat We Eat Bed Bugs: the Pesticide Dilemma Is PTSD Contagious? Suicide, Guns, and Public Policy The New Sex Cancer The Secret Life of Dirt: At the Finnish-Russian Border, Scientists Investigate a Medical Mystery
Chapter 15: Conventional and Complementary Medicine	Consumers Should Drive Medicine Deviated: a Memoir How Government Killed the Medical Profession How Not to Die Problems with Modern Medicine: Too Much Emphasis on Disease, Not Enough on Managing Risk Still Unsafe: Why the American Medical Establishment Cannot Reduce Medical Errors
Chapter 16: Personal Safety	Antibiotics and the Meat We Eat Bed Bugs: the Pesticide Dilemma Hey! Parents, Leave Those Kids Alone Refusing Vaccination Could Put Others at Risk The Secret Life of Dirt: At the Finnish-Russian Border, Scientists Investigate a Medical Mystery The Surprising Reason Why Heavy Isn't Healthy
Chapter 17: The Challenge of Aging	Deviated: a Memoir How Government Killed the Medical Profession How Not to Die Still Unsafe: Why the American Medical Establishment Cannot Reduce Medical Errors

This convenient guide matches the articles in **Annual Editions: Health, 36/e** with **Understanding Your Health, 12/e** by Payne et al.

Understanding Your Health, 12/e	Annual Editions: Health, 36/e
Chapter 1: Shaping Your Health	Crimes of the Heart Solve Your Energy Crisis: A Guide to Finding—and Fixing—the Cause of Your Fatigue The Perils of Higher Education
Chapter 2: Achieving Psychological Health	Giving ADHD a Rest: with Diagnosis Rates Exploding Wildly, Is the Disorder a Mental Health Crisis—or a Cultural One? Go Forth in Anger Internet Addiction Social Withdrawal and Violence—Newtown, Connecticut Sound Mind, Sound Student Body
Chapter 3: Managing Stress	Go Forth in Anger Internet Addiction Social Withdrawal and Violence—Newtown, Connecticut Sound Mind, Sound Student Body
Chapter 4: Becoming Physically Fit	Dieting on a Budget Eat Like a Greek Solve Your Energy Crisis: A Guide to Finding—and Fixing—the Cause of Your Fatigue
Chapter 5: Understanding Nutrition and Your Diet	Fat Facts and Fat Fiction Wonderful Wheat: Why This Ancient Staple Is Still Good for You Yes, Healthful Fast Food Is Possible. But Edible?
Chapter 6: Maintaining a Healthy Weight	Dieting on a Budget Eat Like a Greek The Surprising Reason Why Heavy Isn't Healthy Yes, Healthful Fast Food Is Possible. But Edible?
Chapter 7: Making Decisions About Drug Use	Drowned in a Stream of Prescriptions Philip Seymour Hoffman Death: a Cautionary Tale about Branded Heroin? Pot Goes Legit: What the End of Prohibition Looks Like in Colorado Rethinking Drug Policy Assumptions So Long, Lance. Next, 21st-Century Doping Sparking Controversy

(continued)

(concluded)

Understanding Your Health, 12/e	Annual Editions: Health, 36/e
Chapter 8: Taking Control of Alcohol Drug Use	Drowned in a Stream of Prescriptions Philip Seymour Hoffman Death: a Cautionary Tale about Branded Heroin? Pot Goes Legit: What the End of Prohibition Looks Like in Colorado Rethinking Drug Policy Assumptions So Long, Lance. Next, 21st-Century Doping Sparking Controversy
Chapter 9: Rejecting Tobacco Use	Drowned in a Stream of Prescriptions Philip Seymour Hoffman Death: a Cautionary Tale about Branded Heroin? Rethinking Drug Policy Assumptions So Long, Lance. Next, 21st-Century Doping Sparking Controversy
Chapter 10: Enhancing Your Cardiovascular Health	The Broken Vaccine The High Cost of "Hooking Up"
Chapter 11: Living with Cancer	The Broken Vaccine The High Cost of "Hooking Up" The New Sex Cancer The Surprising Reason Why Heavy Isn't Healthy
Chapter 12: Managing Chronic Conditions	Problems with Modern Medicine: Too Much Emphasis on Disease, Not Enough on Managing Risk The Broken Vaccine The High Cost of "Hooking Up"
Chapter 13: Preventing Infectious Diseases	Antibiotics and the Meat We Eat Refusing Vaccination Puts Others at Risk The Broken Vaccine The High Cost of "Hooking Up" The Secret Life of Dirt: At the Finnish-Russian Border, Scientists Investigate a Medical Mystery
Chapter 14: Exploring the Origins of Sexuality	Masters of Their Domain The Marriage Paradox: Loves, Lies, and the Power of Self-Deception The Mixed-Bag Buddy [and Other Friendship Conundrums] There's No Evidence Online Dating Is Threatening Commitment or Marriage
Chapter 15: Understanding Sexual Behavior and Relationship	Masters of Their Domain The Marriage Paradox: Loves, Lies, and the Power of Self-Deception The Mixed-Bag Buddy [and Other Friendship Conundrums] There's No Evidence Online Dating Is Threatening Commitment or Marriage
Chapter 16: Managing Your Fertility	Masters of Their Domain The Marriage Paradox: Loves, Lies, and the Power of Self-Deception The Mixed-Bag Buddy [and Other Friendship Conundrums] There's No Evidence Online Dating Is Threatening Commitment or Marriage
Chapter 17: Becoming a Parent	Masters of Their Domain The Marriage Paradox: Loves, Lies, and the Power of Self-Deception The Mixed-Bag Buddy [and Other Friendship Conundrums] There's No Evidence Online Dating Is Threatening Commitment or Marriage
Chapter 18: Becoming an Informed Health Care Consumer	Consumers Should Drive Medicine Deviated: a Memoir How Government Killed the Medical Profession How Not to Die Problems with Modern Medicine: Too Much Emphasis on Disease, Not Enough on Managing Risk Still Unsafe: Why the American Medical Establishment Cannot Reduce Medical Errors
Chapter 19: Preventing Injuries	Antibiotics and the Meat We Eat Bed Bugs: the Pesticide Dilemma Hey! Parents, Leave Those Kids Alone Suicide, Guns, and Public Policy The Surprising Reason Why Heavy Isn't Healthy
Chapter 20: The Environment and Your Health	Antibiotics and the Meat We Eat Bed Bugs: the Pesticide Dilemma Is PTSD Contagious? Suicide, Guns, and Public Policy The New Sex Cancer
Chapter 21: Accepting Dying and Death	How Not to Die

Topic Guide

This Topic Guide suggests how the selections in this book relate to the subjects covered in your course.

All the articles that relate to each topic are listed below the bold-faced term.

Unit 1

UNIT

Prepared by: Eileen Daniel, *SUNY College at Brockport*

Promoting Healthy Behavior Change

"Those of us who protect our health daily and those of us who put our health in constant jeopardy have exactly the same mortality: 100 percent. The difference, of course, is the timing." This quotation from Elizabeth M. Whelan, ScD, MPH, reminds us that we must all face the fact that we are going to die sometime. The question that is decided by our behavior is when and, to a certain extent, how. This book, and especially this unit, is designed to assist students to develop the cognitive skills and knowledge that, when put to use, help make the moment of our death come as late as possible in our lives and maintain our health as long as possible. While we cannot control many of the things that happen to us, we must all strive to accept personal responsibility for, and make informed decisions about, things that we can control. This is no minor task, but it is one in which the potential reward is life itself. Perhaps the best way to start this process is by educating ourselves on the relative risks associated with the various behaviors and lifestyle choices we make. To minimize all the risks to life and health would be to significantly limit the quality of our lives, and while this might be a choice that some would make, it certainly is not the goal of health education. A more logical approach to risk reduction would be to educate the public on the relative risks associated with various behaviors and lifestyle choices so that they are capable of making informed decisions. While it may seem obvious that certain behaviors, such as smoking, entail a high level of risk, the significance of others such as toxic waste sites and food additives are frequently blown out of proportion to the actual risks involved. The net result of this type of distortion is that many Americans tend to minimize the dangers of known hazards such as tobacco and alcohol and focus attention instead on potentially minor health hazards over which they have little or no control.

Educating the public on the relative risk of various health behaviors is only part of the job that health educators must tackle in order to assist individuals in making informed choices regarding their health. They must also teach the skills that will enable people to evaluate the validity and significance of new information as it becomes available. Just how important informed decision making is in our daily lives is evidenced by the numerous health-related media announcements and articles that fill our newspapers, magazines, and television broadcasts. Rather than informing and enlightening the public on significant new medical discoveries, many of these announcements do little more than add to the level of confusion or exaggerate or sensationalize health issues.

Let's assume for a minute that the scientific community is in general agreement that certain behaviors clearly promote our health while others damage our health. Given this information, are you likely to make adjustments to your lifestyle to comply with the findings? Logic would suggest that of course you would, but experience has taught us that information alone isn't enough to bring about behavioral change in many people. Why is it that so many people continue to make bad choices regarding their health behaviors when they are fully aware of the risks involved? And why do women take better care of themselves than men? Health behaviors such as alcohol, substance abuse, and lack of consistent health care among men, which contributes to men getting sick younger and dying faster than women. We can take vows to try and undo or minimize the negative health behaviors of our past. However, while strategies such as these may work for those who feel they are at risk, how do we help those who do not feel that they are at risk, or those who feel that it is too late in their lives for the changes to matter? For students, college is a place to learn and grow, but for many it becomes four years of bad diet, too little sleep, and too much alcohol. These negative health behaviors affect not only the students' health but also their grades too.

Article   Prepared by: Eileen L. Daniel, *SUNY Brockport*

Crimes of the Heart

It's time society stopped reinforcing the bad behavior that leads to heart disease—and pursued policies to prevent it.

WALTER C. WILLETT AND ANNE UNDERWOOD

Learning Outcomes

After reading this article, you will be able to:

- Explain how changing an area's environment helps to support healthier lifestyles.

- Describe lifestyles conducive to heart health.

- Describe what specific public health measures can contribute to healthy behaviors.

Until last year, the residents of Albert Lea, Mn., were no healthier than any other Americans. Then the city became the first American town to sign on to the AARP/Blue Zones Vitality Project—the brainchild of writer Dan Buettner, whose 2008 book, *The Blue Zones,* detailed the health habits of the world's longest-lived people. His goal was to bring the same benefits to middle America—not by forcing people to diet and exercise, but by changing their everyday environments in ways that encourage a healthier lifestyle.

What followed was a sort of townwide makeover. The city laid new sidewalks linking residential areas with schools and shopping centers. It built a recreational path around a lake and dug new plots for community gardens. Restaurants made healthy changes to their menus. Schools banned eating in hallways (reducing the opportunities for kids to munch on snack food) and stopped selling candy for fundraisers. (They sold wreaths instead.) More than 2,600 of the city's 18,000 residents volunteered, too, selecting from more than a dozen heart-healthy measures—for example, ridding their kitchens of supersize dinner plates (which encourage larger portions) and forming "walking schoolbuses" to escort kids to school on foot.

The results were stunning. In six months, participants lost an average of 2.6 pounds and boosted their estimated life expectancy by 3.1 years. Even more impressive, health-care claims for city and school employees fell for the first time in a decade—by 32 percent over 10 months. And benefits didn't accrue solely to volunteers. Thanks to the influence of social networks, says Buettner, "even the curmudgeons who didn't want to be involved ended up modifying their behaviors."

Isn't it time we all followed Albert Lea's example? Diet and exercise programs routinely fail not for lack of willpower, but because the society in which we live favors unhealthy behaviors. In 2006, cardiovascular disease cost $403 billion in medical bills and lost productivity. By 2025 an aging population is expected to drive up the total by as much as 54 percent. But creative government programs could help forestall the increases—and help our hearts, too. A few suggestions:

Require graphic warnings on cigarette packages. It's easy to disregard a black-box warning that smoking is "hazardous to your health." It's not so easy to dismiss a picture of gangrenous limbs, diseased hearts, or chests sawed open for autopsy. These are exactly the types of images that the law now requires on cigarette packages in Brazil. In Canada, such warning images must cover at least half the wrapping. In 2001, the year after the Canadian law took effect, 38 percent of smokers who tried to quit cited the images. Think of it as truth in advertising.

Sponsor "commitment contracts" to quit smoking. Yale economist Dean Karlan spearheaded a test program in the Philippines in which smokers who wanted to quit deposited the money they would have spent on cigarettes into a special bank account. After six months those who had succeeded got their money back, while those who had failed lost it. Such a program could be run here by public-health clinics and offer greater incentives, such as letting winners divvy up the money forfeited by losers. Even without such an enhancement, says Karlan, "Filipino participants were 39 percent more likely to quit than those who were not offered the option."

Subsidize whole grains, fruits, and vegetables in the food-stamp program. The underprivileged tend to have disastrously unhealthy diets, and no wonder: $1 will buy 100 calories of carrots—or 1,250 calories of cookies and chips. The government should offer incentives for buying produce. The Wholesome Wave Foundation has shown the way in 12 states, providing vouchers redeemable at farmers' markets to people in the SNAP program (the official name for food stamps). "We've seen purchases of fruits and vegetables double and triple among recipients," says president and CEO Michel Nischan.

Set targets for salt reduction. The average American consumes twice the recommended daily maximum of sodium, most of it from processed foods. The result: high blood pressure, heart attacks, and strokes. But New York City is leading a campaign to encourage food manufacturers to reduce added sodium over the next five years. Consumers will barely notice the changes because they will occur so gradually. The FDA should follow New York's lead.

One urban-planning expert advocates a "road diet" in which towns eliminate a lane or two of traffic and substitute sidewalks. "When roads slim down, so do people," he says.

Incorporate physical education into No Child Left Behind. American children may be prepping like crazy for standardized tests, but they're seriously lagging in physical fitness. Regular exercise improves mood, concentration, and academic achievement. It can also help reverse the growing trend toward type 2 diabetes and early heart disease in children and teenagers.

Require that sidewalks and bike lanes be part of every federally funded road project. The government already spends 1 percent of transportation dollars on such projects. It should increase the level to 2 to 3 percent. When sidewalks are built in neighborhoods and downtowns, people start walking. "The big win for city government is that anything built to a walkable scale leases out for three to five times more money, with more tax revenue on less infrastructure," says Dan Burden, executive director of the Walkable and Livable Communities Institute. He recommends a "road diet" in which towns eliminate a lane or two of downtown traffic and substitute sidewalks. "When roads slim down, so do people," he says.

It's all reasonable. But Dan Buettner isn't waiting for any of these measures to surmount the inevitable industry hurdles. This year he's looking to scale up the Blue Zones Vitality Project to a city of 100,000 or more. "If this works, it could provide a template for the government that's replicable across the country," says his colleague Ben Leedle, CEO of Healthways, which is developing the next phase of the project. The challenges will be much steeper in large cities. But with measures like these, we could one day find ourselves growing fitter without specifically dieting or exercising. Finally, a New Year's resolution we can all keep.

Critical Thinking

1. What does a healthy environment consist of?
2. How can communities go about changing their environments to support a healthy lifestyle?
3. What are examples of public health improvements?

Create Central

www.mhhe.com/createcentral

Internet References

American Heart Association
    www.amhrt.org
U.S. National Institutes of Health (NIH)
    www.nih.gov

WALTER C. WILLETT is a physician, chair of the department of nutrition at the Harvard School of Public Health, and coauthor of *The Fertility Diet*. ANNE UNDERWOOD is a Newsweek contributor.

Willett, Walter and Underwood, Anne. From *Newsweek*, February 15, 2010, pp. 42–43. Copyright © 2010 by Anne Underwood and Walter Willett. Reprinted by permission of Anne Underwood.

Article   Prepared by: Eileen L. Daniel, *SUNY Brockport*

The Perils of Higher Education

Can't remember the difference between declensions and derivatives? Blame college. The undergrad life is a blast, but it may lead you to forget everything you learn.

Steven Kotler

Learning Outcomes

After reading this article, you will be able to:

- Explain how college students' health behaviors impact their academic status.

- Describe student lifestyles that impact health status.

- Discuss the risks associated with sleep deprivation on memory.

We go to college to learn, to soak up a dazzling array of information intended to prepare us for adult life. But college is not simply a data dump; it is also the end of parental supervision. For many students, that translates into four years of late nights, pizza banquets and boozy weekends that start on Wednesday. And while we know that bad habits are detrimental to cognition in general—think drunk driving—new studies show that the undergrad urges to eat, drink and be merry have devastating effects on learning and memory. It turns out that the exact place we go to get an education may in fact be one of the worst possible environments in which to retain anything we've learned.

Dude, I Haven't Slept in Three Days!

Normal human beings spend one-third of their lives asleep, but today's college students aren't normal. A recent survey of undergraduates and medical students at Stanford University found 80 percent of them qualified as sleep-deprived, and a poll taken by the National Sleep Foundation found that most young adults get only 6.8 hours a night.

All-night cramfests may seem to be the only option when the end of the semester looms, but in fact getting sleep—and a full dose of it—might be a better way to ace exams. Sleep is crucial to declarative memory, the hard, factual kind that helps us remember which year World War I began, or what room the

French Lit class is in. It's also essential for procedural memory, the "know-how" memory we use when learning to drive a car or write a five-paragraph essay. "Practice makes perfect," says Harvard Medical School psychologist Matt Walker, "but having a night's rest after practicing might make you even better."

Walker taught 100 people to bang out a series of nonsense sequences on a keyboard—a standard procedural memory task. When asked to replay the sequence 12 hours later, they hadn't improved. But when one group of subjects was allowed to sleep overnight before being retested, their speed and accuracy improved by 20 to 30 percent. "It was bizarre," says Walker. "We were seeing people's skills improve just by sleeping."

For procedural memory, the deep slow-wave stages of sleep were the most important for improvement—particularly during the last two hours of the night. Declarative memory, by contrast, gets processed during the slow-wave stages that come in the first two hours of sleep. "This means that memory requires a full eight hours of sleep," says Walker. He also found that if someone goes without sleep for 24 hours after acquiring a new skill, a week later they will have lost it completely. So college students who pull all-nighters during exam week might do fine on their tests but may not remember any of the material by next semester.

Walker believes that the common practice of back-loading semesters with a blizzard of papers and exams needs a rethink. "Educators are just encouraging sleeplessness," says Walker. "This is just not an effective way to force information into the brain."

Who's up for Pizza?

Walk into any college cafeteria and you'll find a smorgasbord of French fries, greasy pizza, burgers, potato chips and the like. On top of that, McDonald's, Burger King, Wendy's and other fast-food chains have been gobbling up campus real estate in recent years. With hectic schedules and skinny budgets, students find fast food an easy alternative. A recent Tufts University survey found that 50 percent of students eat too much fat, and 70 to 80 percent eat too much saturated fat.

But students who fuel their studies with fast food have something more serious than the "freshman 15" to worry about: They may literally be eating themselves stupid. Researchers have known since the late 1980s that bad eating habits contribute to the kind of cognitive decline found in diseases like Alzheimer's. Since then, they've been trying to find out exactly how a bad diet might be hard on the brain. Ann-Charlotte Granholm, director of the Center for Aging at the Medical University of South Carolina, has recently focused on trans fat, widely used in fast-food cooking because it extends the shelf life of foods. Trans fat is made by bubbling hydrogen through unsaturated fat, with copper or zinc added to speed the chemical reaction along. These metals are frequently found in the brains of people with Alzheimer's, which sparked Granholm's concern.

To investigate, she fed one group of rats a diet high in trans fat and compared them with another group fed a diet that was just as greasy but low in trans fat. Six weeks later, she tested the animals in a water maze, the rodent equivalent of a final exam in organic chemistry. "The trans-fat group made many more errors," says Granholm, especially when she used more difficult mazes.

When she examined the rats' brains, she found that trans-fat eaters had fewer proteins critical to healthy neurological function. She also saw inflammation in and around the hippocampus, the part of the brain responsible for learning and memory. "It was alarming," says Granholm. "These are the exact types of changes we normally see at the onset of Alzheimer's, but we saw them after six weeks," even though the rats were still young.

Students who fuel their studies with fast food have something serious to worry about: They may literally be eating themselves stupid.

Her work corresponds to a broader inquiry conducted by Veerendra Kumar Madala Halagaapa and Mark Mattson of the National Institute on Aging. The researchers fed four groups of mice different diets—normal, high-fat, high-sugar and high-fat/high-sugar. Each diet had the same caloric value, so that one group of mice wouldn't end up heavier. Four months later, the mice on the high-fat diets performed significantly worse than the other groups on a water maze test.

The researchers then exposed the animals to a neurotoxin that targets the hippocampus, to assess whether a high-fat diet made the mice less able to cope with brain damage. Back in the maze, all the animals performed worse than before, but the mice who had eaten the high-fat diets were the most seriously compromised. "Based on our work," says Mattson, "we'd predict that people who eat high-fat diets and high-fat/high-sugar diets are not only damaging their ability to learn and remember new information, but also putting themselves at much greater risk for all sorts of neurodegenerative disorders like Alzheimer's."

Welcome to Margaritaville State University

It's widely recognized that heavy drinking doesn't exactly boost your intellect. But most people figure that their booze-induced foolishness wears off once the hangover is gone. Instead, it turns out that even limited stints of overindulgence may have long-term effects.

Less than 20 years ago, researchers began to realize that the adult brain wasn't just a static lump of cells. They found that stem cells in the brain are constantly churning out new neurons, particularly in the hippocampus. Alcoholism researchers, in turn, began to wonder if chronic alcoholics' memory problems had something to do with nerve cell birth and growth.

In 2000, Kimberly Nixon and Fulton Crews at the University of North Carolina's Bowles Center for Alcohol Studies subjected lab rats to four days of heavy alcohol intoxication. They gave the rats a week to shake off their hangovers, then tested them on and off during the next month in a water maze. "We didn't find anything at first," says Nixon. But on the 19th day, the rats who had been on the binge performed much worse. In 19 days, the cells born during the binge had grown to maturity—and clearly, the neurons born during the boozy period didn't work properly once they reached maturity. "[The timing] was almost too perfect," says Nixon.

While normal rats generated about 2,500 new brain cells in three weeks, the drinking rats produced only 1,400. A month later, the sober rats had lost about half of those new cells through normal die-off. But all of the new cells died in the brains of the binge drinkers. "This was startling," says Nixon. "It was the first time anyone had found that alcohol not only inhibits the birth of new cells but also inhibits the ones that survive." In further study, they found that a week's abstinence produced a twofold burst of neurogenesis, and a month off the sauce brought cognitive function back to normal.

What does this have to do with a weekend keg party? A number of recent studies show that college students consume far more alcohol than anyone previously suspected. Forty-four percent of today's collegiates drink enough to be classified as binge drinkers, according to a nationwide survey of 10,000 students done at Harvard University. The amount of alcohol consumed by Nixon's binging rats far exceeded intake at a typical keg party—but other research shows that the effects of alcohol work on a sliding scale. Students who follow a weekend of heavy drinking with a week of heavy studying might not forget everything they learn. They just may struggle come test time.

Can I Bum a Smoke?

If this ledger of campus menaces worries you, here's something you really won't like: Smoking cigarettes may actually have some cognitive benefits, thanks to the power of nicotine. The chemical improves mental focus, as scientists have known since the 1950s. Nicotine also aids concentration in people who have ADHD and may protect against Alzheimer's disease. Back in 2000, a nicotine-like drug under development by the pharmaceutical company Astra Arcus USA was shown to restore the ability to learn and remember in rats with brain lesions similar to those found in Alzheimer's patients. More recently Granholm, the scientist investigating trans fats and memory, found that nicotine enhances spatial memory in healthy rats. Other researchers have found that nicotine also boosts both emotional memory (the kind that helps us *not* put our hands back in the fire after we've been burned) and auditory memory.

There's a catch: Other studies show that nicotine encourages state-dependent learning. The idea is that if, for example, you study in blue sweats, it helps to take the exam in blue sweats. In other words, what you learn while smoking is best recalled while smoking. Since lighting up in an exam room might cause problems, cigarettes probably aren't the key to getting on the dean's list.

Nonetheless, while the number of cigarette smokers continues to drop nationwide, college students are still lighting up: As many as 30 percent smoke during their years of higher education. The smoking rate for young adults between the ages of 18 and 24 has actually risen in the past decade.

All this news makes you wonder how anyone's ever managed to get an education. Or what would happen to GPAs at a vegetarian university with a 10 P.M. curfew. But you might not need to go to such extremes. While Granholm agrees that the excesses of college can be "a perfect example of what you shouldn't do to yourself if you are trying to learn," she doesn't recommend abstinence. "Moderation," she counsels, "just like in everything else. Moderation is the key to collegiate success."

Critical Thinking

1. What negative health behaviors impact college students' well-being?

2. Why do college students continue to engage in such risky behaviors?

3. How does a poor diet negatively affect learning and memory?

Create Central

www.mhhe.com/createcentral

Internet References

Columbia University's Go Ask Alice!
   www.goaskalice.columbia.edu/index.html
The Society of Behavioral Medicine
   www.sbm.org

STEVEN KOTLER, based in Los Angeles, has written for *The New York Times Magazine, National Geographic, Details, Wired* and *Outside.*

Article Prepared by: Eileen Daniel, *SUNY College at Brockport*

Solve Your Energy Crisis

A Guide to Finding—and Fixing— the Cause of Your Fatigue

CONSUMER REPORTS ON HEALTH

Learning Outcomes

After reading this article, you will be able to:

- Understand the causes of low energy.

- Explain ways to modify sleep habits.

- Describe techniques to enhance energy.

National survey results suggest that "utterly exhausted" may be America's new normal. In one survey, 37 percent of working adults admitted they'd felt fatigued in the previous two weeks. A report by the national Centers for Disease Control and Prevention found that 16 percent of women and 12 percent of men ages 45 to 64 described themselves as wiped out in the prior three months. That's worrisome, because letting fatigue drag on can mess with your mood (and may even boost your risk for depression), as well as with your health, weight, work performance, and sex life.

But there's no need to live in a dog-tired state. "When you find and fix the real cause of your fatigue, you can recover your energy and feel great again," says Martin Surks, MD, program director of the Endocrinology Division at Montefiore and the Albert Einstein College of Medicine. Assuming you're logging 7 to 9 hours of sleep time (and if you aren't, that's what you need to address first), follow these steps, in order, to help you get to the root of your weariness.

Step 1 Improve Your Sleep Hygiene

Sometimes it's not lack of sleep that causes fatigue—it's the lack of refreshing, high-quality slumber. You want to spend the optimal amount of time in deep, restorative sleep and minimize fragmented sleep. (There are several phone apps, such as SleepCycle, that can track sleep quality. The activity monitor Fitbit One does, too.) "Whenever someone is

Beverage Boost

What's the best thing to drink when you're feeling zapped? Here, the pros and cons to the most commonly touted liquid energizers.

Water

This should be your first choice. Being dehydrated, even mildly, may lead to fatigue, lack of energy, loss of concentration, and irritability, studies show.

Tea

It has enough caffeine to perk you up but not enough to cause the jitters. Green tea has 24 to 40 milligrams per eight-ounce cup. Black tea has 14 to 61 milligrams.

Coffee

A cup has 95 to 200 milligrams; most adults should have no more than 400 milligrams per day. It takes almost 6 hours for half of the caffeine you consume to be metabolized by your body, so having it too late in the day can disrupt sleep.

Energy Drinks

Energy drink labels don't always list the caffeine count. Our tests showed that they can have more than double the amount in coffee. Some may contain undesirable ingredients such as sugar. If you're looking for a pick-me-up, you're better off with a cup of tea or coffee.

Is There Such a Thing as an Energy Pill?

Many products promise to fend off fatigue and give you some oomph when you're dragging. Do they work? Are they safe? Here's what you need to know:

Vitamin B12 Shots

How they work: B12 helps your body make red blood cells, convert food into fuel, and maintain healthy nerve cells, all of which can have an effect on energy.

Our take: If you're deficient in vitamin B12, oral supplements have been shown to be as effective as shots, but if you aren't, neither shots nor supplements are likely to raise your energy level.

Armodafinil (Nuvigil) and Modafinil (Provigil)

How they work: These prescription stimulants are FDA-approved for excessive sleepiness due to narcolepsy, sleep apnea, and shift work. They're used off-label to ease fatigue in people with depression, multiple sclerosis, and other conditions.

Our take: They're costly, and have side effects, such as headaches, severe skin rashes, and tremors. They shouldn't be used in place of getting the sleep you need.

Ginseng

How it works: It's used for fatigue in traditional Chinese medicine, but the exact mechanism is unknown.

Our take: Short-term use is safe, but it may cause insomnia and blood-pressure changes. Ask a doctor before trying herbal remedies.

Tired? The Health Problems You Need to Check

If you have fatigue and . . .
difficulty concentrating, sleep disruption, loss of pleasure in activities you once enjoyed
It may be . . .
Depression

If you have fatigue and . . .
morning headaches, excessive daytime sleepiness, dozing while driving, loud snoring, you wake up at night gasping for breath
It may be . . .
Obstructive sleep apnea

If you have fatigue and . . .
frequent urination, increased thirst and hunger, blurry vision, irritability, unexplained weight loss
It may be . . .
Diabetes

If you have fatigue and . . .
weight gain, puffiness, cold sensitivity, dry skin or hair, muscle cramps
It may be . . .
Underactive thyroid

If you have fatigue and . . .
loss of appetite, fever, nausea, dark urine, clay-colored slools
It may be . . .
Hepatitis

If you have fatigue and . . .
muscle weakness, shortness of breath, you look pale
It may be . . .
Anemia

experiencing fatigue on a regular basis, they should look at their sleeping habits," says Babak Mokhlesi, MD, director of the Sleep Disorders Center at the University of Chicago. For example, many people believe that a nightcap before bed will help them sleep soundly, but alcohol can cause disrupted sleep. Snoring bedmates, letting pets sleep with you, and bright lights could be causing you to toss and turn at night without your realizing it.

Step 2 Consult Your Doc

If you still feel pooped during the day after two weeks of sleep upgrades, it's time for a visit to your doctor. Fatigue is a symptom (not a condition) of many treatable health problems. "See your primary physician rather than a sleep specialist," Surks says. "He or she can ask questions that will help pinpoint the cause and run tests to rule out a wide range of conditions like depression, diabetes, or hypothyroidism [underactive thyroid]."

Step 3 Review Your Meds

Bring a list of the drugs you take to your appointment or simply toss the pill bottles into a bag (a drug review with your doctor is a smart thing to do every 6 to 12 months anyway). From antidepressants to blood pressure drugs to cholesterol-lowering statins, many common prescription medications can leave you dragging through the day. Drugs can cause fatigue in many ways, including depressing the central nervous system, lowering heart rate, or reducing the body's stores of nutrients, such as magnesium or potassium. If it turns out that you take a potentially energy-draining drug, ask about alternatives.

Step 4 Move a Little More

We know: "Get up and exercise" is the last thing you want to hear when you're beat. But believe us, it's worth a try. Exercise seems to create energy and alleviate fatigue by reducing stress, helping you sleep, and increasing circulation so that your muscles receive more oxygen and nutrients. And you don't have to train for a marathon to see the effects. In a small University of Georgia study, chronically tired couch potatoes embarked on a low- or moderate-intensity exercise routine three times per week for six weeks while a control group didn't exercise. The low-intensity group got the best results: a 65 percent drop in fatigue. The moderate-intensity group improved too, but less so. The researchers think that's because some of those people may have been working out too hard for their fitness level.

Even easier exercise may have a benefit. When researchers at New York City's Hospital for Special Surgery put seniors on a gentle yoga or chair-based exercise routine, 39 percent reported an increase in energy after eight weeks. Research suggests that specially designed routines can ease tiredness for cancer survivors, people with chronic fatigue syndrome, and heart attack survivors.

Step 5 Clean up Your Diet

Stay fueled with regular meals and healthy snacks that are low in fat and packed with fiber (beans, fruits, whole grains, and vegetables). According to a recent Pennsylvania State University study, the more fat people eat at a meal, the sleepier they become afterward. Researchers from Australia and the U.K. found that people felt more alert in the morning after having a breakfast high in fiber and carbohydrates than they did when they had a high-fat or a high-carb, low-fiber meal. Beware of very high-protein diets; some evidence suggests that they can increase fatigue.

Step 6 Reorganize Your Day

Still having trouble after taking steps 1 through 5? You may think you're tired when you're actually tense. One in three people who say they're stressed attribute their fatigue to their mood, according to a survey from the American Psychological Association. "Stress feels like fatigue—you're not in control of your life, it takes longer to do things, and you may have trouble multitasking. It can also interfere with sleep and healthy eating, and leave you without enough time to recharge or relax," says sleep and fatigue researcher David Dinges, PhD, professor in the department of psychiatry at the University of Pennsylvania School of Medicine.

Adding "learn a stress-reduction technique" to your already-crazy to-do list isn't the answer. "Stop and think about what's important to you," Dinges recommends. Saying "no" more often to obligations and activities that aren't high priority gives you more time for the things you enjoy. Those are the ones that will rejuvenate you, he says. Another tip: spend some time each day away from your computer, tablet, or smartphone. "When you feel as if you always have to respond, always have to be in touch, it's hard to relax," he says. "I try to set aside part of the day when I get away from all the electronic noise."

Critical Thinking

1. What health problems are associated with fatigue?
2. Should individuals suffering from fatigue consider taking drugs to boost their energy?

Create Central

www.mhhe.com/createcentral

Internet References

Ace Fitness
    http://www.acefitness.org/acefit/fitness-programs-article/2742/ACEFit-workout-advice-and-exercise-tips
National Sleep Foundation
    http://sleepfoundation.org

Unit 2

UNIT

Prepared by: Eileen Daniel, *SUNY College at Brockport*

Stress and Mental Health

The brain is one organ that still mystifies and baffles the scientific community. While more has been learned about this organ in the last decade than in all the rest of recorded history, our understanding of the brain is still in its infancy. What has been learned, however, has spawned exciting new research and has contributed to the establishment of new disciplines, such as psychophysiology and psychoneuroimmunology (PNI).

Traditionally, the medical community has viewed health problems as either physical or mental and has treated each type separately. This dichotomy between the psyche (mind) and soma (body) is fading in the light of scientific data that reveal profound physiological changes associated with mood shifts. What are the physiological changes associated with stress? Hans Selye, the father of stress research, described stress as a nonspecific physiological response to anything that challenges the body. He demonstrated that this response could be elicited by both mental and physical stimuli. Stress researchers have come to regard this response pattern as the "flight-or-fight" response, perhaps an adaptive throwback to our primitive ancestors. Researchers now believe that repeated and prolonged activation of this response can trigger destructive changes in our bodies and contribute to the development of several chronic diseases. So profound is the impact of emotional stress on the body that current estimates suggest that approximately 90 percent of all doctor visits are for stress-related disorders. If emotional stress elicits a generalized physiological response, why are there so many different diseases associated with it? Many experts believe that the answer may best be explained by what has been termed "the weak organ theory." According to this theory, every individual has one organ system that is most susceptible to the damaging effects of prolonged stress.

Mental illness, which is generally regarded as a dysfunction of normal thought processes, has no single identifiable etiology. One may speculate that this is due to the complex nature of the organ system involved. There is also mounting evidence to suggest that there is an organic component to the traditional forms of mental illness such as schizophrenia, chronic depression, and manic depression. The fact that certain mental illnesses tend to occur within families has divided the mental health community into two camps: those who believe that there is a genetic factor operating and those who see the family tendency as more of a learned behavior. In either case, the evidence supports mental illness as another example of the weak-organ theory. The reason one person is more susceptible to the damaging effects of stress than another may not be altogether clear, but evidence is mounting that one's perception or attitude plays a key role in the stress equation. A prime example demonstrating this relationship comes from the research that relates cardiovascular disease to stress. The realization that our attitude has such a significant impact on our health has led to a burgeoning new movement in psychology termed "positive psychology." Dr. Martin Segilman, professor of psychology at the University of Pennsylvania and father of the positive psychology movement, believes that optimism is a key factor in maintaining not only our mental health but our physical health as well. Dr. Segilman notes that while some people are naturally more optimistic than others, optimism can be learned.

One area in particular that appears to be influenced by the positive psychology movement is the area of stress management. Traditionally, stress management programs have focused on the elimination of stress but that is starting to change as new strategies approach stress as an essential component of life and a potential source of health. It is worth noting that this concept, of stress serving as a positive force in a person's life, was presented by Dr. Hans Selye in 1974 in his book *Stress without Distress*. Dr. Selye felt that there were three types of stress: negative stress (distress), normal stress, and positive stress (eustress). He maintained that positive stress not only increases a person's self-esteem but also serves to inoculate the person against the damaging effects of distress. Only time will tell if this change of focus, in the area of stress management, makes any real difference in patient outcome.

The causes of stress are many. Researchers have made significant strides in their understanding of the mechanisms that link emotional stress to physical ailments, but they are less clear on the mechanisms by which positive emotions bolster one's health. Although significant gains have been made in our understanding of the relationship between body and mind, much remains to be learned. What is known indicates that perception and one's attitude are the key elements in shaping our responses to stressors.

Article   Prepared by: Eileen Daniel, *SUNY College at Brockport*

Sound Mind, Sound Student Body

Challenges and Strategies for Managing the Growing Mental Health Crisis on College and University Campuses

KRISTEN DOMONELL

Learning Outcomes

After reading this article, you will be able to:

- Understand why there is an increased number of college students with mental illnesses.

- Describe why so many students with mental illness drop out before graduation.

- Explain ways in which colleges and universities can manage mental illness on their campuses.

Before entering college, Nicole, a junior at a small liberal arts college in New England, had been getting treatment for anorexia for two years. Finding a college with adequate mental health services was one of her biggest concerns, so she was relieved when the director of counseling services at the college she selected promised her a full treatment, complete with a weekly dietician meeting and regular sessions with a psychiatrist and a therapist.

"I entered [college] full of hope, but was immediately disenchanted with the counselors," she says, noting that the dietician was in such high demand, she could only see her every three weeks. By the second semester of her freshman year, Nicole had relapsed.

"It was clear that there was no system in place," she says. "The physician did not find my symptoms serious enough, and the psychiatrist had found another job."

Nicole is now seeing a psychiatrist at school who she feels "makes a great effort to meet the medical needs of students on campus." Yet, she is still unsatisfied with the counseling services as a whole, specifically with graduate student interns working in the center who she feels are inexperienced and not equipped to diagnose complex disorders, let alone identify symptoms.

Nicole isn't alone in needing on-campus mental health services. One in four college-aged Americans has a diagnosable mental illness, and severe mental illness is more common among college students than it was a decade ago, according to the American Psychological Association. Meanwhile, state and local funding for higher education declined by 7 percent, to $81.2 billion, in 2012, and per-student funding dropped to the lowest level in 25 years, according to the State Higher Education Executive Officers Association.

With an increased demand for counseling services paired with budget restraints, experiences like Nicole's aren't uncommon.

Why the Increase?

Early intervention and a decreased stigma surrounding mental illness are two reasons campus counseling centers are seeing an increased demand.

After the shootings at **Virginia Tech** and **Northern Illinois University** in 2007 and 2008, most institutions began creating behavioral intervention teams—called early intervention teams, care teams, or threat assessment teams, depending on the campus.

"These intervention teams are keeping students from falling through the cracks—which is a good thing—but it increases the demands on counseling centers," explains Dan L. Jones, president of the Association for University and College Counseling Center Directors.

"It's kind of like a small town with four-lane highways coming into it. All the traffic is able to get into town, and then there's nowhere for it to go," explains Jones, who serves as director of the Counseling & Psychological Services Center at **Appalachian State University** (N.C.), as well.

A decrease in the stigma surrounding mental illness is also responsible for the increased services demand, as more students visit counseling centers from self-referrals.

"This generation of students seems more willing to seek counselling," says Jones. "There used to be more stigma to getting counseling, and since the stigma has diminished, that leads to more counseling."

Difficulty Meeting the Need

A 2012 survey by the American College Counseling Association found that more than one-third (37.4 percent) of college students seeking help have severe psychological problems, up from 16 percent in 2000. Of the 293 counseling centers surveyed, more than three-quarters reported more crises requiring immediate response than in the past five years.

Despite the increased need, tight budgets aren't allowing for many counseling staff hires to pick up the slack, with the number of counselors increasing only marginally over the past 20 or 30 years, shares Drew Walther, national chapter director for Active Minds, Inc., a mental health advocacy organization with more than 400 campus chapters dedicated to outreach.

Active Minds exists to help remove the stigma and start a larger conversation about the issues surrounding mental health. But it also helps fill a hole in the need for outreach. As counseling centers get busier, counselors who would normally be promoting available campus services wind up spending all their time fulfilling an increased need for therapy sessions, so outreach falls to the wayside.

Even with counselors working full throttle, students are still not able to receive as much help as they need. In non-emergency situations, it's common for students to have to sit on a waiting list for a month before getting their first therapy session, and about half of institutions use a short-term model, where students are only allowed 6 to 12 sessions per academic year, shares Jones.

Last February, before hiring a new staff member and taking on additional trainees to help with the client load, Appalachian State referred out 60 percent of the students who came in. Even after referrals, the center still had a waiting list 70 people long, shares Jones.

"Therapy works best in long chunks, and if you're only getting six sessions, how much progress can you be making?" points out Walther.

The most recent AUCCCD survey shows that more institutions are adding counseling positions, which could signal that administrators recognize the greater need for mental health services. But Jones points out that the trend is coming on the heels of the economic downturn when resources remained static, but demand was steadily growing.

"It's not like there's some huge trend of hiring lots of counseling center people. It's just better than the past few years," says Jones. "It's improving, but it's far from meeting the demands of university counseling services to see all the students that need to be seen in a timely manner."

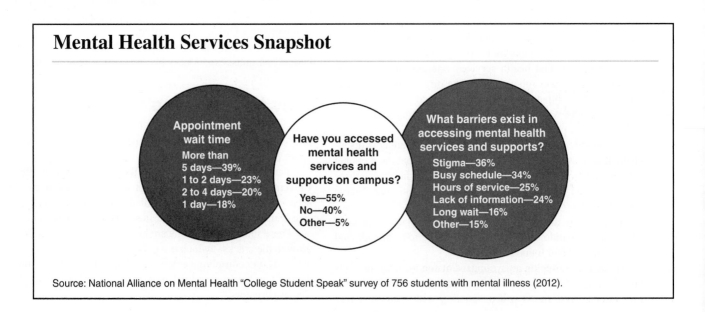

Mental Health Services Snapshot

Appointment wait time
More than 5 days—39%
1 to 2 days—23%
2 to 4 days—20%
1 day—18%

Have you accessed mental health services and supports on campus?
Yes—55%
No—40%
Other—5%

What barriers exist in accessing mental health services and supports?
Stigma—36%
Busy schedule—34%
Hours of service—25%
Lack of information—24%
Long wait—16%
Other—15%

Source: National Alliance on Mental Health "College Student Speak" survey of 756 students with mental illness (2012).

Consequences: Drop Outs, Violence, Litigation

A 2012 National Alliance on Mental Illness survey of 756 college students living with mental health conditions found that 64 percent of those who had stopped attending school within the past five years did so for a mental health-related reason. Half of those students didn't access mental health services and supports while they were attending.

In other words, at-risk students falling between the cracks and being unable to complete could harm a school's ability to retain students. In addition, without proper outreach and care, troubled students could harm themselves or others. Suicide is the second leading cause of death among college students (second to accidents), according to the Centers for Disease Control. Each year, 1,100 students die by suicide—figures that have remained steady in recent years.

There is also a risk for litigation. A noted 2002 wrongful-death lawsuit against MIT was a first in the higher education world. It implied that it's not only medical professionals who legally have a "special relationship" with their patients who could be held responsible for a death or other incident, but schools, administrators, and other employees could, as well.

In 2000, Elizabeth Shin, an MIT student, died from wounds inflicted by a fire in her dorm room. Shin had multiple suicide attempts and hospitalizations for mental illness in the past, although it was never proven whether her death was suicide or an accident.

In 2002, Shin's parents filed a $27 million wrongful death lawsuit against the institution, as well as administrators, campus police, and mental health employees, claiming their daughter did not receive enough mental health treatment and that the fire was not responded to properly. In 2006, the case was settled out of court for an undisclosed amount.

In the wake of a student suicide, the college or university, its administrators, and its other employees could be held financially responsible for the death—not just medical professionals who worked with the student.

"It was never clear what the results might have been, but it really shook up the university world," recalls Jones of AUCCCD.

A more recent example worth considering is the pending litigation over last year's movie theater shooting in Aurora, Colo.

against the **University of Colorado, Denver** and shooter James Holmes' psychiatrist Lynne Fenton.

Although Holmes left the institution a month before the tragedy, at least 20 tort claims have been filed saying that Fenton and the university's threat assessment team should have done more after it was brought to their attention that Holmes could have been dangerous.

Doing More with Less

While increasing resources is the best way to improve services, doing more with less is the option that's more realistic for many schools in the meantime. Here are some strategies that Jones has seen counseling centers across the country adopt to deal with the influx of students seeking services:

- Increased use of group therapy. "Outcome studies report equivalent results between group and individual therapy," says Jones. "Advocates for group therapy point out that it is cost-efficient and time-efficient since more people are served."
- Using trainees (such as field placement students or graduate assistants) to help serve clients with less severe illnesses, and interns or post-docs to help with the more severe clients. This requires adequate office space, which many centers are lacking, notes Jones.
- Increased use of technology and online services, including online and distance tele-counseling to help with excessive demands.
- Hiring part-time temporary contract therapists during peak usage times. Such staff often need advance notice to be available, and institutional administrators would likely need to complete time-consuming background checks before contract therapists can start working, points out Jones.

The Outlook

As with other big issues within higher education and the community at large, reaching agreement on how to improve mental health services won't come easily.

"There are so many decision makers, getting all of them on the same page and getting them all in line to be supportive of counseling centers—financially and resource wise—is difficult," Jones says.

But federal efforts could influence everyone, from state legislators to chancellors to boards of trustees.

The Garrett Lee Smith Memorial Reauthorization Act of 2013, a bill introduced in Congress earlier this year, may be one such step.

The bill would increase grant funding for colleges and universities from $5 million to $7 million for providing counseling services and training mental health providers, according to the office of Senator Jack Reed (D-R.I.), a sponsor of the bill. The original bill, enacted in 2004, provided funding for suicide prevention education and outreach, not for the delivery of services.

The act also funds the Suicide Prevention Resource Center and provides grants to states and tribes to support suicide prevention efforts.

"Over the past 10 years, we've been looking at what's been going on among children and young adults to see where improvements can be made and how schools, colleges, and universities are using their funding," according to the office of Senator Reed. The conclusion was that education institutions needed the flexibility to expand their use of the funds outside of outreach.

"When you think about kids going off to college and the services that universities offer, mental health is a critical component. If we don't have an infrastructure that's capable of providing treatment on those campuses, there are students who will go without."

Resources

Active Minds, Inc., www.activeminds.org
American College Counseling Association,
    www.collegecounseling.org
American Psychological Association, www.apa.org
Association of University and College Counseling Center Directors,
    www.aucccd.org
National Alliance on Mental Illness, www.nami.org

Critical Thinking

1. Why has the number of individuals with mental illnesses increased on college campuses?
2. What is the reason(s) why more students are willing to seek mental health counseling on college and university campuses?

Create Central

www.mhhe.com/createcentral

Internet References

American Psychological Association
    https://www.apa.org
National Alliance on Mental Illness
    http://www.nami.org/Content/NavigationMenu/Find_Support/NAMI_on_Campus1/Mental_Illness_Fact_Sheets/Mental_Health_Conditions_in_College_Students.htm
National Institutes of Mental Health
    http://www.nimh.nih.gov/index.shtml

Kristen Domonell, "Sound Mind, Sound Student Body" from *University Business* (April 2013): 27–30. Copyright © 2013. Reprinted with permission.

Article   Prepared by: Eileen L. Daniel, *SUNY Brockport*

Social Withdrawal and Violence—Newtown, Connecticut

John T. Walkup, M.D., and David H. Rubin, M.D.

Learning Outcomes

After reading this article, you will be able to:

- Understand the complex pathways that lead to mass murder.

- Describe what relationship exists between mental illness and violence.

- Explain barriers to accessing the mental health system.

In the aftermath of the great tragedy in Newtown, Connecticut, the mental health community is responding to our own and others' desperation to understand why this event occurred and is advocating for strategies that might prevent similar events in the future. Discussion has focused on whether Adam Lanza was mentally ill, the risk of violence among the mentally ill, access to high-quality mental health care, gun control, and the relationship between the media and violence. An important dimension that has been less discussed is the question of social withdrawal and isolation, within and beyond the confines of mental illness. For the withdrawn and isolated and the angry and alienated, there are deep-seated barriers to care, and there may exist a small subgroup that is uniquely vulnerable to the seductive power of violence in our culture.

Whether Adam Lanza was mentally ill and whether he had Asperger's syndrome, as has been alleged, will never be known. But it's important to recognize that mental illness is an insufficient explanation for mass murder. The pathway to mass murder is inexplicably complex, involving a confluence of factors that come together only rarely.[1,2] Nevertheless, there appears to be reasonable consensus that Lanza was withdrawn and isolated early in his life and that that condition persisted through adolescence. Withdrawn and isolative behavior is of interest to the medical community for reasons beyond its association with people who have committed school shootings. Indeed, such behavior is quite common, often appears early in childhood, is relatively persistent and stable, and can be very responsive to treatment.[3] Yet withdrawn and isolative behavior usually goes undetected or unaddressed until impairment is obvious; at its extreme, it can manifest in a shocking murder and suicide.

This behavioral dimension actually includes a variety of behaviors and developmental trajectories that have varied and important implications and outcomes; it encompasses the lack of interpersonal reciprocity seen in children with autism spectrum disorders, avoidance and inhibition presenting before puberty in anxious children, withdrawal due to traumatic life-altering experiences, and social withdrawal as observed in adolescent depression. Withdrawal or isolation can also precede the development of schizophrenia and is commonly included as a component of "the schizophrenia prodrome." Finally, there is a very small group of withdrawn and isolated children who lack empathy and are cold and callous toward other human beings. Early identification of withdrawn and isolative behavior can go a long way toward improving outcomes for young people, since effective evidence-based treatments are increasingly available for each of these situations.

The facts about the risk of violence in the mentally ill are relatively straightforward.[4] The vast majority of people with psychiatric disorders are not violent, and the mentally ill do not commit a substantial proportion of violent crimes in the United States. When violence is committed by a mentally ill person, it usually occurs in reaction to an interpersonal provocation and is often charged with emotion. Only rarely do mentally ill people engage in dispassionate, planned, predatory violence toward others. In school shootings, there has been evidence of both a strong emotional component—feelings of anger and alienation—and extended and detailed planning that went undetected or unaddressed.[1]

Even if early signs were noticed, a mentally ill, withdrawn, isolated young man and his family would face barriers to full engagement in psychiatric treatment. Severely mentally ill people, especially if they are angry and alienated, do not often voluntarily seek treatment, and even those who do may not be fully engaged or cooperative. Young adults 18 years of age or older must consent to treatment; their families, as concerned as they may be, aren't necessarily able to bring them to a care provider and can't force them to continue receiving treatment. Moreover, our standards for confidentiality preclude involvement of concerned parents unless it has been specifically authorized by the young person. Also, pursuing care for individuals at risk has become more difficult. Mental health professionals have capitulated to a higher threshold for hospitalization, in part because of standards dictated by insurers; clinicians may also second-guess or fear civil commitment proceedings and so fail to advocate for higher levels of care.

The interface between mental health care providers and these important safeguards of individual liberty can result in delay in, or a complete lack of, a cohesive and comprehensive response to young adults who are experiencing psychiatric difficulties. Particularly, mentally ill young people have the capacity to mask their intent to harm themselves or others.

At the societal level, many challenges confronting efforts to improve access to high-quality mental health care will have to be addressed in upcoming policy discussions. Stigma is still the biggest barrier to effectively engaging individuals and families in the mental health system. But fully addressing the mental health burden in the United States would also be costly. Mental illness is common, often affects people when they're young, can last a long time, and puts people at risk for drug use and other maladaptive behaviors. Though effective treatments exist, some psychiatric disorders are not particularly responsive to treatment and can lead to substantial, sustained, and costly disability. Moreover, given the diverse types of mental health care practitioners and psychiatric practices, patients may not receive the most effective treatments that are known or available. In addition, many practitioners with expertise in evidence-based treatment do not accept insurance, since reimbursement rates are uniformly low.

Psychotherapy and medications can be very effective, but benefit from psychotherapy depends on the patient's motivation and effort, and many patients—and many parents of mentally ill children—don't want to consider the use of medication, even if it has been proven safe and effective. The social contexts of mental health treatment also influence its effectiveness: public uncertainty regarding the safety of medications, past malfeasance by the pharmaceutical industry, and political and religious forces that challenge the fundamental brain basis of mental conditions have affected the use of even safe and effective medications and psychotherapies.

The tragedy in Newtown has revived many Americans' passion for gun control and has drawn attention to the media's influence on violent behavior. What is missing from most related discussions is a focus on the seductive, powerful subculture that celebrates and advocates violent and antisocial behavior. Most people are not interested in and do not engage with this subculture, and most who do so are not seduced into action by antisocial themes and violence in films, video games, written materials, or interest groups. However, a very small minority of angry and alienated mentally ill persons may gain a sense of belonging and support from this subculture and may be particularly vulnerable to being seduced into action.

As we launch into relevant policy debates, mental health professionals are best tasked with addressing the problems in our system that make it difficult for individuals and their loved ones to obtain effective, high-quality mental health care early

in life. Since most psychiatric disorders begin in childhood or adolescence, more research is needed on the progression of mental health problems from childhood through adolescence and into adulthood. More specifically, research is needed to elucidate the multiple trajectories of the early withdrawn and isolated behavior that is so common in the reported histories of people who perform violent acts. Finally, discussions of gun control and violence in the media need to delve deeper and illuminate the dark subculture of alienation and antisocial violence that may engage and seduce rare individuals into performing extreme acts of violence like the one in Newtown.

Disclosure forms provided by the authors are available with the full text of this article at NEJM.org.

From the Division of Child and Adolescent Psychiatry, Department of Psychiatry, Weill Cornell Medical College and New York-Presbyterian Hospital, New York.

This article was published on December 28, 2012, at NEJM.org.

Critical Thinking

1. What is the primary barrier preventing mentally ill people from seeking and getting treatment?
2. Explain how the culture of violence may influence crime.
3. Why is more research needed on early withdrawn and isolated behaviors?

Create Central

www.mhhe.com/createcentral

Internet References

National Mental Health Association (NMHA)
    www.nmha.org/index.html
The American Institute of Stress
    www.stress.org

Notes

1. Flannery DJ, Modzeleski W, Kretschmar JM. Violence and school shootings. Curr Psychiatry Rep 2013,15:331.
2. Follman M, Aronsen G, Pan D. A guide to mass shootings in America Mother Jones December 15, 2012 (www.motherjones.com/politics/2012/07/mass-shootings-map).
3. Rubin DH, Althoff RR, Walkup JT, Hudziak JJ, Cross-informant agreement on child and adolescent withdrawn behavior: a latent class approach. Child Psychiatry Hum Dev 2012 September 12 (Epub ahead of print).
4. Friedman RA. In gun debate, a misguided focus on mental illness. New York Times. December 17, 2012 (www.nytimes.com/2012/12/18/health/a-misguided-focus-on-mental-illness-in-gun-control-debate.html?_r=0).

DOI: 10.1056/NEJMpl215605

Copyright © 2012 Massachusetts Medical Society.

Article   Prepared by: Eileen Daniel, *SUNY College at Brockport*

Go Forth in Anger

JOANN ELLISON RODGERS

Learning Outcomes

After reading this article, you will be able to:

- Explain why people should not work too hard to suppress their anger.

- Understand how and why anger evolved among humans.

- Describe the hormonal changes that occur in the body when we get angry.

Anger gets no respect. It's so yoked to "management" that we give it little consideration on its own. We aspire to the serene sangfroid in comedian John Cleese's description of the British as a people who rarely get more than "miffed" or "peeved," and haven't escalated to "a bit cross" since World War II when the Blitz cut tea supplies. Yoda framed the view well: "Anger leads to hate. Hate leads to suffering." Conclusion: The human race would be far better off without it altogether.

A growing cadre of social and evolutionary biologists, psychologists, and brain scientists begs to differ. With newly detailed neural maps of brain systems that underlie feelings and energize us to act on our goals, they have seriously dented the long-held view of anger as an all-time destructive and negative state worthy mostly of suppression. More to the point, they have uncovered its upside, and proposed a psychological model of anger framed as a positive, a force of nature that has likely fueled the ambitions and creativity of the famous and infamous.

Beethoven, for example, reportedly beat his students but still got the best from them. Mark Rothko's fury at pop art powered his own work and drove his towering mentorship of students. Marlon Brando was an angry young man whose anger later in life informed his bully pulpit for social justice. And Rosie O'Donnell built her career on a foundation of foul-mouthed feistiness—and later on efforts to control it.

Researchers are amassing evidence that anger is a potent form of social communication, a logical part of people's emotional tool kit, an appetitive force that not only moves us toward what we want but fuels optimism, creative brainstorming, and problem solving by focusing mind and mood in highly refined ways. Brainwise, it is the polar opposite of fear, sadness, disgust, and anxiety—feelings that prompt avoidance and cause us to move away from what we deem unpleasant. When the gall rises, it propels the irate toward challenges they otherwise would flee and actions to get others to do what they, the angry, wish.

"We need anger, and there are negative consequences for those without it," says Aaron Sell, a social psychologist at Australia's Griffith University, who, with pioneering evolutionary psychologists Lena Cosmides and John Tooby at the University of California Santa Barbara Center for Evolutionary Psychology, has helped lead the assault on old thinking about anger. It feels rewarding because it moves us closer to our goals. Wielded responsibly, scientists say, it even thwarts aggression.

GRRRR: the Neural Roots of Anger

The idea that anger is a positive feeling is not exactly new. Aristotle in 350 B.C. wrote that "the angry man is aiming at what he can attain, and the belief that you will attain your aim is pleasant." People resort to "mild to moderate" anger as often as several times a day and at least several times a week, finds James Averill, a professor of psychology at the University of Massachusetts. Such universality and frequency suggest that only our Stone Age forebears with the capacity to call forth anger pretty regularly, and get rewarded for it, survived to have descendants with the same makeup—us. "It's no surprise" that babies are born ready to express anger, notes Sell, because it's "the output of a cognitive mechanism engineered by natural

Hooray for Anger

Anger—the feeling—is one thing. Fury—its red-faced, fist-first expression—is another. Fury is hardly a useful modality, but anger has positive value in our emotional lives. Here's what that means for most of us:

Anger Offers a Sense of Control

If the true function of anger is to impose costs or withhold benefits from others to increase our Welfare Tradeoff Ratio, it should follow that people who have enhanced abilities to inflict costs are more likely to prevail in conflicts, consider themselves entitled to better treatment, think better of themselves, and be prone to anger. In other words, they control their destinies more than less angry people do.

Psychologist Aaron Sell and coworkers found that strong men report more success resolving interpersonal conflicts in their favor than weak men and are, by their own account, more prone to anger. They endorse personal aggression and are likely to approve the use of military force in global conflicts. The more a woman considers herself attractive—a counterpart to masculine might—the more she is prone to anger, feelings of entitlement, and success in getting her way.

Anger May Promote Cooperation

The association between attractiveness in women or strength among men and "entitlement anger" also suggests that anger enables cooperative relationships by means of getting two parties to "yes" before hostilities break out.

Harvard's Jennifer Lerner examined Americans' reactions to the terrorist attacks of 9/11 and found that feelings of anger evoked a sense of certainty and control on a mass scale, helping to minimize paralyzing fear and allowing people to come together for common cause. Those who became angry were less likely to anticipate future attacks, while those who were fearful expected more attacks.

Anger preserves a sense of control and the desire to defend what's yours, but only insofar as it leaves both parties more or less OK, because you may need the hungry oaf who stole your dinner to help you hunt down the next meal.

Anger Fuels Optimism

Boston College psychologist Brett Ford has found that anxiety drives people to be extremely vigilant about threats, while a state of excitement makes them hyperaware of rewards within their reach. Anger increases visual attention to rewarding information. It helps people home in on what they hope things can be, rather than on an injury. Fearful people not only have "strikingly different" assessments of the level of risk in the environment compared to angry people, their fear leads to higher perceptions of risk.

Anger Enables Leadership

Dutch psychologist Gerben van Kleef has found that anger deployed by a leader gets underlings to perform well, but only if the underlings are high in their motivation to read the leader. Cheerfulness in a leader is more effective among teams with low interest in reading emotional tea leaves.

Beware of becoming a volcanic Steve Jobs, however. Eventually, the strategy of using either consistent or intermittent explosive anger becomes obvious and may be ignored or resisted. Jobs was notoriously and chronically angry, and he used that emotion to exact extraordinary performance from his most creative employees. But finally, his anger lost its impact and became so dangerous to his effectiveness that he was forced out of the company he had founded.

"If you get a bang for the buck for anger and you don't ever get punished for it and it gets you what you want, you can lose control of the benefit and still keep at it when it's self-destructive," says Michael Cataldo, a psychologist at Johns Hopkins.

Anger Boosts Focus on the Practical

Approach motivation toward anger-related objects occurs only when people perceive they can actually get a reward, finds psychologist Henk Arts of Utrecht University in the Netherlands. In the absence of such a reward context, avoidance motivation prevails. The findings suggest that our anger system is pretty fine-tuned to go after the gettable, not the impossible.

Anger Abets Creativity and Ambition

After establishing that anger often accompanies brainstorming, in which people throw conflicting ideas out for debate, a team of Dutch researchers elicited anger, sadness, or a neutral state from subjects, and then had them brainstorm about ways to protect the environment. Those in the anger group had lots more ideas and more creative ideas than sad or neutral participants—although, over time, things evened out.

Consider the work of superior talents who were famously angry at the world: Francis Bacon's screaming faces. David Mamet's masterful plays, Adrienne Rich's feminist poem, "Diving Into the Wreck," and anything by Virginia Woolf.

It's likely that anger stirs energizing hormones and focuses attention, all while disinhibiting social interactions, creating less "politically correct" behavior.

Anger Is Emotionally Intelligent

People who prefer to feel useful emotions (such as anger) even when they are unpleasant to experience—when confronting others, for example—"tend to be higher in emotional intelligence" than people who prefer to feel happiness, Brett Ford and Maya Tamir report. "Wanting to feel bad may be good at times and vice versa."

Anger Aids Understanding of Others

In advance of an Israeli-Palestinian summit conference convened by President George W. Bush in 2007, a team of Israeli and American psychologists set out to see whether anger would have constructive effects. Experimentally inducing anger in Israelis toward Palestinians several weeks before the summit increased support for making compromises among those with low levels of hatred. Even when anger was evoked just days before the summit, it led to increased support for compromise in the same low-hatred group.

Anger makes people more willing to accept risks, a major feature of leadership.

—*JER*

selection." Nature favored and preserved anger for the same reasons it conserved love, sex, fear, sadness, and anxiety: survival and advantage.

Biologically, when people are aroused to some degree of anger and let off steam, their heart rate, blood pressure, and testosterone levels all increase. This might suggest that anger freaks us out and harms us. But in fact, levels of the stress hormone cortisol drop, suggesting that anger helps people calm down and get ready to address a problem—not run from it. In studies in which she and her colleagues induced indignation among volunteer subjects, Jennifer Lerner, a psychologist at Harvard, found that anger diminished the effects of cortisol on heart reactivity.

Although anger has long been considered a fully negative emotion, recent neuroscience has overturned that view. Scientists know that two basic motivational forces underlie all behavior—the impulse to approach, or move toward something desired, and the impulse to withdraw, or move away from unpleasantness. Hardwired in the brain, these behaviors are headquartered in the frontal cortex, which acts as the executive branch of the emotions. Brain imaging and electrical studies of the brain consistently show that the left frontal lobe is crucial to establishing approach behaviors that push us to pursue desired goals and rewards in rational, logical, systematic, and ordered ways and that activation of the right frontal cortex is tied to the more negative, withdrawal motivational system, marked by inhibition, timidity, and avoidance of punishment and threat.

Brain scans show that anger significantly activates the left anterior cortex, associated with positive approach behaviors. Anger, moreover, appears to be downright rewarding, even pleasurable, in studies showing predominant left-brain activation when angry subjects perceive they can make things better.

"Expecting to be able to act to resolve the [angering] event should yield greater approach motivational intensity," contend social psychologists Charles Carver of the University of Miami and Eddie Harmon-Jones of the University of New South Wales, long-time collaborators in anger scholarship. In a variety of studies, Harmon-Jones has found that subjects who score high on a scale that measures a tendency to anger display a characteristic asymmetry in the prefrontal cortex—they exhibit higher levels of left anterior (frontal) EEG activity and lower levels of right anterior activation. Randomly insulting subjects, compared with treating them neutrally in verbal communications, stimulates greater relative left frontal activity.

Spurred by the findings on anger, neuroscientists have begun to move away from thinking of any emotion as either negative or positive, preferring instead to characterize emotions by "motivational direction"—whether they stimulate approach behaviors or avoidance/withdrawal behaviors. Viewed within this framework, they explain, it's not strange that anger produces happiness. "The case of anger," reports a team of Spanish scientists led by Neus Herrero, "is different because although it is considered or experienced as negative, based on findings of increased left brain activity it produces a motivation of closeness, or approach." When we get mad, in other words, we "show a natural tendency to get closer to what made us angry to try to eliminate it."

Herrero looked at psychological and biological measures—heart rate (increase), testosterone levels (increase), cortisol levels (decrease), and brain activation (asymmetric left activation)—at the same time he induced anger. The findings support the notion that nature intends us to respond to anger in ways that increase motivation to approach what is sending heart rate up and cortisol down and left brains into thinking up creative ways to make it go away. In short, venting calms us enough to think straight.

Harmon-Jones's studies add detail. "When individuals believed there was nothing they could do to rectify an angering situation, they still reported being angry," he reports, "but they did not show increased left frontal activity compared to right frontal activity." Overall, he adds, it's most accurate to say that anger is associated with left frontal activity only when the anger is associated with approach inclinations, the perception that there is an opportunity to fix the situation, at the least cost to oneself.

Director of the University of Wisconsin's influential Laboratory for Affective Neuroscience, Richard Davidson has studied the neural origins of emotions for 40 years. His pioneering investigations of the asymmetric brain response to anger show that the emotion is "intrinsically rewarding, with a positive quality that mobilizes resources, increases vigilance, and facilitates the removal of obstacles in the way of our goal pursuits, particularly if the anger can be divorced from the propensity to harm or destroy."

The Real Function of Anger

Nature wired us over time to get angry when others insult or exploit us or, in the jargon of evolutionary psychologists, impose too high a cost on us (in our opinion) to get an unjustifiably (again in our opinion) small benefit for themselves. So states the Recalibration Theory of Anger put forth by Cosmides, Tooby, and Sell. Moreover, they contend, anger was designed by natural selection to nonconsciously regulate our response to personal conflicts of interest in ways that help us bargain to our advantage. In other words, anger prods the aggrieved to behave in ways that increase the weight the wrongdoer puts on her value and welfare. If the angry person is successful, it not only produces benefits ("I win!") but also pleasure—enough to reinforce deploying anger this way repeatedly.

Using studies that probe people's true emotions by gauging reactions to hypothetical scenarios, along with argument analysis, computerized measures of facial expressions, and voice analysis, Sell finds that anger erupts naturally when someone puts a "too low value, or weight, on your welfare relative to their own when making decisions or taking actions that affect both of you." Sell and his colleagues call this index the Welfare Tradeoff Ratio or WTR. And the purpose of the anger is to recalibrate that ratio.

Anger is likely the primary way people have of addressing conflicts of interest and other "resource conflicts," says Sell. Anger allows us to detect our own value in any conflicting interaction, then motivates us to get others to rethink our positions, to pay a lot more attention to what it will cost us to get what we want—and whether it's worth the cost.

Sell proposes that anger essentially makes the target of the anger "less willing to impose costs and more willing to tolerate costs." Studies conducted with Cosmides and Tooby show that anger, by WTR measure, is more prevalent in physically strong men, who would be perceived as able to get away with anger as a bargaining tactic. The trio has also found when two parties both want exclusive access to, or the lion's share of, something, arguments seasoned with anger work well in divvying up the spoils in ways that allow for winners without destroying the losers.

Recalibration theory explains a lot of everyday human behavior in which anger serves a positive purpose as a social value indicator and regulator and ironically, perhaps, as a check on aggression. "My classmate uses my sleeve to wipe ketchup off his chin in order to keep his shirt clean," Sell offers as an example. Such behavior arouses anger not because he is really harmed by it (no one dies of a ketchup stain), but because it's an indication his classmate has little respect for his worth. The ketchup wipee might respond with a laugh if the wiper is a buddy, but if not, showing anger gets the afflicted to behave in ways that increase the value the wrongdoer puts on him by escalating the social cost of misbehaving.

Standing up for your shirtsleeve is standing up for yourself. You don't need to throw a punch; an angry frown or a loud "Hey!" will probably recalibrate. Anger, then, can be a way of increasing the likelihood of evening out respectful relationships, even among friends—in essence, encouraging cooperation. Without anger, Sell adds, there would be no emotional environment in which to persuade, negotiate, and progress in a relatively safe way without overt war and mayhem at every frustration.

"I keep finding that anger, across different settings, can have positive consequences," says Gerben van Kleef, professor of social psychology at the University of Amsterdam. He has found that negotiators led to believe that their counterparts are angry are more likely to make concessions, a nice edge for those especially good at reading and calculating WTRs. Our innate anger system guides the angered person to do things that encourage an offender to treat the angry person better by some combination of conferring benefits or lowering costs.

If there's a take-home message to all the good news about anger, Davidson says it might be that while anger can be healthy or toxic depending on the situation at hand, people should not work too hard to suppress it. "In general, it's better to let emotions unfold than to externally suppress them," he says.

"Ultimately," insists Harvard's Lerner, "research will provide evidence for the view that the most adaptive and resilient individuals have highly flexible emotional response systems. They are neither chronically angry nor chronically calm." Anger, she adds, is good for you, "as long as you keep the flame low."

Critical Thinking

1. Is it physically and emotionally better to try to suppress anger or let our emotions unfold?
2. How does the recalibration theory explain the positive purpose of anger?
3. Why is anger considered to be a form of social communication?

Create Central

www.mhhe.com/createcentral

Internet References

American Psychological Association
http://apa.org/topics/anger/index.aspx
Psychology Today
http://www.psychologytoday.com/basics/anger

JOANN ELLISON RODGERS is a writer based in Baltimore.

Article   Prepared by: Eileen L. Daniel, *SUNY Brockport*

Internet Addiction

What once was parody may soon be diagnosis.

GREG BEATO

Learning Outcomes

After reading this article, you will be able to:

- Understand why the Internet can become addicting.
- Describe the negative impact the Internet can have on a person's life.
- Understand the types of treatment available for Internet addiction.

In 1995, in an effort to parody the way the American Psychiatric Association's hugely influential *Diagnostic and Statistical Manual of Mental Disorders* medicalizes every excessive behavior, psychiatrist Ivan Goldberg introduced on his website the concept of "Internet Addiction Disorder." Last summer Ben Alexander, a 19-year-old college student obsessed with the online multiplayer game *World of Warcraft,* was profiled by CBS News, NPR, the Associated Press, and countless other media outlets because of his status as client No. 1 at reSTART, the first residential treatment center in America for individuals trying to get themselves clean from Azeroth, iPhones, and all the other digital narcotics of our age.

At reSTART's five-acre haven in the woods near Seattle, clients pay big bucks to detox from pathological computer use by building chicken coops, cooking hamburgers, and engaging in daily therapy sessions with the program's two founders, psychologist Hilarie Cash and clinical social worker and life coach Cosette Rae. With room for just six addicts at a time and a $14,500 program fee, reSTART isn't designed for the masses, and so far it seems to have attracted more reporters than paying clients. When I spoke with Rae in May, she said "10 to 15" people had participated in the 45-day program to date.

Still, the fact that reSTART exists at all shows how far we've progressed in taking Dr. Goldberg's spoof seriously. You may have been too busy monitoring Kim Kardashian's every passing thought-like thing on Twitter to notice, but Digital Detox Week took place in April, and Video Game Addiction Awareness Week followed on its heels in June. Internet addiction disorder has yet to claim a Tiger Woods of its own, but the sad, silly evidence of our worldwide cyber-bingeing mounts on a daily basis. A councilman in the Bulgarian city of Plovdiv is ousted from his position for playing *Farmville* during budget meetings. There are now at least three apps that use the iPhone's camera to show the world right in front of you so you can keep texting while walking down the street, confident in your ability to avoid sinkholes, telephone poles, and traffic. Earlier this year, 200 students taking a class in media literacy at the University of Maryland went on a 24-hour media fast for a group study, then described how "jittery," "anxious," "miserable," and "crazy" they felt without Twitter, Facebook, iPods, and laptops. "I clearly am addicted," one student concluded, "and the dependency is sickening."

In the early days of the Web, dirty talk was exchanged at the excruciatingly slow rate of 14.4 bits per second, connectivity charges accrued by the hour instead of the month, and the only stuff for sale online was some overpriced hot sauce from a tiny store in Pasadena. It took the patience of a Buddhist monk, thousands of dollars, and really bad TV reception to overuse the Web in a self-destructive manner. Yet even then, many people felt Ivan Goldberg's notes on Internet addiction worked better as psychiatry than comedy. A year before Goldberg posted his spoof, Kimberly Young, a psychologist at the University of Pittsburgh, had already begun conducting formal research into online addiction. By 1996 the Harvard-affiliated McLean Hospital had established a computer addiction clinic, a professor at the University of Maryland had created an Internet addiction support group, and *The New York Times* was running op-eds about the divorce epidemic that Internet addiction was about to unleash.

Fifteen years down the line, you'd think we'd all be introverted philanderers by now, isolating ourselves in the virtual Snuggie of *World of Warcraft* by day and stepping out at night to destroy our marriages with our latest hook-ups from AshleyMadison.com. But the introduction of flat monthly fees, online gaming, widespread pornography, MySpace, YouTube, Facebook, WiFi, iPhones, netbooks, and free return shipping on designer shoes with substantial markdowns does not seem to have made the Internet any more addictive than it was a decade ago.

In 1998 Young told the Riverside *Press-Enterprise* that "5 to 10 percent of the 52 million Internet users [were] addicted or 'potentially addicted.'" Doctors today use similar numbers when estimating the number of online junkies. In 2009 David Greenfield, a psychiatrist at the University of Connecticut, told the *San Francisco Chronicle* that studies have shown 3 percent to 6 percent of Internet users "have a problem." Is it possible that the ability to keep extremely close tabs on Ashton Kutcher actually has reduced the Internet's addictive power?

Granted, 3 percent is an awful lot of people. Argue all you like that a real addiction should require needles, or spending time in seedy bars with people who drink vodka through their eyeballs, or at least the overwhelming and nihilistic urge to invest thousands of dollars in a broken public school system through the purchase of lottery tickets. Those working on the front lines of technology overuse have plenty of casualties to point to. In our brief conversation, Cosette Rae tells me about a Harvard student who lost a scholarship because he spent too much time playing games, a guy who spent so many sedentary hours at his computer that he developed blood clots in his leg and had to have it amputated, and an 18-year-old who chose homelessness over gamelessness when his parents told him he either had to quit playing computer games or move out.

A few minutes on Google yields even more lurid anecdotes. In 2007 an Ohio teenager shot his parents, killing his mother and wounding his father, after they took away his Xbox. This year a South Korean couple let their real baby starve to death because they were spending so much time caring for their virtual baby in a role-playing game called *Prius Online*.

On a pound-for-pound basis, the average *World of Warcraft* junkie undoubtedly represents a much less destructive social force than the average meth head. But it's not extreme anecdotes that make the specter of Internet addiction so threatening; it's the fact that Internet overuse has the potential to scale in a way that few other addictions do. Even if Steve Jobs designed a really cool-looking syringe and started distributing free heroin on street corners, not everyone would try it. But who among us doesn't already check his email more often than necessary? As the Internet weaves itself more and more tightly into our lives, only the Amish are completely safe.

As early as 1996, Kimberly Young was promoting the idea that the American Psychiatric Association (APA) should add Internet addiction disorder to the *Diagnostic and Statistical Manual of Mental Disorders* (*DSM*). In February, the APA announced that its coming edition of the *DSM,* the first major

revision since 1994, will for the first time classify a behavior-related condition—pathological gambling—as an "addiction" rather than an "impulse control disorder." Internet addiction disorder is not being included in this new category of "behavioral addictions," but the APA said it will consider it as a "potential addition . . . as research data accumulate."

If the APA does add excessive Internet use to the *DSM,* the consequences will be wide-ranging. Health insurance companies will start offering at least partial coverage for treatment programs such as reSTART. People who suffer from Internet addiction disorder will receive protection under the Americans With Disabilities Act if their impairment "substantially limits one or more major life activities." Criminal lawyers will use their clients' online habits to fashion diminished capacity defenses.

Which means that what started as a parody in 1995 could eventually turn more darkly comic than ever imagined. Picture a world where the health care system goes bankrupt because insurers have to pay for millions of people determined to kick their Twitter addictions once and for all. Where employees who view porn at work are legally protected from termination. Where killing elves in cyberspace could help absolve you for killing people in real life. Is it too late to revert to our older, healthier, more balanced ways of living and just spend all our leisure hours watching *Love Boat* reruns?

Critical Thinking

1. What factors contribute to an Internet addiction?
2. Explain why the Internet can impact a person's normal balanced life.

Create Central

www.mhhe.com/createcentral

Internet References

Center for Online and Internet Addiction
   www.netaddiction.com
National Mental Health Association (NMHA)
   www.nmha.org/index.html

Unit 3

UNIT

Prepared by: Eileen Daniel, *SUNY College at Brockport*

Nutritional Health

For years, the majority of Americans paid little attention to nutrition, other than to eat three meals a day and, perhaps, take a vitamin supplement. While this dietary style was generally adequate for the prevention of major nutritional deficiencies, medical evidence began to accumulate linking the American diet to a variety of chronic illnesses. In an effort to guide Americans in their dietary choices, the U.S. Department of Agriculture and the U.S. Public Health Service review and publish Dietary Guidelines every five years. The recent Dietary Guidelines recommendations are no longer limited to food choices; they include advice on the importance of maintaining a healthy weight and engaging in daily exercise. In addition to the Dietary Guidelines, the Department of Agriculture developed the *Food Guide Pyramid* to show the relative importance of food groups.

Despite an apparent ever-changing array of dietary recommendations from the scientific community, five recommendations remain constant: (1) eat a diet low in saturated fat, (2) eat whole grain foods, (3) drink plenty of fresh water daily, (4) limit your daily intake of sugar and salt, and (5) eat a diet rich in fruits and vegetables. These recommendations, while general in nature, are seldom heeded and in fact many Americans don't eat enough fruits and vegetables and eat too much sugar and saturated fat.

Of all the nutritional findings, the link between dietary fat and coronary heart disease remains the most consistent throughout the literature. Current recommendations suggest that the types of fats consumed may play a much greater role in disease processes than the total amount of fat consumed. As it currently stands, most experts agree that it is prudent to limit our intake of trans fat that appears to raise LDLs (the bad cholesterol) and lower HDLs (the good cholesterol) and thus increases the risk of heart disease. There's also evidence that trans fats increase the risk of diabetes.

While the basic advice on eating healthy remains fairly constant, many Americans are still confused over exactly what to eat. Should their diet be low carbohydrate, high protein, or low fat? When people turn to standards such as the *Food Guide Pyramid,* even here there is some confusion. The *Pyramid,* designed by the Department of Agriculture over 20 years ago, recommends a diet based on grains, fruits, and vegetables with several servings of meats and dairy products. It also restricts the consumption of fats, oils, and sweets. While the *Pyramid* offers guidelines as to food groups, individual nutrients are not emphasized. One nutrient, vitamin D, has been in the news recently. New research on the "sunshine" vitamin suggests current recommendations may not be adequate, especially for senior citizens. The data also indicate that vitamin D may help lower the incidence of cancers, type 1 diabetes, and multiple sclerosis.

Of all the topic areas in health, food and nutrition is certainly one of the most interesting, if for no other reason than the rate at which dietary recommendations change. One recommendation that hasn't changed is the adage that a good breakfast is the best way to start the day. There is a definite link between better grades and breakfast among schoolchildren. Despite all the controversy and conflict, the one message that seems to remain constant is the importance of balance and moderation in everything we eat.

Article   Prepared by: Eileen L. Daniel, *SUNY Brockport*

Fat Facts and Fat Fiction

New research can help you make the best choices for your health.

CONSUMER REPORTS ON HEALTH

Learning Outcomes

After reading this article, you will be able to:

- Explain the difference between healthy and less healthy fats.

- Understand why consumers believe they should try to eliminate most fats from their diets.

- Understand the role of healthy fats in the diet.

If you're confused about fats these days, you're in good company. With research coming in at breakneck speed in recent years, even experts have a hard time agreeing about which fats we should consume, and in what exact proportions, to improve our health and prevent chronic disease. Here we review what the strongest evidence says about healthy choices to make at the grocery store and in your kitchen.

Are Saturated Fats Still "Bad"?

Yes, the best available evidence suggests that saturated fat found in such food as meat, full-fat cheese, ice cream, and cake is still worse for you than the unsaturated fat in vegetable oils, nuts, and avocados. According to a recent report from the United Nations, there is convincing evidence that replacing saturated fat with polyunsaturated fat reduces the risk of heart disease. And a 2012 review of studies by the independent Cochrane Collaboration found that replacing saturated fat with unsaturated fat lowered the risk of cardiovascular events, such as heart attacks and strokes. The authors reported that for every 1,000 people in the studies, there were 77 such events for people on a regular diet compared with 66 for those on a reduced saturated-fat diet.

There's an important caveat, which can make the message here somewhat confusing: When cutting saturated fats, substitute with healthful alternatives, not refined carbohydrates (which are found in such items as white bread, pizza, and snack foods). Otherwise, you probably won't reduce your risk of heart disease and may well increase it, according to the U.N. report. As Penny Kris-Etherton, Ph.D., distinguished professor of nutrition at Penn State University, puts it: "It's not that saturated fats aren't bad anymore. It's that saturated fats and refined carbohydrates are equally bad."

Which Are Better: Mono- or Polyunsaturated Oils?

Nutritionists can't agree about this one, though they do agree that unsaturated fats are better than saturated ones. On the one hand, there is plenty of evidence to support the health benefits of the Mediterranean diet, which calls for generous amounts of olive oil, a mostly mono-unsaturated fat. But when researchers make direct comparisons of mono- and polyunsaturated fats, they generally find stronger evidence of a cardio-protective effect for polyunsaturated fat, found abundantly in safflower, soybean, and sunflower oils.

The American Heart Association recommends minimum dietary intake levels for certain polyunsaturated fats that the body has trouble synthesizing on its own. For example, it suggests getting at least 5 percent to 10 percent of fat calories from omega-6 polyunsaturated fats, and eating at least two servings a week of fish rich in omega-3 polyunsaturated fats. But it makes no specific minimum recommendation for mono-unsaturated fat.

Choosing a variety of plant-based oils, plus low-mercury fish such as salmon twice a week, will help you meet the recommended intake levels and get plenty of all the "good" fats.

Should I Consider the Omega-6 to Omega-3 Ratio?

Omega-6 and omega-3 are two types of polyunsaturated fat—a "good" fat. Many studies suggest that diets rich in two omega-3 fats—eicosapentaenoic acid (EPA) and docosahexaenoic acid (DHA), found in high levels in fish—are linked to lower rates of cardiovascular disease.

To maximize those heart benefits, some experts recommend limiting omega-6 fat found in sources such as corn oil and soybean oil, which have become common in the human diet only in the past 100 years or so, and getting more omega-3s from traditional sources such as fish.

According to some experts, getting too much omega-6 fat might be harmful because it could promote inflammation—which can lead to cardiovascular and other problems—and block the beneficial anti-inflammatory effects of omega-3s. While the jury is still out, recent evidence suggests that omega-6 fats may not in fact increase inflammation.

Can you get enough omega-3 from oils without consuming fish or taking supplements? Probably not. Only a small amount of the alpha-linoleic acid (ALA) found in such oils as canola, flaxseed, and soybean is converted in the body to the more-beneficial omega-3s—EPA and DHA.

The American Heart Association's current position is that both omega-3 and omega-6 fats are beneficial. They say it is more important to meet the minimum recommended intakes for both fats than to try to achieve any specific consumption ratio. Still, there are important gaps and limitations in the research, and conclusions may change as more evidence surfaces.

Can Fats Affect Cancer Risk?

It's your body fat—not the fat in your food—that you should be worrying about most when it comes to cancer risk. According

---

Shopper's guide to fats and oils

Oils with the lowest amount of saturated fat are listed first in each category. Solid fats, such as stick margarine and shortening, are likely to contain trans fats, which should be avoided. Unrefined oils will have a stronger, more distinctive taste than refined oils.

Type of fat/oil	Fatty acids %[1]			Taste	Cost[2]	Best uses
	Mono	Poly	Sat			
Everyday oils						
Safflower	14	75	6	Neutral	$$	Good all-purpose oils for salads and cooking, including pan-frying and deep-frying. Suitable for some baked items (brownies, muffins).
Canola	63	28	7	Neutral	$	
Sunflower	20	66	10	Neutral	$$	
Grapeseed	16	70	10	Neutral	$$	
Corn	28	55	13	Neutral	$	
Olive	73	11	14	Distinctive fruitiness in better virgin oils	$$ to $$$	Extra-virgin is good for salads and light sautéeing. Use lower-grade oils for higher-heat cooking.
Soybean	23	58	16	Neutral	$	Good all-purpose oil; sometimes labeled "vegetable oil."
Peanut	46	32	17	Neutral to mild nutty flavor	$$	Good for all-around use. Unrefined oil adds flavor to Asian dishes.
Tub margarine (vegetable-oil base)	32	46	21	Mild	$	Good substitute for butter for most uses.
Specialty oils (use occasionally)						
Almond	70	17	8	Distinctive	$$$	Unrefined oils are good for dipping, in salads, or drizzled on food. Toasted oils pack extra flavor.
Flaxseed	18	68	9	Distinctive	$$$	
Walnut	23	63	9	Distinctive	$$$	
Sesame	40	42	14	Distinctive	$$$	
Solid fats (use sparingly)						
Stick margarine	39	24	15	Mild	$	Solid fats are best for some baked goods (flaky piecrusts, pastries) or when used judiciously to impart richness (in buttery sauces, for example). Shortening and stick margarine can contain trans fats, which should be avoided.
Shortening	45	26	25	Neutral to mild	$	
Lard (pork fat)	45	11	39	Mild, savory	$	
Palm	37	9	49	Mild	$$	
Butter	21	3	51	Mild	$	
Coconut	6	2	87	Mild	$$ to $$$	

[1] Percentages calculated per 100 grams. Percentages do not add up to 100 because we did not include some minor constituents. "High-oleic" versions of some oils have higher monounsaturated and lower polyunsaturated fat content. [2] Cost calculations based on an informal shopper survey.

to a comprehensive 2007 review of studies by the World Cancer Research Fund and the American Institute for Cancer Research, there is no strong, convincing evidence that eating more or less total fat, or any individual type of fat, has any significant effect on cancer.

Since obesity is one of the few diet-related factors that is strongly and consistently linked to a risk of cancer, the best diet for cancer prevention may be one that can help you maintain a healthy weight.

Are Coconut and Palm Oil Good for You or Not?

The consensus is that those oils are loaded with cholesterol-raising saturated fat. But dissenters say there is emerging evidence that tropical oils, especially coconut oil, behave differently in the body than animal-derived saturated fats, and might have under-appreciated health benefits.

Philip Calder, Ph.D., professor of nutritional immunology at the University of Southampton in England and editor-in-chief of the *British Journal of Nutrition,* notes that while more research is needed, for now, "There's not that much evidence that coconut oil offers an advantage over other types of oil, and it's likely to raise your cholesterol."

What to do? Your best bet for the time being is to limit consumption of those oils but keep an open mind.

How Does Processing Affect the Benefits and Risks of Oil?

Oils may be processed using mechanical pressing or heat and chemicals, a method that can affect its flavor and potentially its health benefits. Olive oil, for example, is prized for the complex flavors that are strongest when the oil is fresh from the fruit. That's why higher grades (extra virgin and virgin) are given only to mechanically pressed oil that hasn't been treated with heat or chemicals. Those premium oils contain higher quantities of antioxidants, which are eliminated or reduced from lesser oils during processing.

Processed or refined oils do have some pluses, though. They are less expensive, last longer, and can hold up to high-heat uses like frying without smoking and breaking down into potentially toxic compounds. On the minus side, refined oils may have been extracted with hexane, an industrial solvent. A form of hexane

is classified as an air pollutant by the Environmental Protection Agency and as a neurotoxin by the Centers for Disease Control and Prevention, and environmental groups have raised concerns about residues that might be left behind in the oil.

Testing by an organic advocacy group found trace amounts of hexane residue (less than 10 parts per million) in a sample of soybean oil. However, almost all of the research on hexane toxicity has involved factory workers breathing in high concentrations of air-borne hexanes.

At very low exposure levels through food, there is no reason to think it should be a health problem, says toxicologist John L. O'Donoghue, Ph.D., of the University of Rochester School of Medicine and Dentistry.

If you're concerned about hexane in oil, look for labels that say it was "expeller pressed." Oils that carry the "USDA Organic" label are also produced without hexane.

Bottom line. According to the 2010 U.S. Dietary Guidelines, 20 to 35 percent of the calories in a healthful diet should come from fats. Most of that total should consist of plant oils such as canola, olive, and soybean oil (usually labeled simply as vegetable oil). Coconut and palm oils are an exception.

Overall, limit your intake of saturated fats to less than 10 percent of your daily calories. That's about 4 teaspoons for someone eating a typical 2,000-calorie-a-day diet. To achieve that, eat less animal-based food (full-fat cheese, processed meats, and dairy desserts like ice cream) and highly processed snack food (cakes and cookies). In addition, reduce saturated fat by filling most of your plate with fruit and vegetables.

Critical Thinking

1. What is the difference between healthy and unhealthy fat in the diet?
2. What type of foods will increase healthy fats in the diet?

Create Central

www.mhhe.com/createcentral

Internet References

The American Dietetic Association
   www.eatright.org
Center for Science in the Public Interest (CSPI)
   www.cspinet.org

Article Prepared by: Eileen L. Daniel, *SUNY Brockport*

Yes, Healthful Fast Food Is Possible. But Edible?

A tofu taco from Lyfe Kitchen, Buffalo "wings" with ranch dressing from Veggie Grill and Veggie Grill's "cheese-burger" on kale.

Mark Bittman

Learning Outcomes

After reading this article, you will be able to:

- Explain what has driven the market for healthy fast food.

- Describe what consumers are seeking besides nutrition when they opt for healthy fast food.

- Understand why so many fast food companies are investing in healthier options.

When my daughter was a teenager, about a dozen years ago, she went through a vegetarian phase. Back then, the payoff for orthodontist visits was a trip to Taco Bell, where the only thing we could eat were bean burritos and tacos. It wasn't my favorite meal, but the mushy beans in that soft tortilla or crisp shell were kind of soothing, and the sweet "hot" sauce made the experience decent enough. I usually polished off two or three.

I was thinking of those Taco Bell stops during a recent week of travel. I had determined, as a way of avoiding the pitfalls of airport food, to be vegan for the length of the trip. This isn't easy. By the time I got to Terminal C at Dallas/Fort Worth, I couldn't bear another Veggie Delite from Subway, a bad chopped salad on lousy bread. So I wandered up to the Taco Bell Express opposite Gate 14 and optimistically asked the cashier if I could get a bean burrito without cheese or sour cream. He pointed out a corner on the overhead display where the "fresco" menu offered pico de gallo in place of dairy, then upsold me on a multilayered "fresco" bean burrito for about 3 bucks. As he was talking, the customers to my right and left, both fit, suit-wearing people bearing expressions of hunger and resignation, perked up. They weren't aware of the fresco menu, either. One was trying to "eat healthy on the road"; the other copped to "having vegan kids." Like me, they were intrigued by a fast-food burrito with about 350 calories, or less than half as many as a Fiesta Taco Salad bowl. It wasn't bad, either.

Twelve years after the publication of "Fast Food Nation" and nearly as long since Morgan Spurlock almost ate himself to death, our relationship with fast food has changed. We've gone from the whistle-blowing stage to the higher-expectations stage, and some of those expectations are being met. Various states have passed measures to limit the confinement of farm animals. In-N-Out Burger has demonstrated that you don't have to underpay your employees to be profitable. There are dozens of plant-based alternatives to meat, with more on the way; increasingly, they're pretty good.

The fulfillment of these expectations has led to higher ones. My experience at the airport only confirmed what I'd been hearing for years from analysts in the fast-food industry. After the success of companies like Whole Foods, and healthful (or theoretically healthful) brands like Annie's and Kashi, there's now a market for a fast-food chain that's not only healthful itself, but vegetarian-friendly, sustainable and even humane. And, this being fast food: cheap. "It is significant, and I do believe it is coming from consumer desire to have choices and more balance," says Andy Barish, a restaurant analyst at Jefferies LLC, the investment bank. "And it's not just the coasts anymore."

I'm not talking about token gestures, like McDonald's fruit-and-yogurt parfait, whose calories are more than 50 percent sugar. And I don't expect the prices to match those of Taco Bell or McDonald's, where economies of scale and inexpensive ingredients make meals dirt cheap. What I'd like is a place that serves only good options, where you don't have to resist the junk food to order well, and where the food is real—by which I mean dishes that generally contain few ingredients and are recognizable to everyone, not just food technologists. It's a place where something like a black-bean burger piled with vegetables and baked sweet potato fries—and, hell, maybe even a vegan shake—is less than 10 bucks and 800 calories (and way fewer without the shake). If I could order and eat that in 15 minutes, I'd be happy, and I think a lot of others would be, too. You can try my recipes for a fast, low-calorie burger, fries and shake.

In recent years, the fast-food industry has started to heed these new demands. Billions of dollars have been invested in more healthful fast-food options, and the financial incentives justify these expenditures. About half of all the money spent on food in the United States is for meals eaten outside the home. And last year McDonald's earned $5.5 billion in profits on $88 billion in sales. If a competitor offered a more healthful option that was able to capture just a single percent of that market share, it would make $55 million. Chipotle, the best newcomer of the last generation, has beaten that 1 percent handily. Last year, sales approached $3 billion. In the fourth quarter, they grew by 17 percent over the same period in the previous year.

Numbers are tricky to pin down for more healthful options because the fast food industry doesn't yet have a category for "healthful." The industry refers to McDonald's and Burger King as "quick-serve restaurants"; Chipotle is "fast casual"; and restaurants where you order at the counter and the food is brought to you are sometimes called "premium fast casual." Restaurants from these various sectors often deny these distinctions, but QSR, an industry trade magazine—"Limited-Service, Unlimited Possibilities"—spends a good deal of space dissecting them.

However, after decades of eating the stuff, I have my own. First, there are those places that serve junk, no matter what kind of veneer they present. Subway, Taco Bell (I may be partial to them, but really. . .), McDonald's and their ilk make up the Junk Food sector. One step up are places with better ambience and perhaps better ingredients—Shake Shack, Five Guys, Starbucks, Pret a Manger—that also peddle unhealthful food but succeed in making diners feel better about eating it, either because it tastes better, is surrounded by some healthful options, the setting is groovier or they use some organic or sustainable ingredients. This is the Nouveau Junk sector.

Chipotle combines the best aspects of Nouveau Junk to create a new category that we might call Improved Fast Food. At Chipotle, the food is fresher and tastes much better than traditional fast food. The sourcing, production and cooking is generally of a higher level; and the overall experience is more pleasant. The guacamole really is made on premises, and the chicken (however tasteless) is cooked before your eyes. It's fairly easy to eat vegan there, but those burritos can pack on the calories. As a competitor told me, "Several brands had a head start on [the Chipotle founder Steve] Ells, but he kicked their [expletive] with culture and quality. It's not shabby for assembly-line steam-table Mexican food. It might be worth $10 billion right now." (It is.)

Chipotle no longer stands alone in the Improved Fast Food world: Chop't, Maoz, Freshii, Zoës Kitchen and several others all have their strong points. And—like Chipotle—they all have their limitations, starting with calories and fat. By offering fried chicken and fried onions in addition to organic tofu, Chop't, a salad chain in New York and Washington, tempts customers to turn what might have been a healthful meal into a calorie bomb (to say nothing of the tasteless dressing), and often raises the price to $12 or more. The Netherlands-based Maoz isn't bad, but it's not as good as the mom-and-pop falafel trucks and shops that are all over Manhattan. There are barely any choices,

nothing is cooked to order, the pita is a sponge and there is a messy serve-yourself setup that makes a $10 meal seem like a bit of a rip-off.

Despite its flaws, Improved Fast Food is the transitional step to a new category of fast-food restaurant whose practices should be even closer to sustainable and whose meals should be reasonably healthful and good-tasting and inexpensive. (Maybe not McDonald's-inexpensive, but under $10.) This new category is, or will be, Good Fast Food, and there are already a few emerging contenders.

Veggie Grill is a six-year-old Los Angeles–based chain with 18 locations. Technically, it falls into the "premium fast casual" category. The restaurants are pleasantly designed and nicely lighted and offer limited service. The food is strictly vegan, though you might not know it at first.

Kevin Boylan and T. K. Pillan, the chain's founders, are vegans themselves. They frequently refer to their food as "familiar" and "American," but that's debatable. The "chickin" in the "Santa Fe Crispy Chickin" sandwich is Gardein, a soy-based product that has become the default for fast-food operators looking for meat substitutes. Although there are better products in the pipeline, Gardein, especially when fried, tastes more or less like a McNugget (which isn't entirely "real" chicken itself). The "cheese" is Daiya, which is tapioca-based and similar in taste to a pasteurized processed American cheese. The "steak," "carne asada," "crab cake" (my favorite) and "burger" are also soy, in combination with wheat and pea protein. In terms of animal welfare, environmental damage and resource usage, these products are huge steps in the right direction. They save animals, water, energy and land.

Boylan wanted to make clear to me that his chain isn't about haute cuisine. "We're not doing sautéed tempeh with a peach reduction da-da-da," he said. "That may be a great menu item, but most people don't know what it is. When we say 'cheese-burger'—or 'fried chickin' with mashed potatoes with gravy and steamed kale—everyone knows what we're talking about." He's probably right, and the vegetables are pretty good, too. The mashed potatoes are cut with 40 percent cauliflower; the gravy is made from porcini mushrooms and you can get your entree on a bed of kale instead of a bun.

When I first entered a Veggie Grill, I expected a room full of skinny vegans talking about their vegan-ness. Instead, at locations in Hollywood, El Segundo and Westwood, the lines could have been anywhere, even an airport Taco Bell. The diners appeared mixed by class and weight, and sure looked like omnivores, which they mostly are. The company's research shows that about 70 percent of its customers eat meat or fish, a fact that seems both reflected in its menu and its instant success. Veggie Grill won best American restaurant in the 2012 Los Angeles Times readers' poll, and sales are up 16 percent in existing stores compared with last year. The plan is to double those 18 locations every 18 months for the foreseeable future—"fast enough to stay ahead of competitors, but not so fast as to lose our cultural DNA," Boylan said. In 2011, the founders brought in a new C.E.O., Greg Dollarhyde, who helped Baja Fresh become a national chain before its sale to Wendy's for nearly $300 million.

Veggie Grill is being underwritten partly by Brentwood Associates, a small private-equity firm that's invested in various consumer businesses, including Zoës Kitchen, a chain that offers kebabs, braised beans and roasted vegetables. "For a firm like us to get involved with a concept like Veggie Grill, we have to believe it's a profitable business model, and we do," Brentwood's managing director, Rahul Aggarwal, told me. "Ten years ago I would've said no vegan restaurant would be successful, but people are looking for different ways to eat and this is a great concept."

I admire Veggie Grill, but while making "chickin" from soy is no crime, it's still far from real food. I have a long-running argument with committed vegan friends, who say that Americans aren't ready for rice and beans, or chickpea-and-spinach stew, and that places like Veggie Grill offer a transition to animal-and-environment-friendlier food. On one level, I agree. Why feed the grain to tortured animals to produce lousy meat when you can process the grain and produce it into "meat"? On another level, the goal should be fast food that's real food, too.

Much of what I ate at Veggie Grill was fried and dense, and even when I didn't overeat, I felt as heavy afterward as I do after eating at a Junk Food chain. And while that Santa Fe Crispy Chickin sandwich with lettuce, tomato, red onion, avocado and vegan mayo comes in at 550 calories, 200 fewer than Burger King's Tendercrisp chicken sandwich, the "chickin" sandwich costs $9. The Tendercrisp costs $5, and that's in Midtown Manhattan.

Future growth should allow Veggie Grill to lower prices, but it may never be possible to spend less than 10 dollars on a meal there. Part of that cost is service: at Veggie Grill, you order, get a number to put on your table and wait for a server. It's a luxury compared with most chains, and a pleasant one, but the combination of the food's being not quite real and the price's being still too high means Veggie Grill hasn't made the leap to Good Fast Food.

During my time in Los Angeles, I also ate at Native Foods Café, a vegan chain similar to Veggie Grill, where you can get a pretty good "meatball" sub (made of seitan, a form of wheat gluten), and at Tender Greens, which, though it is cafeteria-style (think Chipotle with a large Euro-Californian menu), flirts with the $20 mark for a meal. It can't really be considered fast food, but it's quite terrific and I'd love to see it put Applebee's and Olive Garden out of business.

In Culver City, I visited Lyfe Kitchen (that's "Love Your Food Everyday"; I know, but please keep reading). Lyfe has the pedigree, menu, financing, plan and ambition to take on the major chains. The company is trying to build 250 locations in the next five years, and QSR has already wondered whether it will become the "Whole Foods of fast food."

At Lyfe, the cookies are dairy-free; the beef comes from grass-fed, humanely raised cows; nothing weighs in at more than 600 calories; and there's no butter, cream, white sugar, white flour, high-fructose corn syrup or trans fats. The concept was the brainchild of the former Gardein executive and investment banker Stephen Sidwell, who quickly enlisted Mike Roberts, the former global president of McDonald's, and Mike Donahue, McDonald's U.S.A.'s chief of corporate communications. These

three teamed up with Art Smith, Oprah's former chef, and Tal Ronnen, who I believe to be among the most ambitious and talented vegan chefs in the country.

According to Roberts, Lyfe currently has more than 250 angel investors who "represent a group of people that are saying, 'We've been waiting for something like this.'" The Culver City operation opened earlier this year, and two more California locations are scheduled to open before the year is out. New York locations are being actively scouted, and a Chicago franchise is in the works.

When I visited the Culver City operation, shortly before its official opening, I sampled across the menu and came away impressed. There are four small, creative flatbread pizzas under $10; one is vegan, two are vegetarian and one was done with chicken. I tasted terrific salads, like a beet-and-farro one ($9) that could easily pass for a starter at a good restaurant, and breakfast selections, like steel-cut oatmeal with yogurt and real maple syrup ($5) and a tofu wrap ($6.50), were actually delicious.

Lyfe, not unlike life, isn't cheap. The owners claim that an average check is "around $15" but one entree (roast salmon, bok choy, shiitake mushrooms, miso, etc.) costs exactly $15. An "ancient grain" bowl with Gardein "beef tips" costs $12, which seems too much. Still, the salmon is good and the bowl is delicious, as is a squash risotto made with farro that costs $9—or the price of a "chickin" sandwich at Veggie Grill or a couple of Tendercrisp sandwiches at Burger King.

How in the world, I asked Roberts and Donahue, can they expect to run 250 franchises serving that salmon dish or the risotto or their signature roasted brussels sprouts, which they hope to make into the French fries of the 21st century? Donahue acknowledged that it was going to be a challenge, but nothing that technology couldn't solve. Lyfe will rely on digital order-taking, G.P.S. customer location—a coaster will tell your server where you're sitting—online ordering and mobile apps. Programmable, state-of-the-art combination ovens store recipes, cook with moist or dry heat and really do take the guesswork out of cooking. An order-tracking system tells cooks when to start preparing various parts of dishes and requires their input only at the end of each order. Almost all activity is tracked in real time, which helps the managers run things smoothly.

Lyfe isn't vegan, so much as protein-agnostic. You can get a Gardein burger or a grass-fed beef burger, "unfried" chicken or Gardein "chickin." You can also get wine (biodynamic), beer (organic) or a better-than-it-sounds banana-kale smoothie. However, I fear that Lyfe's ambition, and its diverse menu, will drive up equipment and labor costs, and that those costs are going to keep the chain from appealing to less-affluent Americans. You can get a lot done in a franchise system, but its main virtues are locating the most popular dishes, focusing on their preparation and streamlining the process. My hope is that Lyfe will evolve, as all businesses do, by a process of trial and error, and be successful enough that they have a real impact on the way we think of fast food.

Veggie Grill, Lyfe Kitchen, Tender Greens and others have solved the challenge of bringing formerly upscale, plant-based foods to more of a mass audience. But the industry seems to be focused on a niche group that you might call the health-aware sector of the population. (If you're reading this article, you're probably in it.) Whole Foods has proved that you can build a publicly traded business, with $16 billion in market capitalization, by appealing to this niche. But fast food is, at its core, a class issue. Many people rely on that Tendercrisp because they need to, and our country's fast-food problem won't be solved—no matter how much innovation in vegan options or high-tech ovens—until the prices come down and this niche sector is no longer niche.

It was this idea that led me, a few years ago, to try to start a fast-food chain of my own, modeled after Chipotle. I wanted to focus on Mediterranean food, largely on plant-based options like falafel, hummus, chopped salad, grilled vegetables and maybe a tagine or ratatouille. I wanted to prioritize sustainability, minimize meat and eliminate soda, and I'd treat and pay workers fairly. But after chatting with a few fast-food veterans, I soon recognized just how quixotic my ideas seemed. Anyone with industry experience would want to add more meat, sell Coke and take advantage of both workers and customers to maximize profits. I lost my stomach for the project before I even really began, but recent trends suggest that there may have been hope had I stuck to my guns. Soda consumption is down; meat consumption is down; sales of organic foods are up; more people are expressing concern about G.M.O.s, additives, pesticides and animal welfare. The lines out the door—first at Chipotle and now at Maoz, Chop't, Tender Greens and Veggie Grill—don't lie. According to a report in Advertising Age, McDonald's no longer ranks in the top 10 favorite restaurants of Millennials, a group that comprises as many as 80 million people. Vegans looking for a quick fix after the orthodontist have plenty of choices.

Good Fast Food doesn't need to be vegan or even vegetarian; it just ought to be real, whole food. The best word to describe a wise contemporary diet is flexitarian, which is nothing more than intelligent omnivorism. There are probably millions of people who now eat this way, including me. My own style, which has worked for me for six years, is to eat a vegan diet before 6 p.m. and then allow myself pretty much whatever I want for dinner. This flexibility avoids junk and emphasizes plants, and

Lyfe Kitchen, which offers both "chickin" and chicken—plus beans, vegetables and grains in their whole forms (all for under 600 calories per dish)—comes closest to this ideal. But the menu offers too much, the service raises prices too high and speed is going to be an issue. My advice would be to skip the service and the wine, make a limited menu with big flavors and a few treats and keep it as cheap as you can. Of course, there are huge players who could do this almost instantaneously. But the best thing they seem able to come up with is the McWrap or the fresco menu.

In the meantime, I'm throwing out a few recipes to the entire fast-food world to help build a case that it's possible to use real ingredients to create relatively inexpensive, low-calorie, meat-free, protein-dense, inexpensive fast food. If anyone with the desire can produce this stuff in a home kitchen, then industry veterans financed by private equity firms should be able to produce it at scale in a fraction of the time and at a fraction of the price. You think people won't eat it? There's a lot of evidence that suggests otherwise.

Critical Thinking

1. What are consumers looking for in fast food besides good nutrition?
2. Why are so many fast food companies investing in healthier menu options?

Create Central

www.mhhe.com/createcentral

Internet References

The American Dietetic Association
www.eatright.org
Center for Science in the Public Interest (CSPI)
www.cspinet.org

MARK BITTMAN *is a food writer for the magazine.*

Article   Prepared by: Eileen Daniel, *SUNY College at Brockport*

Wonderful Wheat

Why This Ancient Staple Is Still Good for You

Learn which factors determine best uses, nutrition, and flavor.

STAN COX

Learning Outcomes

After reading this article, you will be able to:

- Understand the nutritional differences between whole wheat and unenriched white wheat flour.

- Understand the relationship between wheat consumption and celiac disease and gluten intolerance.

- Describe the different types of wheat.

The great diversity we see today in wheat is the result of millions of years of evolution capped by 100 centuries of breeding by humans. Varieties originating throughout that history—modern types, heirloom varieties from past decades or centuries, and even wheat varieties we can date back to 9,000 B.C.—are still available today. Sorting through the types of wheat and flour to find the most nutritious or flavorful—or the best to use for a specific purpose—requires wading into a deep gene pool. Doing so, however, will give you better breads, more tender cakes and biscuits, and sturdier pastas.

There are no "standard" types of wheat. The term "wheat" encompasses a sprawling family tree of species, and myriad varieties within those species, and no two varieties produce grain that's exactly the same.

Which Wheat for Which Purpose?

Common wheat (*Triticum aestivum*), sometimes called "bread wheat," is the most widely grown species and yields the flout we buy by the bag. This wheat is the chief ingredient in commercial foods, such as loaf and raised breads, tortillas, doughnuts and cakes, and East Asian noodles.

Durum wheat (*T. turgidum ssp. durum*) is used in most dried pasta and couscous, for raised and flat breads in parts of Europe and the Middle East, and, less often, in the United States for raised breads. Although pasta can be made from common wheat as well, durum pasta predominates and is generally considered higher quality.

Ancient wheat varieties ate currently grown on smaller acreages in the United States than common and durum wheats. Whereas the kernels of the latter two are released from their hulls by threshing, those of ancient wheats remain enclosed in inedible hulls after threshing. Each ancient species occupies a different branch of wheats family tree: spelt (*T. aestivum var. spelta*) is an older form of common wheat, emmer (farro) (*T. turgidum* ssp. *dicoccoides*) is the direct ancestor of durum wheat, and einkorn (*T. monococcum*) is closely related to a wild grass species that played a part in the ancestry of all wheats (see the chart "Wheat's Family Tree"). These early wheat varieties are now mechanically dehulled and lend themselves to a variety of products. Some strains of einkorn can make raised bread or pasta. Spelt, too, can create good bread.

Which Wheat Is Most Nutritious?

Whole-wheat products are richer in fiber, minerals, B vitamins and antioxidants than those made from white flour—which, stripped of its nutrient- and fiber-rich germ and bran, provides mostly empty calories (see the chart "Whole-Wheat Flour vs. Unenriched White Flour"). An extra-nutrient-rich wheat variety processed into white flour will be less nutritious than whole-wheat flour from any run-of-the-mill variety. The long-running

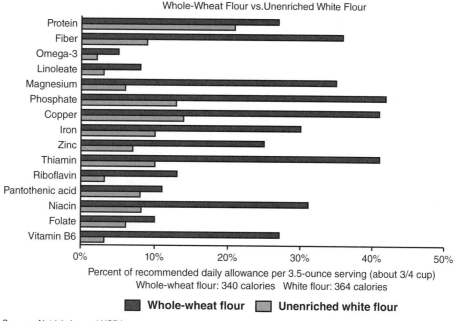

Whole-Wheat Flour vs. Unenriched White Flour

Percent of recommended daily allowance per 3.5-ounce serving (about 3/4 cup)
Whole-wheat flour: 340 calories   White flour: 364 calories

■ **Whole-wheat flour**   ■ **Unenriched white flour**

Sources: Nutricircles and USDA.

Framingham Heart Study in Massachusetts, begun in 1948 and still continuing, found that subjects who ate at least five servings of grains per day, with whole-wheat products prominent, lost more belly fat than those who ate less than five servings of grains.

But if you consume the whole kernel, can you obtain better nutrition from some classes of wheat than from others? Possibly. Each wheat variety has a different profile, higher in some nutrients but lower in others.

Early wheat varieties are usually higher in protein than common wheat. An evaluation of 176 wheat varieties showed that dietary fiber was highest in common wheat, while einkorn and emmer had the lowest amount. (Remember: Everything's relative; all wholewheat varieties in that study would still be good sources of fiber.) Plus, although some published research finds that einkorn, emmer, and spelt typically have mote iron, zinc, copper, and other essential minerals than do common wheats; other researchers have found no differences.

Throughout the past century, wheat breeders' efforts have converged with changes in farming practices—most prominently, chemical soil fertilization—to increase wheat yields per acre. Millers, bakers, nutritionists, and wheat breeders themselves have wondered whether these higher yields have been achieved at the cost of lower nutrition, a theory that has sparked growing interest in ancient varieties and heirloom wheat varieties (strains that were developed by farmers before the age of the university plant breeder).

Recently, researchers in Europe and North America have been studying whether wheat nutrition has indeed declined. The majority have examined old and new wheats grown under the same environmental conditions, often focusing on protein, which is the dominant factor in bread and pasta quality. Most field trials have revealed that early wheat varieties have protein levels that are, on average, equal to or greater than those of modern wheats. In contrast, no strong differences have been found in the few retrospective studies of fiber or antioxidants. Wheat classes rank in protein content from highest to lowest in this order: hard red spring wheats, hard red winter wheats, and then both red and white soft winter wheats (see "Wheat Terminology, Demystified").

Recent trials by North Dakota State University found that the hard red spring wheat varieties "Alsen," "Elgin," and "Glenn" showed the highest amount of protein of the 18 varieties tested. Among hard red winter wheats, the older varieties "Karl" and "Plainsman V" remain among the highest in protein content.

Zinc tends to be lower in newer European and U.S. wheat varieties than in those developed 50 to 100 years ago. Iron has seen a less steep, less consistent decline, while other essential minerals have remained stable for the most part.

White spring wheat—a class grown primarily in the Pacific Northwest—is generally lower in protein than in red wheats. Wholewheat products made from these white wheats may be less bitter than those made from whole red wheat. Commercial millers like white spring wheat because they can mill "closer to

Wheat Terminology, Demystified

Varieties of wheat are classified as either "spring" or "winter" types. Those terms refer to differences in the plant's response to cold weather.

Winter wheats flower only after several weeks of cold weather, so winter wheats are sown in autumn and harvested the following spring or summer in regions that have cold winters. Spring wheats have no such temperature requirement in order to flower. They are sown in spring where winters are cold enough to kill winter wheat, and they can be sown in autumn in regions that are relatively warm year-round. The most commonly grown durum wheat varieties are spring wheats; einkorn, emmer, and spelt wheats can be either.

Wheats are also classified as "red" or "white" and as "hard" or "soft" (based on kernel characteristics). In North America, breads and rolls usually use higher-protein hard-wheat flour (which has more gluten, creating the spongy texture of yeast breads), while lower-protein soft-wheat flour goes into cakes, cookies, crackers, and pastries.

Flours labeled "bread flour" at the supermarket are made from blends of hard wheats, with a protein content of 12 to 14 percent. Products labeled "cake flour" or "pastry flour" are from soft wheats with a protein content of 8 to 10 percent, and "all-purpose flour" is either medium-protein hard-wheat flour or a blend of hard- and soft-wheat flours with a protein content of 10 to 12 percent.

Why Are Wheat Products Making Some People Sick?

Recent books such as Dr. William Davis' *Wheat Belly* and David Perlmutter's *Grain Brain* revile wheat, blaming it for everything from "destroying more brains in this country than all the strokes, car accidents and head trauma combined" (Davis) to depression, schizophrenia, and infertility (Perlmutter).

Seizing on these sensational claims, food manufacturers have flooded the market with "gluten-free" products—many of which are just sugar-laden junk food.

Thousands of people have come to believe that contemporary wheat causes gluten intolerance and they're convinced that they suffer from the ailment.

Nutrition researchers can point to mountains of scientific data demonstrating the health benefits of whole-wheat foods. But that doesn't mean wheat is good for everyone. Just under 1 percent of people in the United States have an autoimmune condition called celiac disease, in which certain peptides—protein fragments produced during digestion of wheat's gluten proteins—severely damage the walls of the intestines.

People who have celiac disease must not eat foods containing wheat of any type. Today, an estimated 5 to 10 percent of the U.S. population not suffering from celiac disease is nevertheless avoiding wheat because they either have, or believe they may have, a digestive intolerance of gluten proteins.

Many people think genetic modification of wheat is behind the apparent rise in gluten sensitivity. They are mistaken.

No transgenic wheats—often called "genetically modified" or "GM"—are currently available to wheat growers. Nor are wheats "hybrids" in the modern meaning of the term.

In *Wheat Belly*, Davis makes the extreme argument that *no one* should eat wheat. He blames wheat for a host of medical problems, including gastrointestinal disruption, obesity, diabetes, and autism.

Food processing and additives are more likely to blame. Because much processed food pairs refined white flour with sugar and industrial fats, some people may feel better when they eliminate wheat—because they're eliminating excess starch, sugar, and fats, too.

In point-by-point reviews of Davis' claims published by the *Journal of Cereal Science* and the American Association of Cereal Chemists International journal, *Cereal Foods World,* little of *Wheat Belly* stood up to scientific scrutiny. These and other examinations of published research reveal no evidence that wheat is a top culprit in modern health problems as Davis and Perlmutter suggest.

While the way wheat is bred may result in nutritional effects, claims that wheat or gluten itself is the source of various health issues remain unproved.

the bran" and extract more flour per ton of wheat. Most wheat exported from the West Coast to East Asia is white because noodles made from red wheat tend to be gray.

Older white spring varieties have distinctly higher levels of copper, iron, magnesium, phosphorus, selenium, and zinc than do modern varieties. Wheat researcher Stephen Jones and his colleagues at Washington State University have surmised that breeders of white wheats have inadvertently driven down mineral content by selecting varieties with higher yields and lighter flour color.

Taking into account all nutrients, wheat from heirloom and ancient varieties could raise your intake of some nutrients while not affecting your intake of others. Wide variation exists, however, among individual wheats in their ability to pack protein, antioxidants, and minerals into the kernel. Furthermore, soil and climate can trump genetic influences on nutritional quality. Thus, regardless of species or class, wheat varieties raised with optimal growing conditions will produce nutrient-dense grain.

Concerns about maximum nutrition and quality mustn't overlook the effects of processing flour on the final food product. Flour improves with age; its gluten strength increases and its color lightens if it is exposed to the air for several days or weeks before baking. Commercial millers often use tricks to shorten the time from grain to bread. They add chemical oxidizing agents to simulate this aging and allow flour to be used soon after milling. Potassium bromate, once the most common such "bleaching" agent, is a potential carcinogen that has been outlawed in many countries, and the Food and Drug Administration discourages its use. One widely used chemical, azodicarbonamide, is not harmful itself, but one of the by-products of its breakdown in the body is semicarbazide, also a potential carcinogen. Buy unbleached flour and read product labels to avoid such chemicals.

Which Wheat Tastes Better?

Texture and flavor in breads and other products rely on many factors. Unlike single-malt Scotch whiskes, prized for their single-source origins, flour milled from only one wheat variety is rarely optimal for baking; blends predominate. Consider an experiment in France, says Julie Dawson, a plant scientist at the University of Wisconsin. Trained panelists tasted sourdough breads made from 12 flours milled from French heirloom wheat varieties, such as "Blé de la Réole," "Bladette de Puylaurens" and "Souris." The highest average score went to a bread made with a blend of flours from several heirloom varieties—a mixture created by a farmer and baker who worked together over several years.

Recent taste research by Maria Jesus Callejo Gonzalez of the Technical University of Madrid compared spelt and common wheat varieties. She found that "one of the spelt breads was more complex with respect to flavor attributes." Available winter spelt varieties include "Champ," "Comet," "Maverick," "Oberkulmer," "Sammy," "Sindelar," "Sungold," "Tiber," and "Tora." "Bavaria," a spring spelt, is also sold. There have not yet been any controlled quality evaluations for flavor on specific spelt varieties.

Randy Metz, a Pennsylvania grower, says a good spelt for baking is "Sungold," but it's new, expensive, and hard to find. He also likes "Maverick," which dehulls easily—about 40 percent clean in the combine, he says, and he recommends it for homestead growers. But dehulled spelt won't grow, Metz says, so to grow your own, plant unprocessed kernels with hulls intact.

Wheat's Family Tree

Wheat's evolution goes back about 4 million years to southwest Asia, where two wild grasses, *Triticum boeoticum* and a species in the genus *Aegilops,* cross-pollinated to produce a hybrid species, *T. dicoccoides.* Between 8,000 and 11,000 years ago, a close relative of *T. boeoticum* was domesticated, creating einkorn (*T. monococcum*); at about that same time, emmer (*T. turgidum* ssp. *dicoccoides*) arose from the domestication of *T. dicoccoides.* Between 6,000 and 8,000 years ago, the wild grass *A. tauschii* pollinated emmer and produced spelt (*I aestivum* var. *spelta*). Further domestication of spelt led to the development of common wheat (*T. aestivum*).

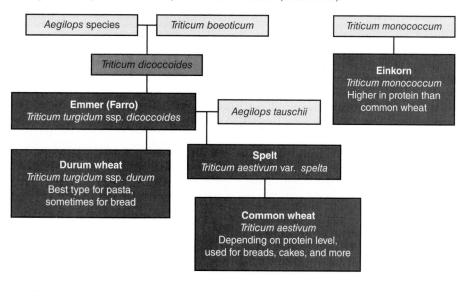

Other early wheat varieties also stand out from the crowd, Dawson says. "We found that einkorn and emmer wheats have their own distinct flavors, and there is diversity among varieties." Today, einkorn is widely sought-after for its unique taste, which Dawson describes as sweet and nutty. Einkorn flour, despite being powdery and having low gluten strength, can still make excellent-tasting pasta.

North American heirloom wheats are treasured for good flavor. In northern climates, the red spring wheat variety "Red Fife" is one such favorite. Among hard winter wheats of the central Plains states, "Turkey Red" is a true heirloom variety that started as a blend of genetic types. Quickly adopted by Mennonite immigrants to Kansas in the 1870s, by 1920 "Turkey Red" constituted a staggering 99 percent of the Great Plains' wheat production. It is the genetic foundation on which today's higher-yielding hard winter wheats were built. Working with Heartland Mill in Marienthal, Kan., artisanal baker Thorn Leonard has helped foster the cultivation of "Turkey Red" for use by other bakers and himself. He says the old variety has a complexity and flavor that, he speculates, may have resulted in part from its diverse genetic makeup.

Flavor is of crucial importance in durum wheat, too. At the Italian National Agricultural Research Council (CRA) in Rome, Dr. Norberto Pogna and his colleagues routinely put durum wheat to the pasta test. Spaghetti is evaluated by a panel of professional tasters, and any flour that creates spaghetti without excellent texture and taste will go no further. Pogna's panels find few differences between older and newer durum varieties in these samplings.

As a home miller or baker, you can craft noodles, bread, and baked delicacies from a diverse set of wheat varieties or blends simply by adjusting ingredients and methods. This allows experimentation with wheats, whether ancient species, heirloom strains, or recently bred varieties. Most will work well, with no chemical additives.

Critical Thinking

1. Does modern wheat cause health problems such as celiac disease or gluten intolerance?

2. Why is there no standard type of wheat?

Create Central

www.mhhe.com/createcentral

Internet References

Celiac Disease Foundation
http://www.celiac.org

Wheat Foods Network
http://www.wheatfoods.org

STAN COX is a sustainable-living activist and plant breeder at The Land Institute in Salina, Kan. He has worked as a USDA wheat geneticist and his most recent book is *Any Way You Slice It: The Past, Present, and Future of Rationing.*

Unit 4

UNIT

Prepared by: Eileen Daniel, *SUNY College at Brockport*

Exercise and Weight Management

Recently, a new set of guidelines, dubbed "Exercise Lite," has been issued by the U.S. Centers for Disease Control and Prevention in conjunction with the American College of Sports Medicine. These guidelines call for 30 minutes of exercise, 5 days a week, which can be spread over the course of a day. The primary focus of this approach to exercise is improving health, not athletic performance. Examples of activities that qualify under the new guidelines are walking your dog, playing tag with your kids, scrubbing floors, washing your car, mowing the lawn, weeding your garden, and having sex. From a practical standpoint, this approach to fitness will likely motivate many more people to become active and stay active. Remember, because the benefits of exercise can take weeks or even months before they become apparent, it is very important to choose an exercise program that you enjoy so that you will stick with it.

While a good diet cannot compensate for the lack of exercise, exercise can compensate for a less than optimal diet. Exercise not only makes people physically healthier, it also keeps their brains healthy. While the connection hasn't been proven, there is evidence that regular workouts may cause the brain to better process and store information, which results in a smarter brain.

Although exercise and a nutritious diet can keep people fit and healthy, many Americans are not heeding this advice. For the first time in our history, the average American is now overweight when judged according to the standard height/weight tables. In addition, more than 25 percent of Americans are clinically obese, and the number appears to be growing. Why is this happening, given the prevailing attitude that Americans have toward fat? One theory that is currently gaining support suggests that while Americans have cut back on their consumption of fatty snacks and desserts, they have actually increased their total caloric intake by failing to limit their consumption of carbohydrates. The underlying philosophy goes something like this: Fat calories make you fat, but you can eat as many carbohydrates as you want and not gain weight. The truth is that all calories count when it comes to weight gain, and if cutting back on fat calories prevents you from feeling satiated, you will naturally eat more to achieve that feeling. While this position seems

reasonable enough, some groups, most notably supporters of the Atkins diet, have suggested that eating a high-fat diet will actually help people lose weight because of fat's high satiety value in conjunction with the formation of ketones (which suppress appetite). Whether people limit fat or carbohydrates, they will not lose weight unless their total caloric intake is less than their energy expenditure.

America's preoccupation with body weight has given rise to a billion-dollar industry. When asked why people go on diets, the predominant answer is for social reasons such as appearance and group acceptance, rather than concerns regarding health. Why do diets and diet aids fail? One of the major reasons lies in the mindset of the dieter. Many dieters do not fully understand the biological and behavioral aspects of weight loss, and consequently they have unrealistic expectations regarding the process. While many people reasonably need to lose weight, many college women strive and compete with each other for the thinnest and most perfect body. This practice has led to an increase in the number of young women suffering from eating disorders.

Being overweight not only causes health problems; it also carries with it a social stigma. Overweight people are often thought of as weak-willed individuals with little or no self-respect. The notion that weight control problems are the result of personality defects is being challenged by new research findings. Evidence is mounting that suggests that physiological and hereditary factors may play as great a role in obesity as do behavioral and environmental factors. Researchers now believe that genetics dictate the base number of fat cells an individual will have, as well as the location and distribution of these cells within the body.

The study of fat metabolism has provided additional clues as to why weight control is so difficult. These metabolic studies have found that the body seems to have a "setpoint," or desired weight, and it will defend this weight through alterations in basal metabolic rate and fat-cell activities. While this process is thought to be an adaptive throwback to primitive times when food supplies were uncertain, today, with our abundant food supply, this mechanism only contributes to the problem of weight control.

It should be apparent by now that weight control is both an attitudinal and a lifestyle issue. Fortunately, a new, more rational approach to the problem of weight control is emerging. This approach is based on the premise that you can be perfectly healthy and good looking without being pencil-thin. The primary focus of this approach to weight management is the attainment of your body's "natural ideal weight" and not some idealized, fanciful notion of what you would like to weigh. The concept of achieving your natural ideal body weight suggests that we need to take a more realistic approach to both fitness and weight control and also serves to remind us that a healthy lifestyle is based on the concepts of balance and moderation.

Article   Prepared by: Eileen L. Daniel, *SUNY Brockport*

Eat Like a Greek

Want flavor plus good health? The Mediterranean style of dining has it all.

Learning Outcomes

After reading this article, you will be able to:

- Identify the components of a Mediterranean diet.

- Describe how a Mediterranean diet can reduce the risk of heart disease, cancer, diabetes, and dementia.

- Describe the style of eating that is characterized as Mediterranean.

Diets are often doomed to fail because they focus more on what you can't eat than what you can. Don't eat bread. Don't eat sugar. Don't eat fat. On some diets, even certain fruits and vegetables are forbidden. After a few weeks of being told "no," our inner toddler throws a tantrum and runs screaming to Krispy Kreme.

That's what is so appealing about the Mediterranean diet, which isn't really a diet at all but a style of eating that focuses on an abundance of delicious, hearty, and nutritious food. Just looking at the pyramid at right, developed by Oldways Preservation Trust, a nonprofit organization that encourages healthy food choices, may be enough to make you look forward to the next meal.

"What I like about this approach to food is that it's very easy," says Sara Baer-Sinnott, executive vice president of Oldways. "It's not a fancy way of eating, but you'll never feel deprived because the foods have so much flavor."

The best part is that eating like a Greek not only satisfies your need to say yes to food, but has been scientifically proven to be good for your health. Decades of research have shown that traditional Mediterranean eating patterns are associated with a lower risk of several chronic diseases, including the big three—cancer, heart disease, and type 2 diabetes. Most recently, a systematic review of 146 observational studies and 43 randomized clinical trials published in the April 13, 2009, issue of the *Archives of Internal Medicine* found strong evidence that a Mediterranean diet protects against cardiovascular disease. Other recent research has linked the eating style to a lower risk of cognitive decline and dementia.

So, where do you start? Your next meal is as good a place as any. Just walk through our guide for menu planning.

Stepping into a Mediterranean Lifestyle

Although a trip to southern Italy or Greece would be nice, you needn't go farther than your local supermarket. If your menu planning usually begins with a meat entrée, then adds a starch and a vegetable side dish as an afterthought, you'll want to reprioritize your food choices. "Think about designing a plate where a good half of it is taken up with vegetables, another one-quarter is healthy grains—whole-grain pasta, rice, couscous, quinoa—and the remaining quarter is lean protein," says Katherine McManus, R.D., director of nutrition at Brigham and Women's Hospital in Boston and a consultant on the most recent version of the Mediterranean pyramid. "Of course, you needn't physically separate your foods in that fashion, but it gives you a good idea of the proportions to aim for."

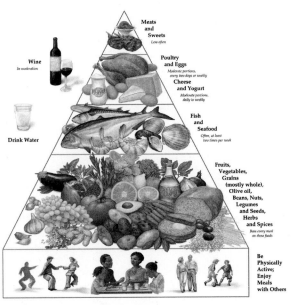

© 2009 Oldways Preservation Trust, www.oldwayspt.org

A Day in the Mediterranean Life

Breakfast

It's hard to go wrong with whole-grain cereal, fruit, and low-fat milk. Variations on the theme include low-fat yogurt with fresh berries and granola, or meaty steel-cut oats topped with fresh fruit, applesauce, whipped yogurt, or a sprinkle of nuts. Enjoy eggs? Try sautéing vegetables or greens in a bit of olive oil until soft and then scramble in a beaten egg. Go Greek with chopped olives and feta, or top with salsa and avocado for a Tex-Mex flair.

Lunch

Whether you're at home or brown-bagging, a Mediterranean lunch is tastier and healthier than drive-through fare and often faster and cheaper, too. Bagged salad greens provide a base for whatever you have on hand—fruit, vegetables, nuts, cheese, or a bit of leftover grilled chicken or fish. Consider topping it with a low-fat ranch dressing, an olive-oil vinaigrette, or just a drizzle of flavorful oil and a squeeze of fresh lemon. Or fill a whole-wheat pita pocket with hummus and as much fresh lettuce, peppers, cucumbers, and tomatoes as you can stuff in. If you're really pressed for time, heat up a can of low-sodium lentil, minestrone, or vegetable soup.

Snack Time

Keep a ready supply of fruit and veggies on hand so you'll grab them at snack time. Hummus, low-fat yogurt, and salad dressings pair nicely with them. If you don't want to invest the prep time, buy pre-cut. It's also a good idea to keep some nonperishable snacks at your desk or in your car—raisins or other dried fruit, nuts, and whole-grain crackers or pretzels.

Dinner

This is when many of us lose sight of nutrition goals because it's so easy after a long day to fall into old, comfortable habits. Fortunately, Mediterranean-style dining emphasizes simple foods and cooking methods.

While your pasta boils, for example, you can sauté a variety of vegetables in olive oil and garlic, then toss in a few shrimp and cook until they turn pink. Mix it all with a sprinkle of cheese, pour yourself a glass of wine, and you're sitting down to a relaxing dinner in less than 20 minutes.

In much the same manner, you can put together a quick stir-fry with slices of chicken breast, vegetables, and rice. Fresh fish is the simplest of entrées because it cooks quickly and doesn't take much dressing up. Spritz it with olive oil and your favorite seasonings and broil it, or coat it in bread crumbs and pan fry in a bit of olive oil. Squeeze on fresh lemon juice and adorn with parsley just before serving.

Two things you should have on hand for your evening meal: frozen vegetables, which are usually just as nutritious as fresh, and a plastic container of salad, preferably filled with a variety of greens. It's also a good idea to stock your crisper with seasonal fruit. A bowl of ripe berries, a chunk of melon, or a soft, farm-fresh peach is a delicious and satisfying end to any meal.

Oldways Preservation Trust, a nonprofit organization that promotes healthful eating, has more recipes and menu ideas on the two websites it sponsors: www.oldwayspt.org and www.mediterraneanmark.org.

STEP 1: Start with plant foods. Build your menus around an abundance of fruits and vegetables (yes, even potatoes); breads and grains (at least half of the servings should be whole grains); and beans, nuts, and seeds. To maximize the health benefits, emphasize a variety of minimally processed and locally grown foods.

STEP 2: Add some lean protein. The Mediterranean diet draws much of its protein from the sea, reflecting its coastal origins. Fish is not only low in saturated fat but can also be high in heart-healthy omega-3 fatty acids. Aim for two servings of fish a week, especially those, such as salmon and sardines, that are high in omega-3s but lower in mercury. You can also include moderate amounts of poultry and even eggs. Or substitute with vegetarian sources of protein, such as beans, nuts, or soy products. Limit red meat to a couple of servings a month, and minimize consumption of processed meats.

STEP 3: Say cheese. Include some milk, yogurt, or cheese in your daily meal. While low-fat versions are preferable, others are fine in small amounts. A sprinkle of high-quality Romano or Parmesan, for example, adds a spark to vegetables and pasta.

Soy-based dairy products are fine, too, if you prefer them or are lactose intolerant.

STEP 4: Use oils high in "good" fats. Canola oil is a good choice, but many Mediterranean recipes call for olive oil. Both are high in unsaturated fat. Minimize artery-clogging saturated fat, which comes mainly from animal sources, and avoid the even more heart-harming trans fat, which comes from partially hydrogenated vegetable oil.

STEP 5: End meals with the sweetness of fruit. Make sugary and fatty desserts just an occasional indulgence.

STEP 6: Drink to your health. A moderate amount of alcohol—especially red wine—may help protect your heart. But balance that against the increased risks from drinking alcohol, including breast cancer in women. A moderate amount is one drink a day for women, two for men.

STEP 7: Step out. "The Mediterranean lifestyle is built around daily activity," McManus says. Go for a walk after dinner. And choose leisure activities that keep you moving.

Critical Thinking

1. Why is the Mediterranean diet not just about foods but about a style of eating?
2. Why is dietary planning important when implementing a Mediterranean diet?

Create Central

www.mhhe.com/createcentral

Internet References

The American Dietetic Association
www.eatright.org

Center for Science in the Public Interest (CSPI)
www.cspinet.org

Article   Prepared by: Eileen L. Daniel, *SUNY Brockport*

Dieting on a Budget

Plus the secrets of thin people, based on our survey of 21,000 readers.

Learning Outcomes

After reading this article, you will be able to:

• Explain how it's possible to lose weight on a limited budget.

• Describe a diet plan of low-cost, low-calorie foods.

• Explain the components of a healthy weight loss program.

With jobs being cut and retirement accounts seemingly shrinking by the day, it's too bad our waistlines aren't dwindling, too. We can't rectify that cosmic injustice, but in this issue we aim to help you figure out the most effective, least expensive ways to stay trim and fit.

Though most Americans find themselves overweight by middle age, an enviable minority stay slim throughout their lives. Are those people just genetically gifted? Or do they, too, have to work at keeping down their weight?

To find out, the Consumer Reports National Research Center asked subscribers to *Consumer Reports* about their lifetime weight history and their eating, dieting, and exercising habits. And now we have our answer:

People who have never become overweight aren't sitting in recliners with a bowl of corn chips in their laps. In our group of always-slim respondents, a mere 3 percent reported that they never exercised and that they ate whatever they pleased. The eating and exercise habits of the vast majority of the always-slim group look surprisingly like those of people who have successfully lost weight and kept it off.

Both groups eat healthful foods such as fruits, vegetables, and whole grains and eschew excessive dietary fat; practice portion control; and exercise vigorously and regularly. The only advantage the always-slim have over the successful dieters is that those habits seem to come a bit more naturally to them.

"When we've compared people maintaining a weight loss with controls who've always had a normal weight, we've found that both groups are working hard at it; the maintainers are just working a little harder," says Suzanne Phelan, Ph.D., an assistant professor of kinesiology at California Polytechnic State University and co-investigator of the National Weight Control Registry, which tracks people who have successfully maintained a weight loss over time. For our respondents, that meant exercising a little more and eating with a bit more restraint than

---

Price vs. Nutrition: Making Smart Choices

Although healthful foods often cost more than high-calorie junk such as cookies and soda, we unearthed some encouraging exceptions. As illustrated below, two rich sources of nutrients, black beans and eggs, cost mere pennies per serving—and less than plain noodles, which supply fewer nutrients. And for the same price as a doughnut, packed with empty calories, you can buy a serving of broccoli.

- **Cooked black beans**
  - Serving size 1/2 cup
  - Calories per serving 114
  - Cost per serving 74¢
- **Hard-boiled egg**
  - Serving size one medium
  - Calories per serving 78
  - Cost per serving 94¢
- **Cooked noodles**
  - Serving size 3/4 cup
  - Calories per serving 166
  - Cost per serving 134¢
- **Glazed doughnut**
  - Serving size 1 medium
  - Calories per serving 239
  - Cost per serving 324¢
- **Cooked broccoli**
  - Serving size 1/2 cup chopped
  - Calories per serving 27
  - Cost per serving 334¢
- **Chicken breast**
  - Serving size 4 oz.
  - Calories per serving 142
  - Cost per serving 364¢

Sources: Adam Drewnowski, Ph.D., director of the Center for Public Health Nutrition, University of Washington: USDA Nutrient Database for Standard Reference.

---

an always-thin person—plus using more monitoring strategies such as weighing themselves or keeping a food diary.

A total of 21,632 readers completed the 2007 survey. The always thin, who had never been overweight, comprised 16 percent

Stay-Thin Strategies

Successful losers and the always thin do a lot of the same things—and they do them more frequently than failed dieters do. For the dietary strategies below, numbers reflect those who said they are that way at least five days a week, a key tipping point, our analysis found. (Differences of less than 4 percentage points are not statistically meaningful.)

Lifetime Weight History

Failed dieters: overweight and have tried to lose, but still close to highest weight. **Always thin:** never overweight. **Successful losers:** once overweight but now at least 10 percent lighter and have kept pounds off for at least three years.

Strength Train at Least Once a Week

Always thin	31%
Successful loser	32%
Failed dieter	23%

Do Vigorous Exercise at Least Four Days a Week

Always thin	35%
Successful loser	41%
Failed dieter	27%

Eat Fruit and Vegetables at Least Five Times a Day

Always thin	49%
Successful loser	49%
Failed dieter	38%

Eat Whole Grains, Not Refined

Always thin	56%
Successful loser	61%
Failed dieter	49%

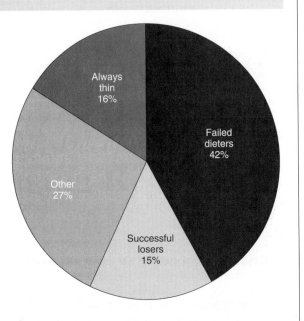

Eat Less Than 1/3 Calories from Fat

Always thin	47%
Successful loser	53%
Failed dieter	35%

Observe Portion Control at Every Meal

Always thin	57%
Successful loser	62%
Failed dieter	42%

Count Calories

Always thin	9%
Successful loser	47%
Failed dieter	9%

of our sample. Successful losers made up an additional 15 percent. We defined that group as people who, at the time of the survey, weighed at least 10 percent less than they did at their heaviest, and had been at that lower weight for at least three years. Failed dieters, who said they would like to slim down yet still weighed at or near their lifetime high, were, sad to say, the largest group: 42 percent. (The remaining 27 percent of respondents, such as people who had lost weight more recently, didn't fit into any of the categories.)

An encouraging note: More than half of our successful losers reported shedding the weight themselves, without aid of a commercial diet program, a medical treatment, a book, or diet pills. That confirms what we found in our last large diet survey, in 2002, in which 83 percent of "superlosers"—people

who'd lost at least 10 percent of their starting weight and kept it off for five years or more—had done it entirely on their own.

6 Secrets of the Slim

Through statistical analyses, we were able to identify six key behaviors that correlated the most strongly with having a healthy body mass index (BMI), a measure of weight that takes height into account. Always thin people were only slightly less likely than successful losers to embrace each of the behaviors—and significantly more likely to do so than failed dieters. By following the behaviors, you can, quite literally, live like a thin person.

Watch portions. Of all the eating behaviors we asked about, carefully controlling portion size at each meal correlated most strongly with having a lower BMI. Successful losers—even those who were still overweight—were especially likely (62 percent) to report practicing portion control at least five days per week. So did 57 percent of the always thin, but only 42 percent of failed dieters.

Portion control is strongly linked to a lower BMI.

Limit fat. Specifically, that means restricting fat to less than one-third of daily calorie intake. Fifty-three percent of successful losers and 47 percent of the always thin said they did that five or more days a week, compared with just 35 percent of failed dieters.

Eat fruits and vegetables. The more days that respondents ate five or more servings of fruits or vegetables, the lower their average BMI score. Forty-nine percent of successful losers and the always thin said they ate that way at least five days a week, while 38 percent of failed dieters did so.

Choose whole grains over refined. People with lower body weights consistently opted for whole-wheat breads, cereals, and other grains over refined (white) grains.

Eat at home. As the number of days per week respondents ate restaurant or takeout meals for dinner increased, so did their weight. Eating at home can save a lot of money, too.

Exercise, exercise, exercise. Regular vigorous exercise—the type that increases breathing and heart rate for 30 minutes or longer—was strongly linked to a lower BMI. Although only about one quarter of respondents said they did strength training at least once a week, that practice was significantly more prevalent among successful losers (32 percent) and always thin respondents (31 percent) than it was among failed dieters (23 percent).

What Didn't Matter

One weight-loss strategy is conspicuously absent from the list: going low-carb. Of course we asked about it, and it turned out that limiting carbohydrates was linked to higher BMIs in our survey. That doesn't necessarily mean low-carb plans such as the Atkins or South Beach diets don't work. "If you go to the hospital and everyone there is sick, that doesn't mean the hospital made them sick," says Eric C. Westman, M.D., associate professor of medicine and director of the Lifestyle Medicine Clinic at Duke University Medical School. "Just as people go to hospitals because they're ill, people may go to carb restriction because they have a higher BMI, not the other way around." At the same time, the findings do suggest that cutting carbs alone, without other healthful behaviors such as exercise and portion control, might not lead to great results.

> ## Are You Overweight?
>
> A body mass index under 25 is considered normal weight; from 25 to 29, overweight; and 30 or above, obese. To calculate your BMI, multiply your weight in pounds by 703, then divide by your height squared in inches.

Eating many small meals, or never eating between meals, didn't seem to make much difference one way or another. Including lean protein with most meals also didn't by itself predict a healthier weight.

Realistic Expectations

Sixty-six percent of our respondents, all subscribers to *Consumer Reports,* were overweight as assessed by their body mass index; that's the same percentage as the population as a whole. One third of the overweight group, or 22 percent of the overall sample, qualified as obese.

Although that might seem discouraging, the survey actually contains good news for would-be dieters. Our respondents did much better at losing weight than published clinical studies would predict. Though such studies are deemed successful if participants are 5 percent lighter after a year, our successful losers had managed to shed an average of 16 percent of their peak weight, an average of almost 34 pounds. They had an impressive average BMI of 25.7, meaning they were just barely overweight.

One key to weight loss success is having realistic goals and our subscribers' responses proved encouraging. A staggering 70 percent of them said they currently wanted to lose weight. But when we asked how many pounds they hoped to take off, we found that their goals were modest: The vast majority reported wanting to lose 15 percent or less of their overall body weight; 65 percent sought to lose between 1 and 10 percent. Keeping expectations in check might help dieters from becoming discouraged when they don't achieve, say, a 70-pound weight loss or drop from a size 20 to a size 6—a common problem in behavioral weight loss studies.

Realistic goals are one key to weight loss.

What You Can Do

Weight loss is a highly individual process, and what matters most is finding the combination of habits that work for you. But our findings suggest that there are key behaviors common to people who have successfully lost weight and to those who have never gained it in the first place. By embracing some or all of those behaviors, you can probably increase your chances of weight-loss success, and live a healthier life in the process. In addition to following the steps above, consider these tips:

Don't get discouraged. Studies show that prospective dieters often have unrealistic ideas about how much weight they can lose. A 10 percent loss might not sound like much, but it significantly improves overall health and reduces risk of disease.

Ask for support. Though only a small minority of respondents overall reported that a spouse or family member interfered with their healthful eating efforts, that problem was much more likely among failed dieters, 31 percent of whom reported some form of spousal sabotage in the month prior to the survey. Ask housemates to help you stay on track by, for example, not pestering you to eat foods you're trying to avoid, or not eating those foods in front of you.

Get up and move. While regular vigorous exercise correlated most strongly with healthy body weight, our findings suggest that any physical activity is helpful, including activities you might not even consider exercise. Everyday activities such as housework, yard work, and playing with kids were modestly tied to lower weight. By contrast, hours spent sitting each day, whether at an office desk or at home watching television, correlated with higher weight.

Critical Thinking

1. What does a healthy weight loss diet consist of?
2. How can one lose weight without spending a fortune on "diet" foods?

Create Central

www.mhhe.com/createcentral

Internet References

The American Dietetic Association
   www.eatright.org
Cyberdiet
   www.cyberdiet.com

Article   Prepared by: Eileen L. Daniel, *SUNY Brockport*

The Hungry Brain

The urge to eat too much is wired into our heads. **Tackling obesity may require bypassing the stomach and short-circuiting our brains.**

DAN HURLEY

Learning Outcomes

After reading this article, you will be able to:

- Discuss the neurological basis for overeating.
- Describe how sleep patterns can influence the desire to eat.
- Describe how the hormones leptin and ghrelin impact weight.
- Understand the relationship between sleep, circadian rhythm, and obesity.

At 10:19 P.M. on a Monday evening in October, I sat in a booth at Chevys Fresh Mex in Clifton, New Jersey, reviewing the latest research into the neurobiology of hunger and obesity. While I read I ate a shrimp and crab enchilada, consuming two-thirds of it, maybe less. With all this information in front of me, I thought, I had an edge over my brain's wily efforts to thwart my months-long campaign to get under 190 pounds. But even as I was taking in a study about the powerful lure of guacamole and other salty, fatty foods, I experienced something extraordinary. That bowl of chips and salsa at the edge of the table? It was whispering to me: *Just one more. You know you want us. Aren't we delicious?* In 10 minutes, all that was left of the chips, and my willpower, were crumbs.

I am not alone. An overabundance of chips, Baconator Double burgers, and Venti White Chocolate Mochas have aided a widespread epidemic of obesity in this country. Our waists are laying waste to our health and to our health-care economy: According to a study published by the Centers for Disease Control and Prevention in 2010, nine states had an obesity rate of at least 30 percent—compared with zero states some 10 years earlier—and the cost of treatment for obesity-related conditions had reached nearly 10 percent of total U.S. medical expenditure. So-called normal weight is no longer normal, with two-thirds of adults and one third of children and adolescents now classified as overweight or obese. Dubbed the "Age of Obesity and Inactivity" by the *Journal of the American Medical Association,* this runaway weight gain threatens to decrease average U.S. life span, reversing gains made over the past century by lowering risk factors from smoking, hypertension, and cholesterol. We all know what we should do—eat less, exercise more—but to no avail. An estimated 25 percent of American men and 43 percent of women attempt to lose weight each year; of those who succeed in their diets, between 5 and 20 percent (and it is closer to 5 percent) manage to keep it off for the long haul.

The urgent question is, why do our bodies seem to be fighting against our own good health? According to a growing number of neurobiologists, the fault lies not in our stomachs but in our heads. No matter how convincing our conscious plans and resolutions, they pale beside the brain's power to goad us into noshing and hanging on to as much fat as we can. With that in mind, some scientists were hopeful that careful studies of the brain might uncover an all-powerful hormone that regulates food consumption or a single spot where the cortical equivalent of a neon sign blinks "Eat Heavy," all the better to shut it off.

After extensive research, the idea of a single, simple cure has been replaced by a much more nuanced view. The latest studies show that a multitude of systems in the brain act in concert to encourage eating. Targeting a single neuronal system is probably doomed to the same ill fate as the failed diets themselves. Because the brain has so many backup systems all geared toward the same thing—maximizing the body's intake of calories—no single silver bullet will ever work.

The brain's prime directive to eat and defend against the loss of fat emerged early in evolution.

"I call it the 'hungry brain syndrome'," says Hans-Rudolf Berthoud, an expert in the neurobiology of nutrition at the Pennington Biomedical Research Center in Baton Rouge, Louisiana. The brain's prime directive to eat and defend against the loss of fat emerged early in evolution, because just about every creature that ever trotted, crawled, swam, or floated was beset by the uncertainty of that next meal. "The system has evolved to defend against the slightest threat of weight loss, so you have to attack it from different directions at once."

With the obesity epidemic raging, the race for countermeasures has kicked into high gear. Neuroscientists are still seeking hormones that inhibit hunger, but they have other tactics as well. One fruitful new avenue comes from the revelation that hunger, blood sugar, and weight gained per calorie consumed all ratchet up when our sleep is disrupted and our circadian rhythms—the 24-hour cycle responding to light and dark—[are] thrown into disarray. All this is compounded by stress, which decreases metabolism while increasing the yen for high-calorie food. We might feel in sync with our high-tech world, but the obesity epidemic is a somber sign that our biology and lifestyles have diverged.

Seeking Silver Bullets, Shooting Blanks

The path forward seemed so simple back in 1995, when three papers in *Science* suggested a panacea for the overweight: A hormone that made animals shed pounds, rapidly losing body fat until they were slim. Based on the research, it seemed that doctors might soon be able to treat obesity the way they treat diabetes, with a simple metabolic drug.

Fat cells release that "diet" hormone—today named leptin, from the Greek *leptos,* meaning thin—to begin a journey across the blood-brain barrier to the hypothalamus, the pea-size structure above the pituitary gland. The hypothalamus serves as a kind of thermostat, setting not only body temperature but playing a key role in hunger, thirst, fatigue, and sleep cycles. Leptin signals the hypothalamus to reduce the sense of hunger so that we stop eating.

In early lab experiments, obese mice given extra leptin by injection seemed sated. They ate less, their body temperature increased, and their weight plummeted. Even normal-weight mice became skinnier when given injections of the hormone.

Once the pharmaceutical industry created a synthetic version of human leptin, clinical trials were begun. But when injected into hundreds of obese human volunteers, leptin's effect was clinically insignificant. It soon became clear why. In humans, as in mice, fat cells of the obese already produced plenty of leptin—more in fact than those of their thin counterparts, since the level of leptin was directly proportional to the amount of fat. The early studies had worked largely because the test mice were, by experimental design, leptin-deficient. Subsequent experiments showed that in normal mice—as in humans—increases in leptin made little difference to the brain, which looked to *low* leptin levels as a signal to eat more, essentially disregarding the kind of high levels that had caused deficient mice to eat less. This made leptin a good drug for maintaining weight loss but not a great candidate for getting the pounds off up front.

Despite that disappointment, the discovery of leptin unleashed a scientific gold rush to find other molecules that could talk the brain into turning hunger off. By 1999 researchers from Japan's National Cardiovascular Center Research Institute in Osaka had announced the discovery of ghrelin, a kind of antileptin that is released primarily by the gut rather than by fat cells. Ghrelin signals hunger rather than satiety to

the hypothalamus. Then, in 2002, a team from the University of Washington found that ghrelin levels rise before a meal and fall immediately after. Ghrelin (from the Indo-European root for the word "grow") increased hunger while jamming on the metabolic brakes to promote the body's storage of fat.

So began another line of attack on obesity. Rather than turning leptin on, researchers began exploring ways to turn ghrelin off. Some of them began looking at animal models, but progress has been slow; the concept of a ghrelin "vaccine" has been floated, but clinical trials are still years off.

Seeking a better understanding of the hormone, University of Washington endocrinologist David Cummings compared ghrelin levels in people who had lost considerable amounts of weight through diet with those who shed pounds by means of gastric bypass surgery—a technique that reduces the capacity of the stomach and seems to damage its ghrelin-producing capacity as well. The results were remarkable. For dieters, the more weight lost, the greater the rise in ghrelin, as if the body were telling the brain to get hungry and regain that weight. By contrast, the big losers in the surgical group saw ghrelin levels fall to the floor. Surgical patients never felt increases in appetite and had an easier time maintaining their weight loss as a result. (A newer weight-loss surgery removes most of the ghrelin-producing cells outright.)

Based on such findings, a ghrelin-blocking drug called rimonabant was approved and sold in 32 countries, though not in the United States. It remained available as recently as 2008, even though it also increased the risk of depression and suicidal thinking; it has since been withdrawn everywhere. The verdict is still out on a newer generation of combination pharmaceuticals, including one that contains synthetic versions of leptin and the neurohormone amylin, known to help regulate appetite. In a six-month clinical trial, the combination therapy resulted in an average weight loss of 25 pounds, or 12.7 percent of body weight, with greater weight loss when continued for a full 52 weeks; those who stopped taking the drug midway regained most of their weight.

The Circadian Connection

The limited results from tackling the hypothalamus sent many scientists looking at the other gyres and gears driving obesity in the brain, especially in regions associated with sleep. The first big breakthrough came in 2005, when *Science* published a landmark paper on mice with a mutated version of the Clock gene, which plays a key role in the regulation of the body's circadian rhythms. The mutant mice not only failed to follow the strict eat-by-night, sleep-by-day schedule of normally nocturnal mice, they also became overweight and developed diabetes. "There was a difference in weight gain based on when the food was eaten, whether during day or night," says the study's senior author, endocrinologist Joe Bass of Northwestern University. "That means the metabolic rate must differ under those two conditions."

Could *my* late-night hours be the undoing of my weight-loss plans? Four days after my humiliating defeat by a bowl of tortilla chips, I met with Alex Keene, a postdoctoral researcher at New York University with a Matisse nude tattooed on his right forearm and a penchant for studying flies. His latest study asked whether a starved fly would take normal naps or sacrifice sleep to keep searching for food. He found that like humans (and most other creatures), flies have a neurological toggle between two fundamental yet incompatible drives: to eat or to sleep. "Flies only live a day or two when they're starved," Keene told me as we walked past graduate students peering at flies under microscopes. "If they decide to sleep through the night when they're starved, it's a bad decision on their part. So their brains are finely tuned to suppress their sleep when they don't have food and to sleep well after a meal."

For a major study published last year, Keene bred flies with dysfunctional mutations of the Clock gene and also of Cycle, another gene involved in circadian rhythms. He found that the genes together regulate the interaction between the two mutually exclusive behaviors, sleep and feeding, kicking in to suppress sleep when a fly is hungry.

Even when fed, flies without working versions of the Clock and Cycle genes tended to sleep poorly—about 30 percent as much as normal flies. "It was as if they were starving right away," Keene explains. Keene went even further, pinpointing where, amid the 100,000 or so neurons in the fly brain, the Clock gene acts to regulate the sleeping-feeding interaction: a region of just four to eight cells at the top of the fly brain.

"My father is an anthropologist," Keene told me as we stood in the fly room, its air pungent with the corn meal and molasses the flies feed on. "It's ironic, right? He looks at how culture determines behavior, while I look at how genes determine behavior. I used to get him so mad he'd storm out of the house."

Perhaps it takes an anthropologist's son to see that the excess availability of cheap, high-calorie chow cannot fully explain the magnitude and persistence of the problem in our culture. The rebellion against our inborn circadian rhythms wrought by a 24-hour lifestyle, lit by neon and fueled by caffeine, also bears part of the blame. The powerful effect of disordered sleep on metabolism has been seen not just in flies but also in humans. A 2009 study by Harvard University researchers showed that in just 10 days, three of eight healthy volunteers developed prediabetic blood-sugar levels when their sleep-wake schedule was gradually shifted out of alignment.

"It's clear from these types of studies that the way we're keeping the lights on until late at night, the way in which society demands that we stay active for so much longer, could well be contributing to aspects of the metabolic disease we're seeing now," says Steve Kay, a molecular geneticist at the University of California, San Diego.

These insights have fostered collaboration between once-diverse groups. "Physicians who specialized in obesity and diabetes for years are now discovering the importance of circadian effects," Kay says. At the same time, "basic research scientists like me, who have been studying the circadian system for so many years, are now looking at its metabolic effects. When so many people's research from so many areas starts to converge, you know we're in the midst of a paradigm shift. This is the slow rumbling before the volcano blows."

This past April, the National Institute of Diabetes and Digestive and Kidney Diseases (NIDDK) of the National Institutes of Health organized a first-ever national conference focused solely on how circadian rhythms affect metabolism. "What has become obvious over the past few years is that metabolism, all those pathways regulating how fats and carbohydrates are used, is affected by the circadian clock," says biochemist Corinne Silva, a program director at the NIDDK. Her goal is to find drugs that treat diabetes and obesity by targeting circadian pathways. "The mechanisms by which circadian rhythms are maintained and the cross talk with metabolic signaling are just beginning to be elucidated," she says, but they should lead to novel therapeutic approaches in the years ahead.

In Keene's view, the newfound link between sleep and obesity could be put to use right now. "People who are susceptible to diabetes or have weight issues might just get more sleep. I get only about six hours of sleep myself. I usually run in the middle of the night. I'm not a morning person," the enviably thin, 29-year-old Keene states.

My visit to his fly room convinced me to try a new angle in my quest to get under 190 pounds: Rather than focus on *how much* food I put in my mouth, I would focus on *when* I eat. I decided I would no longer eat after 10 P.M.

The Pleasure Factor

Timing may be everything for some folks, but it wasn't for me. No wonder: The brain has no shortage of techniques to goad us into eating. Another line of evidence suggests that the brains of overweight people are wired to feel more pleasure in response to food. Sleep deprived or not, they just enjoy eating more. To study such differences, clinical psychologist Eric Stice of the Oregon Research Institute mastered the delicate task of conducting fMRI brain scans while people were eating. The food he chose to give the volunteers inside the tunnel-like scanners was a milk shake. And let the record show, it was a *chocolate* milk shake.

Brains of the overweight are wired to feel more pleasure in response to food.

Obese adolescent girls, Stice found, showed greater activation compared with their lean peers in regions of the brain that encode the sensory experience of eating food—the so-called gustatory cortex and the somatosensory regions, archipelagoes of neurons that reach across different structures in the brain. At the same time, the obese girls sipping milk shakes showed decreased activation in the striatum, a region near the center of the brain that is studded with dopamine receptors and known to respond to stimuli associated with rewards. Stice wondered whether, even among normal-weight girls, such a pattern might predict an increased risk of overeating and weight gain.

To test his hypothesis, he followed a group of subjects over time, finding that those with reduced activation in the dorsal (rear) region of the striatum while sipping a milk shake were ultimately more likely to gain weight than those with normal activation. The most vulnerable of these girls were also more likely to have a DNA polymorphism—not a mutation, per se, but a rather routine genetic variation—in a dopamine receptor gene, causing reduced dopamine signaling in the striatum and placing them at higher risk. "Individuals may overeat," Stice and his colleagues concluded, "to compensate for a hypofunctioning dorsal striatum, particularly those with genetic polymorphisms thought to attenuate dopamine signaling in this region."

Stice was initially surprised by the results. "It's totally weird," he admits. "Those who experienced less pleasure were at increased risk for weight gain." But his more recent studies have convinced him that the reduced pleasure is a result of years of overeating among the obese girls—the same phenomenon seen in drug addicts who require ever-greater amounts of their drug to feel the same reward. "Imagine a classroom of third graders, and everyone is skinny," he says. "The people who initially find that milk shake most orgasmic will want more of it, but in so doing they cause neuroplastic changes that downregulate the reward circuitry, driving them to eat more and more to regain that same feeling they crave."

Even among people of normal weight, individual differences in brain functioning can directly affect eating behaviors, according to a 2009 study by Michael Lowe, a research psychologist at Drexel University. He took fMRI brain scans of 19 people, all of them of normal weight. Nine of the volunteers reported following strict diets; the other 10 typically ate whenever and whatever they wanted. Lowe had all of them sip a milk shake immediately before getting scanned. The brains of the nondieters, he found, lit up just as one would expect, showing activations in areas associated with satiation and memory, as if saying, "Mmmm, that was good." The chronic dieters showed activations in areas of the brain associated with desire and expectation of reward, however. If anything, the milk shake had made them hungrier.

"What we have shown is that these chronic dieters may actually have a reason to restrain themselves, because they are more susceptible than average to overeating," Lowe says.

Yet inborn differences in hunger and desire, too, turn out to be only part of the weighting game. Eating behaviors are also linked to areas of the brain associated with self-control (such as the left superior frontal region) and visual attention (such as the right middle temporal region). A recent fMRI study led by Jeanne McCaffery, a psychologist at Brown Medical School, showed that successful weight losers had greater activation in those regions, compared with normal-weight people and obese people, when viewing images of food.

The effects of stress on eating behaviors also has a neurobiological basis, according to University of Pennsylvania neurobiologist Tracy Bale. She showed that neural pathways associated with stress link directly to areas of the brain associated with seeking rewards. "Few things are more rewarding evolutionarily than calorie-dense food," Bale told me a few days after presenting a seminar on the subject at last fall's Society for Neuroscience meeting in San Diego. "Under stress people don't crave a salad; they crave something high-calorie. It's because

those stress pathways in the limbic system feed into the reward centers, and they drive reward-seeking behaviors. What that tells us is that in addition to drug companies' trying to target appetite, they need to look at the reward centers. We're not necessarily fat because we're hungry but because we're looking for something to deal with stress."

Aha! Perhaps it was stress that was messing with my latest, clock-based diet. Back in March 2010, a tree had fallen on my family's home during a major storm, crushing the roof, destroying half the house, and forcing us to flee to a nearby apartment. By November, as I researched this story, we had finally moved back into our rebuilt house. With nerves fully frayed, I found myself drawn as never before to the Tick Tock Diner, where the motto literally is "Eat Heavy," and where the french fries never tasted better. Instead of losing a few pounds to get under 190, by Thanksgiving I had hit 196.

How to Fix a Hungry Brain

Neuroscience has yet to deliver a weight-loss elixir for paunchy 53-year-old journalists like me, much less for those suffering from serious obesity. But that day will come, Steve Kay asserts, once researchers figure out the correct combination of drugs that work simultaneously on multiple triggers of eating and metabolism, just as hypertension is now routinely treated with two- or three-drug combinations.

Some scientists think a more radical approach is called for. Since the triggers of obesity lie in the brain, neurosurgeons at West Virginia University Health Sciences Center are attempting to rewire those triggers directly using deep brain stimulation (DBS). Since 2009 they have performed surgery on three obese patients to implant electrodes that emit rhythmic electric shocks into the hypothalamus. Having failed other medical therapies for obesity, the three agreed to volunteer for DBS, a treatment already approved for treating the tremors and dystonia of Parkinson's disease. "These patients weren't eating all that much; it was mainly a problem of having very slow metabolisms," says Donald M. Whiting, one of the neurosurgeons leading the study. "Our goal was to speed it up." On the basis of successful animal studies, he adds, "we thought we'd switch on the energy and collect our Nobel Prize."

All three patients experienced significantly less hunger when the electrodes were switched on, and all regained their normal hunger when the electrodes were switched off. Unfortunately, none lost a significant amount of weight in the study's first year. The problem, Whiting concludes, is that there are many ways to adjust DBS. With four contact points on the electrodes, each placed half a millimeter apart and each adjustable for voltage, frequency, and pulse width, the research team has been seeking the combination of settings that most effectively rev up metabolism. So far they have found settings that work only temporarily.

"The brain is really pretty smart," Whiting says. "It tends to want to reboot to factory settings whenever it can. We find that we can reset things for a week or two, but then the brain gets back to where it wants." Despite the challenges, Whiting remains convinced that finding a safe and effective medical treatment for weight control will be essential to turn the obesity epidemic around—and that no amount of preaching from Oprah, no behavior program from Weight Watchers nor food from Jenny Craig, will ever suffice.

"This mystification that obesity is caused by a lack of will-power or just eating the wrong foods is simply a misconception," Joe Bass of Northwestern told me. "There is so much social stigma attached to weight that we make a lot of value judgments. The effort in science is to peel back those layers of belief and try to understand things in an experimental, rational mode. Just as we have made progress against heart disease with statins and blood pressure drugs, we will find medications that can safely and substantially lower weight."

Months after my investigation of the brain-gut connection began, I faced the acid test. In early March I stepped back onto my bathroom scale for a final weigh-in. Rather than slip below 190, for the first time in my life I had tipped, by a single pound, over 200. You might blame it on insufficient exercise or on the cheese and crackers I failed to remove from my late-night work ritual. I'm blaming it on my brain.

Critical Thinking

1. Explain the neurological basis for overeating.
2. How do sleep patterns influence overeating and obesity?
3. How do hormones effect obesity?

Create Central

www.mhhe.com/createcentral

Internet References

National Sleep Foundation
www. sleep foundation.org
Center for Science in the Public Interest (CSPI)
www.cspinet.org
U.S. Department of Agriculture (USDA)/Food and Nutrition Information Center (FNIC)
www.nal.usda.gov/fnic

Unit 5

UNIT

Prepared by: Eileen Daniel, *SUNY College at Brockport*

Drugs and Health

As a culture, Americans have come to rely on drugs not only as a treatment for disease but also as an aid for living normal, productive lives. This view of drugs has fostered a casual attitude regarding their use and resulted in a tremendous drug abuse problem. Drug use and abuse has become so widespread that there is no way to describe the typical drug abuser. There is no simple explanation for why America has become a drug-taking culture, but there certainly is evidence to suggest some of the factors that have contributed to this development.

From the time that we are children, we are constantly bombarded by advertisements about how certain drugs can make us feel and look better. While most of these ads deal with proprietary drugs, the belief created is that drugs are a legitimate and effective way to help us cope with everyday problems. Certainly drugs can have a profound effect on how we feel and act, but research has also demonstrated that our mind plays a major role in the healing process. For many people, it's easier to take a drug than to adopt a healthier lifestyle.

Growing up, most of us probably had a medicine cabinet full of prescription and over-the-counter (OTC) drugs, freely dispensed to family members to treat a variety of ailments. This familiarity with drugs, coupled with rising health-care costs, has prompted many people to diagnose and medicate themselves with OTC medications without sufficient knowledge of the possible side effects. Although most of these preparations have little potential for abuse, it does not mean that they are innocuous. Generally speaking, OTC drugs are relatively safe if taken at the recommended dosage by healthy people, but the risk of dangerous side effects rises sharply when people exceed the recommended dosage. Another potential danger associated with the use of OTC drugs is the drug interactions that can occur when they are taken in conjunction with prescription medications. The gravest danger associated with the use of OTC drugs is that an individual may use them to control symptoms of an underlying disease and thus prevent its early diagnosis and treatment.

While OTC drugs can be abused, an increasing number of drug-related deaths over the past five years have been linked to prescription drugs. These drugs, opiate-based painkillers such as OxyContin, Darvon, and Vicodin are often used as an alternative to an illicit high. Ironically, however, there has been a recent surge in heroin use as these prescription drugs become harder to get.

As a culture, we have grown up believing that there is, or should be, a drug to treat any malady or discomfort that befalls us. Would we have a drug problem if there was no demand for drugs? One drug which is used widely in the United States is alcohol, especially on college campuses. Every year over 1,000 students die from alcohol-related causes, mostly drinking and driving. Other risks associated with students' drinking include missed classes, falling behind in schoolwork, damage to property, and injuries, which occur while under the influence of alcohol.

While alcohol abuse among college students is a serious issue, drinking among pregnant women is also a concern. Women who drink during their pregnancies risk delivering a baby who could suffer from a range of effects including physical, emotional, mental, behavioral, and cognitive abnormalities.

In addition to alcohol, another widely used legal drug is tobacco. Millions still smoke despite all the well-publicized health effects linked to smoking. Many Americans have quit and many others would like to quit. To facilitate this process, some companies have developed programs to help employees stop smoking. Because smoking and its related diseases cost approximately $150 billion each year, the stakes are enormous. A recent introduction, electronic cigarettes are considered controversial relative to their safety. While the research is limited, some smokers use electronic cigarettes to help quit the habit while others use the product to reduce the effects of secondhand smoke. One concern over electronic cigarettes is their appeal to minors. E-cigarettes often come in flavors that appear to be targeted toward children.

Article   Prepared by: Eileen Daniel, *SUNY College at Brockport*

Pot Goes Legit

What the End of Prohibition Looks Like in Colorado

JACOB SULLUM

Learning Outcomes

After reading this article, you will be able to:

- Explain the restrictions imposed on marijuana sellers in Colorado.
- Understand the provisions of Colorado's Amendment 64.
- Describe the 70/30 rule regarding marijuana growing and selling.

"What we need," said Norton Arbelaez, a thirty-something attorney and businessman in a suit and tie, "is a vertically integrated, closed-loop regulatory framework." The bureaucrats, politicians, and entrepreneurs crowding the conference room took notes, watched his PowerPoint slides, and furrowed their brows. This was the fourth meeting of a working group set up by a task force appointed by the governor of Colorado, and if you happened to wander by you would think, it sounded as dull as the average subcommittee session anywhere.

Until you discerned the subject of the meeting. "We will be, and are, the cannabis industry in Colorado," Arbelaez proclaimed. "It is our necks that are on the line."

Last November, 75 years after Congress enacted national marijuana prohibition, voters in Colorado and Washington decided to opt out. After Coloradans approved Amendment 64, which legalized the production, possession, and distribution of marijuana for recreational use, Gov. John Hickenlooper appointed the Amendment 64 Implementation Task Force to advise state legislators on how to regulate the nascent cannabis industry, which for years had served patients under Colorado's medical marijuana law but now was authorized to supply any adult 21 or older. And as in all sorts of industries, the incumbents were trying to write the rules in their favor.

"We need to maintain the edifice of what continues to work in Colorado," said Arbelaez, who co-owns two medical marijuana dispensaries in Denver and serves on the board of the Medical Marijuana Industry Group. Among other things, he said that means retaining a rule that requires pot retailers to grow at least 70 percent of what they sell while selling no more than 30 percent of what they grow to other outlets. Arbelaez argued that the 70/30 rule, designed to prevent recreational consumers from obtaining medical marijuana, would help stop diversion of recreational marijuana to minors or other states and thereby discourage federal interference.

The other members of the working group seemed unpersuaded. Liquor stores do not make the distilled spirits they stock, and pharmacies do not produce the drugs they sell. Why should pot stores have to grow their own marijuana?

"I am still left scratching my head about vertical integration and why it's so important," said Denver City Councilman Chris Nevitt. "The 70 percent rule is endlessly complicated and confusing." Nevitt alluded to the financial interests at stake: when the rule took effect in 2011, more than a decade after Colorado voters approved the medical use of marijuana, dispensaries had to invest in growing space and equipment, and they were forced into sometimes awkward business partnerships with growers. "I totally understand the anxiety of an industry that has made all of these investments," Nevitt said. "But I am still scratching my head."

Jessica LeRoux, owner of Twirling Hippy Confections, a Denver business that supplies cannabis-infused chocolates and cheesecakes to medical marijuana centers (MMCs) across the state, concurred. "The 70/30 rule does notwork," LeRoux stated flatly. "This is not vertical integration. This is vertical protectionism."

But most MMC owners in the room seemed to support the 70/30 rule. "The current medical marijuana system works for us," said Erica Freeman of Choice Organics in Fort Collins.

"Changing the rules again will force new mergers," warned Tad Bowler of Rocky Road Remedies in Steamboat Springs. "The small centers won't be able to compete." Michael Elliott, executive director of the Medical Marijuana Industry Group, declared "we are united" in supporting the 70/30 rule.

A straw poll of the working group revealed that its members were overwhelmingly opposed to requiring vertical integration, instead favoring a more flexible approach that would allow retailers to grow whatever percentage of their inventory they wanted, including zero. But in the end, after several more weeks of meetings, the dispensaries represented by Elliott's group prevailed. In its March 13 report, the task force recommended that the 70/30 rule remain in effect for at least three years and that new entrants be excluded from the market for 12 months. Two months later, Gov. Hickenlooper signed a marijuana regulation bill that included watered-down versions of both ideas, extending 70/30 until October 2014 and giving MMCs a three-month head start in the licensing process.

"The industry did a really good job of building a coalition" explains University of Denver law professor Sam Kamin, a member of the task force. "They convinced law enforcement and public health that part of keeping the industry in check and part of keeping it diverse and keeping the feds at bay was the current model."

Rob Corry, a Denver attorney and longtime marijuana activist, is less polite, calling the 70/30 rule "completely unworkable and economically illiterate." But Corry sees a bright side to the dispute over vertical integration. "On the one hand," he says, "I'm disappointed at rent seeking behavior and businesses that seek the heavy hand of government to prevent new competition. On the other hand, it means that our industry has grown up and is behaving like every other industry out there."

Conservatives for Cannabis

Normalizing a formerly criminal business is the avowed goal of Amendment 64, which declares that "marijuana should be regulated in a manner similar to alcohol." The initiative will succeed to the extent that it transforms a countercultural symbol into a capitalist commodity. Dutch officials like to say, regarding their policy of tolerating the retail sale of cannabis, that they made marijuana boring by making it legal. Something similar is happening in Colorado, where the head rush of passing Amendment 64 has given way to the headache of implementing it.

That process, which is supposed to culminate in state-licensed pot stores by next January, aims to address the concerns of marijuana's detractors as well as its fans. Among other things, that means trying to avoid a crackdown by the federal government, which cannot force Colorado to ban marijuana but can make trouble for businesses openly selling a product that

remains illegal under the Controlled Substances Act. Wariness of the feds has shaped every aspect of the new legal regime, from the size of store signs to the size of marijuana brownies, from the amount of tax charged on a quarter-ounce of Hidden Valley Kush to the amount of THC allowed in a driver's bloodstream. These are the mundane details that will define Colorado's momentous experiment in pharmacological tolerance. Boring debates about vertical integration could signal the beginning of the end for the war on drugs.

Colorado and Washington are 2 of the 11 states that opted out of alcohol prohibition through ballot initiatives that voters approved in November 1932, more than a year before the 21st Amendment (which repealed alcohol prohibition nationally) was ratified. Eighty years later, Colorado and Washington used the same method to opt out of marijuana prohibition, by surprisingly strong margins of about 10 points in both states. The victory was especially striking in Colorado, which is more Republican than both Washington and California, where a marijuana legalization initiative lost by seven points just two years earlier. Four years before that Colorado voters had resoundingly rejected Amendment 44, which would have merely made it legal to possess up to an ounce of marijuana. Amendment 64 accomplished that while also legalizing home cultivation and authorizing commercial production and distribution. Yet it was supported by 55 percent of voters, compared to the 41 percent who went for Amendment 44 in 2006.

Former Colorado congressman Tom Tancredo, a conservative Republican, supported Amendment 64 but did not expect it to pass. "The only thing I can attribute it to [is that] we presented a case for conservatives to vote for it," Tancredo says. "The exit polling showed that we had a much stronger support from Republicans and conservatives than they ever had in the past." Mason Tvert, who spearheaded both the 2006 and 2012 campaigns, notes that "we won El Paso County, which is insane." El Paso County—which includes Colorado Springs, home of the U.S. Air Force Academy and Focus on the Family—is "considered one of the most conservative parts of the country," he says. "We won it by 10 votes, but if we lost by 5,000 I would still tout it as unbelievable."

In an op-ed piece published by the Colorado Springs Gazette about six weeks before the election, Tancredo announced that "I am endorsing Amendment 64 not despite my conservative beliefs, but because of them." He compared the ban on marijuana to alcohol prohibition, "a misguided big-government policy experiment," and argued that legalizing marijuana would strike a blow against murderous Mexican drug cartels. Tancredo, who had criticized aspects of the war on drugs during his decade in Congress, combined practical arguments with an explicitly libertarian appeal. "Our nation is spending tens of billions of dollars annually in an attempt to prohibit adults from using a substance objectively less harmful than alcohol," he wrote. "Marijuana prohibition is perhaps the oldest and most persistent nanny-state law we have in the U.S. We simply cannot afford a government that tries to save people from themselves. It is not the role of government to try to correct bad behavior, as long as those behaviors are not directly causing physical harm to others."

The wastefulness and unfairness of enforcing marijuana prohibition was underlined by a report released a month later. Queens College sociologist Harry Levine and two co-authors showed that police in Colorado were arresting more than 10,000 pot smokers every year, even though the state legislature supposedly had decriminalized marijuana possession in 1975. Possession of small amounts (initially less than an ounce, raised to two ounces in 2010) remained a crime, albeit a "petty offense." Pot smokers were not doing hard time, but they were still burdened by the cost, inconvenience, and humiliation associated with an arrest, not to mention the lasting disadvantage of a criminal record.

Tvert says several factors help explain why Coloradans decided it was time to treat pot smokers like consumers instead of criminals. Nationwide support for legalization has been rising more or less steadily since the 1980s, hitting 50 percent in the Gallup Poll for the first time in 2011. And unlike in 2006, voters were picking a president in 2012. "We see much greater turnout in presidential election years ('Tvert says') and when there is more turnout, there is virtually always more support for making marijuana legal." He also credits six years of public persuasion emphasizing the theme reflected in the name of the group he co-founded in 2005, SAFER (Safer Alternative for Enjoyable Recreation), and the tide of the 2009 book he co-wrote, *Marijuana Is Safer.* Tvert cites polling data indicating that people who accept that premise are much more likely to support legalization than people who don't. "Our strategy all along," he says, "was to bring that message and break people's fears of marijuana down to the point where they would go ahead and go with their gut feeling on making it legal."

Supporters of Amendment 64 had a big financial advantage in getting their message across (although not as big as the one enjoyed by legalizers in Washington, who outspent their opponents by 400 to 1). According to campaign finance reports, seven groups backing the initiative raised about $2.7 million, the vast majority of it from out-of-state donors, including the Marijuana Policy Project and the Drug Policy Alliance. The opposition, which consisted largely of law enforcement groups, raised about $560,000, half of it from out-of-state donors. The biggest backer of the No on 64 campaign was Save Our Society From Drugs, a Florida-based group cofounded by Mel Sembler, a Republican fundraiser and drug treatment entrepreneur who co-founded Straight Inc., the notorious (and now-defunct) chain of behavior modification centers for troubled teenagers.

Tvert argues that, contrary to what you might expect, the switch from merely decriminalizing use to legalizing the marijuana business improved Amendment 64's prospects because it promised to eliminate the black market and addressed the question of where people would get the pot they were now allowed to smoke. Voters' familiarity with state-regulated medical marijuana centers also helped. "When you talk about legalizing marijuana in the abstract," says Rob Kampia, executive director of the Marijuana Policy Project, "people say, 'I don't understand. What does it look like?' The visual matters. The medical marijuana dispensaries have been regulated since 2010, and there were already hundreds of stores voters would walk past every day."

"Like Any Other Business"

On the first floor of a professional building at the foot of Broadway in Colorado's capital is a black awning displaying the words "Denver Relief" in sans-serif type next to a green cross. Inside you find a waiting room with tan walls and brown leather couches flanking an Oriental rug on which sits a coffee table displaying issues of National Geographic. The shop—which began in May 2009 as a delivery service, making it "the second-oldest continuously operating medical marijuana center in the state of Colorado," according to co-owner Kayvan Khalatbari—is located in the same complex as an urgent care clinic. It looks like a cross between a dentist's office and a law firm. "There are no Bob Marley posters," notes Khalatbari, a 30-year-old Nebraska native who moved to Denver in 2004 for a job in electrical engineering, became an active member of SAFER, and now has a stake in two pizza places as well as the dispensary. "We want to be treated like any other business."

At the intake window, customers have to show their state-issued medical marijuana cards, which indicate that they have "a debilitating medical condition" for which a doctor has recommended cannabis as a treatment. Then they can gain entry to a back room, through two locked steel doors, where they will find a partitioned black granite counter of the sort where people might sit to try on sunglasses or lipstick. Displayed on racks attached to a brick wall behind the counter is an array of marijuana products, including drinks, pastries, lollipops, chocolate bars, sunflower seeds, e-cigarette cartridges, and two dozen varieties of buds in glass jars.

For visitors accustomed to the black market's meager selection, iffy quality, and high prices, the back room at Denver Relief is a revelation. The prices range from $30 to $40 for an eighth of an ounce. Other Denver dispensaries, such as Medicine Man on Nome Street, charge as little as $20, with $25 being fairly typical. According to data collected by the website Price of Weed, Americans commonly spend twice as much, around $50, for the same quantity of high-quality marijuana in the black market.

Denver Relief's grow operation, which produces several hundred pounds of marijuana a year, occupies a nondescript warehouse in an area of the city zoned for light industry. There is a separate room for each stage of growth, each with its own "lighting" scheme, calculated to maximize the production of psychoactive resin. The process, which starts with cuttings from mother plants and ends in a drying room where buds are packed in plastic crates, takes about five months.

The operation produces more than 30 strains of pot, with names like Hashberry, Daywrecker, Durban Poison, Q3 (Purple Urkle crossed with Space Queen), and Blue Dream (DJ Short's Blueberry crossed with Santa Cruze Haze). "There is way more of a difference than most laymen or novices imagine," says Nick Hice, Khalatbari's partner and Denver Relief's cultivation manager. "People think 'it's all green.' That's like someone who doesn't drink beer or wine saying 'it's all beer' or 'it's all wine.' Every one of these strains is different, and there are connoisseurs out there who can pull out the different aromas." Even to my uneducated nose, the strains have distinctive smells, including not just the hops and pine you might expect but surprising fruit notes such as lemon, orange, mango, banana, and pineapple.

The different varieties also have noticeably different psychoactive effects, says Hice, especially when you compare the two major types of marijuana, Cannabis sativa and Cannabis indica. "For medical purposes," he says, "we would usually recommend a sativa for the beginning of the day or early in the day when you still have things to do and you still need to function, whereas the indicas can be more lethargic and give you more of a whole-body high, where your whole body becomes slower and sluggish." According to Denver Relief's website, for example, Ghost Train Haze, a sativa-dominant hybrid, "will keep you active while letting you maintain lucidity." By contrast, Bio-Jesus, an indica-dominant strain, "is recommended for evening pain relief when functionality is not a requirement."

The quality and variety on which connoisseurship depends are an important but rarely mentioned benefit of legalization. While alcohol prohibition may have inspired creative cocktail recipes aimed at disguising the taste of black-market booze, it was hardly conducive to the enjoyment of fine liquor. The difference between black-market pot and the cannabis products available at a shop like Denver Relief is the difference between bathtub gin and the dozens of premium gin brands available today, each with its own aroma and flavor.

The Myth of "Seed-to-Sale" Oversight

While today's medical marijuana centers give you a sense of what fully legal cannabis will look like in Colorado, they operate under restrictions that make little or no sense for businesses serving the recreational market. To begin with, there's that requirement that customers have "a debilitating medical condition." To qualify, a condition must be either listed in Amendment 20, the 2000 initiative that legalized medical use of marijuana, or approved by the Colorado Department of Public Health and Environment, which is charged with maintaining the state's registry of approved patients. Those rules are stricter than California's Compassionate Use Act, which allows people to use marijuana for treatment of six specified conditions (including chronic pain), plus "any other illness for which marijuana provides relief."

Under Colorado law, a medical marijuana center is allowed to grow up to six plants for each patient who designates it as his "provider" in the registry. Denver Relief, for example, has about 400 members, meaning it is allowed to grow around 2,400 plants. Every plant is notionally assigned to a patient, but patients are not limited to pot from "their" plants, and they need not buy exclusively from their designated provider. Furthermore, MMCs can sell marijuana to each other, as long as it's no more than 30 percent of what they grow. MMCs are supposed to account for every last gram they produce and file reports whenever they transport marijuana. The rules are aimed at preventing diversion to people who are not registered patients, whereas in the recreational market the government's main concern will be preventing diversion to minors (defined as people younger than 21) and other states.

Although Colorado's regulations are often credited with allowing dispensaries there to operate relatively unmolested by the federal government, a state audit released in March revealed that all the talk of strict oversight was more aspirational than descriptive. Colorado's vaunted "seed-to-sale" monitoring system, which was supposed to include electronic plant tags, 24-hour video surveillance, and records of every marijuana transfer, was never actually implemented. "The envisioned seed-to-sale model does not currently exist in Colorado," said State Auditor Dianne Ray, and in any case "may not make sense," especially with the legal marijuana market expanding to include recreational users.

As a result of inadequate manpower, funding shortages, and poor financial management, Ray said, the Medical Marijuana Enforcement Division (MMED) not only had failed to create the planned high-tech tracking system; it did not even "review forms designed to track medical marijuana activities and inventories and ensure that medical marijuana is not being diverted from the system." That's right: although medical marijuana businesses were required to file forms whenever they moved any of their product, no one ever looked at them.

Furthermore, state inspectors would visit medical marijuana businesses during the application process but generally did not check in again after they were up and running, so it was hard to say how many of 1,440 or so operations officially overseen by the MMED (including dispensaries, their growing operations, and producers of cannabis edibles) were actually complying with regulations such as the 70/30 rule or the limit of six plants per patient. "The current code is extremely difficult to regulate," MMED Director Laura Harris, now head of the repurposed Marijuana Enforcement Division, told me in January. "What you will hear from many in industry is that this works. Well, I'm not as optimistic about it working."

Harris said enforcement was "complaint-driven," although "we have to prioritize our complaints because we have a limited number of investigators whose primary mission at this point has to be conducting pre-licensing inspections." The auditor's report recommended discontinuing those inspections in favor of "risk-based on-site inspections of the licensed businesses as part of a comprehensive monitoring program." The report estimated that pre-approval inspections of all 2,400 applicants who sought state licenses prior to a two-year moratorium that began in August 2010 "would take about 12,300 hours, which equals the work of six full-time equivalent staff in a year." It added that "the number of Division staff available to perform these on-site inspections has been as high as 19 but has been reduced to 10 as of February 2013." You can start to see why it took so long to obtain a license. According to the audit, "The shortest approval time was 436 days, while the longest approval time was 807 days." The average was about two years. "Out of about 2,400 pre-moratorium applications," the report said, "the Division has approved or denied only 622, or about 26 percent [as of October 2012]. The rest of the applications were still pending (41 percent) or were voluntarily withdrawn by the applicant (33 percent)." Pre-moratorium cannabis businesses were allowed to continue operating in the meantime.

Marijuana taxes are supposed to change all this, giving Harris' agency the resources to regulate in reality as well as theory. In addition to existing state and local sales taxes (which total 7.6 percent in Denver), a bill signed by Gov. Hickenlooper in May would impose an excise tax of 15 percent, as envisioned by Amendment 64, and a special sales tax of 10 percent. Both levies are subject to approval by voters this fall, as required by Colorado's constitution. An April report by researchers at Colorado State University estimated that, together with the standard state sales tax of 2.9 percent, a 15 percent excise tax and a 15 percent special sales tax (which legislators were considering at the time) would add $34 or so to the retail price of an ounce, making it about 23 percent higher than it would otherwise be. The estimated final price, based on a production cost of $600 a pound, was $185 an ounce, about the same as the price many dispensaries currently charge. The report's estimate of total state revenue, which hinged on various questionable assumptions about total consumption and other factors, was $131 million a year, which would go mainly to the Department of Revenue and a school construction fund.

Legalize It, but Don't Advertise It

In addition to the taxes, the legislature enacted various restrictions on the production and sale of marijuana, many of them suggested by the Amendment 64 Implementation Task Force. While visitors to Colorado will be allowed to buy marijuana, for instance, they will be limited to a quarter of an ounce per transaction. Residents, by contrast, can buy up to an ounce at a time. The idea is to discourage interstate smuggling by making it more difficult to accumulate large quantities. But the residence-based restriction may be vulnerable to challenge under both the state and federal constitutions.

One regulation approved by the legislature was so clearly unconstitutional that the state decided not to enforce it. A provision introduced by state Rep. Bob Gardner (R-Colorado Springs) would have required that "magazines whose primary focus is marijuana or marijuana businesses" be kept out of sight in stores open to people younger than 21. Gardner, who likened marijuana magazines to pornography, imagined that his rule would be upheld as reasonable restriction on commercial speech. But as the American Civil Liberties Union of Colorado pointed out in a federal lawsuit it filed on behalf of bookstores and newsstands, "the government's content-based restriction on non-commercial truthful information cannot pass constitutional muster" because marijuana magazines "are not within a recognized category of unprotected speech." Colorado Attorney General John Suthers agreed in a June 5 memo advising the Department of Revenue to refrain from enforcing Gardner's amendment in light of its conflict with the free speech guarantees of the state and federal constitutions. Denver attorney David Lane, who represented High Times in another lawsuit challenging the magazine rule, told Westword, "You would think a responsible adult in the legislature would have spoken up."

Other restrictions on marijuana-related speech may also be constitutionally vulnerable. The new marijuana law requires state regulators to ban "mass-market campaigns that have a high likelihood of reaching minors," for instance. The U.S. Supreme Court has rejected more modest restrictions on tobacco advertising that were likewise aimed at shielding minors from messages about products they are not allowed to buy. In the 2001 case *Lorillard Tobacco v. Reilly,* the Court overturned a Massachusetts ban on tobacco billboards within 1,000 feet of a school or playground, saying the rule banned outdoor tobacco advertising from "a substantial portion of Massachusetts' largest cities" and in some places amounted to "nearly a complete ban on the communication of truthful information about smokeless tobacco and cigars to adult consumers." Although it's not clear how federal courts would view restrictions on ads for products banned by federal law, Colorado courts traditionally have read the state constitution's free speech guarantee even more broadly than the Supreme Court has read the First Amendment.

Child protection is also the rationale for a provision calling upon the Marijuana Enforcement Division to create "requirements similar to the federal Poison Prevention Packaging Act of 1970," which describes "special packaging" that is "designed or constructed to be significantly difficult for children under five years of age to open or obtain a toxic or harmful amount of the substance contained therein within a reasonable time and not difficult for normal adults to use properly." But while it may be relatively straightforward to put marijuana buds in bottles with childproof caps, it's not clear how "special packaging" for cannabis-infused brownies or candy bars will work. Laura Harris, head of the Marijuana Enforcement Division, notes that legislators contemplated a similar requirement for medical marijuana. "They said you create a rule that describes a kind of packaging we want that will be child resistant" ["Harris says"]. It was never done, she adds, because "that's a thorny issue. What does that look like?"

Although the childproof packaging mandate will raise prices and may cause some inconvenience, the rules about what you can do inside a pot shop are more significant from a consumer's point of view. Customers will not be able to buy alcohol, tobacco, or cannabis-free snacks or drinks, and they will not be allowed to consume marijuana on the premises. The latter rule apparently puts the kibosh on dreams of Amsterdam-style cannabis cafes sprouting on the streets of Denver and Fort Collins. But what if you buy marijuana in a pot shop and take it with you to a bar or restaurant? In an effort to forestall such BYOW arrangements, legislators added marijuana to Colorado's Clean Indoor Air Act, which bans smoking in bars and restaurants. But as amended, the law applies only to "combustible marijuana" and "marijuana smoke," leaving open the possibility that bars and restaurants could allow patrons to use vaporizers or consume cannabis-infused foods purchased elsewhere.

There may be other legal options for people who want to consume marijuana in a social environment similar to a cafe or tavern. Last New Year's Eve, after the Amendment 64 provisions protecting possession and home cultivation took effect, Rob Corry, the attorney and marijuana activist, held the first meeting of a floating pot party he dubbed Club 64 at a hemp clothing store in Denver. "We had a DJ, lights, dancing, good music," Corry says. "We did serve alcohol, [but] we gave it away because we didn't have a liquor license for that event. We also had marijuana that we were giving away. We weren't selling it. The main way we raised revenue was with an event fee of $30." A variation on this theme would be charging for food and coffee but giving pot away, which could result in something like Amsterdam's so-called coffee shops.

Either operation seems to satisfy Amendment 64's requirements, although much depends on how the initiative's ban on consuming marijuana "openly and publicly" is interpreted. Corry argues that the phrase imposes two distinct conditions: to be prohibited, marijuana use must be "open" (visible to passers-by) and "public" (occurring on public property). Smoking pot while walking down a crowded sidewalk would be the paradigmatic example. But according to Corry's reading of the law, smoking pot in a secluded area of a park would be public without being open, while smoking pot on your front porch or on the patio of a restaurant (where the Clean Indoor Air Act does not apply) would be open without being public.

Denver Relief's Kayvan Khalatbari takes a different view. "On-site consumption is not going to happen," he asserts. "This is not going to be an Amsterdam. It's supposed to be done in the privacy of your own home behind drawn shades. You're not supposed to use it in front of anybody in public. Period."

Free Pot! (Donation Encouraged)

Another gray area is the nonprofit production and distribution of marijuana. Under Amendment 64, Coloradans may privately grow up to six plants and possess the marijuana from them (which could be a lot more than an ounce) on the premises where it was produced. They are also allowed to "assist" others in growing and possessing marijuana, and they can legally transfer up to an ounce at a time "without remuneration." These provisions seem to leave considerable leeway for various cooperative arrangements. Corry advises clients that seeking compensation for the costs they incur in growing marijuana, including rent, supplies, and utilities, is perfectly legal. Even seeking compensation for one's time should be acceptable, he says, although it is risky because that could be interpreted as "remuneration."

Last January police in Colorado Springs busted three guys for running Billygoatgreen MMJ, which was giving away marijuana while accepting "suggested donation[s] toward researching [marijuana] and improving our cultivation operation." The suggested donation for a quarterounce of Sour Kush, for instance, was $55. A spokeswoman for Attorney General Suthers told the The Denver Post such operations were clearly illegal, since "distributing marijuana in exchange for suggested donations is a scam to get around the laws against the sale of marijuana." Colorado Springs Police Lt. Mark Comte, who works in the Metro Vice, Narcotics, and Intelligence Division, seemed to disagree in an interview with The Colorado Springs Independent: "If I show up at your house with less than an ounce of marijuana, I'm 21, you're 21, and I say, 'Hey dude, it cost me 50 bucks in gas to get over here,' and you give me 50 bucks for my gas, there's nothing illegal. I mean, you and I both know what's going on with it, but they know what the loopholes are right now." Comte nevertheless defended the Billygoatgreen arrests, saying those guys were transferring more than an ounce at a time.

In May, The Denver Post reported that "an untold number" of cannabis collectives "have formed in Colorado since Amendment 64's passage." They included MJ Proper, a 501(c)(3) organization that sought to "foster the charitable [activity], scientific investigation, and education necessary to safely grow and consume recreational cannabis responsibly." According to MJ Proper's website, the benefits of joining the organization included eighth-ounce bags of Dark Star buds and six packs of cannabis-infused beer, both delivered for $37.50 each. Offended by such creative interpretations of the law, state legislators banned distribution of marijuana by any unlicensed "business or non-profit, including but not limited to a sole proprietorship, corporation, or other business enterprise." Although that provision led MJ Proper to suspend operations, it apparently does not apply to less formally organized efforts. In any case, it is hard to see how the legislature can ban cooperative cultivation without violating Amendment 64, which is now part of the state constitution.

The provisions allowing home cultivation and nonprofit transfers, which cops tend to view as dangerous loopholes, are actually a pretty clever insurance policy. If state-licensed pot shops open as planned, the do-it-yourself sector will account for a tiny share of marijuana consumption, just as home brewing accounts for a tiny share of beer consumption. Why grow your own if retailers are offering a nice selection of high-quality marijuana at reasonable prices? But unless and until that scenario materializes, the allowance for noncommercial production provides an alternative.

In a Brookings Institution paper published last April, legal analyst Stuart Taylor cites that alternative as a reason for federal drug warriors to think twice before trying to stop legalization in Colorado. Taylor warns that "a federal crackdown would backfire by producing an atomized, anarchic, state-legalized but unregulated marijuana market that federal drug enforcers could neither contain nor force the states to contain." The feds could use threats of prosecution and forfeiture to shut down state-licensed stores or prevent them from opening. That approach worked well for John Walsh, the U.S. attorney in Colorado, who last year sent threatening letters to the landlords and operators of more than 50 medical marijuana centers he deemed too close to schools. According to Laura Harris, all of them closed, with nary a raid or arrest. But if the Justice Department succeeded in blocking recreational pot shops, it would be confronted by thousands of small, inconspicuous growers instead of a few hundred openly operating retailers. Taylor argues that if the feds cooperate with Colorado officials to prevent diversion of marijuana, they will have a better chance of limiting the impact on states that continue to treat cannabis as contraband.

For those who favor confrontation, aggressive enforcement is not the only option. Opponents of legalization, including anti-drug activists, former heads of the Drug Enforcement Administration, and several members of Congress, want the Justice Department to fight it in court. They argue that Colorado's marijuana laws are invalid under the Constitution's Supremacy Clause (which says federal statutes are "the supreme law of the land") because they are pre-empted by the Controlled Substances Act (CSA). They note that the Supreme Court, based on a very broad interpretation of the power to regulate interstate commerce, has upheld enforcement of the CSA's ban on marijuana even in states that allow medical use.

But the fact that the feds can continue to enforce marijuana prohibition in Colorado does not mean they can compel Colorado to help. Under our federal system, states have no obligation to punish every action that Congress decides to treat as a crime, and Congress cannot command state officials to enforce its laws. Furthermore, the CSA itself expressly limits pre-emption to situations where there is "a positive conflict" between state and federal law "so that the two cannot consistently stand together."

As Vanderbilt University law professor Robert Mikos explains in a Cato Institute paper published last December, "a positive conflict would seem to arise anytime a state engages in, or requires others to engage in, conduct or inaction that violates the CSA." If state officials grew medical marijuana or distributed it to patients, for example, they would be violating the CSA, and the law establishing that program would be pre-empted. But specifying the criteria for exemption from state penalties does not require anyone to violate the CSA. Mikos concludes that Congress "has left [states] free to regulate marijuana, so long as their regulations do not positively conflict with the CSA."

It is notable that in the 17 years since states began legalizing marijuana for medical use, the Justice Department has never tried to overturn those laws in court with a pre-emption argument, even though it has interfered with the distribution of cannabis to patients in various other ways. "They know they can't force a state to criminalize a given behavior, which is why the federal government has never tried to push a pre-emption argument [against] these medical marijuana laws," Alex Kreit, a professor at the Thomas Jefferson School of Law who has studied the pre-emption issue, told the Drug War Chronicle last year. "Opponents of these laws would love nothing more than to be able to preempt them, but there is not a viable legal theory to do that. The federal government recognizes that's a losing batde. I would be surprised if they filed suit against Colorado or Washington saying their state laws are pre-empted. It would be purely a political maneuver because they would know they would lose in court."

A Yellow Light for Legalization

At the end of August, nearly 10 months after Colorado and Washington voters decided to legalize marijuana, the Justice Department finally responded. In a memo to U.S. attorneys, Deputy Attorney General James Cole indicated that if the two states adequately address federal concerns about issues such as drugged driving, sales to minors, and diversion to other states, the feds will allow their experiments to proceed. But if regulation and enforcement are not strict enough, he said, the Justice Department may yet decide to prosecute growers and sellers who comply with the new marijuana laws or challenge the laws themselves in federal court.

A bill introduced by Rep. Dana Rohrabacher (R-Calif.) in April would take the decision away from the Obama administration by barring federal prosecution of people who grow, possess, transport, or sell marijuana in compliance with state laws. The Respect State Marijuana Laws Act of 2013 has 18 cosponsors, including three Republicans in addition to Rohrabacher: Justin Amash and Dan Benishek of Michigan, which has a medical marijuana law, and Don Young of Alaska, where it is legal to possess less than four ounces of cannabis in your home.

A more modest bill introduced last November by Rep. Diana DeGette (D-Colo.), clarifying that state regulation of marijuana does not violate the Controlled Substances Act, attracted the support of another Republican, Mike Coffman, a conservative who succeeded Tom Tancredo as representative of Colorado's 6th Congressional District in 2009. Coffman had never before shown any inclination to favor drug policy reform. But Amendment 64 won about 52 percent of the vote in Adams, Arapahoe, and Douglas counties, which make up Coffman's district. That's 4 percent points more than Coffman, who was re-elected with a 48 percent plurality. "I think he's a smart guy," says Christian Sederberg, a Denver lawyer who was involved in passing and implementing Amendment 64. Coffman, Sederberg suggests, realized that "if this issue got more votes than I did, that's a very clear signal that it's time to evolve." Amendment 64, incidentally, also received more votes in Colorado than Barack Obama did.

Wanda James, co-owner of a marijuana edibles business in Denver called Simply Pure, argues that politicians ignore growing public support for legalization at their peril. "Three million people in America on election night voted to legalize marijuana," says James, who plans on jumping into the recreational market with both feet. "I can't imagine the United States government starting some arrest campaign on people who are compliant with their state laws. I just can't see the American government doing this when the will of the people is saying 'enough.'" Anyway, she says, "What court in Colorado is going to convict me?"

Critical Thinking

1. Will the restrictions imposed by Amendment 64 adequately prevent the sale of marijuana to minors?

2. Should marijuana be regulated in a manner similar to alcohol?

3. Why do many conservatives support the legal sale of marijuana?

Create Central

www.mhhe.com/createcentral

Internet References

Norml
   http://www.norml.org
State Marijuana Laws Map
   http://www.governing.com

JACOB SULLUM is a nationally syndicated columnist and the author of *Saying Yes: In Defense of Drug Use* (Tarcber Penguin).

Article   Prepared by: Eileen L. Daniel, *SUNY Brockport*

Rethinking Drug Policy Assumptions

Jefferson M. Fish

Learning Outcomes

After reading this article, you will be able to:

- Explain why the war on drugs has not been successful.

- Describe drug legalization options.

- Describe why therapy for substance abuse is less successful than treatment for anxiety and depression.

The so-called war on drugs has lasted more than four decades and increasing numbers of people are convinced that it is not only unwinnable but also misguided. From foreign policy to domestic policy to drug treatment, U.S. drug policy has been based on inaccurate assumptions and incorrect causal models that have led to an ever-escalating failure. The attempt here is to identify some of the principal errors, point out their shortcomings, and offer more plausible assumptions and models in their stead. These alternatives point not simply to downsizing the war and decriminalizing marijuana, as voters in Colorado and Washington State recently did, but to ending the war on drugs altogether by considering a range of legalization options.

Attacking Drugs vs. the Black Market

Current U.S. policy is based on the assumption that drugs cause crime, corruption, and disease. Hence, we label and ban some substances as "dangerous drugs." It follows that bad people supply these drugs, so we lock them up, but the supply keeps getting through. Engagement between police and criminal suppliers ramps up, leading only to more crime, corruption, and disease at home, while the battle spreads around the world.

It looks as if the more we clamp down, the worse the problem gets. Up until now the response has been not to question the underlying assumption, but to further escalate the war, hoping the right side will eventually achieve victory. There seems to be no consideration of the possibility that it's the policy itself that's making matters worse.

Here is an alternative causal model, one that actually explains the failure of our longstanding policy: drug prohibition—that

is, the war on drugs—causes an illegal, or black market, which in turn causes crime, corruption, and disease. With this model, the goal of drug policy should be to attack the black market instead of attacking drugs because the market undermines the stability of friendly countries (witness Colombia and Mexico) and finances our enemies (al-Qaeda and the Taliban, for example). Attempts to suppress the black market by force merely spread it, from one country to another or, in response to local police crackdowns, from one neighborhood to another.

The way to attack an illegal market is to create a legal one. As we learned when Prohibition ended and it became possible to buy alcohol legally, crime, corruption, and disease (such as blindness or even death from contaminated or substitute products sold as alcohol) fell dramatically.

Decriminalization won't work—even though not locking people up for using a substance is a more humane policy—because it does nothing about the black market. Most people are unaware that Prohibition, with its rampant crime and gang violence, was actually a decriminalization regime for alcohol. The Eighteenth Amendment criminalized "the manufacture, sale, or transportation of intoxicating liquors" but not possession for personal use.

Degrees and Types of Legalization

The question of *how* to legalize drugs (as opposed to whether to legalize) is a complex one that I have dealt with in three separate works offering a wide range of policy alternatives. While the question is too broad to be settled here, let me at least call attention to two of the most important issues that need to be addressed. First, for each substance, one has to consider whether it should be as legal as tomatoes, or if it should be regulated akin to aspirin, or as alcohol and tobacco, or as antibiotics. That is, there are many forms of "legalization," and the term has different meanings for agricultural products, over-the-counter medications, legal psychoactive substances, and prescription medications.

Second, there are two basic approaches to legalization. The first, a rights-based, civil liberties, or libertarian approach, argues that individuals should be free, in private, to have control over their own bodies as long as they don't directly harm other people. This approach tends to be favored by lawyers, judges, police, and others in the criminal justice system because it makes the rules of the game clear to all. The second approach, considered a public health or harm reduction, cost-benefit approach, emphasizes preventing the spread of disease and protecting the health of users. It attempts to devise a different strategy for each substance based on the best scientific knowledge available, and tends to be favored by physicians, psychologists, and those in the biomedical and social sciences. There are many varieties of each kind of approach, and many instances where they agree—but there are also points at which they propose quite different policies; and these differences would need to be addressed in any debate over legalization legislation.

Another key assumption underlying drug prohibition is that drugs "hook" victims, so that making drugs illegal will prevent addiction and the spread of associated diseases. There are many problems with this assumption, but I will only discuss a few. First of all, to simply focus on "drugs" while ignoring dosage level and mode of administration is a mistake. (Other relevant variables include the situation in which the substance is used and the effects users expect it to have.) Higher dosage levels are associated with an increased risk of more serious problems, from dependency to death. Similarly, administering a substance by injecting it is a very efficient means of getting it into your system, but also a dangerous one because of the increased risk of transmitting diseases like HIV and hepatitis through shared needles.

Contrary to the above assumption, the "Iron Law of Prohibition" states that prohibition leads to higher dosage levels and more dangerous modes of administration. These consequences follow naturally from the illegal market. Black marketeers want to pack as much of an outlawed substance as possible into the minimum volume, which is the definition of a high-dosage level; and purchasers, because of the inflated black market price, want the biggest bang for their buck. Similarly, because injecting is so efficient a way of using an expensive substance, there is an economic motivation to use this more dangerous means of administration.

Under Prohibition, the United States went from a nation of drinkers of safe beer (low-dosage alcohol) to drinkers of higher-dosage and often contaminated whiskey. After Prohibition the country gradually returned to its preference for beer. Similarly, over time users have gone from smoked opium to injected heroin; from low-dosage cocaine in the original Coca-Cola to inhaled powdered cocaine to crack; and from lower THC levels in marijuana to higher levels. In addition, because marijuana is bulky and has a strong odor it has the black market disadvantages of taking up a lot of space and being relatively easy to detect. This drives up the price of marijuana relative to cocaine and heroin, and creates an economic incentive for users to switch from soft to hard drugs.

A major study published in *American Psychologist* back in 1990 contradicted the assumption that drugs "hook" victims. Its findings, summarized in the study's Abstract, have long been known, but are startling to many non-experts, and are worth quoting here:

The relation between psychological characteristics and drug use was investigated in subjects studied longitudinally, from preschool through age 18. Adolescents who had engaged in some drug experimentation (primarily with marijuana) were the best-adjusted in the sample. Adolescents who used drugs frequently were maladjusted, showing a distinct personality syndrome marked by interpersonal alienation, poor impulse control, and manifest emotional distress. Adolescents who, by age 18, had never experimented with any drug were relatively anxious, emotionally constricted, and lacking in social skills. Psychological differences between frequent drug users, experimenters, and abstainers could be traced to the earliest years of childhood and related to the quality of parenting received. The findings indicate that (a) problem drug use is a symptom, not a cause, of personal and social maladjustment, and (b) the meaning of drug use can be understood only in the context of an individual's personality structure and developmental history. It is suggested that current efforts at drug prevention are misguided to the extent that they focus on symptoms, rather than on the psychological syndrome underlying drug abuse.

In other words, instead of saying that drugs hook victims, a better causal model for drug abuse is to say that people with significant problems self-medicate. In addition, this description of drug use fits with what we know about adolescence. That is, in our individualistic culture, adolescence is a time of experimentation with different options during the transition from childhood to adulthood. Teenagers work summer or part-time jobs, and they are exposed to courses in a variety of disciplines so that they can make informed career decisions. Dating is an institution that provides young people with experience in forming, maintaining, and dissolving intimate relationships, so that they have a basis for selecting a life partner. In a similar way, teen experimentation with forbidden psychoactive substances can be seen as a way of learning their effects so that people can decide whether to use them in the future.

Punishment vs. Reintegration and Mandatory vs. Voluntary Treatment

Another set of mistaken assumptions underlies current policy regarding prevention and treatment. When it comes to illegal substances, current policy argues that (1) all use is abuse; (2) zero tolerance will discourage use and therefore abuse; (3) punishing users will send a powerful message to others and prevent them from going down the wrong path; and (4) mandatory drug treatment, offered by the courts as an alternative to imprisonment, is an effective and enlightened policy.

An alternative set of assumptions is that (1) only some use, when it is out of control and self-destructive, is abuse; (2) for many individuals and many psychoactive substances, both legal and illegal, controlled, non-problematic use is possible; (3) marginalizing problem users is counterproductive—a more effective strategy is to reduce the harm they do to themselves and others and attempt to reintegrate them into society; and (4) mandatory treatment (for example, in drug courts) undermines the institution of psychotherapy, and is less effective than voluntary treatment.

Tolerance is a virtue, so it's unfortunate that a slogan like "zero tolerance" has become part of the world of prevention and treatment. A better slogan might be "get a life."

When the Vietnam War ended and the troops came home, there was great anxiety in the law enforcement community. Tens of thousands of drug-addicted, trained killers were about to descend on American society. The fear was that their cravings for illegal substances, such as marijuana and heroin, would lead to an unprecedented crime wave as their addictions forced them to come up with the money to support their habits.

It never happened. Yes, some continued to have drug problems and others sought treatment, but for the great majority of problem users, they simply stopped. On their own. With no professional help.

This non-crime wave makes no sense according to the "drugs hook victims" ideology, but it is easily understandable if you employ the point of view that people with significant problems self-medicate. In Vietnam, soldiers faced constant danger and staying high made them feel better. Back home, staying high interfered with their reintegration into society. Work, family, love, a better future—all of these depended on attending to and living in reality, not blotting it out.

Years ago, I had a conversation with a marijuana activist. He was an intelligent, college-educated young man who could have earned much more in another line of work, but whose revulsion at our drug policy led him to sacrifice income for what he viewed as a worthy cause. "You know," he said, "I've actually been smoking very little these days." He described his situation—he worked long hours and needed to keep a clear head; he was in a serious relationship with a woman and wanted to focus his attention on her when they were together; and as a single adult he had responsibilities for feeding himself and maintaining his apartment. In essence, he had a life and was involved with highly valued activities, so that marijuana functioned for him the way alcohol functions for occasional users of that substance—now and then providing a few hours of an altered state of consciousness, integrated responsibly as part of a fulfilling life.

By criminalizing all use we marginalize problem users, which diminishes their likelihood of recovery; and we also marginalize non-problem users who've had the bad luck to get caught up in the criminal justice system—thereby creating serious problems for them where none existed before.

Supposedly, mandatory drug treatment offers an enlightened option for users who've been arrested. To understand why this is not the case, it's necessary to have a basic understanding of the way therapy works. To begin with, therapy is based on trust. In voluntary therapy, the therapist is working for the client, and what happens in therapy is protected by confidentiality, which allows the client to candidly discuss anything, including illegal drug use. If the client feels that therapy isn't working, that client is free to leave altogether, or to seek another therapist. In mandatory drug treatment, the therapist is working for the court, and a client seeking to leave therapy can be labeled as uncooperative, which can result in imprisonment.

For non-problem users, therapy turns into a charade. The individual has to pretend he or she has a drug problem to avoid going to jail. The user then has to pretend to cooperate with the therapist, since lack of cooperation could result in jail time. In this situation, therapists get paid for their time, which provides an incentive to maintain the charade. Eventually, the client is deemed cured and has succeeded in avoiding jail by undergoing the lesser punishment of pretend therapy. (Some people may actually benefit from the process by dealing better with various aspects of their lives, but this is hardly a justification for undermining the institution of therapy by making therapist and client co-conspirators in a lie.)

In order to understand the situation for problem users it's necessary to consider the role of motivation in therapy. ("How many therapists does it take to change a light bulb?" the relevant joke goes. "Only one, but the light bulb has to *want* to change.") Why is it that the success rates in therapy are so much better for anxiety and depression than they are for substance abuse? The reason is that anxiety and depression are unpleasant, so clients are motivated to change. They are likely to cooperate with therapists because they want to experience less of those unpleasant feelings, and more positive feelings instead. The situation is the opposite for overeating, risky sexual behavior, gambling, and substance abuse. These are pleasurable activities, so change—even if it is clearly better for the client—entails a loss of an important source of pleasure. Thus, when clients are self-motivated to change, because they see that they are headed in a bad direction, they are more likely to cooperate with a therapist who suggests difficult or unpleasant tasks than they are with a court-ordered therapist who says "Change, or else!" This is one reason for the slogan "drug treatment on demand." You'll get better results with people who want to change than with those who are forced to change against their will.

One form of brief therapy, known as solution-focused therapy, describes three kinds of therapeutic relationships. In a customer relationship, the individual wants to change (technically, the individual is "willing to construct a solution"), and the therapist helps that person to change. In a complainant relationship, the client wants to complain but is unwilling to change (one who might say, "I'd be fine if only my spouse would change"). In a visitor relationship, the individual has neither a complaint nor an interest in changing (such as a child who has problems at school, whose mother brings him or her for therapy, and whose father [the visitor] comes because the therapist asked him to, although he isn't sure what he's doing there). In general, solution-focused therapists work directly toward change with customers, and try to convert complainants and visitors into customers.

A colleague of mine suggested that mandatory treatment deserved a separate label as a fourth kind of relationship—a hostage relationship.

In short, replacing the inaccurate assumptions and causal models underlying the war on drugs with better alternatives points to a different way of understanding drug use and abuse and to different drug policy options. These alternatives include shifting our primary aim from attacking drugs to shrinking the black market through a targeted policy of legalization for adults, and differentiating between problem users (who should be offered help) and non-problem users (who should be left alone). We must also shift from a policy of punishing and marginalizing problem users to one of harm reduction and reintegration into society, while shifting from a mandatory treatment policy to one of voluntary treatment. Moreover, abstention need not be the only acceptable treatment outcome—we must recognize that many (but not all) problem users can become occasional, non-problematic users. Finally, moving away from a near-exclusive treatment focus on the substance itself to building on positive aspects of people's lives, such as work, family, friends, and interests, will enable us to forge a more successful, more humanistic approach to drug use.

Critical Thinking

1. Why is the war on drugs considered unwinnable?
2. What are some of the ranges of legalized options relative to drug legalization?
3. Why are the success rates in therapy so much better for anxiety and depression than they are for substance abuse?

Create Central

www.mhhe.com/createcentral

Internet References

Food and Drug Administration (FDA)
   www.fda.gov

National Institute on Drug Abuse (NIDA)
   www.nida.nih.gov

JEFFERSON M. FISH *is professor emeritus, former Psychology Department chair, and former director of clinical psychology at St. John's University, New York City. He is the author or editor of twelve books, most recently* **The Myth of Race.** *His Psychology Today blog is called "**Looking in the Cultural Mirror**" and his website is* **www.jeffersonfish.com.** *You can also find him on* **Facebook** *and* **Twitter**.

Article   Prepared by: Eileen Daniel, *SUNY College at Brockport*

Sparking Controversy

Rise in e-cigarette use has public health experts questioning their safety, effectiveness as harm-reduction device.

STEVEN ROSS JOHNSON

Learning Outcomes

After reading this article, you will be able to:

- Explain why e-cigarettes, which do not contain tobacco, are in regulatory limbo.

- Understand why many physicians do not support the use of e-cigarettes

- Describe why e-cigarettes may offer quitters an advantage over nicotine patches

It has been a year since Travis Legge, 34, of Rockford, Ill., made the switch from smoking two packs of cigarettes a day to becoming a regular user of electronic cigarettes. "It became apparent that it was time to make a change," said Legge, who has smoked for more than 20 years. "Since I started using them, I feel like I got more energy and it's easier to breathe."

Legge is one of the millions of people around the world who now puff e-cigarettes instead of smoking tobacco. The rise of the new industry has triggered a sharp debate over whether the devices can play a major role in helping the nation's estimated 44 million adult smokers kick their unhealthy habit.

While critics say there's not enough research to determine the long-term health effects of e-cigarettes, proponents of the increasingly popular devices contend they are a safe alternative and could provide a major public health benefit if millions of smokers switched. Inhaling nicotine and other additives through a vapor doesn't expose users to all the harmful chemicals that accompany cigarette smoke, they say.

Clearly, better anti-smoking aids are needed. One-third of smokers who use Food and Drug Administration-approved nicotine replacement therapies such as patches or drugs are likely to relapse, according to a study by researchers at the Harvard School of Public Health, which was published in a January 2012 issue of the journal Tobacco Control. If e-cigarettes could improve the quit rate without causing as much harm, cancer rates several decades out might plummet.

"In an ideal world, if, in fact, everybody switched to a non-combustible form of nicotine, yes, from a public health point-of-view that would be very good," said Dr. Paul Cinciripini, director of the Tobacco Treatment Program at M.D. Anderson Cancer Center in Texas. "But it doesn't have to be e-cigarettes."

Smoking remains the largest cause of preventable death, killing nearly a half-million people in the U.S. annually. It costs businesses and their employees an estimated $193 billion a year in lost productivity and heath-related expenses. Left untreated, an estimated 60 percent of smokers will die of tobacco-caused diseases such as lung cancer and chronic obstructive pulmonary disease.

It now costs smokers even before they get sick. The Patient Protection and Affordable Care Act allows insurers to charge individuals or small group plans as much as 50 percent more in premiums for "tobacco use," although the term isn't rigidly defined in the law. A number of large employers, including Wal-Mart and UPS, that already charge smokers higher insurance premiums as part of their wellness programs have included e-cigarettes among those products that incur the penalty.

But are e-cigarettes the same as smoking? The FDA attempted to answer that question in 2009 when it looked to ban e-cigarettes on the grounds the products were "an unapproved drug-device combination" under the Food, Drug, and Cosmetics Act. The FDA's attempt to label e-cigarettes as a drug-delivery device would suggest the agency at least considered the possibility that e-cigarettes might be used to help people quit smoking.

But a federal appeals court in 2010 ruled in favor of the manufacturers, who argued that e-cigarettes were not medical devices and should be regulated like tobacco products. The decision allowed e-cigarette manufacturers, who never claimed the puffable nicotine delivery devices helped people stop smoking, to continue marketing their products without having to go through stringent FDA testing. Regulating e-cigarettes as an anti-smoking device would subject them to lengthy clinical trials to determine their safety and effectiveness.

In the wake of the court's ruling, the FDA reversed field. A 2011 letter announced it would seek to establish rules that treated e-cigarettes the same as traditional cigarettes and other tobacco products.

The FDA has yet to establish guidelines regarding the production and marketing of e-cigarettes. Last July, the agency stated it expected to issue rules on unspecified "tobacco products," which many think will include e-cigarettes, later this year. FDA spokeswoman Jennifer Haliski said the agency does not speculate on the timing of its rulings.

That leaves e-cigarettes, which do not contain tobacco, in regulatory limbo. Supporters, opponents, clinicians, and policymakers are on their own to determine whether the devices can significantly reduce the enormous economic damage caused by smoking or will simply become one more drag on public health.

Smoking-Cessation Device?

Electronic cigarettes were first developed in China in 2003 and made their way to the U.S. and Europe three years later. Sales have been increasing every year, and with an estimated 3 million users, total revenue is expected to reach more than $1 billion by the end of 2013. Many analysts believe that within the next decade, e-cigarettes will outsell traditional tobacco cigarettes, which is now an $80 billion-a-year market.

While many physicians and anti-smoking advocates concede e-cigarettes, along with other noncombustible forms of nicotine delivery, are probably less harmful than smoking tobacco cigarettes, none said they were prepared to endorse their patients using them as a smoking alternative.

"I think there is potential for e-cigarettes to help people stop," said Thomas Glynn, director of cancer science and trends for the American Cancer Society. "It's probably not going to be a panacea or magic bullet. But to date, the information we have on whether they help people to stop or not is mostly anecdotal. There have been a few studies and a number of ones ongoing, and the data have been mixed."

Danny McGoldrick, vice president for research at the Campaign for Tobacco-Free Kids, said the problem with people using e-cigarettes as a way to quit smoking lies with the lack of information about their safety. People who use them could stop using nicotine replacement therapy (NRT) products that have been federally proven to be safe and effective.

"Everyone wants more effective smoking-cessation devices, and what we need is some science and some evidence," McGoldrick said. "We need innovative products to help people quit smoking, but they need to be safe and effective, and they need to not encourage new smoking or relapse for former smokers."

An e-cigarette basically consists of a solution containing propylene glycol, which is used as a food preservative; vegetable glycerin, a sugar substitute; polyethylene glycol, a compound used in medicines and skin creams; and concentrated levels of nicotine, none of which are known to cause cancer. By contrast, there are approximately 600 ingredients in a tobacco cigarette, which can create an estimated 4,000 chemicals when smoked, according to the American Lung Association. Such chemicals include lead, ammonia, a household cleaner, and formaldehyde, all of which are known carcinogens, according to HHS.

Prices can vary, ranging from $12 to $15 for disposable units that last for a day or two to higher-range devices that run about $200. Popular brands such as Blu and NJoy usually start between $60 and $70 for a starter kit, which consists of a pack to hold the e-cigs, two rechargeable batteries, a USB charger and wall charger, and up to five flavor cartridges.

E-cigarette supporters tout the devices' ability to mimic smoking by requiring users to inhale and exhale the vapor. That offers a behavioral advantage over products such as the nicotine patch or gum.

Dr. Michael Siegel, a physician and professor of community health sciences at Boston University, compared the use of e-cigarettes with the way methadone is prescribed to heroin addicts. "This is basically what I would call a harm reduction strategy," he said.

But much is still unknown about the potential health effects of the chemicals in e-cigarettes, said Dr. D. Kyle Hogarth, medical director for the University of Chicago Medical Center's Pulmonary Rehabilitation Program. "These are like vitamins, supplements and everything else that's a complete Wild West," he said. There could be "a lot of other garbage in there."

So far, studies have offered conflicting results on the potential health impact of e-cigarettes. One study of 10 reusable and disposable e-cigarette models by the French magazine 60 Million Consumers claimed levels of formaldehyde close to the levels in tobacco cigarettes.

A 2009 FDA study reported finding toxic chemicals in e-cigarette vapors such as diethylene glycol, an ingredient used in antifreeze. A 2012 study published in the journal Chest by Greek researchers at the University of Athens found changes in the lung function of healthy smokers who puffed on an e-cigarette for as long as five minutes.

But an independent analysis conducted by Drexel University School of Public Health Professor Igor Burstyn found the contaminants in e-cigarettes did not pose a significant health risk.

"There is no serious concern about the contaminants such as volatile organic compounds in the liquid or vapor produced by heating," he said.

Dr. Richard Hurt, founder and director of the Mayo Clinic's Nicotine Dependence Center, said if e-cigarettes were proven to be an effective means of helping people quit smoking, then many clinicians would most likely be on board with their use considering the devastating effects tobacco has on the health of the smoker and bystanders. "It's one of those things where the cart is way out before the horse—and the horse would be the science," he said.

Marketing Intensifying

Critics cite the lack of regulation as the driving force behind the large-scale marketing push by e-cigarette makers, some of which are owned by tobacco companies. Actor Stephen Dorff, actress Jenny McCarthy and singer Courtney Love have all appeared on television commercials endorsing the devices.

And that has started to affect sales of FDA-approved nicotine replacement therapy devices. An analysis of the NRT market released in April by the consumer strategy research firm Euromonitor International found sales of Nicoderm CQ patches, which release nicotine through the skin, fell by 8 percent in 2012 as a result of "competitive disadvantages against oral NRTs (nicotine gum and lozenges) and e-cigarettes."

The marketing push has led anti-smoking advocates to push the FDA to move faster in issuing rules. They believe heavy advertising by e-cigarette makers will encourage ex-smokers and some nonsmokers, such as children, to start using the product. They fear e-cigarettes may become a gateway drug to regular smoking.

"We are certainly concerned about the claims that are being made with regard to e-cigarettes," said Erika Sward, assistant vice president at the American Lung Association. "We're concerned that they may start kids on a lifetime of nicotine addiction."

In the Centers for Disease Control and Prevention's most recent National Youth Tobacco Survey, the number of middle school and high school students who reported using an e-cigarette doubled, from 3.3 percent in 2011 to 6.8 percent in 2012.

"The increased use of e-cigarettes by teens is deeply troubling," said CDC Director Dr. Tom Frieden. "Nicotine is a highly addictive drug. Many teens who start with e-cigarettes may be condemned to struggling with a lifelong addiction to nicotine and conventional cigarettes."

Mayo's Hurt said the question people should be asking is whether e-cigarettes are as effective as traditional nicotine replacement therapies in helping people to quit smoking. "The comparator should not be comparing what's in an e-cigarette with what's in a traditional cigarette," he said. "The comparator should be with what's in an e-cigarette to a comparable,

medicinal nicotine delivery device that's been approved by the Food and Drug Administration as being safe and effective—and that would be the nicotine inhaler."

Studies on the effectiveness of e-cigarettes as a smoking cessation device are sparse since manufacturers don't want to go that route and haven't sponsored research. A recent study in The Lancet from researchers at the National Institute for Health Innovation at the University of Auckland in New Zealand found e-cigarettes were at least as effective in helping smokers quit as the nicotine patch.

E-cigarette makers have steered clear of claiming their products help people to quit. Such claims would subject them to government regulation as a medical device. "We're not making any cessation claims on this," said David Sylvia, spokesman for Nu Mark, the manufacturer of MarkTen e-cigarettes and a subsidiary of tobacco maker Altria Group.

What Would Regulation Look Like?

While opponents and supporters alike recognize the need for federal regulation on the sale and production of e-cigarettes, the two sides greatly differ on how those rules should look.

Anti-smoking advocates believe the agency should simply impose the same rules on e-cigarettes that it has on tobacco. That would ban TV and radio advertising and place restrictions on where and how they can be sold.

But industry officials are resisting that approach. "We don't believe that the Tobacco (Control) Act is the appropriate regulatory framework for electronic cigarettes," said Cynthia Cabrera, executive director of the Smoke-Free Alternatives Trade Association, one of the largest trade groups for e-cigarette manufacturers. "The compliance and regulatory burden that being designated a tobacco product would bring with it would wipe out quite a lot of the industry."

Regulation can have consequences that go beyond restrictions on how e-cigarettes are sold. Treating them like tobacco products could subject them to local and state government "sin taxes," which would make them more expensive and discourage use.

Moreover, since the ACA does not define what is considered "tobacco use," designating e-cigarettes as a tobacco product could trigger higher health insurance premiums for users—an assumption already made by some insurers and employers.

The designation would also hurt low-income users who turn to the new exchanges for health insurance. Those receiving a federal subsidy to buy health coverage could be hit with higher out-of-pocket costs because the subsidy would not increase to cover the smoker's premium, which could be 50 percent higher.

A number of businesses have already begun banning e-cigarette use inside their establishments while some employers have started to prohibit their employees from using them at the workplace.

Helen Darling, president of the National Business Group on Health, said the use of e-cigarettes would be considered tobacco use under the ACA, although the health law does not specifically name e-cigarettes as falling under that designation.

"Any employer that has a tobacco surcharge or penalty of any kind would count e-cigarettes as use of tobacco," Darling said, "And they will already be counted in however that's treated."

Boston University's Siegel said the ambiguity over e-cigarettes' status underscores the need for regulation that clearly separates the devices from their tobacco cigarette cousins. "I'm hoping the FDA will recognize that there are major differences in risks between electronic cigarettes and regular cigarettes," he said. "To regulate them in the exact same way would make no sense at all."

Critical Thinking

1. Why would regulating e-cigarettes the same as tobacco cigarettes discourage their use:?

2. Overall, does it appear that e-cigarettes are safe or safer than tobacco cigarettes?

Create Central

www.mhhe.com/createcentral

Internet References

American Lung Association
http://www.lung.org/press-room/press-releases/advocacy/FDA-ECig-Deeming-Reg-Statement.html

Food and Drug Adminstration
http://www.fda.gov

***

STEVEN ROSS JOHNSON covers public health issues and news for *Modern Healthcare Magazine*.

Article   Prepared by: Eileen L. Daniel, *SUNY Brockport*

Drowned in a Stream of Prescriptions

Before his addiction, Richard Fee was a popular college class president and aspiring medical student. "You keep giving Adderall to my son, you're going to kill him," said Rick Fee, Richard's father, to one of his son's doctors.

ALAN SCHWARZ

Learning Outcomes

After reading this article, you will be able to:

- Explain the risks associated with the use of non-prescribed prescription drugs.

- Describe the mechanisms in which drugs such as Ritalin and Adderall work.

- Understand the reasons for the widespread use of these drugs among college students.

Virginia beach—Every morning on her way to work, Kathy Fee holds her breath as she drives past the squat brick building that houses Dominion Psychiatric Associates.

It was there that her son, Richard, visited a doctor and received prescriptions for Adderall, an amphetamine-based medication for attention deficit hyperactivity disorder. It was in the parking lot that she insisted to Richard that he did not have A.D.H.D., not as a child and not now as a 24-year-old college graduate, and that he was getting dangerously addicted to the medication. It was inside the building that her husband, Rick, implored Richard's doctor to stop prescribing him Adderall, warning, "You're going to kill him."

It was where, after becoming violently delusional and spending a week in a psychiatric hospital in 2011, Richard met with his doctor and received prescriptions for 90 more days of Adderall. He hanged himself in his bedroom closet two weeks after they expired.

The story of Richard Fee, an athletic, personable college class president and aspiring medical student, highlights widespread failings in the system through which five million Americans take medication for A.D.H.D., doctors and other experts said.

Medications like Adderall can markedly improve the lives of children and others with the disorder. But the tunnel-like focus the medicines provide has led growing numbers of teenagers and young adults to fake symptoms to obtain steady prescriptions for highly addictive medications that carry serious psychological dangers. These efforts are facilitated by a segment of doctors who skip established diagnostic procedures, renew prescriptions reflexively and spend too little time with patients to accurately monitor side effects.

Richard Fee's experience included it all. Conversations with friends and family members and a review of detailed medical records depict an intelligent and articulate young man lying to doctor after doctor, physicians issuing hasty diagnoses, and psychiatrists continuing to prescribe medication—even increasing dosages—despite evidence of his growing addiction and psychiatric breakdown.

Very few people who misuse stimulants devolve into psychotic or suicidal addicts. But even one of Richard's own physicians, Dr. Charles Parker, characterized his case as a virtual textbook for ways that A.D.H.D. practices can fail patients, particularly young adults. "We have a significant travesty being done in this country with how the diagnosis is being made and the meds are being administered," said Dr. Parker, a psychiatrist in Virginia Beach. "I think it's an abnegation of trust. The public needs to say this is totally unacceptable and walk out."

Young adults are by far the fastest-growing segment of people taking A.D.H.D medications. Nearly 14 million monthly prescriptions for the condition were written for Americans ages 20 to 39 in 2011, two and a half times the 5.6 million just four years before, according to the data company I.M.S. Health. While this rise is generally attributed to the maturing of adolescents who have A.D.H.D. into young adults—combined with a greater recognition of adult A.D.H.D. in general—many experts caution that savvy college graduates, freed of parental oversight, can legally and easily obtain stimulant prescriptions from obliging doctors.

"Any step along the way, someone could have helped him—they were just handing out drugs," said Richard's father. Emphasizing that he had no intention of bringing legal action against any of the doctors involved, Mr. Fee said: "People have to know that kids are out there getting these drugs and getting addicted to them. And doctors are helping them do it."

" . . .when he was in elementary school he fidgeted, daydreamed and got A's. he has been an A-B student until mid college when he became scattered and he wandered while reading He never had to study. Presently without medication, his mind thinks most of the time, he procrastinated, he multitasks not finishing in a timely manner."

Dr. Waldo M. Ellison
Richard Fee initial evaluation
Feb. 5, 2010

Richard began acting strangely soon after moving back home in late 2009, his parents said. He stayed up for days at a time, went from gregarious to grumpy and back, and scrawled compulsively in notebooks. His father, while trying to add Richard to his health insurance policy, learned that he was taking Vyvanse for A.D.H.D.

Richard explained to him that he had been having trouble concentrating while studying for medical school entrance exams the previous year and that he had seen a doctor and received a diagnosis. His father reacted with surprise. Richard had never shown any A.D.H.D. symptoms his entire life, from nursery school through high school, when he was awarded a full academic scholarship to Greensboro College in North Carolina. Mr. Fee also expressed concerns about the safety of his son's taking daily amphetamines for a condition he might not have.

"The doctor wouldn't give me anything that's bad for me," Mr. Fee recalled his son saying that day. "I'm not buying it on the street corner."

Richard's first experience with A.D.H.D. pills, like so many others', had come in college. Friends said he was a typical undergraduate user—when he needed to finish a paper or cram for exams, one Adderall capsule would jolt him with focus and purpose for six to eight hours, repeat as necessary.

So many fellow students had prescriptions or stashes to share, friends of Richard recalled in interviews, that guessing where he got his was futile. He was popular enough on campus—he was sophomore class president and played first base on the baseball team—that they doubted he even had to pay the typical $5 or $10 per pill.

"He would just procrastinate, wait till the last minute and then take a pill to study for tests," said Ryan Sykes, a friend. "It got to the point where he'd say he couldn't get anything done if he didn't have the Adderall."

Various studies have estimated that 8 percent to 35 percent of college students take stimulant pills to enhance school performance. Few students realize that giving or accepting even one Adderall pill from a friend with a prescription is a federal crime. Adderall and its stimulant siblings are classified by the Drug Enforcement Administration as Schedule II drugs, in the same category as cocaine, because of their highly addictive properties.

"It's incredibly nonchalant," Chris Hewitt, a friend of Richard, said of students' attitudes to the drug. "It's: 'Anyone have any Adderall? I want to study tonight,'" said Mr. Hewitt, now an elementary school teacher in Greensboro.

After graduating with honors in 2008 with a degree in biology, Richard planned to apply to medical schools and stayed in Greensboro to study for the entrance exams. He remembered how Adderall had helped him concentrate so well as an undergraduate, friends said, and he made an appointment at the nearby Triad Psychiatric and Counseling Center.

According to records obtained by Richard's parents after his death, a nurse practitioner at Triad detailed his unremarkable medical and psychiatric history before recording his complaints about "organization, memory, attention to detail." She characterized his speech as "clear," his thought process "goal directed" and his concentration "attentive."

Richard filled out an 18-question survey on which he rated various symptoms on a 0-to-3 scale. His total score of 29 led the nurse practitioner to make a diagnosis of "A.D.H.D., inattentive-type"—a type of A.D.H.D. without hyperactivity. She recommended Vyvanse, 30 milligrams a day, for three weeks.

Phone and fax requests to Triad officials for comment were not returned.

Some doctors worry that A.D.H.D. questionnaires, designed to assist and standardize the gathering of a patient's symptoms, are being used as a shortcut to diagnosis. C. Keith Conners, a longtime child psychologist who developed a popular scale similar to the one used with Richard, said in an interview that scales like his "have reinforced this tendency for quick and dirty practice."

Dr. Conners, an emeritus professor of psychiatry and behavioral sciences at Duke University Medical Center, emphasized that a detailed life history must be taken and other sources of information—such as a parent, teacher or friend—must be pursued to learn the nuances of a patient's difficulties and to rule out other maladies before making a proper diagnosis of A.D.H.D. Other doctors interviewed said they would not prescribe medications on a patient's first visit, specifically to deter the faking of symptoms.

According to his parents, Richard had no psychiatric history, or even suspicion of problems, through college. None of his dozen high school and college acquaintances interviewed for this article said he had ever shown or mentioned behaviors related to A.D.H.D.—certainly not the "losing things" and "difficulty awaiting turn" he reported on the Triad questionnaire—suggesting that he probably faked or at least exaggerated his symptoms to get his diagnosis.

That is neither uncommon nor difficult, said David Berry, a professor and researcher at the University of Kentucky. He is a co-author of a 2010 study that compared two groups of college students—those with diagnoses of A.D.H.D. and others who were asked to fake symptoms—to see whether standard symptom questionnaires could tell them apart. They were indistinguishable.

"With college students," Dr. Berry said in an interview, "it's clear that it doesn't take much information for someone who wants to feign A.D.H.D. to do so."

Richard Fee filled his prescription for Vyvanse within hours at a local Rite Aid. He returned to see the nurse three weeks later and reported excellent concentration: "reading books—read 10!" her notes indicate. She increased his dose to 50 milligrams a day. Three weeks later, after Richard left a message for her asking for the dose to go up to 60, which is on the high end of normal adult doses, she wrote on his chart, "Okay rewrite."

Richard filled that prescription later that afternoon. It was his third month's worth of medication in 43 days.

"The patient is a 23-year-old Caucasian male who presents for refill of vyvanse—recently started on this while in NC b/c of lack of motivation/loss of drive. Has moved here and wants refill"

Dr. Robert M. Woodard
Notes on Richard Fee
Nov. 11, 2009

Richard scored too low on the MCAT in 2009 to qualify for a top medical school. Although he had started taking Vyvanse for its jolts of focus and purpose, their side effects began to take hold. His sleep patterns increasingly scrambled and his mood darkening, he moved back in with his parents in Virginia Beach and sought a local physician to renew his prescriptions.

A friend recommended a family physician, Dr. Robert M. Woodard. Dr. Woodard heard Richard describe how well Vyvanse was working for his A.D.H.D., made a diagnosis of "other malaise and fatigue" and renewed his prescription for one month. He suggested that Richard thereafter see a trained psychiatrist at Dominion Psychiatric Associates—only a five-minute walk from the Fees' house.

With eight psychiatrists and almost 20 therapists on staff, Dominion Psychiatric is one of the better-known practices in Virginia Beach, residents said. One of its better-known doctors is Dr. Waldo M. Ellison, a practicing psychiatrist since 1974.

In interviews, some patients and parents of patients of Dr. Ellison's described him as very quick to identify A.D.H.D. and prescribe medication for it. Sandy Paxson of nearby Norfolk said she took her 15-year-old son to see Dr. Ellison for anxiety in 2008; within a few minutes, Mrs. Paxson recalled, Dr. Ellison said her son had A.D.H.D. and prescribed him Adderall.

"My son said: 'I love the way this makes me feel. It helps me focus for school, but it's not getting rid of my anxiety, and that's what I need,'" Mrs. Paxson recalled. "So we went back to Dr. Ellison and told him that it wasn't working properly, what else could he give us, and he basically told me that I was wrong. He basically told me that I was incorrect."

Dr. Ellison met with Richard in his office for the first time on Feb. 5, 2010. He took a medical history, heard Richard's complaints regarding concentration, noted how he was drumming his fingers and made a diagnosis of A.D.H.D. with "moderate symptoms or difficulty functioning." Dominion Psychiatric records of that visit do not mention the use of any A.D.H.D.

symptom questionnaire to identify particular areas of difficulty or strategies for treatment.

As the 47-minute session ended, Dr. Ellison prescribed a common starting dose of Adderall: 30 milligrams daily for 21 days. Eight days later, while Richard still had 13 pills remaining, his prescription was renewed for 30 more days at 50 milligrams.

Through the remainder of 2010, in appointments with Dr. Ellison that usually lasted under five minutes, Richard returned for refills of Adderall. Records indicate that he received only what was consistently coded as "pharmacologic management"—the official term for quick appraisals of medication effects—and none of the more conventional talk-based therapy that experts generally consider an important component of A.D.H.D. treatment.

His Adderall prescriptions were always for the fast-acting variety, rather than the extended-release formula that is less prone to abuse.

"Patient doing well with the medication, is calm, focused and on task, and will return to office in 3 months"

Dr. Waldo M. Ellison
Notes on Richard Fee
Dec. 11, 2010

Regardless of what he might have told his doctor, Richard Fee was anything but well or calm during his first year back home, his father said.

Blowing through a month's worth of Adderall in a few weeks, Richard stayed up all night reading and scribbling in notebooks, occasionally climbing out of his bedroom window and on to the roof to converse with the moon and stars. When the pills ran out, he would sleep for 48 hours straight and not leave his room for 72. He got so hot during the day that he walked around the house with ice packs around his neck—and in frigid weather, he would cool off by jumping into the 52-degree backyard pool.

As Richard lost a series of jobs and tensions in the house ran higher—particularly when talk turned to his Adderall—Rick and Kathy Fee continued to research the side effects of A.D.H.D. medication. They learned that stimulants are exceptionally successful at mollifying the impulsivity and distractibility that characterize classic A.D.H.D., but that they can cause insomnia, increased blood pressure and elevated body temperature. Food and Drug Administration warnings on packaging also note "high potential for abuse," as well as psychiatric side effects such as aggression, hallucinations and paranoia.

A 2006 study in the journal Drug and Alcohol Dependence claimed that about 10 percent of adolescents and young adults who misused A.D.H.D. stimulants became addicted to them. Even proper, doctor-supervised use of the medications can trigger psychotic behavior or suicidal thoughts in about 1 in 400 patients, according to a 2006 study in The American Journal of Psychiatry. So while a vast majority of stimulant users will not experience psychosis—and a doctor may never encounter it in decades of careful practice—the sheer volume of prescriptions leads to thousands of cases every year, experts acknowledged.

When Mrs. Fee noticed Richard putting tape over his computer's camera, he told her that people were spying on him. (He put tape on his fingers, too, to avoid leaving fingerprints.) He cut himself out of family pictures, talked to the television and became increasingly violent when agitated.

In late December, Mr. Fee drove to Dominion Psychiatric and asked to see Dr. Ellison, who explained that federal privacy laws forbade any discussion of an adult patient, even with the patient's father. Mr. Fee said he had tried unsuccessfully to detail Richard's bizarre behavior, assuming that Richard had not shared such details with his doctor.

"I can't talk to you," Mr. Fee recalled Dr. Ellison telling him. "I did this one time with another family, sat down and talked with them, and I ended up getting sued. I can't talk with you unless your son comes with you."

Mr. Fee said he had turned to leave but distinctly recalls warning Dr. Ellison, "You keep giving Adderall to my son, you're going to kill him."

Dr. Ellison declined repeated requests for comment on Richard Fee's case. His office records, like those of other doctors involved, were obtained by Mr. Fee under Virginia and federal law, which allow the legal representative of a deceased patient to obtain medical records as if he were the patient himself.

As 2011 began, the Fees persuaded Richard to see a psychologist, Scott W. Sautter, whose records note Richard's delusions, paranoia and "severe and pervasive mental disorder." Dr. Sautter recommended that Adderall either be stopped or be paired with a sleep aid "if not medically contraindicated."

Mr. Fee did not trust his son to share this report with Dr. Ellison, so he drove back to Dominion Psychiatric and, he recalled, was told by a receptionist that he could leave the information with her. Mr. Fee said he had demanded to put it in Dr. Ellison's hands himself and threatened to break down his door in order to do so.

Mr. Fee said that Dr. Ellison had then come out, read the report and, appreciating the gravity of the situation, spoke with him about Richard for 45 minutes. They scheduled an appointment for the entire family.

"meeting with parents—concern with 'metaphoric' speaking that appears to be outside the realm of appropriated one to one conversation. Richard says he does it on purpose—to me some of it sounds like pre-psychotic thinking."

Dr. Waldo M. Ellison
Notes on Richard Fee
Feb. 23, 2011

Dr. Ellison stopped Richard Fee's prescription—he wrote "no Adderall for now" on his chart and the next day refused Richard's phone request for more. Instead he prescribed Abilify

and Seroquel, antipsychotics for schizophrenia that do not provide the bursts of focus and purpose that stimulants do. Richard became enraged, his parents recalled. He tried to back up over his father in the Dominion Psychiatric parking lot and threatened to burn the house down. At home, he took a baseball bat from the garage, smashed flower pots and screamed, "You're taking my medicine!"

Richard disappeared for a few weeks. He returned to the house when he learned of his grandmother's death, the Fees said.

The morning after the funeral, Richard walked down Potters Road to what became a nine-minute visit with Dr. Ellison. He left with two prescriptions: one for Abilify, and another for 50 milligrams a day of Adderall.

According to Mr. Fee, Richard later told him that he had lied to Dr. Ellison—he told the doctor he was feeling great, life was back on track and he had found a job in Greensboro that he would lose without Adderall. Dr. Ellison's notes do not say why he agreed to start Adderall again.

Richard's delusions and mood swings only got worse, his parents said. They would lock their bedroom door when they went to sleep because of his unpredictable rages. "We were scared of our own son," Mr. Fee said. Richard would blow through his monthly prescriptions in 10 to 15 days and then go through hideous withdrawals. A friend said that he would occasionally get Richard some extra pills during the worst of it, but that "it wasn't enough because he would take four or five at a time."

One night during an argument, after Richard became particularly threatening and pushed him over a chair, Mr. Fee called the police. They arrested Richard for domestic violence. The episode persuaded Richard to see another local psychiatrist, Dr. Charles Parker.

Mrs. Fee said she attended Richard's initial consultation on June 3 with Dr. Parker's clinician, Renee Strelitz, and emphasized his abuse of Adderall. Richard "kept giving me dirty looks," Mrs. Fee recalled. She said she had later left a detailed message on Ms. Strelitz's voice mail, urging her and Dr. Parker not to prescribe stimulants under any circumstances when Richard came in the next day.

Dr. Parker met with Richard alone. The doctor noted depression, anxiety and suicidal ideas. He wrote "no meds" with a box around it—an indication, he explained later, that he was aware of the parents' concerns regarding A.D.H.D. stimulants.

Dr. Parker wrote three 30-day prescriptions: Clonidine (a sleep aid), Venlafaxine (an antidepressant) and Adderall, 60 milligrams a day.

In an interview last November, Dr. Parker said he did not recall the details of Richard's case but reviewed his notes and tried to recreate his mind-set during that appointment. He said he must have trusted Richard's assertions that medication was not an issue, and must have figured that his parents were just philosophically anti-medication. Dr. Parker recalled that he had been reassured by Richard's intelligent discussions of the ins and outs of stimulants and his desire to pursue medicine himself.

"He was smart and he was quick and he had A's and B's and wanted to go to medical school—and he had all the deportment of a guy that had the potential to do that," Dr. Parker said. "He didn't seem like he was a drug person at all, but rather a person that was misunderstood, really desirous of becoming a physician. He was very slick and smooth. He convinced me there was a benefit."

Mrs. Fee was outraged. Over the next several days, she recalled, she repeatedly spoke with Ms. Strelitz over the phone to detail Richard's continued abuse of the medication (she found nine pills gone after 48 hours) and hand-delivered Dr. Sautter's appraisal of his recent psychosis. Dr. Parker confirmed that he had received this information.

Richard next saw Dr. Parker on June 27. Mrs. Fee drove him to the clinic and waited in the parking lot. Soon afterward, Richard returned and asked to head to the pharmacy to fill a prescription. Dr. Parker had raised his Adderall to 80 milligrams a day.

Dr. Parker recalled that the appointment had been a 15-minute "med check" that left little time for careful assessment of any Adderall addiction. Once again, Dr. Parker said, he must have believed Richard's assertions that he needed additional medicine more than the family's pleas that it be stopped.

"He was pitching me very well—I was asking him very specific questions, and he was very good at telling me the answers in a very specific way," Dr. Parker recalled. He added later, "I do feel partially responsible for what happened to this kid."

"Paranoid and psychotic . . . thinking that the computer is spying on him. He has also been receiving messages from stars at night and he is unable to be talked to in a reasonable fashion . . . The patient denies any mental health problems . . . fairly high risk for suicide."

Dr. John Riedler
Admission note for Richard Fee
Virginia Beach Psychiatric Center
July 8, 2011

The 911 operator answered the call and heard a young man screaming on the other end. His parents would not give him his pills. With the man's language scattered and increasingly threatening, the police were sent to the home of Rick and Kathy Fee.

The Fees told officers that Richard was addicted to Adderall, and that after he had received his most recent prescription, they allowed him to fill it through his mother's insurance plan on the condition that they hold it and dispense it appropriately. Richard was now demanding his next day's pills early.

Richard denied his addiction and threats. So the police, noting that Richard was an adult, instructed the Fees to give him the bottle. They said they would comply only if he left the house for good. Officers escorted Richard off the property.

A few hours later Richard called his parents, threatening to stab himself in the head with a knife. The police found him and took him to the Virginia Beach Psychiatric Center.

Described as "paranoid and psychotic" by the admitting physician, Dr. John Riedler, Richard spent one week in the hospital denying that he had any psychiatric or addiction issues. He was placed on two medications: Seroquel and the antidepressant Wellbutrin, no stimulants. In his discharge report, Dr. Riedler noted that Richard had stabilized but remained severely depressed and dependent on both amphetamines and marijuana, which he would smoke in part to counter the buzz of Adderall and the depression from withdrawal.

(Marijuana is known to increase the risk for schizophrenia, psychosis and memory problems, but Richard had smoked pot in high school and college with no such effects, several friends recalled. If that was the case, "in all likelihood the stimulants were the primary issue here," said Dr. Wesley Boyd, a psychiatrist at Children's Hospital Boston and Cambridge Health Alliance who specializes in adolescent substance abuse.)

Unwelcome at home after his discharge from the psychiatric hospital, Richard stayed in cheap motels for a few weeks. His Adderall prescription from Dr. Parker expired on July 26, leaving him eligible for a renewal. He phoned the office of Dr. Ellison, who had not seen him in four months.

"moved out of the house—doesn't feel paranoid or delusional. Hasn't been on meds for a while—working with a friend wiring houses rto 3 months—doesn't feel he needs the abilify or seroquel for sleep."

Dr. Waldo M. Ellison
Notes on Richard Fee
July 25, 2011

The 2:15 p.m. appointment went better than Richard could have hoped. He told Dr. Ellison that the pre-psychotic and metaphoric thinking back in March had receded, and that all that remained was his A.D.H.D. He said nothing of his visits to Dr. Parker, his recent prescriptions or his week in the psychiatric hospital.

At 2:21 p.m., according to Dr. Ellison's records, he prescribed Richard 30 days' worth of Adderall at 50 milligrams a day. He also gave him prescriptions postdated for Aug. 23 and Sept. 21, presumably to allow him to get pills into late October without the need for follow-up appointments. (Virginia state law forbids the dispensation of 90 days of a controlled substance at one time, but does allow doctors to write two 30-day prescriptions in advance.)

Virginia is one of 43 states with a formal Prescription Drug Monitoring Program, an online database that lets doctors check a patient's one-year prescription history, partly to see if he or she is getting medication elsewhere. Although pharmacies are required to enter all prescriptions for controlled substances into the system, Virginia law does not require doctors to consult it.

Dr. Ellison's notes suggest that he did not check the program before issuing the three prescriptions to Richard, who filled the first within hours.

The next morning, during a scheduled appointment at Dr. Parker's clinic, Ms. Strelitz wrote in her notes: "Richard is progressing. He reported staying off of the Adderall and on no meds currently. Focusing on staying healthy, eating well and exercising."

About a week later, Richard called his father with more good news: a job he had found overseeing storm cleanup crews was going well. He was feeling much better.

But Mr. Fee noticed that the more calm and measured speech that Richard had regained during his hospital stay was gone. He jumped from one subject to the next, sounding anxious and rushed. When the call ended, Mr. Fee recalled, he went straight to his wife.

"Call your insurance company," he said, "and find out if they've filled any prescriptions for Adderall."

"spoke to father—richard was in VBPC [Virginia Beach Psychiatric Center] and OD on adderall—NO STIMULANTS—HE WAS ALSO SEEING DR. PARKER"

Dr. Waldo M. Ellison
Interoffice e-mail
Aug. 5, 2011

An insurance representative confirmed that Richard had filled a prescription for Adderall on July 25. Mr. Fee confronted Dr. Ellison in the Dominion Psychiatric parking lot.

Mr. Fee told him that Richard had been in the psychiatric hospital, had been suicidal and had been taking Adderall through June and July. Dr. Ellison confirmed that he had written not only another prescription but two others for later in August and September.

"He told me it was normal procedure and not 90 days at one time," Mr. Fee recalled. "I flipped out on him: 'You gave my son 90 days of Adderall? You're going to kill him!'"

Mr. Fee said he and Dr. Ellison had discussed voiding the two outstanding scripts. Mr. Fee said he had been told that it was possible, but that should Richard need emergency medical attention, it could keep him from getting what would otherwise be proper care or medication. Mr. Fee confirmed that with a pharmacist and decided to drive to Richard's apartment and try to persuade him to rip up the prescriptions.

"I know that you've got these other prescriptions to get pills," Mr. Fee recalled telling Richard. "You're doing so good. You've got a job. You're working. Things with us are better. If you get them filled, I'm worried about what will happen."

"You're right," Mr. Fee said Richard had replied. "I tore them up and threw them away."

Mr. Fee spent two more hours with Richard making relative small talk—increasingly gnawed, he recalled later, by the sense that this was no ordinary conversation. As he looked at Richard he saw two images flickering on top of each other—the boy he had raised to love school and baseball, and the desperate addict he feared that boy had become.

Before he left, Mr. Fee made as loving a demand as he could muster.

"Please. Give them to me," Mr. Fee said.

Richard looked his father dead in the eye.

"I destroyed them," he said. "I don't have them. Don't worry."

"Richard said that he has stopped adderall and wants to work on continuing to progress."

Renee Strelitz
Session notes
Sept. 13, 2011

Richard generally filled his prescriptions at a CVS on Laskin Road, less than three miles from his parents' home. But on Aug. 23, he went to a different CVS about 11 miles away, closer to Norfolk and farther from the locations that his father might have called to alert them to the situation. For his Sept. 21 prescription he traveled even farther, into Norfolk, to get his pills.

On Oct. 3, Richard visited Dr. Ellison for an appointment lasting 17 minutes. The doctor prescribed two weeks of Strattera, a medication for A.D.H.D. that contains no amphetamines and, therefore, is neither a controlled substance nor particularly prone to abuse. His records make no mention of the Adderall prescription Richard filled on Sept. 21; they do note, however, "Father says that he is crazy and abusive of the Adderall—has made directives with regard to giving Richard anymore stimulants—bringing up charges—I explained this to Richard."

Prescription records indicate that Richard did not fill the Strattera prescription before returning to Dr. Ellison's office two weeks later to ask for more stimulants.

"Patient took only a few days of Strattera 40 mg—it calmed him but not focusing," the doctor's notes read. "I had told him not to look for much initially—He would like a list of MD who could rx adderall."

Dr. Ellison never saw Richard again. Given his patterns of abuse, friends said, Richard probably took his last Adderall pill in early October. Because he abruptly stopped without the slow and delicate reduction of medication that is recommended to minimize major psychological risks, especially for instant-release stimulants, he crashed harder than ever.

Richard's lifelong friend Ryan Sykes was one of the few people in contact with him during his final weeks. He said that despite Richard's addiction to Adderall and the ease with which it could be obtained on college campuses nearby, he had never pursued it outside the doctors' prescriptions.

"He had it in his mind that because it came from a doctor, it was O.K.," Mr. Sykes recalled.

On Nov. 7, after arriving home from a weekend away, Mrs. Fee heard a message on the family answering machine from Richard, asking his parents to call him. She phoned back at 10 that night and left a message herself.

Not hearing back by the next afternoon, Mrs. Fee checked Richard's cellphone records—he was on her plan—and saw no calls or texts. At 9 p.m. the Fees drove to Richard's apartment in Norfolk to check on him. The lights were on; his car was in the driveway. He did not answer. Beginning to panic, Mr. Fee found the kitchen window ajar and climbed in through it.

He searched the apartment and found nothing amiss.

"He isn't here," Mr. Fee said he had told his wife.

"Oh, thank God," she replied. "Maybe he's walking on the beach or something."

They got ready to leave before Mr. Fee stopped.

"Wait a minute," he said. "I didn't check the closet."

"Spoke with Richard's mother, Kathy Fee, today. She reported that Richard took his life last November. Family is devasted and having a difficult time. Offered assistance for family."

Renee Strelitz
Last page of Richard Fee file
June 21, 2012

Friends and former baseball teammates flocked to Richard Fee's memorial service in Virginia Beach. Most remembered only the funny and gregarious guy they knew in high school and college; many knew absolutely nothing of his last two years. He left no note explaining his suicide.

At a gathering at the Fees' house afterward, Mr. Fee told them about Richard's addiction to Adderall. Many recalled how they, too, had blithely abused the drug in college—to cram, just as Richard had—and could not help but wonder if they had played the same game of Russian roulette.

"I guarantee you a good number of them had used it for studying—that shock was definitely there in that room," said a Greensboro baseball teammate, Danny Michael, adding that he was among the few who had not. "It's so prevalent and widely used. People had no idea it could be abused to the point of no return."

Almost every one of more than 40 A.D.H.D. experts interviewed for this article said that worst-case scenarios like Richard Fee's can occur with any medication—and that people who do have A.D.H.D., or parents of children with the disorder, should not be dissuaded from considering the proven benefits of stimulant medication when supervised by a responsible physician.

Other experts, however, cautioned that Richard Fee's experience is instructive less in its ending than its evolution—that it underscores aspects of A.D.H.D. treatment that are mishandled every day with countless patients, many of them children.

"You don't have everything that happened with this kid, but his experience is not that unusual," said DeAnsin Parker, a clinical neuropsychologist in New York who specializes in young adults. "Diagnoses are made just this quickly, and medication is filled just this quickly. And the lack of therapy is really sad. Doctors are saying, 'Just take the meds to see if they help,' and if they help, 'You must have A.D.H.D.'"

Dr. Parker added: "Stimulants will help anyone focus better. And a lot of young people like or value that feeling, especially those who are driven and have ambitions. We have to realize that these are potential addicts—drug addicts don't look like they used to."

The Fees decided to go. The event was sponsored by the local chapter of Children and Adults with Attention Deficit Disorder (Chadd), the nation's primary advocacy group for A.D.H.D. patients. They wanted to attend the question-and-answer session afterward with local doctors and community college officials.

The evening opened with the local Chadd coordinator thanking the drug company Shire—the manufacturer of several A.D.H.D. drugs, including Vyvanse and extended-release Adderall—for partly underwriting the event. An hourlong film directed and narrated by two men with A.D.H.D. closed by examining some "myths" about stimulant medications, with several doctors praising their efficacy and safety. One said they were "safer than aspirin," while another added, "It's O.K.—there's nothing that's going to happen."

Sitting in the fourth row, Mr. Fee raised his hand to pose a question to the panel, which was moderated by Jeffrey Katz, a local clinical psychologist and a national board member of Chadd. "What are some of the drawbacks or some of the dangers of a misdiagnosis in somebody," Mr. Fee asked, "and then the subsequent medication that goes along with that?"

Dr. Katz looked straight at the Fees as he answered, "Not much."

Adding that "the medication itself is pretty innocuous," Dr. Katz continued that someone without A.D.H.D. might feel more awake with stimulants but would not consider it "something that they need."

"If you misdiagnose it and you give somebody medication, it's not going to do anything for them," Dr. Katz concluded. "Why would they continue to take it?"

Mr. Fee slowly sat down, trembling. Mrs. Fee placed her hand on his knee as the panel continued.

Critical Thinking

1. Discuss the risk of addiction, dependence, and overdose from prescription drug abuse.

2. What are reasons college students use prescription drugs they don't need and were not prescribed for them?

Create Central

www.mhhe.com/createcentral

Internet References

Food and Drug Administration (FDA)
www.fda.gov
National Institute on Drug Abuse (NIDA)
www.nida.nih.gov

ALAN SCHWARZ is a Pulitzer-Prize nominated reporter for the *New York Times.*

Article   Prepared by: Eileen L. Daniel, *SUNY Brockport*

So Long, Lance. Next, 21st-Century Doping.

David Ewing Duncan

Learning Outcomes

After reading this article, you will be able to:

- Explain the risks associated with the use of bio enhancers by athletes.

- Identify the various types of bio enhancers.

- Describe how users avoid detection.

Lance Armstrong's sad saga of doping and lying is over, allowing us to turn our attention to a far more important issue arising from the Armstrong era: what to do about the rise of ever more potent bio-enhancers in sports.

The "arms race" in this new age of augmentation has already begun, said the bioethicist Thomas Murray, former president of the Hastings Center in Garrison, N.Y. It pits enforcers like the World Anti-Doping Agency, armed with strict bans on certain enhancers, against elite athletes—and their trainers, technicians and financers—who are determined to get away with doping.

Antidopers justify their crackdown as a means of protecting athletes from potentially dangerous enhancers, and because the use of bio-boosters is unfair to nondoping competitors. Enhancers also threaten the "spirit of sports," in the words of the World Anti-Doping Code, which now guides most elite sports.

Currently, WADA bans a growing list of enhancers, including anabolic steroids, human growth hormone, amphetamines, beta-2 agonists (which relax the muscles around the airways and make breathing easier) and erythropoietin, or EPO (which increases oxygen levels in the blood). In future years this list might also include an arsenal of as-yet unimagined chemical compounds and technologies. Those could include everything from genetic alterations (so-called gene doping) to the regeneration of tissue using stem cells.

Today's dopers try to avoid detection by administering microdoses of enhancers that quickly clear the body, and by using natural versions of growth hormone and erythropoietin that cannot be easily differentiated from an athlete's own onboard supplies. They also use the Lance Armstrong techniques of avoiding testing when possible, and timing the use of banned substances to appear clean.

"The technology is there to detect minute levels of most substances," said Matthew Fedoruk, science director at the United States Anti-Doping Agency. "The challenge is that athletes are turning to substances that mimic natural substances in your body." Dr. Fedoruk added that resource constraints and athletes' sophisticated schemes to avoid detection can thwart investigators.

Drug companies, meanwhile, are developing a raft of new medications for diseases like muscular dystrophy and anemia that could one day be used as enhancers. Scientists are studying genes associated with physical performance and muscle growth to see if drugs—or, someday, gene-modulating technologies—can be developed to activate the strengthening or other positive effects of those genes.

Beyond chemical fixes, neuroscientists are experimenting with noninvasive technologies that augment brain activity by bathing targeted regions in low levels of electricity (transcranial electrical stimulation) or a magnetic field (transcranial magnetic stimulation). Both appear to enhance cortical excitability and cognitive performance.

Bioengineers are in the early stages of developing artificial limbs and exoskeletons that one day may be better than real limbs. Andy Miah, an ethicist at the University of the West of Scotland, has suggested that scientists in the future might create embedded nano-devices to stimulate muscles to a sustained peak of performance. Hugh Herr, a biomechanical engineer at the M.I.T. Media Lab, recently told the journal Nature that "stepping decades into the future, I think one day the field will produce a bionic limb that's so sophisticated that it truly emulates biological limb function." He predicts the emergence of new human-machine sports. These might combine, say, track and field and Nascar.

The motivation of athletes to win at all costs remains a potent incentive to gain an edge. Competitors in the ancient Greek Olympics tried enhancers that ranged from exotic herbs to animal testicles. Nothing was banned, however, except the fixing of competitions, and also the use of black magic—a prohibition that didn't keep some athletes from casting spells against their competitors.

Not even the reported dangers of using enhancers have stopped millions of amateur and elite athletes from taking

So Long, Lance. Next, 21st-Century Doping. by David Ewing Duncan

89

them. One reason is that the side effects stemming from the use of lower doses of some boosters are poorly understood. Studies indicate that healthy people taking anabolic steroids raise their risk of increasing LDL (bad) cholesterol levels and of having blood clots, though much more research is needed. Higher doses increase the odds of damage to the heart, mood shifts, reduced sperm counts and masculinization in women.

For other popular enhancers, like human growth hormone and erythropoietin, the evidence of harm is less clear. Large numbers of people take them with no obvious injury, though again more research is needed. "We don't really understand the long-term implications of many of these compounds," said Dr. Fedoruk of the United States Anti-Doping Agency. For some bioethicists, the risks of taking enhancers must be compared to the dangers inherent in many sports. "You are at risk for head injuries in football," said David Magnus of Stanford, a bioethicist. "Throwing a baseball at 100 miles per hour at a batter is dangerous. So is riding a bicycle at 60 m.p.h. with no protection. Are steroids really more dangerous than this?"

Dr. Magnus and others also challenge the idea that the use of certain enhancers is inherently cheating. "Of course it is if rules are violated, whatever they are; that's the definition of cheating," he said. "But what if the rules make no sense?"

He and others complain that rules are arbitrary and unevenly applied to some athletes and not others. For instance, erythropoietin is banned because it increases oxygen-rich red blood cells, but the use of special tents and rooms that mimic high altitudes that also increase red blood cell production is not. Amphetamines are banned, but not caffeine, nicotine and other "natural" stimulants. Elite athletes also have the resources to fine-tune their bodies by using food chemists, physiologists and other enhancement experts that most competitors can't afford.

Ultimately, the decision to enhance or not will ride on how society views the value of sports. For some people, the purity comes from competition among untainted humans. For others it's about speed and strength and taking risks—with many in this group embracing whatever excesses might be allowed.

Freakishly huge wrestlers and monstrous right tackles? Machine-men with bionic wheels instead of legs racing across the Bonneville Salt Flats? Bring it on!

Dr. Miah of the University of the West of Scotland and others have proposed holding enhanced sports contests, including an enhanced Olympics. "If the goal is to protect health, then medically supervised doping is likely to be a better route," Dr. Miah told the journal Nature. "If athletes want to use these substances, they should be up front about it and compete just against each other," said Dr. Linn Goldberg, a sports medicine doctor and researcher at the Oregon Health and Science University.

The question would then become: which version of sports would you watch—the natural or the enhanced?

Critical Thinking

1. What is the motivation to use bio-enhancers?
2. How do athletes manage to avoid detection?
3. What are the health concerns surrounding the use of bio-enhancers?

Create Central

www.mhhe.com/createcentral

Internet References

American College of Sports Medicine
   www.acsm.org
American Society of Exercise Physiologists (ASEP)
   www.asep.org
Food and Drug Administration (FDA)
   www.fda.gov

David Ewing Duncan *is a journalist who has contributed to the science section of The New York Times.*

Article   Prepared by: Eileen Daniel, *SUNY College at Brockport*

Philip Seymour Hoffman Death: a Cautionary Tale about Branded Heroin?

ELIZABETH BARBER

Learning Outcomes

After reading this article, you will be able to:

• Understand the reason for dealers branding heroin.

• Explain why the use of heroin has been increasing lately.

• Describe why heroin use is such a high risk.

He had about 50 bags of heroin, law enforcement officials say. Some of the envelopes were branded with an "Ace of Spaces" stamp. Others were labeled "Ace of Hearts." There were used syringes, some prescription-pill bottles, and a small amount of cocaine.

This was the scene police describe at actor Philip Seymour Hoffman's Manhattan apartment after he was found dead Sunday of an apparent (but still unconfirmed) drug overdose. A needle was in his arm, empty heroin packets in his waste-bin, according to news reports.

That scene reflects a larger-scale one on the rise in New York City, the proverbial hub of potent recreational drugs, and in heroin-laced towns and hamlets up and down the East Coast, where city dealers run a lucrative business.

It also offers a window into a seedy underworld of "branded" heroin, in which the drug is peddled in stamped bags and marketed with names that range from whimsical, such as the "Ace" stamps, to sinister. The brand names are an attempt to boost a product's popularity, promising that the product will be the same every time, but they have no relevance at all to the drug and offer no such guarantee, experts say. Buyers have no way to know with what substances the dose of heroin has been cut—suppliers often cut costs by diluting their product—and that not-knowing can be lethal.

"You're playing Russian roulette every time," says Joseph Moses, a spokesman for the US Drug Enforcement Administration (DEA).

Heroin is a sedative processed from morphine, and about 23 percent of users become addicted, according to the National Institute on Drug Abuse (NIDA). For reasons that remain unclear, its rate of use has been growing rapidly during the past decade. The rise appears to be associated, in an unexpected and unfortunate twist, with the success of initiatives to curb prescription-drug abuse: opiate addicts have not gotten clean but have switched to heroin. It has also been linked to Mexican cartels raising their stake in the trade by expanding operations from America's Southwest to the Northeast, once dominated by South American suppliers.

Whatever the reason, heroin use has been on an upswing for at least a decade: some 3,038 people died from heroin overdoses in the US in 2010, the most recent year for which DEA data are available, up from 1,879 heroin overdose deaths in 2004.

The geographic scope of the problem is also expanding. Last month, Vermont Gov. Peter Shumlin (D) devoted his entire State of the State speech to the heroin problem. In Vermont, the number of people receiving treatment for heroin addiction has jumped 250 percent since 2000, and about 40 percent of that uptick occurring just in the past year, the governor said in his speech.

Vermont, home to sleepy towns clinging to mountainsides, may seem an odd candidate for a drug problem associated with high-octane cities, but it is in good company. Even quiet swaths of New England have become hotbeds for heroin use, with dealers enjoying big price markups in out-there communities, according to statistics from the US Department of Justice. A bag of heroin that would net $6 in New York City fetches about $30 to $40 in parts of rural New England, according to figures Mr. Shumlin cited in his Jan. 8 speech.

"Heroin is no longer just an urban issue," says Jack Stein, director of the Office of Science Policy and Communications at NIDA. "We've seen it pop up in suburbs and rural communities across the country."

But if the problem has expanded to the rural and suburban US, it has not ebbed in its longtime hotbed, New York City. There, heroin remains cheap, or at least much cheaper than it is further down the distribution line, out in New England or on Long Island.

From 2010 to 2012, heroin-involved deaths jumped 71 percent in New York, up to 352 people in 2012, according to figures from the city's Department of Health and Mental Hygiene. That year, heroin accounted for more than half of all drug overdose deaths, those data show.

New York is where heroin, smuggled in from south of the US border, is sneaked into home-based production mills, diluted in coffee filters with chemicals that range from benign (such as cornmeal) to toxic (like powerful sedatives), divided into envelopes, and stamped with brand names.

The practice of stamping envelopes with brands has been around for decades—and it is not universal. In Detroit, dealers put heroin in lotto tickets—but the brand names themselves are always changing, keeping pace with trends, says the DEA's Mr. Moses. In those names are nods to pop culture—"Twilight" and "Lady Gaga"—and to political hot buttons—"Obama Care" and "Government Shutdown." They range from mundane to blithe to tongue-in-cheek morbid—from "Starbucks" to "iPhone" to "D.O.A."

Three days before Mr. Hoffman's death, city and state police, in tandem with the US DEA's New York Drug Enforcement Task Force, raided a Bronx apartment and confiscated 33 pounds of heroin worth about $8 million, authorities say. The drug was branded with names such as "NFL" and "Olympics 2012."

But these brand names, if catchy, indicate little about the product: how potent is it? Is it cut with baking soda—or with something much more lethal, like powerful painkillers?

That's because dealers who stamp the packets often get heroin from different suppliers, says Moses. Individual dealers might not even know what's in their product, but they stamp each batch with the same brand regardless, creating the illusion of a consistent product, he says. The exact same batch of heroin is also often distributed by different dealers under different labels, he says.

That means it's impossible for buyers to tell what they're buying, even if they're buying the same label each time, Moses says.

"You just don't know what's in the substance you're using," he warns.

The consequences of not knowing can be dire. In late January, heroin branded as "Theraflu" was linked to 22 deaths in Pennsylvania. The drug, it turns out, was cut with fentanyl, a painkiller 50 to 100 times more potent than morphine, and 30 times more powerful than undiluted heroin, says Moses. Fentanyl-laced versions of the drug sold under different brands have also been implicated in overdose deaths elsewhere across the Northeast and the mid-Atlantic in recent months.

Investigators have suggested that the heroin Hoffman used may have been cut with fentanyl, Reuters reports. The toxicology report, yet to be released, will show what was in it, and police are hunting for the dealers who sold Hoffman the Ace of Spades and Ace of Hearts heroin, the New York Post reports. It's unknown what substances, if anything, the "Ace" brands of heroin include, or even if the "Ace" packets said to be in Hoffman's home are related to "Ace" envelopes seen before.

Regardless of what substance is used to dilute a batch of heroin, the odds that the drug is safe are still zero, says Dr. Stein. Heroin is, of course, still heroin, and overdose is always a possibility.

"Pure heroin is bad enough. This drug literally hijacks the brain." He adds: "Every time someone uses heroin, they are putting their life at risk."

Critical Thinking

1. Could branding heroin influence its use? Explain.
2. Why is it so risky to use heroin?
3. Why has the use of the drug increased in recent times?

Create Central

www.mhhe.com/createcentral

Internet References

National Institutes of Health
http://www.nlm.nih.gov/medlineplus/heroin.html
National Institute on Drug Abuse
http://www.drugabuse.gov

Elizabeth Barber, "Philip Seymour Hoffman Death: A Cautionary Tale about Branded Heroin?" from *The Christian Science Monitor* (February 2, 2014).

Unit 6

UNIT

Prepared by: Eileen Daniel, *SUNY College at Brockport*

Sexuality and Relationships

Sexuality is an important part of both self-awareness and intimate relationships. But how important is physical attraction in establishing and maintaining intimate relationships? Researchers in the area of evolutionary psychology have proposed numerous theories that attempt to explain the mutual attraction that occurs between the sexes. The most controversial of these theories postulates that our perception of beauty or physical attractiveness is not subjective but rather a biological component hardwired into our brains. It is generally assumed that perceptions of beauty vary from era to era and culture to culture, but evidence is mounting that suggests that people all over share a common sense of beauty that is based on physical symmetry and scent.

While physical attraction is clearly an important issue when it comes to dating, how important is it in long-term loving relationships? For many Americans, the answer may be very important because we tend to be a "Love Culture" that places a premium on passion in the selection of our mates. Is passion an essential ingredient in love, and can passion serve to sustain a long-term meaningful relationship? Because most people can't imagine marrying someone that they don't love, we must assume that most marriages are based on this feeling we call love. That being the case, why is it that so few marriages survive the rigors of day-to-day living? Perhaps the answer has more to do with our limited definition of love rather than love itself. It appears that married individuals tend to see any unhappiness they experience as a failure of their partner to satisfy their needs. It's common for couples to search for perfection because people believe that they are entitled to the best option there is. Spending time together in challenging activities is suggested to couples to enhance the feelings of closeness and satisfaction with the relationship.

Pornography can be another reason for dissatisfaction in a relationship. The idea that pornography is related to marital infidelity has been a topic of discussion in recent years. With the increase in online options to view pornography, there appears to be a connection to divorce as well.

Two additional topics of interest and controversy in the area of human sexuality are sex education and sex selection. First,

although most states mandate some type of school-based sex education, many parents believe that they should be the only source for their children's sex education. Next, should couples have the option of choosing the sex of their baby? Some doctors are willing to accommodate parents' choices, while others question the ethics of choosing gender.

Perhaps no topic in the area of human sexuality has garnered more publicity and public concern than the dangers associated with unprotected sex. Although the concept of "safe sex" is nothing new, the degree of open and public discussion regarding sexual behaviors is. With the emergence of AIDS as a disease of epidemic proportions and the rapid spreading of other sexually transmitted diseases (STDs), the surgeon general of the United States initiated an aggressive educational campaign, based on the assumption that knowledge would change behavior. If STD rates among teens are any indication of the effectiveness of this approach, then we must conclude that our educational efforts are failing. Conservatives believe that while education may play a role in curbing the spread of STDs, the root of the problem is promiscuity and that promiscuity rises when a society is undergoing a moral decline. The solution, according to conservatives, is a joint effort between parents and educators to teach students the importance of values such as respect, responsibility, and integrity. Liberals, on the other hand, think that preventing promiscuity is unrealistic and instead the focus should be on establishing open and frank discussions between the sexes. Their premise is that we are all sexual beings and the best way to combat STDs is to establish open discussions between sexual partners, so that condoms will be used correctly when couples engage in intercourse.

While education undoubtedly has had a positive impact on slowing the spread of STDs, perhaps it is unrealistic to think that education alone is the solution, given the magnitude and the nature of the problem. Most experts agree that for education to succeed in changing personal behaviors, the following conditions must be met: (1) the recipients of the information must first perceive themselves as vulnerable and, thus, be motivated to explore replacement behaviors and (2) the replacement behaviors must satisfy the needs that were the basis of the problem behaviors. To date, most education programs have failed to meet these criteria. Given all the information that we now have on the dangers associated with AIDS and STDs, why is it that people do not perceive themselves at risk? It is not so much the denial of risks as it is the notion of most people that they use good judgment when it comes to choosing sex partners. Unfortunately, most decisions regarding sexual behavior are based on subjective criteria that bear little or no relationship to one's actual risk. Even when individuals do view themselves as vulnerable to AIDS and STDs, there are currently only two viable options for reducing the risk of contracting these diseases. The first is the use of a condom and the second is sexual abstinence, neither of which is an ideal solution to the problem.

Article   Prepared by: Eileen L. Daniel, *SUNY Brockport*

The Mixed-Bag Buddy [And Other Friendship Conundrums]

Any relationship that holds the power to buoy us can also sink us, or set us adrift. From the ambiguous to the truly bad, friends come in many shades.

CARLIN FLORA

Learning Outcomes

After reading this article, you will be able to:

- Explain how friendship can impact blood pressure.
- Describe how negative friendships can be profoundly hurtful.
- Discuss how changes in marital status can dismantle friendships.

Shane Shaps remembers the day her friend Claudia pushed her to climb the monkey bars when they were little girls in Louisville, Kentucky. Terrified of heights, Shane fell and broke her wrist. That type of pressure from Claudia was typical. But they had been companions since they were infants, and Claudia continued to be an important—yet on balance negative—figure in Shane's life. "Our parents were close friends," says Shane, now 40 and a social-media consultant and mother of two. "It was a codependent relationship: She bossed me around, and I let her do it."

During college, the two lived together for a few summers, and they moved into the same building after graduation. But the push-pull dynamic continued, with Shane intermittently receiving support from her more confident friend. During one low point, Claudia never received an anniversary card Shane had sent her. Furious, Claudia called Shane to complain that her friend had forgotten her wedding anniversary.

When Claudia later hosted a bridal shower for Shane, their relationship had become so awkward that Shane tried to demote her from bridesmaid to guest. Claudia responded by writing her: "I'll be there and I'll be in the pictures. You can look at me for all of time." Claudia's parents hosted a dinner party for the bride the night before the wedding, but once Claudia's father learned of the underlying drama, he refused to speak to Shane. The familial meshing had frayed, and soon Shane had

the courage to end it. "Our friendship never grew up," she says. "We could not get past the fifth grade."

Since "friendfluence" is so powerful, our pals can just as easily have negative effects as positive ones. Even caring, compatible friends can vex or hurt us. And the fluid nature of friendship sometimes makes its darker waters harder to navigate than conflicts in romantic or family relationships.

The Problem of Drift

Your friends may be perfectly considerate companions, but they can still have a subtly negative influence on you. These are friends whose goals, values, or habits are misaligned with your ideals—often in subtle ways—causing you to drift away from your core self and, consequently, from the aspirations most suited to you. Gretchen Rubin, author of *The Happiness Project*, defines the concept of "drift" as "the decision you make by not deciding." If you're drifting, you might feel that you are living someone else's life, and you might daydream about escaping your circumstances. Drift often comes about when you do things because the people around you are doing them.

"Your sense of what is right for you becomes clouded by what other people think is right," Rubin notes. For example, you drift into marriage because all your friends are getting married. Drift in friendships can also happen when you grow and change while your friends do not, or when you haven't quite figured out your own talents and beliefs and are susceptible to conforming to the values of those around you. One friend of mine wonders: Would I have been more thoughtful as a young man if I'd had more conscientious and studious buddies back in college, instead of a group of hedonistic frat guys?

The right group—one that validates who you are and also projects an ideal version of yourself—can lift you up almost effortlessly over time. In contrast, staying with the wrong crowd will leave you walking against the wind, having to exert more and more effort just to move forward.

Avoiding drift shouldn't be confused with ladder climbing, or using people to get ahead. Blunt networking is anathema to making friends. Yet forging sincere friendships with people who bring out your potential will likely help you get ahead and bring you more contentment than could any amount of card swapping.

The Mixed-Bag Buddy

The late Ray Pahl, a British sociologist, conducted a poll of about a thousand people and discovered that almost two-thirds identified friends as one of the biggest sources of stress in their lives. Whether it's the friend who criticizes your fiance or the one who clings to you with a needy grip, friendship is not as rosy as it's sometimes portrayed. Journalist and philosopher Mark Vernon, who has examined Pahl's research, notes: "Friends are the main cause of arguments with partners and families." And many people admit to wanting to lose at least five "flabby" friends—those akin to the extra pounds that a regular workout would shed. Think of the flabby as those who don't necessarily incite strong emotions, negative or positive. Maybe you feel a vague obligation to keep up with them, but you don't feel nourished by their company.

Friends who stir up both affection and annoyance, however, are much harder to manage or shed. Julianne Holt-Lunstad, of Brigham Young University, has studied ambivalent friendships—those that are both agreeable and disagreeable. Subjects in one of her studies wore a blood-pressure monitor that recorded every interaction they had. Unsurprisingly, encounters with people the subjects felt primarily positive toward were associated with their lowest blood-pressure rates. Intriguingly, blood pressure is higher when we're in the company of "ambivalent" friends than when we're among people we describe as "negative" forces in our lives. "Because ambivalent friends are unpredictable, the subjects probably had a heightened level of vigilance while with them, which could explain the blood-pressure spike," Holt-Lunstad says. True "frenemies" may be less taxing than those sometimes great, sometimes not so much pals.

Why do we keep these ambivalent companions? Are they part of a dense network we can't escape? That was the case with some of the subjects in Holt-Lunstad's follow-up study, but the top reason for maintaining these relationships was not external but internal pressure. "Subjects wanted to see themselves as the type of person who can keep friends," she says.

Teasing banter with pals is an entertaining release for many, yet outright negative and competitive encounters with friends might wreak havoc on your health by unleashing inflammation in the body. Jessica Chiang, a graduate student at UCLA, and colleagues had volunteers keep diaries documenting all of their good, bad, and competitive interactions (from games and sports to work or academic rivalry to interpersonal competition—say, vying for attention at a party). She then measured subjects' levels of pro-inflammatory cytokines. Higher levels of these cytokines were found in those who had told more negative and competitive tales in their journals.

"Inflammation is a healthy response," Chiang says. "We need it to heal wounds, for example. But activating that system when you don't have to, in the absence of physical injury, is dangerous over time. Those who suffer from chronic inflammation can develop cardiovascular problems, arthritis, and depression." Chiang notes that leisurely competition, such as playing games or sports, did not increase inflammation, while the other forms of competition did. "The media coverage of 'toxic friends' might be an exaggeration," she says, "but over years, an accumulation of social stressors really could cause physical damage."

The Mirror-Image Trap

"A true friend stabs you in the front," Oscar Wilde said. True friends by this definition may be rare indeed: Our close buddies, in fact, avoid extreme honesty when it might hurt us. They may even misperceive reality because they are so invested in the relationship—they need to discount truths that could rock its foundation. That's the conclusion that Weylin Sternglanz and Bella DePaulo came to after they found that while friends are better than strangers at using nonverbal cues to identify emotions, less close friends are better than closer ones at sniffing out hidden negative emotions. The idea that good friends are motivated to maintain a certain image of one another echoes advice some psychologists dole out to couples: Having positive illusions about your beloved can hold the two of you together longer than a cold, clear view will.

One honesty killer is the need to believe a friend is exactly like you. Friendship researcher Jan Yager discusses the "mirror-image trap" in her book *When Friendship Hurts.* "Does your friend fall into the trap of assuming everyone should approach life the same way that she does? Instead of respecting your differences, does she try to change you or tell you that you are wrong?"

Dissecting the latest political scandal with buddies can set off personal conflicts. It's easy to feel so passionately about an issue that you assume all good and rational human beings—including your friends, naturally—will take your side. Some can relish a rousing debate and appreciate friendly sparring. But for those who themselves fall into the mirror-image trap, disagreement on a social issue can feel like a personal affront, one with a scary underlying message: "We're not as close and mutually admiring as we thought."

If you're on the other end of a debate with a friend who insists the two of you remain "twinsies," Yager suggests that you might keep your opinions to yourself, or even lie. You'll just have to bite your tongue on charter schools or the death penalty; otherwise you risk having a distinctly unproductive conversation that leaves you less enlightened about the issue at hand and more frustrated with your friendship.

Brutal Betrayal and Natural Demise

A pal who broadcasts our most sensitive secrets is going beyond the normal human instinct to gossip. Certainly, friends have the power to hurt us profoundly. When people pull away or use their knowledge about us to create emotional weapons, their behavior can be scarring.

Sixty-eight percent of those Jan Yager surveyed for her book had been betrayed by a friend. In addition to repeating confidences, common betrayals include spreading lies or rumors, stealing a lover, and not paying back financial loans. Betrayals are more common among friends who have grown apart. For that reason, Yager recommends letting those friendships wither rather than ending them outright, which could spark a desire for revenge.

Shedding friends naturally is quite common. Psychologist Laura Carstensen mapped friend quantity over time and found that the number of people we hang out with dwindles after age 17, increases in our 30s and declines again from age 40 to 50. Losing friends is inevitable—some sort of pruning as we travel through different life stages only makes sense. Keeping up with all the friends we've ever had would be very taxing and would surely cancel out the good influence of friends who can best support us through each era. Still, when two friends are not on the same timetable or of the same opinion about how close they should be, egos get bruised.

Also, changes in marital status often dismantle friendships. When a spouse dies, friends may not feel comfortable with the newly single, and they may end up choosing sides when a couple divorces. Indeed, parting ways with a buddy can be more difficult and complicated than breaking up with a boyfriend, says Susan Shapiro Barash, author of *Toxic Friends*. Though it might be naïve, we have a belief that friendships are forever, whereas most dating relationships are expected to end. Friend breakups, she adds, can challenge our sense of self, especially if we've been invested in and intertwined with a friend for many years.

Such breakups are especially difficult for women. Clinical psychologist Terri Apter has studied friendship in women and girls, noting that women have higher expectations for friendships than do men. Some think that for a friendship to be viable it has to be pretty perfect: When there are differences or a change in the emotional weather, they may feel it's all coming apart. If something is a little bit bad, they want to make it all bad.

But as complex as friendships can be, a life without them is likely more devastating. Social neuroscientist John Cacioppo describes loneliness as the fallout from not fulfilling a biological need for social contact, one almost as strong as thirst or hunger. Thanks to his work, we know that loneliness is associated with the progression of Alzheimer's disease, obesity, diminished immunity, alcoholism, and suicidal thoughts. Exposing yourself to the vulnerabilities that come with intimacy, withstanding the discomfort of connecting to people who are different from you, and striving to assert your authentic self among pals eager to sway you in other directions are most certainly worthwhile struggles compared with the bleak alternative of friendlessness.

Critical Thinking

1. Why does a change in marital status often dismantle friendships?
2. How do negative friendships cause profound hurt?

Create Central

www.mhhe.com/createcentral

Internet References

American Psychological Association
   www.apa.org
Columbia University's Go Ask Alice!
   www.goaskalice.columbia.edu/index.htm

Article   Prepared by: Eileen Daniel, *SUNY College at Brockport*

Masters of Their Domain

More and more young men believe that swearing off porn—and the sob act that goes with it—is improving their lives.

TAMSIN MCMAHON

Learning Outcomes

After reading this article, you will be able to:

- Explain why many young men are trying to wean themselves from viewing porn.

- Understand why the organization NoFap is fundamentally different from traditional campaigns that look at masturbation as a religious issue.

- Describe how swearing off pornography can improve the lives of young men.

Earlier this year, Armando, a 23-year-old technician from Oklahoma (who didn't want to give his last name), was browsing the online news and discussion board Reddit when he clicked a button called "random." It took him to a forum filled with guys his age discussing what guys his age tend to discuss on the Internet: porn. Only, this forum wasn't dedicated to sourcing the most explicit sites, but to how people could wean themselves off porn forever. Participants were asked to challenge themselves by giving up porn and masturbation for at least a week. Those who had done so claimed it gave them more energy and confidence and boosted their self-esteem, something they dubbed "superpowers."

For Armando, who had recently broken up with his girlfriend, it sounded worth a try. His first attempt to give up what he considered a casual daily habit of surfing the web for porn lasted three days. So did his second and third. By his fourth attempt, Armando says he had come to the realization that what had once seemed like a perfectly normal pastime might not be so healthy after all. He's been porn-free for two months. He has also remained "master of his own domain," in Seinfeld parlance

(after the episode where Jerry, George, Elaine, and Kramer have a contest over who can refrain from masturbation the longest). He reads more and works out twice as hard at the gym. One day, after he'd read a book, exercised and taken two cold showers, he dug out the violin he hadn't played since high school.

He's now aiming to quit porn forever, convinced that his porn habit was responsible for the failure of his past two relationships. "It really messes up your mind for what sex is actually supposed to be," he says. "It sets the hopes too high for normal men and women to be able to perform at that level. I believe that's causing a lot of relationship problems among my peers." He's also gained enough confidence in his willpower to take on a new challenge: to stop smoking.

Armando is part of "NoFap," a growing online movement among young men who pledge to give up both guilty pleasures for a period of time in hopes of improving their lives. ("Fapping" is Internet slang for masturbation.) When it started two years ago, it was a lighthearted experiment to test whether giving up porn for a week could make you more productive. Today, NoFap has grown to more than 80,000 members, many of whom pledge to swear off porn entirely, saying it contributed to low self-esteem, problems with women and lack of career ambition. Recent forum discussions include a debate on the effectiveness of male chastity belts (yes, they exist) and the best software to block Internet porn pop-ups. One post from a college freshman says giving up porn suddenly made him want to cuddle with a girl. "I just want to lie in bed, fully clothed . . . holding hands and being really close," he writes.

"I've started to view myself the same way I view a heroin addict nodding off right after getting high," writes another about his attempt to give up his nighttime solo activity. A professional guitar player announced that his month-long abstention from porn gave him the courage to get over his ex-girlfriend and focus on his music. "Every walk through a public place feels like I'm 14 years old again, searching for beauty, but not in an objectified way," he writes. "My mind is more free for things that give me joy."

Despite the evangelical tone, NoFap is fundamentally different from traditional campaigns that view masturbation as an assault on religious values. Instead, it is developing as a secular movement popular among young men, many of whom identify as liberal and atheist. The majority of No Fap members are men in their teens and early 20s, though there are women, too, says Alexander Rhodes, the 23-year-old web developer from Pittsburgh who founded the movement two years ago. He estimates about 60 percent are atheists; the site is also home to a fair number of Christians and some Muslims, all in broad agreement that porn is harmful.

A significant number are teenaged virgins worried that their porn habits will ruin their future chances with women. They're tapping into a broader cultural moment. A similar idea inspired Joseph Gordon-Levitt's directorial debut *Don Jon,* where he plays a swaggering womanizer whose budding romance with Scarlett Johansson is nearly destroyed by his addiction to Internet porn.

While many adherents are ardently opposed to porn, they also tend to be vehemently against any form of online censorship. Rhodes describes himself as "an Internet-freedom zealot" who thinks the dangerous effects of porn are best dealt with in sex-ed class and not through government regulation. His views are broadly echoed by others on NoFap who say porn between consenting adults is both deeply harmful and an inviolable act of free speech.

"It's made me realize that even Playboy, even Miley Cyrus doing her thing, isn't healthy for anybody," says James, a graphic designer from southern California, on Day 37 of his NoFap challenge. "But absolutely, I would defend it. She has every right to do that and Hugh Hefner has every right to do what he does." Now 40, James (not his real name) was raised by parents who taught him masturbation was healthy and viewing pornography was a valid form of sexual expression.

But that was in the days when porn for teens meant sneaking off to see what was on late-night television. The advent of high-speed Internet changed the game, he says, allowing anyone with a computer to access an endless array of extreme content that he found both deeply destructive and difficult to resist.

Since swearing off porn, James says he's noticed small but significant changes in his life. He realized his Internet habits had been feeding his social anxiety by allowing him to substitute online fantasies for conversations with real women. Shortly after joining NoFap, he found himself doing what he had previously considered unthinkable: sharing a casual joke with a female cashier at the grocery store. Recently, he fell into conversation with an attractive young woman in line. "Before, I would have probably just stood there stonily and wanted to talk to her but resented her for being hot," he says. "Instead, she smiled at me, I smiled at her and we had a really nice conversation and ended up walking down the street for several blocks together. That never would have happened 37 days ago."

Like others, James found his way to NoFap through an online video of a 2011 TED Talk by psychologist Philip Zombardo, leader of the 1971 Stanford prison experiment. (One of the most famous studies of the psychology of evil, the experiment divided 21 students into guards and prisoners in a simulated prison.) In his TED talk, Zombardo blames declining marriage rates and rising rates of school dropout among boys on the widespread effects of Internet porn. "Boys' brains are being digitally rewired in a totally new way for change, novelty, excitement and constant arousal" that makes it difficult for them to commit to anything or anyone, he says.

That talk was followed by an independent TEDx Talk video last year by Gary Wilson, a past adjunct professor in anatomy at an Oregon university. In it, he claims porn is deeply addictive because it causes the brain to become desensitized to dopamine. The video has been viewed more than 1.3 million times and Wilson's website, YourBrainonPorn.com, which he runs with his wife, a former Campbell Soup executive, has been the source for much of the scientific theorizing about porn addiction that gets passed around the NoFap community.

But the kind of definitive research that could explain what happens to the brain while watching porn simply hasn't been done, says Dr. Richard Krueger, associate clinical professor of psychiatry at Columbia University's college of physicians and surgeons. Kruger helped revise the sexual disorders section of the latest edition of the psychiatric bible, the Diagnostic and Statistical Manual of Mental Disorders, which doesn't include sex or porn addiction due to lack of academic evidence that they exist. "The whole notion of what goes on in someone's brain when they're sexually excited is just starting to be evaluated," he says.

He has little doubt porn addiction is real and will eventually garner enough attention to be recognized as a mental illness. But he's skeptical it has the kind of universal neurological effects that some suggest. Other behaviours such as drinking alcohol or gambling are addictive to only a small minority of the people who engage in them—between 1 and 10 percent, Krueger says. "I would argue for the same sort of hit rate with exposure to Internet pornography, that most people would do it and it won't become a problem."

Meanwhile, Rhodes is pushing ahead with his plans for NoFap. The movement now has a dedicated website and he's working on an education and awareness campaign to reduce incidence of sexual assault. Though NoFap began as an experiment in productivity, it has morphed into a movement with a loftier goal. "My No. 1 goal in life isn't to improve people's sex lives," Rhodes says. "I want society to value sex as something meaningful."

For some, it's already working. Midway through his NoFap challenge, Armando says he began noticing changes in the way he looks at women. "Before, whenever I'd see a woman, the first thing I would look for is what have they got hanging on back there, or how big are their breasts," he says. "Lately, I've been catching myself looking at their eyes."

Critical Thinking

1. Why is viewing porn harmful?
2. How does giving up masturbation and swearing off porn better one's life?
3. Should pornography be outlawed by the government or dealt by with by sex education?

Create Central

www.mhhe.com/createcentral

Internet References

NoFap
   http://www.nofap.org
SIECUS-Comprehensive Sex Education
   http://www.siecus.org

Tamsin McMahon, "Masters of Their Domain" from *Maclean's* 127.5 (January 27, 2014): 52–54.

Article Prepared by: Eileen Daniel, *SUNY College at Brockport*

The Marriage Paradox

Love, Lies, and the Power of Self-Deception

CLANCY MARTIN

Learning Outcomes

After reading this article, you will be able to:

- Explain why political, educational, and labor equality for women has changed marriage.

- Understand why the author considers marriage to be a "leap of faith."

- Describe why Martin calls marriage a kind of self-deception.

Last thanksgiving, at the turn-of-the-century house Amie and I just bought in old Kansas City: Amie, my third wife; Rebecca, my second; Alicia, my first; Amie's mom, Pat; and my three daughters sat around the harvest table. My first wife, Alicia, who has a large, ambitious heart, had proposed this act of holiday lunacy. My second wife, Rebecca, had suggested we just have fun without her, but then came anyway. Amie had felt powerless to say no, and now it was taking place.

Once the guests arrived, Amie hid in the kitchen until dinner. She spent most of her time there, making eggnog cappuccinos, roasting sweet potatoes, and baking pumpkin pies. I was afraid of the dinner table but took the head, my daughters flanking me on either side. Amie's mother was at the other end. The four women and three girls all seemed to have a good time. My first wife and my third wife discussed cleaning supplies and ghosts. Three of the four women—everyone but Amie—were single mothers, I realized. They'd all been married; they were all presently single.

Coming out of the kitchen with a roasted chicken on a platter, I listened nervously to the conversation:

"I know the wood needs oil," Amie said, gesturing to the mahogany paneling in the dining room. "But you can't really do it before company comes."

My eldest daughter was musing aloud about what she would do if she accidentally killed someone. She thought it would be best to hide the body.

"No," her mother, my first wife, said. "You would call me."

"I'd call my attorney!" my daughter said, and she pointed to my second wife (a divorce lawyer), who laughed.

Two ex-wives and my present wife all together: my divorce mediator had warned against it. I stood at the end of the table, amateurishly carved the chicken—these were the first I'd roasted in a few years—and talked with my daughters.

Dinner and dessert went well. Every time I looked up to check on Amie, she was smiling and chatting. When they all left, the hugs were natural. They all took pumpkin pies home with them.

Good luck always makes me anxious. That night I woke at 3 A.M. in a sweat. Why had those once-married women stayed single? Did they understand something I didn't? Did Amie and I get married too quickly? Was it because I need someone to love me? Did she love me? But if not, why marry a twice-divorced man with three children? I couldn't get back to sleep.

I went downstairs to the study, sat at our new desk, and made a list of all the reasons I'd married for a third time. I decided to be as rough on myself as I could. The first reason I wrote was: "I fell madly in love with Amie. She's the one." Wait, that's a cop-out. That was what I would say in a Nora Ephron play. I started a new list. Tougher.

"Reason No. 1: I don't like to be alone. Reason No. 2: Life seems mostly sane when I am with the person who is my best friend." The list had 11 reasons. I could have kept going.

After my second divorce, a friend and mentor said to me, "Give me this much: You'll wait as long as I did before trying it again." This friend had an interval of about 15 years between his two marriages. I reassured him that there was no chance I was getting married again. Then, a few months after my promise, less than two weeks after the signing of my divorce decree, at the beginning of the monsoon season in a Tibetan colony in the Himalayas, I married for the third time. "For Christ's sake, why?" my married male friends asked me. My single male friends were quiet. My female friends laughed or shook their heads. My brothers were relieved. My ex-wives were emphatic: "Promise you won't have any more children." My mother said: "Listen to me. There's only one way to make a marriage work, Clancy. You simply refuse to let it fail."

"Marriage is like a cage," Montaigne wrote. "One sees the birds outside desperate to get in, and those inside equally desperate to get out." The metaphor is hardly value-neutral; there is something noble if frightening about living outside the cage, secure but slavish within. (My father, himself twice married, used to quote Groucho Marx: "Marriage is a wonderful institution, but who wants to live in an institution?") For better or worse, Montaigne was right to point out that so many people who are married confess, after half a bottle of wine, that they would rather not be; catch a single person in a weak moment and he will often admit his longing for a lover who is more than temporary.

Divorce and the fortunate trend toward political, educational, and labor equality for women have changed the way we understand and practice marriage (in the West, anyway), but most of us continue to value the ideal of dedicating one's erotic and affectionate attention to another human being for a lifetime. The story of Odysseus striving to get back to Penelope, of Penelope weaving and unweaving her tapestry to delay her suitors while she hopes for the return of her husband, is no less compelling today than it was more than 3,000 years ago.

In the first months of our marriage, when Amie told me she loved me, she often added, "I've never loved anyone like this since my best friend in the third grade." Best friendship in childhood is something like marriage. Kierkegaard had the idea that, in every life, there was both a first and a second "immediacy." The first is the kind you enjoy when you are encountering the world for the first time: the smell of snow in your first few winters (even as a teenager, I could smell the snow in a way I no longer can), the first times you swim, what food tasted like. Then life proceeds: familiarity and habit creep in, and the world loses its newness, its ease, and its golden quality. For many of us, perhaps, we never recapture that immediacy of youth. But there can be a second immediacy, experienced perhaps through love, perhaps only through faith (the Danish word, *tro,* or faith, also means "belief").

This second immediacy sometimes sounds like a mystical state in Kierkegaard's writing, but sometimes like the very ordinary, though uncommon, experience of rediscovering the newness of something you've experienced before—as when you reread a favorite book or swim in the ocean after you haven't done so for a few years. Most simply, I think, it's re-experiencing what it's like to feel fully alive. In this state, we do not forget what the world was like before, when we were satiated with it; rather, we rediscover its wonder, and appreciate it more because of all that we've been through. The world is, as Max Weber (writing under Kierkegaard's influence) put it, "re-enchanted."

Having a best friend as a kid, or falling in love: these are good examples of first immediacy. The world is an enchanted place. Then the disappointments of love disenchant us. But marriage might offer the possibility of re-enchantment. The idea is that in first immediacy, you don't know how lucky you are. In the second immediacy, you bring both the knowledge that you have chosen this situation and your understanding of the past to your new way of looking at the world, your new appreciation of love.

For this reason, a good remarriage might be a particularly powerful case of re-enchantment. I bring to my new marriage everything I learned from my previous two: the immediacy I once had in those marriages; the knowledge of how I lost that freshness and what it is like to lose that; and, consequently, a deeper appreciation of the preciousness of that kind of love when you experience it again. Clearly I'm a slow learner. But I think that, in my third marriage, for the first time, I am starting to understand gratitude.

One of my philosopher friends would argue: how about a fourth marriage, then? Better still! And a fifth! Well, there's a practical limit to human resilience. You love a second child as much as the first; a new career revives you, and so does exotic travel; but most of us don't pursue those goods endlessly. And most long-term love relationships go through phases of enchantment, disenchantment, and re-enchantment: it's not required and probably not recommended that one change partners to appreciate what I'm trying to describe.

The truth is, there's not just one best mate out there waiting for us. If we allow that love relies not just on luck but also on our own ability to choose our partners and creatively apply our minds to romantically loving well, then there might be many potential lifelong mates who can fulfill us. And so we might need to search for re-enchantment following a disenchantment in love. The term "codependent" has gone out of style, and it is not fashionable to suggest that I am "more me" when I am with someone else. But what if it's simply true that—to quote from my list (No. 4)—"I am at my best when I am sharing my life with someone with whom I am deeply in love?"

The contemporary American philosopher Eric Schwitzgebel has identified what he calls a paradox in the marriage vow: to promise to love for a lifetime, while recognizing that both life and love are unpredictable, seems like a risky move. But as Schwitzgebel correctly argues, to promise to love a partner for a lifetime is both to acknowledge the future's unpredictability ("for better, for worse, for richer, for poorer, in sickness, and in health") and to insist that one part of life won't change: one's commitment to one's partner. Which is not to say that the feelings of both partners won't change along the way.

If this vow is paradoxical the first time it's made, think how much more so it is a second time and, in my case, a third. But belief in the meaning of that vow, despite its inherent paradox, despite the evidence that many of us don't live up to it, adds to the passion that one brings to it. Kierkegaard observed that if we knew that God existed, we wouldn't need to believe in him; it's precisely the irrationality of faith that gives its punch.

Marriage as a slightly crazy promise—even, perhaps, a special kind of self-deception: to believe a proposition and at the same time not to believe it. Psychologically, self-deception is even more paradoxical than the marriage vow; it ought to be impossible, and yet we do it with fluency from a young age.

One side of the self-deception allows us to get ourselves into the kinds of love-destroying situations that I created when I ended my first two marriages. Like lying to others, lying to yourself can lead to a whole lot of trouble—as in, for example, sliding into bed with someone while telling yourself (and even telling your new lover), "No, this needn't be the first step toward destroying my happy marriage." Self-deception may also keep people in certain marriages long after they should have left them. The difference between bad self-deception and good, I think, is that in the latter kind you know that you're doing it and you know why you're doing it. The benevolent power of self-deception is, in fact, what makes long, happy marriages—and all successful relationships—possible.

Shakespeare's "Sonnet 138" shows how this works:

When my love swears that she is made of truth
I do believe her, though I know she lies,
That she might think me some untutor'd youth,
Unlearned in the world's false subtleties.
Thus vainly thinking that she thinks me young,
Although she knows my days are past the best,
Simply I credit her false speaking tongue:
On both sides thus is simple truth suppress'd.
But wherefore says she not she is unjust?
And wherefore say not I that I am old?
O, love's best habit is in seeming trust,
And age in love loves not to have years told:
    Therefore I lie with her and she with me,
    And in our faults by lies we flatter'd be.

The first two lines are a terrific double paradox: he believes her, though he knows she's lying—but for him to believe her, he can't know she's lying. Given our facility with the pretzel logic that enables us to believe the lies we tell ourselves, how do we believe a lie someone else is telling us, while knowing it's a lie? The poet admits that he lets his lover believe that he believes her lies so that she will think he is young, which is also the lie she is telling him, and he uses his performance in the same way he believes her lie—to convince himself of the lie she is telling him ("thus vainly thinking that she thinks me young"). This is subtle, convoluted, hilarious, and yet entirely true to the phenomenology of love.

My favorite line: "O, love's best habit is in seeming trust." Real trust in love comes in trusting even when we know there may be reason for distrust, when we recognize that complete trust is an illusion and should not even be a goal. To truly trust is to *seem* to trust, to trust with the acceptance of doubt, to be willing to extend the feigning of trust while hoping, even expecting, that the feint will be returned.

As Nietzsche observed, the wisdom of the ancient Greeks was in the fact that, at least before Socrates, they preferred seeming to being. They understood that "the naked truth" was not what good lovers seek: "It is necessary to keep bravely to the surface, the fold and the skin; to worship appearance, to believe in forms, tones, and words, in the whole Olympus of appearance! Those Greeks were superficial—from profundity!"

Do we really want to know the truth about our lovers? We don't even know that about ourselves—it's simply too elusive, too protean, too complex.

Do we really want to know the truth about our lovers? We don't even know that about ourselves—it's simply too elusive, too protean, and too complex—and we don't want to know it, we don't need to know it. Would I love my wife more, would our marriage be stronger, if we knew every detail of each other's past lovers and love affairs? Even writing this essay about marriage is scary. I am wildly in love; my marriage, though it has its ups and downs, is splendid: Do I really want to put it under a microscope? Will my commitment be stronger because of a 3 A.M. dissection?

In love we are artists, not scientists. Who among us hasn't had the feeling, when first falling in love, of "wait, but aren't I making this all up?" That can be a bad thing, as when the young narrator, at the close of James Joyce's story "Araby," concludes that all of love is a kind of vain trick one plays on oneself. Yet deceptions and self-deceptions are a desirable, vital part of falling and staying in love. The make-believe of first love (and first heartbreak) is just warm-up for the game to come. We have to creatively participate in the romantic appreciation of our beloved—just as we creatively participate in the romantic enhancement of ourselves (both consciously and unconsciously).

Hans Vaihinger called that kind of instrumentally false belief a "necessary fiction"; Coleridge called it "the willing suspension of disbelief." Kids call it playing (although it crucially excludes the illusion-killing cynicism of the "player"). In Shakespeare's sonnet, healthy illusions are being championed, not ironized away.

This is what being married three times has taught me: engaging in this kind of playful, open-eyed deception and self-deception is how love is fostered, nurtured, and maintained. It is necessary to learn how to do it. "Couples last longer if they tend to overrate each other compared to the other's self-evaluation," the evolutionary biologist Robert Trivers teaches us. (That sounds awfully similar to No. 9 on my 3 A.M. Thanksgiving list: "I have doubts about myself and even tend to fail when I don't have a partner who believes in me. When I have a partner who believes in me, I tend to be a better person.")

In his 1996 book, Monogamy, the psychotherapist Adam Phillips succinctly views the same idea in a more negative light: "The point about trust is that it is impossible to establish. It is a risk masquerading as a promise." But we can take blind risks, foolish risks, ill-advised risks; we can also take practiced risks; we can enjoy risk; we can risk because to risk is to live.

A friend of mine, the philosopher R.J. Hankinson, who is a scholar of the ancient skeptic Sextus Empiricus, once raised the argument that being a skeptic might not be all that attractive a way to live, because skepticism—despite or because of the tranquilizing benefits that *ataraxia* ("freedom from disturbance") might have—threatens to take the fun out of life. If you aren't willing to be swayed by appearances, if you aren't stimulated and even scared once in a while, what's the point of it all?

Yes, to get married is a leap of faith. But really, who would want to be marriage because "it makes sense"?

Yes, to get married is a leap of faith: Hell, it's not a rational thing to do, but how much of life is rational? Is it rational to have kids, to chase a career, to write books, to believe that tomorrow will be better than yesterday? If it is all a dream, is a nightmare more honest? And really, who would want to be in a marriage because "it makes sense"?

The Buddhist lama Dzongsar Khyentse Rinpoche (also known as Khyentse Norbu) gave a famous lecture on love and relationships in 2010, in Bir, in northern India. With romantic relationships, he said, "We don't really have a choice. When it comes, it comes. What is important about relationships is not to have expectations. If you are a couple, your attitude should be that you have checked into a hotel for a few days together. I might never see her again tomorrow. This might be our last goodbye, our last kiss, together. Maybe it will help; it will bring out the preciousness of the relationship. When the relationship comes, you should not be afraid."

Or, as Mark Twain wrote in a letter, sounding very Buddhist himself: "Marriage—yes, it is the supreme felicity of life. I concede it. And it is also the supreme tragedy of life. The deeper the love, the surer the tragedy."

When Khyentse Rinpoche married my wife and me, he warned us: "You know, Buddhism doesn't have a marriage ceremony. We don't really believe in marriage." To married couples, he says: "The best thing you can do is live in the world. I would tell you from the day you are married, your practice is, let's forget about giving freedom to the sentient beings"—a fundamental Buddhist motivation—"but start with giving freedom to your husband, and husband to the wife."

In this view, marriage is not supposed to constrain but to liberate. What does that mean, practically speaking? I think it means that I am supposed to help Amie pursue the things that matter most to her—many of which will also, with luck, turn out to be the things that matter most to me.

The lama goes on to say that marrying can be good practice for freeing oneself from the selfish cravings that we all suffer from. In the ideal marriage, which is understood as a goal, Amie's well-being will matter to me more than my own. We do love our children this way, and sometimes one or two friends. Of course we should acknowledge that, if life is impermanent (as indeed it is), marriage may be much more so—but here we are, stuck in the world, so why not risk it? Part of the risk is honestly acknowledging that the other human being, your spouse, is free: there's no telling what he or she might do. You're free, too, and sometimes there's no telling what you might do.

Of course all of this is just a philosopher stumbling awkwardly around the real story, which is that Amie called one afternoon to do a tarot-card reading on me for a column she eventually wrote for a magazine (the cards said I should work and avoid romance). I Google-imaged her and, single at the time, flirted with her. Facebook led to emails led to texts and then long phone calls. I flew Amie to Kansas City, and one morning, coming upstairs from the basement of my apartment with laundry in my arms, I caught sight of her in the eastern sunlight making coffee, smiling with that half-frown she makes when she's working, her long, dark brown hair in her face and on her shoulders. I flew back with her to Seattle, and walking through the jewelry department of Barney's, I saw a ring. That afternoon I proposed. That's the truth of it. We met; we fell in love; I asked her to spend the rest of her life with me; she said yes.

Yes, you might have your heart broken; yes, the whole thing might be an impossible joke, a game with outrageous odds; yes, you might have failed at it twice before, and there's no guarantee—just the opposite, really—that the third time's the charm. Life is risky; love, riskier still; marriage might be riskiest of all. But to choose to be married is, *contra* Montaigne, a paradoxical expression of one's freedom. It's not the only game in town, but it's one helluva good game.

Critical Thinking

1. Why does the author believe that divorce has changed the way we practice marriage?

2. Why does the author believe that there's not just one best mate out there waiting for us?

Create Central

www.mhhe.com/createcentral

Internet References

American Psychological Association
http://www.apa.org/topics/divorce

Psychology Today
http://www.psychologytoday.com/basics/marriage

CLANCY MARTIN is a professor of philosophy at the University of Missouri at Kansas City and the author of the novel *How to Sell* (2009) and the forthcoming nonfiction book *Love, Lies, and Marriage* (both Farrar, Straus and Giroux).

Clancy Martin, "The Marriage Paradox: Loves, Lies, and the Power of Self Deception" from *The Chronicle Review* (February 28, 2014): 7–10.

Article   Prepared by: Eileen L. Daniel, *SUNY Brockport*

There's No Evidence Online Dating Is Threatening Commitment or Marriage

One guy's commitment issues don't mean the end of monogamy for the country. The first in a series of responses to Dan Slater's article "A Million First Dates."

ALEXIS C. MADRIGAL

Learning Outcomes

After reading this article, you will be able to:

- Explain how Internet dating has affected our thinking about commitment.
- Describe the effect online dating has on monogamy.
- Describe why relationships that begin online may move more quickly than conventional dating.

The question at hand in Dan Slater's piece in the latest *Atlantic* print edition, "A Million First Dates: How Online Dating is Threatening Monogamy," is whether online dating can change some basic settings in American heterosexual relationships such that monogamy and commitment are less important.

Narratively, the story focuses on Jacob, an overgrown man-child jackass who can't figure out what it takes to have a real relationship. The problem, however, is not him, and his desire for a "low-maintenance" woman who is hot, young, interested in him, and doesn't mind that he is callow and doesn't care very much about her. No, the problem is online dating, which has shown Jacob that he can have a steady stream of mediocre dates, some of whom will have sex with him.

"I'm 95 percent certain," Jacob says of a long-term relationship ending, "that if I'd met Rachel offline, and I'd never done online dating, I would've married her. Did online dating change my perception of permanence? No doubt."

This story forms the spineless spine of a larger argument about how online dating is changing the world, by which we mean yuppie romance. The argument is that online dating expands the romantic choices that people have available, somewhat like moving to a city. And more choices mean less satisfaction. For example, if you give people more chocolate bars to choose from, the story tells us, they think the one they choose tastes worse

than a control group who had a smaller selection. Therefore, online dating makes people less likely to commit and less likely to be satisfied with the people to whom they do commit.

But what if online dating makes it too easy to meet someone new? What if it raises the bar for a good relationship too high? What if the prospect of finding an ever-more-compatible mate with the click of a mouse means a future of relationship instability, in which we keep chasing the elusive rabbit around the dating track?

Unfortunately, neither Jacob's story nor any of the evidence offered compellingly answers the questions raised. Now, let's stipulate that there is no dataset that perfectly settles the core question: Does online dating increase or decrease commitment or its related states, like marriage?

But I'll tell you one group that I would not trust to give me a straight answer: People who run online dating sites. While these sites may try to attract some users with the idea that they'll find everlasting love, how great is it for their marketing to suggest that they are so easy and fun that people can't even stay in committed relationships anymore? As Slater notes, "the profit models of many online-dating sites are at cross-purposes with clients who are trying to develop long-term commitments." Which is exactly why they are happy to be quoted talking about how well their sites work for getting laid and moving on.

It should also be noted: There isn't a single woman's perspective in this story. Or a gay person's. Or someone who was into polyamory before online dating. Or some kind of historical look at how commitment rates have changed in the past and what factors drove those increases or decreases. Instead we get eight men from the industry that, as we put it on our cover, "works too well."

But hey, maybe these guys are right. Maybe online dating and social networking is tearing apart the fabric of society. How well does the proposition actually hold up?

First off, the heaviest users of technology—educated, wealthier people—have been using online dating and networking sites to find each other for years. And yet, divorce rates among this exact group have been declining for 30 years. Take a look at these statistics. If technology were the problem, you'd expect that people who can afford to use the technology, and who have been using the technology, would be seeing the impacts of this new lack of commitment. But that's just not the case.

Does it follow that within this wealthy, educated group, online daters are less likely to commit or stay married? No, it does not.

Like I said, there's no data to prove that question one way or the other. But we have something close. A 2012 paper in the American Sociological Review asked, are people who have the Internet at home more or less likely to be in relationships? Here was the answer they found:

One result of the increasing importance of the Internet in meeting partners is that adults with Internet access at home are substantially more likely to have partners, even after controlling for other factors. Partnership rate has increased during the Internet era (consistent with Internet efficiency of search) for same sex couples, but the heterosexual partnership rate has been flat.

So, we have, at worst, that controlling for other factors, the Internet doesn't hurt and sometimes helps. That seems to strike right at the heart of Slater's proposition.

A 2008 paper looked at the Internet's ability to help people find partners and postulated who might benefit the most. "The Internet's potential to change matching is perhaps greatest for those facing thin markets or difficulty in meeting potential mates." This could increase marriage rates as people with smaller pools can more easily find each other. The paper also proposes that perhaps people would be better matched through online dating and therefore have higher-quality marriages. The available evidence, though, suggests that there was no difference between couples who met online and couples who met offline. (Surprise!)

So, here's the way it looks to me: Either online dating's (and the Internet's) effect on commitment is nonexistent, the effect has the opposite polarity (i.e. online dating creates more marriages), or whatever small effect either way is overwhelmed by other changes in the structure of commitment and marriage in America.

The possibility that the relationship "market" is changing in a bunch of ways, rather than just by the introduction of date-matching technology, is the most compelling to me. That same 2008 paper found that the biggest change in marriage could be increasingly "co-ed" workplaces. Many, many more people work in places where they might find relationship partners more easily. That's a big confounding variable in any analysis of online dating as the key causal factor in any change in marital or commitment rates.

But there's certainly more complexity than that lurking within what was left out of Jacob's story: how about changing gender norms a la Hanna Rosin's *End of Men?* How about changes that arose in the recent difficult economic circumstances? How about changes in where marriage-age people live (say, living in a walkable core versus the exurbs)? How about the spikiness of American religious observance, as declining church attendance rates combine with evangelical fervor? How about changing cultural norms about childrearing and marriage? How about the increasing acceptance of homosexuality across the country, particularly in younger demographics?

All of these things could bring about changes in the likelihood of people to meet and stay in relationships. And none of them have much to do with online dating. Yet our story places all of the emphasis for Jacob's drift on his desire to browse online dating profiles.

Is online dating a trend that's worth us looking into? Certainly. And there are even things that online dating sites may be able to do within their technical systems to negate the effects of thinking about possible partners as profiles rather than people. Slater cited Northwestern's Eli Finkel, who appears to have legitimate concerns about the structure of search and discovery on dating sites.

But the jumps and leaps from that observation—and Finkel's academic assessment in a recent paper—to blaming online dating for "threatening monogamy"? There's just so little support there.

And if you are going to make a hard deterministic argument, you better have some good evidence that it is the technology itself that is the actor, and not someone or something else. At any time in this big old world, there are lots of changes happening slowly. So many trend lines, so much data. In that world, there appears some undeniably shiny new thing: a technology! People—TED speakers, teenage skateboarders, venture capitalists, a grandfather, advertisers, deli counter clerks, accountants—standing amidst the swirl of the white swirl of the onrushing future look out and say, "This technology is changing everything!"

Flush with this knowledge of the one true cause of good/bad in the _____ Age, the magic technology key seems to unlock every room in the house, and all the doors on every neighbor's house, and the vault at Fort Knox, and the highest office at 30 Rock.

Of course, technology does have impacts. Certain types of technology, say, nuclear reactors, have politics in that they "are man-made systems that appear to require or to be strongly compatible with particular kinds of political relationships," as the political scientist Langdon Winner has shown. Some technological systems, the electric grid or cell phone networks, prove difficult to change, and make some kinds of behavior really easy, and others more difficult. A technology can tilt a set of interactions towards certain outcomes, which is precisely why some people want to ban specific types of guns.

So, you can say, in some sense, that a technology "wants" certain outcomes. Jacob from the story might say that online dating wants him to keep browsing and not commit. The electrical grid wants you to plug in. Or, the owners of Facebook want you to post more photographs, so they design tools—technical and statistical—to make you more likely to do so.

And it's not wrong to say that Facebook wants us to do things. But if you stop talking to your cousins because it's easier to update Facebook than give them a call, it's not right to say that Facebook made you do that. If you stop reading novels because you find Twitter more compelling, it's not correct to say that Twitter made you do that. Maybe you like real-time news more than the Bronte sisters, no matter what your better conception of yourself might say.

Maybe Jacob doesn't want to get married. Maybe he wants to get drunk, have sex, watch basketball, and never deal with the depths of a real relationship. OK, Jacob, good luck! But that doesn't make online dating an ineluctable force crushing the romantic landscape. It's just the means to Jacob's ends and his convenient scapegoat for behavior that might otherwise lead to self-loathing.

Create Central

www.mhhe.com/createcentral

Critical Thinking

1. Does Internet dating affect our thinking about commitment in relationships?
2. Will online dating have an impact on divorce rates?

Internet References

Sexuality Information and Education Council of the United States (SIECUS)
  www.siecus.org
Columbia University's Go Ask Alice!
  www.goaskalice.columbia.edu/index.html

Unit 7

UNIT

Prepared by: Eileen Daniel, *SUNY College at Brockport*

Preventing and Fighting Disease

Cardiovascular disease and cancer are the leading killers in this country. This is not altogether surprising given that the American population is growing increasingly older, and one's risk of developing both of these diseases is directly proportional to one's age. Another major risk factor, which has received considerable attention over the past 30 years, is one's genetic predisposition or family history. Historically, the significance of this risk factor has been emphasized as a basis for encouraging at-risk individuals to make prudent lifestyle choices, but this may be about to change as recent advances in genetic research, including mapping the human genome, may significantly improve the efficacy of both diagnostic and therapeutic procedures.

Just as cutting-edge genetic research is transforming the practice of medicine, startling new research findings in the health profession are transforming our views concerning adult health. This new research suggests that the primary determinants of our health as adults are the environmental conditions we experienced during our life in the womb. According to Dr. Peter Nathanielsz of Cornell University, conditions during gestation, ranging from hormones that flow from the mother to how well the placenta delivers nutrients to the tiny limbs and organs, program how our liver, heart, kidneys, and especially our brains function as adults. While it is too early to draw any firm conclusions regarding the significance of the "life in the womb factor," it appears that this avenue of research may yield important clues as to how we may best prevent or forestall chronic illness.

Of all the diseases in America, coronary heart disease is this nation's number one killer. Frequently, the first and only symptom of this disease is a sudden heart attack. Epidemiological studies have revealed a number of risk factors that increase one's likelihood of developing this disease. These include hypertension, a high serum cholesterol level, diabetes, cigarette smoking, obesity, a sedentary lifestyle, a family history of heart disease, age, sex, race, and stress. In addition to these well-established risk factors, scientists think they may have discovered several additional risk factors. These include the following: low birth weight, cytomegalovirus, *Chlamydia pneumoniae,* porphyromonasgingivalis, and c-reactive protein (CRP). CRP is a measure of inflammation somewhere in the

body. In theory, a high CRP reading may be a good indicator of an impending heart attack.

One of the most startling and ominous health stories was the recent announcement by the Centers for Disease Control and Prevention (CDC) that the incidence of Type 2 adult onset diabetes increased significantly over the past 15 years. This sudden rise appears to cross all races and age groups, with the sharpest increase occurring among people ages 30 to 39 (about 70 percent). Health experts at the CDC believe that this startling rise in diabetes among 30 to 39 year olds is linked to the rise in obesity observed among young adults (obesity rates rose from 12 to 20 percent nationally during this same time period). Experts at the CDC believe that there is a time lag of about 10–15 years between the deposition of body fat and the manifestation of Type 2 diabetes. This time lag could explain why individuals in their 30s are experiencing the greatest increase in developing Type 2 diabetes today. Current estimates suggest that 16 million Americans have diabetes, and it kills approximately 180,000 Americans each year. Many experts now believe that our couch potato culture is fueling the rising rates of both obesity and diabetes. Given what we know about the relationship between obesity and Type 2 diabetes, the only practical solution is for Americans to watch their total calorie intake and exercise regularly. Currently, there has been a rise in the incidence of Type 2 diabetes among our youth and young adults, and the term *adult onset diabetes* may be a misnomer, given the growing number of young adults and teens with this form of diabetes.

Cardiovascular disease is America's number one killer, but cancer takes top billing in terms of the "fear factor." This fear of cancer stems from an awareness of the degenerative and disfiguring nature of the disease. Today, cancer specialists are employing a variety of complex agents and technologies, such as monoclonal antibodies, interferon, and immunotherapy, in their attempt to fight the disease. Progress has been slow, however, and the results, while promising, suggest that a cure may be several years away. A very disturbing aspect of this country's battle against cancer is the fact that millions of dollars are spent each year trying to advance the treatment of cancer, while the funding for the technologies used to detect cancer in its early stages is quite limited. A reallocation of funds would seem appropriate, given the medical community posits that early detection and treatment are the key elements in the successful cure of cancer. An interesting issue related to early detection has arisen. A government task force recently announced that women in their 40s do not need annual mammograms, a long-held belief. Until we have more effective methods for detecting cancer in the early stages, our best hope for managing cancer is to prevent it through our lifestyle choices. The same lifestyle choices that may help prevent cancer can also help reduce the incidence of heart disease and diabetes.

Article   Prepared by: Eileen Daniel, *SUNY College at Brockport*

Refusing Vaccination Puts Others at Risk

Ronald Bailey

Learning Outcomes

After reading this article, you will be able to:

- Explain why vaccine refusal puts others at risk.
- Understand why defenseless people such as infants who are too young to be vaccinated and individuals whose immune systems are compromised are at particular risk for disease prevented by vaccination.
- Understand the concept of herd immunity.

Millions of Americans believe it is perfectly all right to put other people at risk of death and misery. These people are your friends, neighbors, and fellow citizens who refuse to have themselves or their children vaccinated against preventable infectious diseases.

Aside from the issue of child neglect, there would be no argument against allowing people to refuse government-required vaccination if they and their families were the only ones who suffered the consequences of their fool-hardiness. But that is not the case in the real world. Let's first take a look at how vaccines have improved health, then consider the role of the state in promoting immunization.

Vaccines are among the most effective health care innovations ever devised. A November 2013 New England Journal of Medicine article, drawing on the University of Pittsburgh's Project Tycho database of infectious disease statistics since 1888, concluded that vaccinations since 1924 have prevented 103 million cases of polio, measles, rubella, mumps, hepatitis A, diphtheria, and pertussis. They have played a substantial role in greatly reducing death and hospitalization rates, as well as the sheer unpleasantness of being hobbled by disease.

A 2007 article in the Journal of the American Medical Association compared the annual average number of cases and resulting deaths of various diseases before the advent of vaccines to those occurring in 2006. Before an effective diphtheria vaccine was developed in the 1930s, for example, the disease infected about 21,000 people in the United States each year, killing 1,800. By 2006, both numbers were zero. Polio, too, went from deadly (16,000 cases, 1,900 deaths) to nonexistent after vaccines were rolled out in the 1950s and 1960s. Chickenpox used to infect 4 million kids a year, hospitalize 11,000, and kill 105; within a decade of a vaccine being rolled out in the mid-1990s, infections had dropped to 600,000, resulting in 1,276 hospitalizations and 19 deaths. Similar dramatic results can be found with whooping cough, measles, rubella, and more.

And deaths don't tell the whole story. In the case of rubella, which went from infecting 48,000 people and killing 17 per year, to infecting just 17 and killing zero, there were damaging pass-on effects that no longer exist. Some 2,160 infants born to mothers infected by others were afflicted with congenital rubella syndrome-causing deafness, cloudy corneas, damaged hearts, and stunted intellects—as late as 1965. In 2006 that number was one.

It is certainly true that much of the decline in infectious disease mortality has occurred as a result of improved sanitation and water chlorination. A 2004 study by the Harvard University economist David Cutler and the National Bureau of Economic Research economist Grant Miller estimated that the provision of clean water "was responsible for nearly half of the total mortality reduction in major cities, three-quarters of the infant mortality reduction, and nearly two-thirds of the child mortality reduction." Providing clean water and pasteurized milk resulted in a steep decline in deadly waterborne infectious diseases. Improved nutrition also reduced mortality rates, enabling infants, children, and adults to fight off diseases that would have more likely killed their malnourished ancestors. But it is a simple fact that vaccines are the most effective tool yet devised for preventing contagious airborne diseases.

Vaccines do not always produce immunity, so a percentage of those who took the responsibility to be vaccinated remain vulnerable. Other defenseless people include infants who are too young to be vaccinated and individuals whose immune systems are compromised. In America today, it is estimated that about 10 million people are immunocompromised through no fault of their own.

This brings us to the important issue of "herd immunity." Herd immunity works when most people in a community are immunized against an illness, greatly reducing the chances that an infected person can pass his microbes along to other susceptible people.

People who refuse vaccination for themselves and their children are free riding off of herd immunity. Even while receiving this benefit, the unvaccinated inflict the negative externality of being possible vectors of disease, threatening those 10 million most vulnerable to contagion.

Vaccines are like fences. Fences keep your neighbor's livestock out of your pastures and yours out of his. Similarly, vaccines separate people's microbes. Anti-vaccination folks are taking advantage of the fact that most people around them have chosen differently, thus acting as a firewall protecting them from disease. But if enough people refuse, that firewall comes down, and innocent people get hurt.

Oliver Wendell Holmes articulated a good libertarian principle when he said, "The right to swing my fist ends where the other man's nose begins." Holmes' observation is particularly salient in the case of whooping cough shots.

Infants cannot be vaccinated against whooping cough (pertussis), so their protection against this dangerous disease depends upon the fact that most of the rest of us are immunized. Unfortunately, as immunization refusals have increased in recent years, so have whooping cough infections. The annual number of pertussis cases fell from 200,000 pre-vaccine to a low of 1,010 in 1976. Last year, the number of reported cases rose to 48,277, the highest since 1955. Eighteen infants died of the disease in 2012, up from just four in 1976.

The trend is affecting other diseases as well. In 2005, an intentionally unvaccinated 17-year-old Indiana girl brought measles back with her from a visit to Romania and ended up infecting 34 people. Most of them were also intentionally unvaccinated, but a medical technician who had been vaccinated caught the disease as well, and was hospitalized.

Another intentionally unvaccinated 7-year-old boy in San Diego sparked an outbreak of measles in 2008. The kid, who caught the disease in Switzerland, ended up spreading his illness to 11 other children, all of whom were also unvaccinated, putting one infant in the hospital. Forty-eight other children younger than vaccination age had to be quarantined.

Some people object to applying Holmes' aphorism by arguing that aggression can only occur when someone intends to hit someone else; microbes just happen. However, being intentionally unvaccinated against highly contagious airborne diseases is, to extend the metaphor, like walking down a street randomly swinging your fists without warning. You may not hit an innocent bystander, but you've substantially increased the chances. Those harmed by the irresponsibility of the unvaccinated are not being accorded the inherent equal dignity and rights every individual possesses. The autonomy of the unvaccinated is trumping the autonomy of those they put at risk.

As central to libertarian thinking as the non-aggression principle is, there are other tenets that also inform the philosophy. One such is the harm principle, as outlined by John Stuart Mill. In On Liberty, Mill argued that "the only purpose for which power can be rightfully exercised over any member of a civilized community, against his will, is to prevent harm to others." Vaccination clearly prevents harm to others.

So what are the best methods for increasing vaccination? Education and the incentives of the market have encouraged many Americans to get themselves and their children immunized, and surely those avenues of persuasion can and should be used more. Perhaps schools and daycare centers and pediatric clinics could attract clients by advertising their refusal to admit unvaccinated kids. Or social pressure might be exercised by parents who insist on assurances from other parents that their children are vaccinated before agreeing to playdates.

But it would be naive not to acknowledge the central role of government mandates in spreading immunization. By requiring that children entering school be vaccinated against many highly contagious diseases, states have greatly benefited the vast majority of Americans.

For the sake of social peace, vaccine opt-out loopholes based on religious and philosophical objections should be maintained. States should, however, amend their vaccine exemption laws to require that people who take advantage of them acknowledge in writing that they know their actions are considered by the medical community to be putting others at risk. This could potentially expose vaccine objectors to legal liability, should their decisions lead to infections that could have been prevented.

In terms of net human freedom, the trade-off is clear: in exchange for punishment-free government requirements that contain opt-out loopholes, humans have freed themselves from hundreds of millions of infections from diseases that maimed and often killed people in recent memory. People who refuse vaccination are asserting that they have a right to "swing" their microbes at other people. That is wrong.

Being intentionally unvaccinated against highly contagious airborne diseases is like walking down a street randomly swinging your fists without warning.

Critical Thinking

1. Why don't vaccines always produce immunity and who is most at risk?
2. What are some of the best ways to increase the vaccination rates?

Create Central

www.mhhe.com/createcentral

Internet References

Centers for Disease Control and Prevention
http://www.cdc.gov/vaccines

National Vaccine Information Center
http://www.nvic.org

Article   Prepared by: Eileen L. Daniel, *SUNY Brockport*

The High Cost of "Hooking Up"

KURT WILLIAMSEN

Learning Outcomes

After reading this article, you will be able to:

- Explain the health risks associated with promiscuous sex.

- Describe the types of pathogenic organisms that can be transmitted sexually.

- Describe why there is such a high rate of sexually transmitted diseases among teenagers.

Hydeia Broadbent became somewhat of a mini-celebrity 20 years ago as a seven-year-old when she appeared on a Nickelodeon AIDS special. She appeared on the show with basketball great and HIV-positive athlete Magic Johnson—she had been diagnosed with AIDS, basically believed at the time to be a death sentence. She is still alive, and is a public-speaking dynamo. As an early recipient of anti-viral treatments that made AIDS a livable disease, one might expect her to be one of the many who reiterate their positive experiences having the disease, also inadvertently pooh-poohing the seriousness of the disease.

Not her. She does the opposite. She lays bare the consequences of having the disease, in order to encourage people to abstain from behaviors that might lead them to acquire it. She explained in a story for CNN: "If you're HIV-negative, I would say 'Stay that way.' If you're positive, I would say, 'There's life after a positive test, but it is a hassle.'"

As she told CNN last year, what she accomplishes in a day depends on how she feels:

There are days when Hydeia can't get out of bed. Sometimes she is so sick her mornings are spent with her head hung over the toilet.

Every morning, she must take her cocktail of five pills. Her tiny frame is partly a result of medicine stunting her growth.

If it's a good day, she goes to the gym to exercise. Staying fit is key to living with AIDS, she says. She eats healthy too, because a person with HIV/AIDS is more prone to cancer and heart disease. . . .

"There's so much misinformation. People think there's a cure . . .," she said. "There is no cure." . . .

Although a positive test result is no longer a death sentence, Hydeia says, "it's a life sentence."

"It's always there. You're always going to have HIV or AIDS. You're always going to be taking medicine. You're always going to be going to the doctor's office. You're always going to be getting your blood drawn."

Her medicine costs $3,500 to $5,000 a month.

The story soberly added that "16,000 Americans will die this year from AIDS."

Yet despite the very harsh realities of HIV/AIDS, according to the National Center for Health Statistics, in 2010, in the United States, "for all races combined in the age group 15–24 years, HIV disease moved from the 12th leading cause of death in 2009 to the 11th leading cause of death in 2010." It is the "7th leading cause of death in 2010 for the age group 25–44 years."

Moreover, there are, according to the Centers for Disease Control's "2010 Sexually Transmitted Diseases Surveillance," about 47,000 new diagnoses of HIV made each year, with a lifetime cost for each person conservatively estimated at $379,668—that's $17,844,396,000 of medical costs added to an already overwhelmed and over-budgeted U.S. medical system yearly. (Note: Many people catch HIV by sharing intravenous needles, not via sex.)

There are also 19 million new infections of sexually transmitted gonorrhea, chlamydia, and syphilis yearly, which cost $17 billion to treat each year. Then there are the costs to treat all of the other STDs—human papillomavirus, herpes, genital warts, hepatitis, trichomoniasis, scabies, etc. The World Health Organization says that there "are more than 30 different sexually transmissible bacteria, viruses and parasites." Treatment for those in the United States is also in the billions of dollars per year—when they're treatable and not drug resistant.

Whooping It Up over Whooppee

Though it's likely that literally everyone who is having sex is aware of STDs, such as herpes and HIV, and that STDs have consequences that include death, casual sex in our country is practically revered by youths and leftists. Sex on a whim, to them, is the be-all and end-all of life.

Accordingly, public schools, Hollywood celebs, and teen magazines often teach youths that no one should be allowed to tell them that they should not have sex until they are married, that every type and manner of sex is OK, and that having sex is just another bodily function and should be considered only with the same level of care as eating: Be careful about what you put in your body; try to prevent the transmission of pathogens via hygienic practices and barriers to disease transmission, such as latex products; and then dig in.

As well, even network TV tantalizes viewers with titillation and works to convince viewers that bed hopping is no big deal—everyone does it, with ones they love or ones they merely like. The term "friends with benefits"—friends who have sex with each other when no one better is available—is now such common slang that Hollywood used it as the basis for a movie.

Human nature being what it is, it's really no surprise to learn that there's not much difference between the percentage of youths who latch on to the "safe sex" message and the percentage of those who heed the appeals to participate in "uninhibited sex." A CDC survey showed that about 60 percent of high-school students who have had sex used a condom the last time they had sex, and 50 percent of them say they've had sex at least once. That's a lot of young people, with a lot of exposure to STDs. (Of course, in both cases there's probably some false data: In the case of the number of youths having sex, many youths don't consider oral sex to be sex at all, and so don't count it.)

In 2008, according to an AP article entitled "1 in 4 teen girls has sexually transmitted disease," not only did 25 percent of teenage girls have an STD, "among those who admitted to having sex, the rate was even more disturbing—40 percent had an STD." Black girls suffered worst: 48 percent of them had an STD, though blacks as a group are the most likely to use condoms, using them between 65 and 70 percent of the time.

Lest one believe the oft-cited refrain that such high rates of venereal disease in the United States demonstrate, as stated by Cecile Richards, the head of Planned Parenthood, that "the national policy of promoting abstinence-only programs is a . . . failure," know that "abstinence-only" is far from national policy—with only 34 percent of school principals in a Kaiser study saying that their school's "main message was abstinence-only" and with two-thirds of U.S. teens having had school lessons about condom usage. More importantly, it should be clear to all by studying France that sex-ed programs are a proven failure at eliminating such problems.

In France, sex education has been part of the school curricula since 1973, and students are given condoms in eighth and ninth grades. Moreover, in that country there can be no claims of hidden sexual repression influencing findings: Sex is not only part of the national dialogue, it's part of the country's national pride—alongside French cuisine—and public sex is not uncommon. Yet according to the World Health Organization, nearly 45 percent of French women tested under 25 years of age had sexually transmitted human papillomavirus (HPV). When women of all ages are considered, the evidence is equally damning: 12.8 percent of French women had HPV versus 7.3 percent for women of Western Europe as a whole. The worldwide HPV rate is 11.4 percent.

One Disease, Then Another

But sex-related diseases and costs go far beyond those directly associated with STDs. The National Cancer Institute at the National Institutes of Health stated that the human papillomavirus, which is "spread through direct skin-to-skin contact during vaginal, anal, and oral sex," causes "virtually all cervical cancers" and "most anal cancers and some vaginal, vulvar, penile, and oropharyngeal cancers [cancers in the middle part of the throat]." And the risk isn't limited to women. The title of a 2011 NBCNews.com article adequately sums up the situation: "Cancer spike, mainly in men, tied to HPV from oral sex." The article added that "we can expect some 10,000 to 15,000 patients with (the [oropharyngeal] cancers) per year in the United States, with the great majority having HPV-positive (cancers)." All told, "High risk HPV infections account for approximately 5 percent of cancers worldwide."

With the total cost of treating cancer in the United States in excess of $124.6 billion in 2010, the cost of treating cancer caused by HPV infections is likely upward of $6.23 billion per year—five percent of $124.6 billion. (This total is based on average costs from 2001 to 2006, before many expensive treatments were introduced, so costs now are likely higher.)

Also, according to the CDC, "Chlamydia and gonorrhea are important preventable causes of infertility," even though "most women infected with chlamydia or gonorrhea have no symptoms." There are "an estimated 2.8 million cases of chlamydia and 718,000 cases of gonorrhea [that] occur annually in the United States." "Each year untreated STDs cause 24,000 women in the United States to become infertile." STDs cause approximately one-fourth of all infertility in women, and treatment to rectify infertility can be very costly.

STDs also cause ectopic pregnancy, wherein a woman's egg gets fertilized in her fallopian tubes, instead of her uterus, again causing a life-threatening situation.

And the effects of STDs travel further than between the couple having sex: The effects can get passed on to newborns. The CDC commented:

STDs can be passed from a pregnant woman to the baby before, during, or after the baby's birth. Some STDs (like syphilis) cross the placenta and infect the baby while it is in the uterus (womb). Other STDs (like gonorrhea, chlamydia, hepatitis B, and genital herpes) can be transmitted from the mother to the baby during delivery as the baby passes through the birth canal. . . .

A pregnant woman with an STD may also have early onset of labor, premature rupture of the membranes surrounding the baby in the uterus, and uterine infection after delivery.

The harmful effects of STDs in babies may include stillbirth (a baby that is born dead), low birth weight (less than five pounds), conjunctivitis (eye infection), pneumonia, neonatal sepsis (infection in the baby's blood stream), neurologic damage, blindness, deafness, acute hepatitis, meningitis, chronic liver disease, and cirrhosis.

STDs truly are the gifts that keep on giving.

Too, taking "the pill" to avoid begetting any infants increases the risk of getting blood clots, strokes, and heart attacks.

A study published in the June *New England Journal of Medicine* determined that some types of pill double the risk of heart attack and stroke. (Much of this extra risk is borne by smokers.) For every 10,000 pill users, there is approximately one extra heart attack and one extra stroke. Combined with the fact that the pill can cause high blood pressure, possibly damaging organs; more than double the increase in risk of blood clots in veins, called deep venous thrombosis; and cause pulmonary embolism, which is when blood clots break loose from a vein and go into the lungs—potentially causing death—taking the pill is akin to playing bingo in a very large room and waiting for your chance to "win" an ailment.

Taking the pill also frequently results in increased headaches and, rarely, in liver tumors.

And the pill isn't the birth-control choice only of women in long-term monogamous relationships. A May report released by the CDC said that 60 percent of teen girls who have sex use the pill.

Though this is admittedly already a horrific list of physical consequences of sexual promiscuity—accompanied with a tab of many billions of dollars—it is far from an all-encompassing list. It really only covers some of the obvious "biggies." It ignores such things as the blisters, lesions, sores, and pain that come with STDs and their complications, such as pelvic inflammatory disease.

Moreover, to fully account for costs of the free-sex ethic, we must add emotional trauma and its consequences and treatment to the list of physical ailments.

Ouch, My Head/Heart Hurts

The emotional trauma that often comes with promiscuity includes, but is definitely not limited to, the embarrassment of having to tell someone with whom you want to become intimate that you have incurable herpes or HIV, telling your family that you're dying of AIDS, or grieving over the knowledge that your herpes caused your newborn to be blind or brain damaged.

The online article "Life With Herpes: One Woman's Story" recounts a woman named Angela's experience with contracting herpes:

In the summer of 1995, Angela, who was 25 at the time, felt like she had the flu and found it difficult and painful to urinate. She saw a doctor and, after being treated with several different medications for a possible bladder infection, felt worse than ever. "At the end of the three weeks I was miserable, couldn't walk and the pain was beyond description," she said.

Angela finally insisted on a vaginal examination and was diagnosed with genital herpes. . . .

She later realized she had contracted the virus from a sexual contact two weeks earlier. She was angry that her partner hadn't informed her he had herpes. . . . Shocked, terrified and alone, she struggled to find support and information about her disease.

Her physician wasn't helpful. "He basically handed me a box of tissues and told me my life would never be the same and sent me on my way." . . .

The emotional effects of having genital herpes have been as painful for Angela as the physical effects. "The first year I was ashamed, got flare ups all the time and didn't have anybody I trusted to talk to about what was happening in my life," she said. Frustrated by the lack of support systems where she lived, Angela started her own support group . . .

The HELP group meets monthly and offers a confidential environment where people can relate to others experiencing similar difficulties. . . . Herpes support groups allow attendees to vent their feelings, which can range from denial, depression, isolation and intense anger.

The CDC states that "nationwide, 16.2% [of], or about one out of six, people aged 14 to 49 years have genital HSV-2 infection"—one of two types of genital herpes. Women are more apt to catch it than men. Insidiously, the disease can move to different areas of the body: "If a person with genital herpes touches their sores or the fluids from the sores, they may transfer herpes to another part of the body. This is particularly problematic if it is a sensitive location such as the eyes."

Then there's the litany of findings that were released in 2003 by the Heritage Foundation, compiled from the U.S. Department of Health and Human Services' National Survey of Family Growth, in which 10,000 sexually active women between the ages of 15 and 44 were interviewed about both their sex lives and their lives in general.

The study, which asked women about how early in their lives they initiated voluntary sexual encounters, found that the younger a girl is when she becomes sexually active, the more likely she is to give birth out of wedlock. (At the time of the study, "nearly 40 percent of girls who commence sexual activity at ages 13 or 14 will give birth outside of marriage [versus] . . . 9 percent of women who begin sexual activity at ages 21 or 22.") Starting sex earlier also correlated to higher levels of child and maternal poverty, increased single motherhood, more abortions, more unstable marriages (once they did get married), decreased personal happiness, and increased depression.

Servings of sex came with heaping helpings of emotional pain, mental pain, and stress.

Please, Sir, May I Have Some More

Here again, the negative effects snowball. It's clearly evident in a Heritage Foundation study entitled "Marriage: America's Greatest Weapon Against Child Poverty" that over the years as the free-sex ideology has increasingly found acceptance, single motherhood has jumped dramatically—"in 2010 nearly 60 percent of all births in the U.S. were to single mothers," while "in 1964, 93 percent of children born in the United States were born to married parents." Moreover, as "free sex" and single motherhood took hold, poverty has prospered.

As the report says,

According to the U.S. Census, the poverty rate for single parents with children in the United States in 2009 was 37.1 percent. The rate for married couples with children was 6.8 percent. Being raised in a married family reduced a child's probability of living in poverty by about 82 percent.

And single motherhood costs this country dearly. In terms of dollars, the Heritage report stated:

In fiscal year 2011, federal and state governments spent over $450 billion on means-tested welfare for low-income families with children. Roughly three-quarters of this welfare assistance, or $330 billion, went to single-parent families. Most nonmarital births are currently paid for by the taxpayers through the Medicaid system, and a wide variety of welfare assistance will continue to be given to the mother and child for nearly two decades after the child is born. On average, the means-tested welfare costs for single parents with children amount to around $30,000 per household per year.

And that's just a part of the "economic costs." There are other heavy costs.

Studies have shown that 63 percent of youth suicides are from fatherless homes, as are 90 percent of all homeless and runaway children, 85 percent of all children that exhibit behavioral disorders, 80 percent of rapists motivated with displaced anger, and 85 percent of youths in prison. As well, single parenting results in a lower likelihood of graduating from high school for kids.

And women, who are already more inclined to abuse their children than are men, become more likely to abuse their children when they have a heavier "parenting and housework load." Even when the children of single-mother homes do have a man in the picture, it's not all good. According to the U.S. Department of Health and Human Services' Administration for Children and Families, "Unrelated male figures and stepfathers in households tend to be more abusive than biological, married fathers." The report specifically says:

Children who live in father-absent homes often face higher risks of physical abuse, sexual abuse, and neglect than children who live with their fathers. A 1997 Federal study indicated that the overall rate of child maltreatment among single-parent families was almost double that of the rate among two-parent families: 27.4 children per thousand were maltreated in single-parent families, compared to 15.5 per thousand in two-parent families. One national study found that 7 percent of children who had lived with one parent had ever been sexually abused, compared to 4 percent of children who lived with both biological parents.

And the wounds from maltreatment run deep. Remuda Ranch, which bills itself as "the nation's leading eating disorder treatment center," said that "more than 50 percent of its patients have experienced trauma in their lives. The trauma is usually sexual, physical and emotional abuse." It added: "Forty-nine percent of our patients have experienced childhood sexual abuse."

Remuda gave a brief explanation of how eating disorders may be generated from abuse:

Research has shown that childhood sexual abuse increases binge-eating, purging, restricting calories, body shame and body dissatisfaction. Eating disorders become a way of helping victims cope with shame. They feel they may need to modify their body in ways that reduce shame or distress. For example, a woman suffering from trauma and an eating disorder may wish to reduce her breast size in order to appear less feminine and therefore, less appealing to men because of her past history of abuse.

A girl named Kacy at Pandora's Project, a resource for victims of rape and sexual abuse, related the story of her abuse:

About twice a year my family would fly out to where my grandparents lived. Thats how my young life started, being violently raped and abused over and over again [by my grandfather]. And thats how the sexual abuse continued throughout my entire childhood.

When I reached 9th grade, I was sent away to an all girls boarding school. I had been in and out of schools every year of high school and when I was in 11th grade (in yet again, a new school) thats where I met perp #2. She was my teacher, and I confided in her, the secret that I had been holding in all those years. She responded with kindness and compassion. But soon after, she went on to take advantage of my vulnerability, and continued the horrid pattern that my life had claimed. She would crawl into my bed at night and exploit and shatter whatever human part of me my grandfather had left behind. She stole any innocence that had been forgotten, she tore me apart once again—leaving me more broken than I had ever been.

The next two years went by, filled with numbness and unbearable pain. Filled with emotions I had never known existed. Filled with an emptiness that was so hollow, I was a walking dead person. The endless amount of sleepless nights became a ritual in my twisted schedule. The daily confusion and absolute loss that consumed me is indescribable. This torturous hell was my life as I had come to know it.

Porn's Part

Sadly, according to Dr. Laura Berman, "up to one-third of the sexual abuse in this country is committed by minors. (It is worth noting that while a small percentage of those who are sexually abused become abusers, almost all child abusers—adult or otherwise—are victims of sexual abuse)." And for this, pornography—another segment of the "sexual freedom" mantra—can be partially blamed.

An article entitled "Children as Victims," about the effect of porn on children, reported the following statistic: "A Los Angeles Police Department study of every child molestation case referred to them over a ten-year period, found that in 60% of the cases adult or child pornography was used to lower the inhibitions of the children molested and/or to excite and sexually arouse the pedophile." Also, "87% of convicted molesters of girls and 77% of convicted molesters of boys admit to using pornography, most often in the commission of their crimes." Let's not forget that, as Massachusetts U.S. Attorney Carmen Diaz said in an AP article, demand for child porn—images and videos of children being "raped by adults"—is increasing rapidly, and increasing numbers of children are abused to satisfy the demand: "This demand leads to the abuse of children, yet there is this misconception that somehow, viewing child pornography is a victimless crime." Diaz prosecuted one member of a global child porn ring, a ring in which the members had hundreds of thousands of images on their computers of children being abused.

Many users of porn would likely dismiss its use as innocuous, but the preponderance of evidence shows that it has a cost far beyond its huge—but unknowable—dollar costs. (The most popular "adult website" on the Web gets "32 million visitors a month, or almost 2.5% of all Internet users!" according to a *Forbes* interview of scientists who crunched the numbers.) Not only do children act out things they see during porn viewing, even committing rape, but, according to psychologist Steve

Livingston, porn may similarly affect "vulnerable" adults by "strengthen[ing] existing violent proclivities." Moreover, he added, experts haven't yet investigated whether there are ties between jurors using porn and the likelihood they'll convict rapists.

Additionally, porn has the same addicting physiological effects as gambling; it causes men to desire more and more graphic sexual imagery to remain stimulated; it causes men to objectify women and see them merely as sperm receptacles; and it causes men and women to have problems with emotional intimacy. According to a news release entitled "Internet Porn Ruining Male-Female Relationships, Studies Show" for Jim Wysong, the author of *The Neutering of the American Male*, "In a 20,000-person study recently conducted by TED.com [a website containing "remarkable" speeches], porn is the most prevalently cited obstacle for romantic relationships between men and women in their teens and 20s. Women say guys are emotionally unavailable, and men say porn makes them less interested in pursuing a relationship."

One woman told about her porn experience with the man in her life:

My ex told me that he knew porn was an "addiction" for him. He used that term, and he said he wanted to stop and that because he couldn't porn had "ruined his life." He also showed me a scar from [performing a sex act] to the point of bleeding because he was unable to stop.

He said porn made him want to cheat all the time, and made him constantly fantasize about "nasty" sex with strangers, and young (teen) girls. . . . He would become agitated, irritable and mean when he could not look at porn because I was home, and he would become so angry and abusive due to frustration that I would unwittingly give him what he wanted by leaving. He would also abandon me places and run home and get online.

And porn has other, even more dramatic, effects: It causes men both to instigate sex that is actually physically painful to the woman and to even completely lose the ability to have sex with an actual woman. Sex, for a heavy porn user, often becomes reduced to self-stimulation while watching pornographic videos.

And that's what some people call sexual freedom.

Sex and Security

The problems with porn and a lack of sexual restraint are societal and, believe it or not, actually even have a negative effect on U.S. national defense and crime-fighting. During the Cold War with Russia, it was common to hear of diplomats and military personnel turning traitor through a "honeytrap"—an intelligence operative using sex. Even now weak willpower and sex could easily lead to secrets being leaked. In recent months, nine Secret Service agents responsible for protecting the president were forced out of their positions after they engaged in liaisons with prostitutes while doing advanced work for the president's trip to Colombia; four-star general and director of the CIA David Petreaus admitted to having an extramarital affair with a woman named Paula Broadwell and resigned; presidential candidates Newt Gingrich, John Edwards, and Herman Cain were involved in trysts with women who were not their wives; and Bill Clinton had a sexual encounter with Monica Lewinsky in the White House. Who knows what deals these men were willing to make—or did make—to protect their prestige and not get exposed diddling around. Meanwhile, last July the Pentagon's Missile Defense Agency had to warn its staff not to watch porn on U.S. government computers. (Gee, I wonder if computer viruses embedded in porn videos could allow hackers to gain access to government computers?)

Dangers and crimes that threaten U.S. citizens have been allowed to slide because of sexual obsessions: Dozens of members of the Securities and Exchange Commission, tasked with monitoring the country's financial system, watched porn at work—for up to eight hours a day—instead of responding to credible, repeated accusations against Bernie Madoff, who was eventually caught running a $50 billion Ponzi scheme.

The list of problems and costs associated with the free-sex mantra go on and on. Not covered here are its implications for abortion, sex trafficking, and drug and alcohol use, among others.

In response to the weighty evidence aligned against them, the best libertines could do in the way of defense of their ideology—the best defense I could find—came from a young woman writing for Salon.com in an article entitled "In defense of casual sex." She claims that numerous sexual exploits "lead to better adult relationships." She believes that it's good to try "on different men to see how they fit." Women are "romantically vetting—and being vetted. . . . Hopefully, by taking several test-drives before buying, we'll be happier with our final investment." (And as a feminist she likes "empowerment," "respect," and "choice"—meaning she wants to do what she feels, whenever she feels.)

Of course, studies don't back her up (and it *is* possible to vet possible spouses without having sex), but there it is.

U.S. Representative Joe Pitts (R-Pa.) makes a good point about the propensity of schools—and others—to promote sexual freedom:

How would it look if the federal government took the same approach to reducing teenage drinking that it takes to reducing teenage pregnancies? . . . School programs would teach teens how to drink, but also encourage them to use good judgment through messages like: "Wait until you know you are ready before you have your first drink." . . . They would be told: "The only one who can decide when you are ready to drink is you."

Knowing what we know about teenagers and their ability to assess risk and act accordingly, this sort of approach sounds ludicrous. Nevertheless, that's precisely the approach we've been taking to sex ed for decades. . . . We do it right in other areas. Teens are simply told "no" when it comes to other risky activities like smoking, drinking, and driving below a certain age.

He added that a government report entitled "A Better Approach to Teenage Pregnancy Prevention: Sexual Risk Avoidance" gave the science fortifying his claims.

Moreover, it seems as if liberals subconsciously acknowledge the damage that's done by their teachings, even as they promulgate their views: In so-called sex-ed classes, students learn little about STDs (except perhaps HIV/AIDS), according to a study reported on by ScienceDaily, even though additional details go a long way toward keeping youth abstinent.

In a sense liberals are correct: Sex *is* just another physical activity that people do—such as eating, sleeping, and exercising—but it is also much more than that. It changes behavior, moods, attitudes, views of self-worth, moral constraints, and more, and so-called free sex is nowhere near being "free." It imposes heavy costs on both individuals and society, and the chance that anyone who participates in the free-sex lifestyle—or their children—will remain unscathed is low.

Since this information is not hard to find, any individual or organization that takes a public position pushing a free-sex ideology goes far beyond the point of being simply ignorant to being brainwashed, stupid, depraved, or in serious denial. Where do you stand on the issue?

Critical Thinking

1. What are the health and social risks associated with promiscuous sex?
2. What types of organisms can cause sexually transmitted diseases?

Create Central

www.mhhe.com/createcentral

Internet References

National Institute of Allergy and Infectious Diseases (NIAID)
www3.niaid.nih.gov

Planned Parenthood
www.plannedparenthood.org

Sexuality Information and Education Council of the United States (SIECUS)
www.siecus.org

Article   Prepared by: Eileen Daniel, *SUNY College at Brockport*

The Secret Life of Dirt

At the Finnish-Russian Border, Scientists Investigate a Medical Mystery

ANDREW CURRY

Learning Outcomes

After reading this article, you will be able to:

- Understand why exposure to dirt in childhood may lead to lower rates of certain diseases.

- Describe why allergies are less common in areas that resemble a "pre-hygiene" past.

- Explain the relationship between exposure to dirt and the risk of childhood diabetes.

After eight hours in an overheated Soviet-era sleeper car, we pull into the Petrozavodsk train station just after 1 A.M. The streets are silent, the night air chilly. Our taxi shudders and swerves along roads pitted with axle-gulping potholes. Identical concrete apartment blocks built in the 1960s flash by in a blur. Winter temperatures here, some 250 miles northeast of St. Petersburg, sometimes plunge to minus 40 degrees Fahrenheit. A traffic circle in the middle of town boasts what locals claim is Russia's only statue of Lenin holding a fur hat.

I'm traveling with Mikael Knip, a short, energetic Finnish physician and University of Helsinki researcher with a perpetual smile under his bushy mustache. He has come to Petrozavodsk—an impoverished Russian city of 270,000 on the shores of Lake Onega and the capital of the Republic of Karelia—to solve a medical mystery, and perhaps help explain a scourge increasingly afflicting the developed world, the United States included.

For reasons that no one has been able to identify, Finland has the world's highest rate of Type 1 diabetes among children.

Out of every 100,000 Finnish kids, 64 are diagnosed annually with the disease, in which the body's immune system declares war on the cells that produce insulin. Type 1 diabetes is usually diagnosed in children, adolescents, and young adults.

The disease rate wasn't always so high. In the 1950s, Finland had less than a quarter of the Type 1 diabetes it has today. Over the past half-century, much of the industrialized world has also seen a proliferation of the once rare disease, along with other autoimmune disorders such as rheumatoid arthritis and celiac disease. Meanwhile, such afflictions remain relatively rare in poorer, less-developed nations.

Why?

Petrozavodsk, only about 175 miles from the Finland border, may be the perfect place to investigate the question: The rate of childhood Type 1 diabetes in Russian Karelia is one-sixth that of Finland. That stark difference intrigues Knip and others because the two populations for the most part are genetically similar, even sharing risk factors for Type 1 diabetes. They also live in the same subarctic environment of pine forests and pristine lakes, dark, bitter winters, and long summer days. Still, the 500-mile boundary between Finland and this Russian republic marks one of the steepest standard-of-living gradients in the world: Finns are seven times richer than their neighbors across the border. "The difference is even greater than between Mexico and the U.S.," Knip tells me.

Since 2008, Knip and his colleagues have collected tens of thousands of tissue samples from babies and young children in Russia and Finland, as well as in nearby Estonia. In his spotless lab on the fourth floor of a modern research complex in Helsinki, nearly two dozen freezers are filled with bar-coded vials of, among other things, umbilical cord blood, stool samples, and nasal swabs. The freezers also hold tap water and dust collected at the different locations. By comparing the samples, Knip hopes to isolate what's driving Finland's diabetes rate up—or what's keeping Russian Karelia's low.

For all the sophisticated analysis involved, the theory that Knip is testing couldn't be more basic. He thinks the key difference between the two populations is . . . dirt. In a sense, he wonders if kids in Finland, and in the United States and other developed nations as well, are too clean for their own good.

The idea that dirt, or the lack of it, might play a role in autoimmune disease and allergy gained support along another border. In the late 1980s, Erika von Mutius was studying asthma in and around Munich. At the time, researchers thought air pollution was the cause. But after years of work, the young German researcher couldn't clearly link Munich's pollution and respiratory disease.

On November 9, 1989, an unusual opportunity came along: The Berlin Wall fell. For the first time since the 1940s, West Germans could conduct research in the East. Von Mutius, of Ludwig-Maximilians University Munich, seized the opportunity, expanding her study to include Leipzig, a city of 520,000 deep in East Germany.

The countryside around Leipzig was home to polluting chemical plants and was pocked with open-pit coal mines; many residents heated their apartments with coal-burning ovens. It was a perfect experiment: two groups of children with similar genetic backgrounds, divided by the Iron Curtain into dramatically different environments. If air pollution caused asthma, Leipzig's kids should be off the charts.

Working with local doctors, von Mutius studied hundreds of East German schoolchildren. "The results were a complete surprise," von Mutius says. "In fact, at first we thought we should re-enter the data." Young Leipzigers had slightly lower rates of asthma than their Bavarian counterparts—and dramatically less hay fever, a pollen allergy.

Puzzling over her results, von Mutius came across a paper by David Strachan, a British physician who had examined the medical records of 17,000 British children for clues to what caused allergies later in life. Strachan found that kids with a lot of older brothers and sisters had lower rates of hay fever and eczema, probably because the siblings brought home colds, flus, and other germs.

After learning of Strachan's study, von Mutius wondered whether air pollution might somehow protect East Germans from respiratory allergies.

Soon, studies from around the world showed similarly surprising results. But it was germ-laden dirt that seemed to matter, not air pollution. The children of full-time farmers in rural Switzerland and Bavaria, for example, had far fewer allergies than their non-farming peers. And a study following more than 1,000 babies in Arizona showed that, unless parents also had asthma, living in houses with dogs reduced the chances of

wheezing and allergies later in life. Researchers proposed that the more microbial agents that children are exposed to early in life, the less likely they are to develop allergies and autoimmune diseases later on. Studies also showed that baby mice kept in sterile environments were more likely to face autoimmune disease, seeming to back what came to be called the "hygiene hypothesis."

"It was so unexpected," says von Mutius, who now believes air pollution was a red herring. Instead, East German children may have benefited from time spent in daycare.

Think about it this way: At birth, our immune cells make up an aggressive army with no sense of who its enemies are. But the more bad guys the immune system is exposed to during life's early years, the more discerning it gets. "The immune system is programmed within the first two years of life," says Knip. "With less early infection, the immune system has too little to do, so it starts looking for other targets."

Sometimes the immune system overreacts to things it should simply ignore, like cat dander, eggs, peanuts, or pollen. Those are allergies. And sometimes the immune system turns on the body itself, attacking the cells we need to produce insulin (Type 1 diabetes) or hair follicles (alopecia) or even targeting the central nervous system (multiple sclerosis). Those are autoimmune disorders.

Both appear to be mostly modern phenomena. A century ago, more people lived on farms or in the countryside. Antibiotics hadn't been invented yet. Families were larger, and children spent more time outside. Water came straight from wells, lakes, and rivers. Kids running barefoot picked up parasites like hookworms. All these circumstances gave young immune systems a workout, keeping allergy and autoimmune diseases at bay.

In places where living conditions resemble this "prehygiene" past-rural parts of Africa, South America, and Asia—the disorders remain uncommon. It can be tempting to dismiss the differences as genetic. But disease rates in the industrialized world have risen too fast, up to 3 or 4 percent a year in recent decades, to be explained by evolutionary changes in DNA "You can see quite clearly in a pre-hygiene situation you don't see allergic disease," says Thomas Platts-Mills, an allergy specialist at the University of Virginia. "Move to a hygiene society, and it does not matter your race or ethnicity—allergy rises."

These findings don't mean that people should eschew basic hygiene. Its benefits are clear: In the past 60 years or so, our overall life expectancy has continued to rise. The trick for scientists is to determine exactly which early life exposures to germs might matter and identify the biology behind their potentially protective effect.

That's one big way Knip's research on the Finland-Russia border can contribute. The accident of geography and history playing out there offers a chance to work in what Knip calls a "living laboratory."

"It's really an exciting opportunity," says Richard Insel, chief scientific officer for the New York City-based Juvenile Diabetes Research Foundation.

Just a few hours after we arrive in Petrozavodsk, I follow Knip and his team to a morning meeting at the Karelian Ministry of Health. Russian officials on the other side of a long conference table explain through an interpreter that they haven't recruited as many study participants as their Finnish and Estonian colleagues. Parents in Petrozavodsk are unfamiliar with the practice of conducting medical studies, reluctant to submit their babies to what they see as painful blood tests and too stressed to fill out long surveys on diet and family history.

If Knip is frustrated, he hides it well. The recruitment phase of the study was supposed to end in 2012. He's trying to buy his Russian colleagues another year to conduct their work, he says, smiling and shaking hands before heading to a taxi waiting outside. "It's turned out to be a lot more complicated than we expected," Knip tells me later. "Cultural differences have been a big learning process for us."

The next stop is Petrozavodsk Children's Hospital, a building on the city's outskirts surrounded by concrete apartments. While Knip gives a pep talk to pediatricians charged with gathering study samples, I sit down with Tatyana Varlamova, a young doctor in a thigh-length white lab coat and black pumps. Varlamova's drab exam room is a world away from Knip's gleaming lab in Helsinki. It's equipped with a plug-in space heater and particleboard desk. Wilted potted plants sit next to an open window. In a long corridor outside are wood benches filled with exhausted-looking parents and children edging toward tears.

Varlamova is clear-eyed about the differences between Russian Karelia and Finland. "Karelia is poorer," she says, "there's no hysterical cleaning of apartments and a lot more physical activity."

Conducting the study in Russia has been a struggle, she says. While extra attention from doctors encourages Finnish and Estonian parents to participate, that's not the case in Russia. Babies here are already required to visit a pediatrician once a month in the first year of life, more often than in Finland. Enrolling young children has also been challenging. Since 2008, doctors have seen 1,575 children in Es-poo, a suburb of Helsinki; 1,681 have been sampled in Estonia, where the diabetes rate falls between that of Finland and of Russian Karelia. But after three years, researchers had recruited only 320 Russian children.

"People don't need more time with the doctor," Varlamova tells me softly in Russian. "They're not as motivated to take part in scientific investigations. They have more important problems in their life."

Then there's the Russian bureaucracy. All the samples taken for the study have to be analyzed in the same Finnish lab for consistency. But just as Knip's study was taking shape, Russian legislators passed a law requiring special permission to export human tissue samples. (Some lawmakers argued that foreigners might use the samples to develop biological weapons targeting Russians.) As a result, Varlamova explains, thousands of study samples from Petrozavodsk had to be individually reviewed by three ministries, including the dauntingly named Federal Agency for the Legal Protection of Military, Special, and Dual-Use Intellectual Property, before being exported. Finally, though, samples going all the way back to 2008 and filling two industrial freezers crossed the border into Finland last December, along with a 30-pound stack of paperwork.

Early results are pointing to different immune system challenges during infancy in the study regions. Russian children, Knip says, spend the first years of their lives fighting off a host of infections virtually unknown in Finland. The Russian kids, as other studies have shown, have signs of regular exposure to hepatitis A, the parasite Toxoplasma gondii and the stomach bug Helicobacter pylori. "Helicobacter pylori antibodies are 15 times more common in children in Russian Karelia than in Finland," says Knip. "We did expect more microbial infections. But we didn't expect such a huge difference."

Identifying important differences may lead to a Type 1 diabetes prevention strategy, for kids in Finland and the rest of the developed world. "If one could identify specific microbes, you'd have to consider whether you could expose children—in a safe way—to those microbes," Knip says.

Such an intervention could prime the immune system much like a vaccine but might use a collection of bacteria rather than a specific microbe.

Knip's in a hurry to find out: Living laboratories don't last forever. Von Mutius, for her part, says she might have missed her chance to prove her hypothesis that crowded daycare centers, not pollution, protected kids in East Germany. Leipzig's coal pits have been flooded and turned into lakes ringed with beaches and bike paths. "We cannot go back—the East and West German phenomenon will remain an enigma," von Mutius says.

In Russia, Karelia's living standards, though they lag behind those in the most developed nations, have been rising slowly—alongside cases of Type 1 diabetes, celiac disease, hay fever, and asthma.

If Knip and his team can identify the culprits soon enough, perhaps Karelia, and other developing regions, can enjoy the upsides of modernity without some of the disorders that have accompanied economic advancement elsewhere in the world.

Kids with a lot of older brothers and sisters had lower rates of hay fever and eczema, probably because the siblings brought home colds, flus, and other germs.

Sometimes, the immune system overreacts to things that it should simply ignore, like cat dander, eggs, peanuts, or pollen. And sometimes the immune system turns on the body itself.

"People don't need more time with the doctor. They're not as motivated to take part in scientific investigations. They have more important problems in their life."

A poorly trained immune system may overreact to allergens such as pollen.

Critical Thinking

1. Because better hygiene has improved health overall, why should we consider increasing exposure to dirt?
2. In what ways does the immune system respond to dirt and microbes in childhood?

Create Central

www.mhhe.com/createcentral

Internet References

American Academy of Allergy, Asthma, and Immunology
http://www.aaaai.org/conditions-and-treatments/allergies.aspx

National Institutes of Health
http://www.ncbi.nlm.nih.gov/pubmed/15167035

Andrew Curry, "The Secret Life of Dirt: At the Finnish-Russian Border, Scientists Investigate a Medical Mystery" from *Smithsonian* (April 2013): 40–45.

Article   Prepared by: Eileen L. Daniel, *SUNY Brockport*

The Broken Vaccine

Whooping cough is on the rise, exposing a worrisome trend: The vaccine that holds it in check is losing its potency, and nobody is sure why.

MELINDA WENNER MOYER

Learning Outcomes

After reading this article, you will be able to:

- Explain why the pertussis vaccine is losing its effectiveness.
- Describe how the Centers for Disease Control and Prevention tracks outbreaks and epidemics.
- Discuss why there is an increase in the number of pertussis cases in the United States since the 1990s.

Seth Fikkert had a head cold. The 30-year-old worked in a hospital and had two kids, so he didn't think much of it. But after three weeks, he still felt short of breath, and his 2-year-old son was coughing a little, too.

Fikkert, who resembles Jim from the NBC television show *The Office* in both his boyish good looks and his sharp sense of humor (he jokes about the mispronunciations his last name inspires), lived in Everett, Washington, which last summer was in the midst of one of the country's most serious whooping cough epidemics. So he thought it best to get tested.

"I just wanted to rule it out," Fikkert says. He had gotten his adult booster for pertussis, the bacterium that causes whooping cough, only a year before, so it was highly unlikely that he had the infection. On the morning of Thursday, June 28, he walked into the employee health clinic at Providence Regional Medical Center, where he worked, and asked for a test.

The clinic did not take his concern lightly. Fikkert recalls that afterward, "they masked me up, sent me down for a Z-Pak [the antibiotic Zithromax] at the pharmacy, and sent me directly home."

And for good reason: Four days later, Fikkert learned he had tested positive. "It was a huge surprise," he says. His daughter also tested positive; his son tested negative, though if a test is administered more than two weeks after symptoms arise, it may yield a false negative. To keep the infection from spreading, the hospital and the local health department in Snohomish County gave antibiotics to 35 hospital patients and 77 employees that Fikkert had been in close contact with over the 28 days before his diagnosis, despite the fact that almost all of the staff had had boosters.

Before pertussis vaccines came into use in the 1930s, the infection killed about 4,000 Americans (mostly infants) a year—10 times as many as the number of people who died annually from measles and 12 times more than died from smallpox.

Although infection rates dropped dramatically with the vaccine, pertussis has recently returned with dangerous fervor: 2012 was the country's worst year for pertussis since 1959, with more than 38,000 cases reported nationally, 16 deaths of infants and children, and large spikes in every state except California. Most health officials believe that because many cases go undetected, the actual infection numbers are far higher. Pertussis is now considered the most poorly controlled vaccine-preventable bacterial disease in the developed world.

The resurgence is not the fault of parents who haven't immunized their kids. "We don't think those exemptors are driving this current wave," Anne Schuchat, director of the National Center for Immunization and Respiratory Diseases at the Centers for Disease Control and Prevention (CDC), told reporters at a July press briefing.

Indeed, 73 percent of kids aged 7 to 10 who caught pertussis last year in Washington State—where the infection hit particularly hard—had been fully vaccinated. And 81 percent of adolescents had not only had full childhood vaccinations, but also a booster shot.

The problem is the pertussis vaccine itself. In 1992, U.S. doctors began switching to a new formulation with fewer side effects. But the CDC, which monitors infectious disease outbreaks, is learning the hard way that it just doesn't work very well. "It wanes, and it wanes more quickly than we expected," says CDC epidemiologist Stacey Martin. Scientists are trying hard to find out why.

In the meantime, more than 228 million Americans—some kids and teens, as well as most adults—think that they are protected from whooping cough, but they are not.

Pertussis is caused by *bordetella pertussis,* a bacterium that has been around for at least 400 years. The microbes attach to tiny, hairlike structures in the lungs and release toxins that cause a terrible and persistent cough. Every outburst projects live bacteria into the air, and anyone within three feet can breathe them in and become infected.

Often the relentless hacking causes people to throw up, or to have so much trouble catching their breath that they make a "whooping" sound while inhaling. Antibiotics stop a person from being contagious but do not always ease symptoms.

Babies younger than 3 months are particularly vulnerable. They can suffocate because of the cough, and since their immune systems are undeveloped, their white blood cells can spike so high that they literally clog the veins, obstructing blood flow and causing cardiovascular problems. Babies get their first pertussis vaccine at 2 months, but it provides only a small amount of protection.

Prior to 1992, children in the United States were inoculated with whole-cell pertussis vaccines, which were made using whole killed bacteria. These were quite effective but often caused side effects like local swelling, fevers, and, in rare instances, neurological problems.

That year, the CDC began recommending a new vaccine that contained two to five proteins isolated from *B. pertussis* rather than the entire bacterium. While these acellular vaccines, as they are called, cause fewer side effects, they do not seem to last very long.

In 2010 California experienced a particularly devastating pertussis outbreak that sickened 9,000 people and killed 10 babies. At the time, David Witt, an infectious disease specialist at Kaiser Permanente Medical Center in San Rafael, assumed that most of the infected kids were unvaccinated; the very first patient he treated, for instance, was from a non-vaccinating family.

To confirm his suspicions, Witt assigned a project to his son, a University of California, Berkeley, public health major who was home for the Christmas holiday: Check the vaccination records of all of the kids the medical center had treated so far that year.

"The original impetus was just to show how virulent an effect not being vaccinated has," Witt explains. Instead, Witt's son found that whooping cough rates were not significantly different in vaccinated, unvaccinated and undervaccinated children between the ages of 8 and 12.

Kids typically finish their initial vaccine series between ages 4 and 6, and the results suggested that protection starts to wane three years later—a big problem, considering that they don't get another shot until they're 11 or 12. "It's awfully worrisome," Witt says.

In November 2012, the CDC announced the results of its own analysis of the California outbreak. The agency found that the vaccine's effectiveness begins to drop after one year, and that five years after the final dose, it provides only 70 percent protection. An Australian study recently reported that kids who were given the acellular vaccine as infants were more than three times as likely to get pertussis between 2009 and 2011 than were those who received the whole-cell version.

No one knows why the acellular vaccine is so ineffective. It exposes the immune system to only a handful of bacterial proteins, and it may be that exposure to more—as occurred when people were inoculated with the whole-cell vaccine—is more powerful. But the CDC's Martin notes that the United States will probably never use the whole cell vaccine again because of concerns about its possible side effects.

Frits Mooi, a molecular microbiologist at the Centre for Infectious Disease Control in the Netherlands, has a controversial theory about the acellular version: The pertussis bacteria may have adapted to it, much like bacteria become resistant to antibiotics.

Mooi sequenced the genomes of today's *B. pertussis* strains and found they have acquired mutations in each of the proteins used to make the acellular vaccines. This means, he says, that our immune systems are being primed to fight an attacker that is slightly different from what they actually encounter. While Martin agrees that the vaccine does not precisely match today's circulating strains, she says it is unclear whether this mismatch is actually causing the observed vaccine failure.

Jean Zahalka, a soft-spoken public health nurse with shortly cropped gray hair, sat in a small office at the headquarters of the Snohomish Health District, conducting a phone interview with the mother of a 7-month-old baby who had just been diagnosed with whooping cough.

Luckily, the little boy didn't attend daycare, which meant that he hadn't had many opportunities to infect others. And despite his persistent cough, he was holding up well, possibly because he'd already had two doses of DTaP, the childhood vaccine for diphtheria, tetanus, and pertussis.

But then the mom told Zahalka that the boy's 3-year-old sister was also coughing. Zahalka winced. Next, it came to light that the mother's 14-year-old niece had spent three days with the family earlier that week, which meant she was probably infected as well. The niece's mother had just lost her job and could not afford to buy antibiotics, so the health department was going to have to cover the cost of her treatment in order to curb the spread of the infection.

As health departments across the country are coming to learn, it is extremely difficult to monitor and control pertussis outbreaks. For one thing, many cases go undetected. "We're reporting just the tip of the iceberg," says Sandi Paciotti, communicable disease manager at the Skagit County Health Department, which tallied the most pertussis cases in Washington State in 2012. Paciotti estimates that three to five times more people have been infected than are reflected in her official numbers.

One reason is that 15 percent of the Skagit County population is uninsured and unwilling to pay for the $300 test. Teens are another overlooked pertussis reservoir; the director of the Skagit County Health Department, Peter Browning, says his 13-year-old son caught pertussis early in the outbreak, but since he had been immunized, Browning didn't suspect it. "We don't stop loving our kids after age 13, but we don't rush them to the doctor, either," he says.

The vaccine's effectiveness begins to drop after one year. Five years after the final dose, it provides only 70 percent protection.

There are probably also thousands of adults who have suffered through the infection without seeking treatment. Adults who have been vaccinated, like Fikkert, often have milder symptoms, but they are still contagious. Some do go to the doctor but only after they have been sick for several weeks, at which point the test can come back negative even if they had the infection. And some doctors do not even consider pertussis when adults come in complaining of a persistent cough. "They don't think adults can get it," the CDC's Martin says.

With an infection so difficult to control, the best hope is prevention. But a better vaccine may be years, if not decades, away. "We just don't know what we should be targeting," says Martin, pointing out that no one knows what parts of the bacterium should be included in the vaccine to make it more effective.

Scott Halperin, the director of the Canadian Center for Vaccinology in Halifax, believes that changing the immune-boosting chemicals, called adjuvants, in the vaccine could make a difference. Camille Locht, a microbiologist at Inserm and Institut Pasteur de Lille in France, is developing a live vaccine for newborns; he says it could give infants enough protection to survive until they get their childhood series, but so far he has tested the vaccine only in adults.

The CDC began recommending a tetanus, diphtheria, and pertussis (Tdap) booster shot for most people over age 11, including adults up to age 64, in 2005. But as of 2010, only 8 percent of the adult population had actually received one. Moreover, an ongoing CDC investigation suggests that, like the childhood vaccine, the adult Tdap booster lasts only a few years at most.

Yet with the exception of childbearing women, who are advised to get the booster during every pregnancy, Tdap is licensed only for one-time use in adults. "That probably isn't enough," says Amie Tidrington, the immunization clinic manager for the Skagit County Health Department.

Still, it is crucial to vaccinate as many people as possible, says Gary Goldbaum, the health officer of the Snohomish Health District in Everett. Unprotected people are much less likely to encounter the infection if most of the population is protected. Despite a slew of recent funding cuts, Goldbaum's district has held 20 vaccination clinics since the outbreaks started.

Last spring the American Congress of Obstetricians and Gynecologists sent pertussis information packets to more than 33,000 of its members to increase awareness among doctors, and a joint program between the AmeriCares charity and pharmaceutical company Sanofi-Pasteur has given more than 117,000 free Tdap booster shots to health clinics around the country to immunize uninsured, low-income families. "If we are serious about trying to protect the most vulnerable," Goldbaum says, "the rest of us have to be fully protected too."

Critical Thinking

1. Why is the number of cases of pertussis increasing?
2. How does the Centers for Disease Control and Prevention track disease outbreaks and epidemics?

Create Central

www.mhhe.com/createcentral

Internet References

Centers for Disease Control and Prevention
cdc.gov
National Institute of Allergy and Infectious Diseases (NIAID)
www3.niaid.nih.gov

Unit 8

UNIT

Prepared by: Eileen Daniel, *SUNY College at Brockport*

Health Care and the Health Care System

Americans are healthier today than they have been at any time in this nation's history. Americans suffer more illness today than they have at any time in this nation's history. Which statement is true? They both are, depending on the statistics you quote. According to longevity statistics, Americans are living longer today and, therefore, must be healthier. Still, other statistics indicate that Americans today report twice as many acute illnesses as did our ancestors 60 years ago. They also report that their pain lasts longer. Unfortunately, this combination of living longer and feeling sicker places additional demands on a health-care system that, according to experts, is already in a state of crisis.

Despite the clamor about the problems with our health-care system, if you can afford it, then the American health-care system is one of the best in the world. However, being the best does not mean that it is without problems. Each year, more than half a million Americans are injured or die due to preventable mistakes made by medical-care professionals. In addition, countless unnecessary tests are preformed that not only add to the expense of health care but may actually place the patient at risk. Reports such as these fuel the fire of public skepticism toward the quality of health care that Americans receive. While these aspects of our health-care system indicate a need for repair, they represent just the tip of the iceberg. Despite the implementation of the Affordable Care Act (Obama care), there are calls for the government to develop a better universal system that covers all. Many believe that universal coverage will not only insure all Americans but it will also help to reduce the cost of health care. A number of Americans also believe that costs continue to rise due to the blockage of price controls by the pharmaceutical industry. Laws that affect the way health care is provided and fewer regulations that impact market forces might reduce the overall cost of medical care and medications. While choices in health-care providers are increasing, paying for services continues to be a challenge as medical costs continue to rise. In addition, it appears that the uninsured have more health risks because they're more likely to be poor, smokers, less educated, obese, and unemployed.

Why have health-care costs risen so much? The answer to this question is multifaceted and includes such factors as physicians' fees, hospital costs, insurance costs, pharmaceutical costs, and health fraud. It could be argued that while these factors operate within any health-care system, the lack of a meaningful form of outcomes assessment has permitted and encouraged waste and inefficiency within our system. Ironically, one of the major factors for the rise in the cost of health care is our rapidly expanding aging population—tangible evidence of an improving health-care delivery system. This is obviously one factor that we hope will continue to rise. Another significant factor that is often overlooked is the constantly expanding boundaries of health care. It is somewhat ironic that as our success in treating various disorders has expanded, so has the domain of health care, often into areas where previously health care had little or no involvement.

Traditionally, Americans have felt that the state of their health was largely determined by the quality of the health care available to them. This attitude has fostered an unhealthy dependence upon the health-care system and contributed to the skyrocketing costs. It should be obvious by now that while there is no simple solution to our health-care problems, we would all be a lot better off if we accepted more personal responsibility for our health. While this shift would help ease the financial burden of health care, it might necessitate a more responsible coverage of medical news in order to educate and enlighten the public on personal health issues.

Article

Prepared by: Eileen L. Daniel, *SUNY Brockport*

Deviated: A Memoir

A cautionary tale from the brave new world of health-care coverage

JESSE KELLERMAN

Learning Outcomes

After reading this article, you will be able to:

- Explain an insurance company's rationale for denying coverage based on a preexisting condition.

- Describe symptoms of a nasal deviated septum.

- Describe why surgery was required by the insurance company before issuing a policy.

Aside from a brief stint as a writing tutor during graduate school, I have managed to avoid respectable employment all my adult life. There was a time, after I earned my graduate degree and before I sold my first novel, when it looked like I might have to get an office job. I remember one interview with one stultifying prospective boss; it took him a half hour to describe the important tasks I would be called upon to perform, such as licking envelopes—a half hour I spent steadily withdrawing into a cocoon of self-pity, so that when he finally paused to ask if I was up for the challenge, I said, "Huh?" and wasn't called back.

I don't take my self-employment for granted. I commute 30 feet. I have the privilege to spend a great amount of time watching my son grow up. I have access to a supply of snacks rivaling that of a Silicon Valley start-up circa 1997. Still, there are drawbacks, most of them courtesy of the federal government. Some are minor, like having to pay estimated quarterly taxes, which for a writer with multiple contracts coming due at unpredictable times is a bewildering process akin to picking the next eight winners of the Kentucky Derby. More painfully, I am subject to the full amount of Medicare and Social Security tax, a burden more often shared with one's employer.

Until recently, though, I had never given much thought to one of the clearest benefits forfeited by the self-employed: simplified access to health insurance. I'd never given it much thought because for years I'd been covered by my wife's policy. Then she left her hospital job to work at home, and both of us were self-employed. The law entitled us to extend her coverage for an additional 18 months at the same rate paid by her former employer. After that, we knew, we were on our own. As a deadline, it seemed very abstract, and very far away. I don't remember hearing a ticking clock, anyway. Today I look back and speculate that its sound was smothered by red tape.

With our extension used up, we sat down to begin the paperwork. By *we*, I mean my wife, who took it upon herself to price out every plan under the California sun. Numbers were crunched, contingencies planned for. In the end we decided to reapply for coverage with the same provider. On some level, we had the idea that this would simplify things.

All was in *Ordnung,* or so it seemed, until the day we opened the mailbox to find a big fat envelope waiting for us. We tore it open like excited high schoolers awaiting SAT scores and unfolded the pages in search of our little plastic cards, the ones that would entitle us to stand before the gum-chewing receptionists at our local internal medicine clinic and declare, "Behold, I am a member of the working world, gainfully self-employed and nominally self-sufficient, evinced by the way I wield this card plus a $40 office visit co-pay."

There weren't any cards.

There was, rather, a lot of tiny black type.

"I'm approved," my wife said, squinting to read. "The baby's approved."

She frowned.

"You've been declined," she said.

I chuckled, mentally. Declined? Impossible. I was a healthy 33-year-old man with an unremarkable medical history. I took no medications other than the odd Claritin or Advil. I'd never broken a bone. I'd never had a hospital stay. At 17 I'd had my one and only surgery, performed under local anaesthetic, to remove a benign bone spur in my toe. I ate well. I exercised daily. And talk about blood work—oh, my blood work! It runs in the family. Many of my forebears on both sides lived well into their 90s. My 89-year-old grandmother recently complained to me that she can no longer play mah-jongg because "all my girls are dead." My 92-year-old grandmother does Israeli dance with a group of women half her age. Like my mother, who has a rare and beneficent gene variant, I have more good cholesterol than bad. A high triglyceride level is 200; 150–199 is borderline; lower than 150 is considered normal. Mine: 15.

"It's about your nose," my wife said, turning pages.

I instantly suspected anti-Semitism. "What about it?"

She showed me the page. In the interest of full disclosure, I suppose I ought to revise the rosy medical self-portrait a tad. One thing I have endured, from about fourth grade on, is insomnia. It gets better or worse depending on my stress level, and even when I do manage to fall asleep, I tend to wake up every three hours. The year that I spent abroad prior to college, learning in an Israeli yeshiva, was probably the roughest I ever had, sleepwise. At least once a week I was up all night, with the result that I rarely attended the regular 7 a.m. prayer service. Either I waited for the sunrise minyan, or I skipped services entirely and slept in. When I started writing full time, I embraced my inner night owl, often working until two or three in the morning and sleeping until nine.

A sour man with a badly patterned tie, Dr. K. regarded me distastefully from behind thick aviator glasses. He asked me what I did. I told him I wrote novels.

The arrival of my son forced me to get on his schedule. I could never quite manage it, though, and long after he had learned to sleep through the night, I would still spend hours at a stretch tossing and turning. Concerned that I might have apnea, I made an appointment with an ear-nose-and-throat man, whom I'll call Dr. K. I chose him because the practice he belonged to told me he had the first available opening. I've since learned that the person with the first available opening is seldom the person you want to see.

A sour man with a badly patterned necktie, he regarded me distastefully from behind thick aviator glasses. He asked me what I did. I told him I wrote novels. He asked if he had heard of any of them. I told him probably not. Then he shoved a wad of cotton soaked in topical anaesthetic up my nose. There was nothing gentle about the way he did this. Indeed, it seemed to be something of a game to him: *How much can I cram in there?* I shudder to imagine what the inside of his garage looks like. The anaesthetic still hadn't taken effect when he yanked the cotton out and impaled my face on a plastic scope. I gagged and choked. "Sorry," he said, smiling faintly. I tried to hold still while he rooted around up there, sighing and saying things like "hmm" and "yup." Finally he pointed to the live feed of my sinuses on the screen and turned to the terrified medical student standing in the corner, her notebook at the ready.

"Deviated septum," he said to her. She wrote it down. Then he flashed me a Bond villain smile. "*Severe.*"

I had three options. The first was a course of nasal steroids to reduce the swelling, although Dr. K. made it clear that this was a giant waste of time, strictly a formality to secure permission from my insurance company to proceed to option two: corrective surgery.

"What's option three?" I asked.

"You could try those little plastic thingies," he said, stroking the bridge of his nose. I couldn't afford to be laid out for a week

or more. I had a novel to write and a toddler to manage. I said I'd give the plastic thingies a shot. I could tell he was disappointed. "Suit yourself," he said, walking away to dictate his note into a pocket recorder.

My first few nights wearing Breathe Right Nasal Strips weren't all that different. Then I discovered that I had accidentally purchased the wrong size, the large ones, "for adults with larger noses." (Self-anti-Semitism?) Once I got hold of the small/mediums, my life literally changed overnight. For the first time in 20 years I slept seven straight hours. I called Dr. K.'s office and left a message saying I had the problem under control. And I did. The only apparent downside was that I developed, over the next few months, a semi-permanent red stripe across the bridge of my nose where the adhesive attached. It seemed a small price to pay. Every morning my wife would look at me and say, in the Jamaican accent of the guy from the beer commercials, "Reeeed Stripe."

We laughed the laugh of the young and able-bodied.

Back to the letter. "'Health history,'" my wife read. "'Deviated septum, surgery recommended. Should Jesse Kellerman wish reconsideration of our underwriting decision, he must, one, be sign-, symptom-, and treatment-free from the deviated septum, not a surgical candidate and no symptoms documented by your physician and no further treatment needed, and, two, meet the Medical Underwriting Guidelines in effect at the time of application.'"

It took a hard charge through several layers of voicemail and an hour on hold, but at last I found myself talking to the medical underwriting department.

"It's nice that they're employing the illiterate," I said.

"Here," she said. "Call them."

It took a hard charge through several layers of voicemail and an hour on hold, but at last I found myself talking to the underwriting department.

"You have failed to meet the underwriting criteria," the underwriter said.

"I realize that," I said. "My question is what I can do to qualify."

"You must be sign-, symptom-, and treatment-free—"

"But I *am* sign- and symptom-free. I wear those little plastic thingies. I pay for them myself."

"I understand, sir."

"So what's the problem, then?"

"You must be sign-, symptom-, and treatment-free, and not a surgical candidate, and if you meet the underwriting criteria at the time of application, you may qualify."

"That's what I'm trying to tell you. I feel fine."

"I understand."

"OK, so, just to be clear, here, if I get reevaluated and I'm OK, then I'll qualify."

"You must be—"

"Janet. Janet. Janet. May I call you Janet?"

"Sir."

"Janet, I understand that you have a script to follow. I understand that. I'm just trying to get some information here, like a normal person. And what I'm trying to understand, Janet, is what *else* I have to do to qualify, because, Janet, I *am* sign- and symptom-free."

"I understand that, sir, but until you are no longer a surgical candidate, and until you meet the underwriting criteria, we are declining to offer you coverage."

"My nose is shaped in a certain way. It's not going to change, magically."

"Sir."

"So as long as I have this nose, I'm always going to be a surgical candidate."

"Sir."

"The only way *not* to be a surgical candidate is to have surgery."

"Sir."

"But I don't want surgery. I don't need it. I'm *fine*. Janet, I promise you that I will not have surgery."

"I'm sorry, sir, but we can't offer you coverage based on your promises."

"Okay, well, what can I do to convince you?"

"You must be sign-, symptom-, and treatment-free, and not a surgical candidate, and if you meet the underwriting criteria at the time of application, you may qualify."

I paused. "Let's try another approach here."

"Sir?"

"Right now I'm covered by your company, right?"

"I don't know, sir. Are you?"

"Yes. I am. And I'm reapplying to be covered by your company."

"Sir."

"So you're telling me," I said, "that the only way for me to get new coverage is to no longer be a surgical candidate."

"If you meet the underwriting criteria at the time of application, you will qualify."

"Fine. Got it. So. I have the surgery, and now I meet the underwriting criteria, right?"

"I can't promise you that."

"*I'm not asking you to.*"

"There's no need to yell."

"I'm not asking you to promise me that. I'm asking you, Janet, my love, to follow me, please, down this theoretical path. OK? Let's say I get surgery. And I am no longer a surgical candidate. *And* I meet the underwriting criteria when I reapply. Then what happens?"

"Then you may be eligible for coverage."

"'May?'"

"Yes, sir, you may qualify."

"Okay. I 'may' qualify. Fine. Excellent. Super. Now answer me this. To not be a surgical candidate, I actually have to have this surgery. So let's say I decide to go for it. I'm gonna have this surgery. All right? So. Riddle me this, Janet: *Who's going to pay for it?*"

"I don't know, sir."

"You will. You will, Janet. *You* will pay for it, because you already *are* my insurance provider. Do you see what's

happening here? You're incentivizing me to have an operation, which I neither need nor want, and which *you will pay for,* in order to *avoid* paying for that same operation in the future." I paused. "Janet?"

"Yes, sir," she said. "That sounds about right."

"And that doesn't strike you as odd?"

At last a hint of humanity crept into her voice. "I guess it does, a little."

"Well," I said. "As long as we're clear on that."

I had surgery. I had alternatives, of course. I could have bought into a pre-existing condition plan, or a HIPAA plan, either of which would have covered me and my bent septum. But these plans were extremely expensive, and when we amortized the cost of the operation over a year, it turned out to be cheaper to have it than not, even if I had to pay for it in full.

So, I had surgery.

I didn't go back to Dr. K. First, he creeped me out, and moreover he was booked. Everyone in San Diego was. I had to drive two hours north to Los Angeles to find someone who could operate soon enough for me to recover (and thereby qualify for the underwriting criteria) before our coverage ran out. I chose my parents' ENT. The walls of Dr. R.'s Beverly Hills practice were hung with the gold and platinum albums of pop stars whose nodules he had soothed. He booked me into a surgical center within 48 hours. My mother drove me over at five in the morning. I handed my credit card to a young woman who had no right to look that beautiful at that hour. She ran the card, and I signed for several thousand dollars.

"At least I'll get miles," I told my mother.

The surgery went well, and for the next few days I sat in bed and watched TV. When it came time to remove the packing from my nose, Dr. R. was good enough to come in on a Sunday morning.

The walls of Dr. R.'s practice in Beverly Hills were hung with the gold and platinum albums of pop stars whose nodules he had soothed.

"Don't blow, don't pick, don't futz with it at all," he said. I obeyed. Still, the incision kept on bleeding, so he had me return for a chemical cauterization. I drove back to San Diego with the smell of it in my nostrils. My wife met me at the door, scrutinizing me before she let me back in.

"I'm checking to see if you look different," she said.

"Do I?"

"No."

"Do I sound different?"

"You're bleeding," she said.

I ran to the bathroom. Sure enough, a little ruby droplet had formed near the inside corner of the left nostril—the one Dr. R. had just cauterized.

I called him.

"Don't futz with it," he said.

I didn't futz. Three days later, it was still bleeding.

"Come back in."

I drove to L.A. He cauterized the incision a second time.

"It has to scab and heal," he said. "Don't futz with it."

I drove back to San Diego. I didn't futz. It was hard not to; it itched like hell. And it was still bleeding.

"Come back in."

I got into the car.

An ENT's tools are either extremely sophisticated or else positively medieval, and I had discovered that Dr. R., for all his charm, shared Dr. K.'s enthusiasm for ramming larger-than-reasonable objects in my face. Before cauterizing the incision a third time, he pried the offending nostril open with pliers and gazed contemplatively into my sinuses.

"How's your breathing been?" he said.

"Pretty good," I said.

"Mm." He reached for the cauterization stick. "It's amazing, how the cartilage has a memory. It's curving back a bit. You can breathe, though?"

"Pretty well."

"Well, good enough."

The third cauterization took. The bleeding tapered off, and within a few weeks I was back to blowing my nose like normal. But in the interim, a new problem had arisen: The left nostril had turned shiny and crimson and tender to the touch. "It looks infected," my wife said.

I called my primary-care physician.

"He can see you in February."

"It's May."

"Do you want to see someone else?"

I saw an intern, who looked at my nose and wrote me a prescription for an antibiotic. It didn't work. I called the practice and spoke to a nurse, who told me I needed to come back in.

"I'm pretty sure it's one of those drug-resistant strains," I said. "You can't have them just write me a new prescription?"

"Not without seeing you first."

I went back in. A different intern looked at my nose.

"It's one of those drug-resistant strains," he said, writing me a new prescription.

Twice a day for the next seven days, I swallowed a pill the size of a ping-pong ball. The infection abated, and I stood victorious in front of the mirror, prodding my nose.

My wife entered with a torn envelope. "We've been approved."

"Great," I said. At that moment, it all seemed worth it. To celebrate, I reached for a tissue and blew my nose, expelling a massive quantity of bright red blood.

Eight months later, I've recovered, for the most part. The surgeon was right: Cartilage does have a memory. Every day I feel my septum curve a little bit more as it struggles to regain its original shape. After the surgery, flush with optimism, I threw away all my Breathe Right strips; I have since bought more, for use in the event of a cold or bad allergies, which render my nose just as obstructed as it ever was.

And so, some nights, I lie awake, gasping for air.

Critical Thinking

1. Why does an insurance company have the right to deny coverage based on a pre-existing condition?

2. What symptoms does a deviated septum produce?

Create Central

www.mhhe.com/createcentral

Internet References

American Medical Association (AMA)
www.ama-assn.org

MedScape: The Online Resource for Better Patient Care
www.medscape.com

JESSE KELLERMAN *is the author of four novels, including* The Genius *and, most recently,* The Executor. *His novel* Potboiler *will be published by Putnam in June. His April 2009* Commentary *article, "Let My People Go to the Buffet," was included in* The Best Spiritual Writing 2011.

Article   Prepared by: Eileen L. Daniel, *SUNY Brockport*

How Government Killed the Medical Profession

JEFFREY A. SINGER

Learning Outcomes

After reading this article, you will be able to:

- Explain how hospitals' reimbursements for their Medicare-patient treatments are determined.

- Understand how Diagnosis Related Groups incentivize hospitals to attach multiple codes in order to increase Medicare reimbursement.

- Describe how data accuracy is compromised with the coding system.

I am a general surgeon with more than three decades in private clinical practice. And I am fed up. Since the late 1970s, I have witnessed remarkable technological revolutions in medicine, from CT scans to robot-assisted surgery. But I have also watched as medicine slowly evolved into the domain of technicians, bookkeepers, and clerks.

Government interventions over the past four decades have yielded a cascade of perverse incentives, bureaucratic diktats, and economic pressures that together are forcing doctors to sacrifice their independent professional medical judgment, and their integrity. The consequence is clear: Many doctors from my generation are exiting the field. Others are seeing their private practices threatened with bankruptcy, or are giving up their autonomy for the life of a shift-working hospital employee. Governments and hospital administrators hold all the power, while doctors—and worse still, patients—hold none.

The Coding Revolution

At first, the decay was subtle. In the 1980s, Medicare imposed price controls upon physicians who treated anyone over 65. Any provider wishing to get compensated was required to use International Statistical Classification of Diseases (ICD) and Current Procedural Terminology (CPT) codes to describe the service when submitting a bill. The designers of these systems believed that standardized classifications would lead to more accurate adjudication of Medicare claims.

What it actually did was force doctors to wedge their patients and their services into predetermined, ill-fitting categories. This approach resembled the command-and-control models used in the Soviet bloc and the People's Republic of China, models that were already failing spectacularly by the end of the 1980s.

Before long, these codes were attached to a fee schedule based upon the amount of time a medical professional had to devote to each patient, a concept perilously close to another Marxist relic: the labor theory of value. Named the Resource-Based Relative Value System (RBRVS), each procedure code was assigned a specific value, by a panel of experts, based supposedly upon the amount of time and labor it required. It didn't matter if an operation was being performed by a renowned surgical expert—perhaps the inventor of the procedure—or by a doctor just out of residency doing the operation for the first time. They both got paid the same.

Hospitals' reimbursements for their Medicare-patient treatments were based on another coding system: the Diagnosis Related Group (DRG). Each diagnostic code is assigned a specific monetary value, and the hospital is paid based on one or a combination of diagnostic codes used to describe the reason for a patient's hospitalization. If, say, the diagnosis is pneumonia, then the hospital is given a flat amount for that diagnosis, regardless of the amount of equipment, staffing, and days used to treat a particular patient.

As a result, the hospital is incentivized to attach as many adjunct diagnostic codes as possible to try to increase the Medicare payday. It is common for hospital coders to contact the attending physicians and try to coax them into adding a few more diagnoses into the hospital record.

Medicare has used these two price-setting systems (RBRVS for doctors, DRG for hospitals) to maintain its price control system for more than 20 years. Doctors and their advocacy associations cooperated, trading their professional latitude for the lure of maintaining monopoly control of the ICD and CPT codes that determine their payday. The goal of setting their own prices has proved elusive, though—every year the industry's biggest trade group, the American Medical Association, squabbles with various medical specialty associations and the Centers for Medicare and Medicaid Services (CMS) over fees.

As goes Medicare, so goes the private insurance industry. Insurers, starting in the late 1980s, began the practice of using the Medicare fee schedule to serve as the basis for negotiation of compensation with the doctors and hospitals on their preferred provider lists. An insurance company might offer a hospital 130 percent of Medicare's reimbursement for a specific procedure code, for instance.

The coding system was supposed to improve the accuracy of adjudicating claims submitted by doctors and hospitals to Medicare, and later to non-Medicare insurance companies. Instead, it gave doctors and hospitals an incentive to find ways of describing procedures and services with the cluster of codes that would yield the biggest payment. Sometimes this required the assistance of consulting firms. A cottage industry of fee-maximizing advisors and seminars bloomed.

I recall more than one occasion when I discovered at such a seminar that I was "undercoding" for procedures I routinely perform; a small tweak meant a bigger check for me. That fact encouraged me to keep one eye on the codes at all times, leaving less attention for my patients. Today, most doctors in private practice employ coding specialists, a relatively new occupation, to oversee their billing departments.

Another goal of the coding system was to provide Medicare, regulatory agencies, research organizations, and insurance companies with a standardized method of collecting epidemiological data—the information medical professionals use to track ailments across different regions and populations. However, the developers of the coding system did not anticipate the unintended consequence of linking the laudable goal of epidemiologic data mining with a system of financial reward.

This coding system leads inevitably to distortions in epidemiological data. Because doctors are required to come up with a diagnostic code on each bill submitted in order to get paid, they pick the code that comes closest to describing the patient's problem while yielding maximum remuneration. The same process plays out when it comes to submitting procedure codes on bills. As a result, the accuracy of the data collected since the advent of compensation coding is suspect.

Command and Control

Coding was one of the earliest manifestations of the cancer consuming the medical profession, but the disease is much more broad-based and systemic. The root of the problem is that patients are not payers. Through myriad tax and regulatory policies adopted on the federal and state level, the system rarely sees a direct interaction between a consumer and a provider of a health care good or service. Instead, a third party—either a private insurance company or a government payer, such as Medicare or Medicaid—covers almost all the costs. According to the National Center for Policy Analysis, on average, the consumer pays only 12 percent of the total health care bill directly out of pocket. There is no incentive, through a market system with transparent prices, for either the provider or the consumer to be cost-effective.

As the third party payment system led health care costs to escalate, the people footing the bill have attempted to rein in costs with yet more command-and-control solutions. In the 1990s, private insurance carriers did this through a form of health plan called a health maintenance organization, or HMO. Strict oversight, rationing, and practice protocols were imposed on both physicians and patients. Both groups protested loudly. Eventually, most of these top-down regulations were set aside, and many HMOs were watered down into little more than expensive prepaid health plans.

Then, as the 1990s gave way to the 21st century, demographic reality caught up with Medicare and Medicaid, the two principal drivers of federal health care spending.

Twenty years after the fall of the Iron Curtain, protocols and regimentation were imposed on America's physicians through a centralized bureaucracy. Using so-called "evidence-based medicine," algorithms and protocols were based on statistically generalized, rather than individualized, outcomes in large population groups.

While all physicians appreciate the development of general approaches to the work-up and treatment of various illnesses and disorders, we also realize that everyone is an individual—that every protocol or algorithm is based on the average, typical case. We want to be able to use our knowledge, years of experience, and sometimes even our intuition to deal with each patient as a unique person while bearing in mind what the data and research reveal.

Being pressured into following a pre-determined set of protocols inhibits clinical judgment, especially when it comes to atypical problems. Some medical educators are concerned that excessive reliance on these protocols could make students less likely to recognize and deal with complicated clinical presentations that don't follow standard patterns. It is easy to standardize treatment protocols. But it is difficult to standardize patients.

What began as guidelines eventually grew into requirements. In order for hospitals to maintain their Medicare certification, the Centers for Medicare and Medicaid Services began to require their medical staff to follow these protocols or face financial retribution.

Once again, the medical profession cooperated. The American College of Surgeons helped develop Surgical Care Improvement Project (SCIP) protocols, directing surgeons as to what antibiotics they may use and the day-to-day post-operative decisions they must make. If a surgeon deviates from the guidelines, he is usually required to document in the medical record an acceptable justification for that decision.

These requirements have consequences. On more than one occasion I have seen patients develop dramatic postoperative bruising and bleeding because of protocol-mandated therapies aimed at preventing the development of blood clots in the legs after surgery. Had these therapies been left up to the clinical judgment of the surgeon, many of these patients might not have had the complication.

Operating room and endoscopy suites now must follow protocols developed by the global World Health Organization—an even more remote agency. There are protocols for cardiac catheterization, stenting, and respirator management, just to name a few.

Patients should worry about doctors trying to make symptoms fit into a standardized clinical model and ignoring the vital nuances of their complaints. Even more, they should be alarmed that the protocols being used don't provide any measurable health benefits. Most were designed and implemented before any objective evidence existed as to their effectiveness.

A large Veterans Administration study released in March 2011 showed that SCIP protocols led to no improvement in surgical-site infection rate. If past is prologue, we should not expect the SCIP protocols to be repealed, just "improved"—or expanded, adding to the already existing glut.

These rules are being bred into the system. Young doctors and medical students are being trained to follow protocol. To them, command and control is normal. But to older physicians who have lived through the decline of medical culture, this only contributes to our angst.

One of my colleagues, a noted pulmonologist with over 30 years' experience, fears that teaching young physicians to follow guidelines and practice protocols discourages creative medical thinking and may lead to a decrease in diagnostic and therapeutic excellence. He laments that "'evidence-based' means you are not interested in listening to anyone." Another colleague, a North Phoenix orthopedist of many years, decries the "cookie-cutter" approach mandated by protocols.

A noted gastroenterologist who has practiced more than 35 years has a more cynical take on things. He believes that the increased regimentation and regularization of medicine is a prelude to the replacement of physicians by nurse practitioners and physician-assistants, and that these people will be even more likely to follow the directives proclaimed by regulatory bureaus. It is true that, in many cases, routine medical problems can be handled more cheaply and efficiently by paraprofessionals. But these practitioners are also limited by depth of knowledge, understanding, and experience. Patients should be able to decide for themselves if they want to be seen by a doctor. It is increasingly rare that patients are given a choice about such things.

The partners in my practice all believe that protocols and guidelines will accomplish nothing more than giving us more work to do and more rules to comply with. But they implore me to keep my mouth shut—rather than risk angering hospital administrators, insurance company executives, and the other powerful entities that control our fates.

Electronic Records and Financial Burdens

When Congress passed the stimulus, a.k.a. the American Reinvestment and Recovery Act of 2009, it included a requirement that all physicians and hospitals convert to electronic medical records (EMR) by 2014 or face Medicare reimbursement penalties. There has never been a peer-reviewed study clearly demonstrating that requiring all doctors and hospitals to switch to electronic records will decrease error and increase efficiency, but that didn't stop Washington policymakers from repeating that claim over and over again in advance of the stimulus.

Some institutions, such as Kaiser Permanente Health Systems, the Mayo Clinic, and the Veterans Administration Hospitals, have seen big benefits after going digital voluntarily. But if the same benefits could reasonably be expected to play out universally, government coercion would not be needed.

Instead, Congress made that business decision on behalf of thousands of doctors and hospitals, who must now spend huge sums on the purchase of EMR systems and take staff off other important jobs to task them with entering thousands of old-style paper medical records into the new database. For a period of weeks or months after the new system is in place, doctors must see fewer patients as they adapt to the demands of the technology.

The persistence of price controls has coincided with a steady ratcheting down of fees for doctors. As a result, private insurance payments, which are typically pegged to Medicare payment schedules, have been ratcheting down as well. Meanwhile, Medicare's regulatory burdens on physician practices continue to increase, adding on compliance costs. Medicare continues to demand that specific coded services be redefined and subdivided into ever-increasing levels of complexity. Harsh penalties are imposed on providers who accidentally use the wrong level code to bill for a service. Sometimes—as in the case of John Natale of Arlington, Illinois, who began a 10-month sentence in November because he miscoded bills on five patients upon whom he repaired complicated abdominal aortic aneurysms—the penalty can even include prison.

For many physicians in private practice, the EMR requirement is the final straw. Doctors are increasingly selling their practices to hospitals, thus becoming hospital employees. This allows them to offload the high costs of regulatory compliance and converting to EMR.

As doctors become shift workers, they work less intensely and watch the clock much more than they did when they were in private practice. Additionally, the doctor-patient relationship is adversely affected as doctors come to increasingly view their customers as the hospitals' patients rather than their own.

In 2011, The New England Journal of Medicine reported that fully 50 percent of the nation's doctors had become employees—either of hospitals, corporations, insurance companies, or the government. Just six years earlier, in 2005, more than two-thirds of doctors were in private practice. As economic pressures on the sustainability of private clinical practice continue to mount, we can expect this trend to continue.

Accountable Care Organizations

For the next 19 years, an average of 10,000 Americans will turn 65 every day, increasing the fiscal strain on Medicare. Bureaucrats are trying to deal with this partly by reinstating an old concept under a new name: Accountable Care Organization, or ACO, which harkens back to the infamous HMO system of the early 1990s.

In a nutshell, hospitals, clinics, and health care providers have been given incentives to organize into teams that will get assigned groups of 5,000 or more Medicare patients. They will be expected to follow practice guidelines and protocols approved by Medicare. If they achieve certain benchmarks established by Medicare with respect to cost, length of hospital stay, re-admissions, and other measures, they will get to share a portion of Medicare's savings. If the reverse happens, there will be economic penalties.

Naturally, private insurance companies are following suit with non-Medicare versions of the ACO, intended primarily for new markets created by ObamaCare. In this model, an ACO is given a lump sum, or bundled payment, by the insurance company. That chunk of money is intended to cover the cost of all the care for a large group of insurance beneficiaries. The private ACOs are expected to follow the same Medicare-approved practice protocols, but all of the financial risks are assumed by the ACOs. If the ACOs keep costs down, the team of providers and hospitals reap the financial reward: surplus from the lump sum payment. If they lose money, the providers and hospitals eat the loss.

In both the Medicare and non-Medicare varieties of the ACO, cost control and compliance with centrally planned practice guidelines are the primary goal.

ACOs are meant to replace a fee-for-service payment model that critics argue encourages providers to perform more services and procedures on patients than they otherwise would do. This assumes that all providers are unethical, motivated only by the desire for money. But the salaried and prepaid models of provider-reimbursement are also subject to unethical behavior in our current system. There is no reward for increased productivity with the salary model. With the prepaid model there is actually an incentive to maximize profit by withholding services.

Each of these models has its pros and cons. In a true market-based system, where competition rewards positive results, the consumer would be free to choose among the various competing compensation arrangements.

With increasing numbers of health care providers becoming salaried employees of hospitals, that's not likely. Instead, we'll see greater bureaucratization. Hospitals might be able to get ACOs to work better than their ancestor HMOs, because hospital administrators will have more control over their medical staff. If doctors don't follow the protocols and guidelines, and desired outcomes are not reached, hospitals can replace the "problem" doctors.

Doctors Going Galt?

Once free to be creative and innovative in their own practices, doctors are becoming more like assembly-line workers, constrained by rules and regulations aimed to systemize their craft. It's no surprise that retirement is starting to look more attractive. The advent of the Affordable Care Act of 2010, which put the medical profession's already bad trajectory on steroids, has for many doctors become the straw that broke the camel's back.

A June 2012 survey of 36,000 doctors in active clinical practice by the Doctors and Patients Medical Association found 90 percent of doctors believe the medical system is "on the wrong track" and 83 percent are thinking about quitting. Another 85 percent said "the medical profession is in a tailspin." 65 percent say that "government involvement is most to blame for current problems." In addition, 2 out of 3 physicians surveyed in private clinical practice stated they were "just squeaking by or in the red financially."

A separate survey of 2,218 physicians, conducted online by the national health care recruiter Jackson Healthcare, found that 34 percent of physicians plan to leave the field over the next decade. What's more, 16 percent said they would retire or move to part-time in 2012. "Of those physicians who said they plan to retire or leave medicine this year," the study noted, "56% cited economic factors and 51% cited health reform as among the major factors. Of those physicians who said they are strongly considering leaving medicine in 2012, 55% or 97 physicians, were under age 55."

Interestingly, these surveys were completed two years after a pre-ObamaCare survey reported in The New England Journal of Medicine found 46.3 percent of primary care physicians stated passage of the new health law would "either force them out of medicine or make them want to leave medicine."

It has certainly affected my plans. Starting in 2012, I cut back on my general surgery practice. As co-founder of my private group surgical practice in 1986, I reached an arrangement with my partners freeing me from taking night calls, weekend calls, or emergency daytime calls. I now work 40 hours per week, down from 60 or 70. While I had originally planned to practice at least another 12 to 14 years, I am now heading for an exit—and a career change—in the next four years. I didn't sign up for the kind of medical profession that awaits me a few years from now.

Many of my generational peers in medicine have made similar arrangements, taken early retirement, or quit practice and gone to work for hospitals or as consultants to insurance companies. Some of my colleagues who practice primary care are starting cash-only "concierge" medical practices, in which they accept no Medicare, Medicaid, or any private insurance.

As old-school independent-thinking doctors leave, they are replaced by protocol-followers. Medicine in just one generation is transforming from a craft to just another rote occupation.

In the not-too-distant future, a small but healthy market will arise for cash-only, personalized, private care. For those who can afford it, there will always be competitive, market-driven clinics, hospitals, surgicenters, and other arrangements—including "medical tourism," whereby health care packages are offered at competitive rates in overseas medical centers. Similar healthy markets already exist in areas such as Lasik eye surgery and cosmetic procedures. The medical profession will survive and even thrive in these small private niches.

In other words, we're about to experience the two-tiered system that already exists in most parts of the world that provide "universal coverage." Those who have the financial means will still be able to get prompt, courteous, personalized, state-of-the-art health care from providers who consider themselves professionals. But the majority can expect long lines, mediocre and impersonal care from shift-working providers, subtle but definite rationing, and slowly deteriorating outcomes.

We already see this in Canada, where cash-only clinics are beginning to spring up, and the United Kingdom, where a small but healthy private system exists side-by-side with the National Health Service, providing high-end, fee-for-service, private health care, with little or no waiting.

Ayn Rand's philosophical novel *Atlas Shrugged* describes a dystopian near-future America. One of its characters is Dr. Thomas Hendricks, a prominent and innovative neurosurgeon who one day just disappears. He could no longer be a part of a medical system that denied him autonomy and dignity. Dr. Hendricks' warning deserves repeating:

"Let them discover the kind of doctors that their system will now produce. Let them discover, in their operating rooms and hospital wards, that it is not safe to place their lives in the hands of a man whose life they have throttled. It is not safe, if he is the sort of man who resents it—and still less safe, if he is the sort who doesn't."

Critical Thinking

1. What problems arose with the coding system from a doctor's perspective? A patient's?

2. Why has the persistence of price controls coincided with a steady ratcheting down of physician's fees?

Create Central

www.mhhe.com/createcentral

Internet References

American Medical Association (AMA)
www.ama-assn.org
Medicare.gov: the official U.S. government site for Medicare
www.medicare.gov
MedScape: The Online Resource for Better Patient Care
www.medscape.com

Article   Prepared by: Eileen Daniel, *SUNY College at Brockport*

Problems with Modern Medicine: Too Much Emphasis on Disease, Not Enough on Managing Risk

Maciej Zatonski

Learning Outcomes

After reading this article, you will be able to:

- Explain why medicine today is more about risk management than treating sick people.

- Understand the concept of defensive medicine.

- Understand that every abnormality does not develop into disease.

I am a doctor. A surgeon. I was taught to make sick people healthy and to make those who cannot be cured comfortable. I am lucky also. Major advances have benefited us all. We have learned how to put people to sleep during surgery; we have developed antibiotics to battle bacteria; we have started to transplant organs from the deceased. We have created technology that allows us to look into a living body and even observe metabolic processes on the cellular level in real time. We developed effective vaccinations and prevented millions from dying in accidents, from strokes, or from complications of chronic diseases. We have used modern scientific methods to analyze huge amounts of data, and we have managed to change the perception of medicine as a form of art and turn it into a hard science.

But it all happened at a price.

Nowadays, we try to improve our past discoveries, but we probably will need to wait for another breakthrough. In the meanwhile, our old discoveries are becoming available to increasingly larger numbers of people. And the more people we

diagnose, the more diseases we find. But are doctors still making sick people healthy? Our definition of sickness and health is evolving but does not seem to catch up with current medical advances. We can detect cancers before they give us any symptoms. We scan, screen, and diagnose more and more individuals using the most advanced technology. But are we always helping our patients? Who actually benefits from early treatments? How many suffer from complications? How many are harmed, physically or emotionally? These are hard questions to answer, and we are looking into them.

We know that every advanced disease (cancer, for example) had to have a very early stage. It can start as a single mutation in our DNA. Historically, we were not able to pick those things early enough. The tumor had to be of a size that would be detectable with our fingers or eyes—and it often meant that it was too late for a cure. We have learned to look inside our bodies to identify tiny lumps that are invisible to the eye and impossible to feel or touch. Later came newer technologies that allowed us to spot abnormalities in tissues, cells, and even on the molecular level. We thought that this was good because every advanced disease had to start early. And the earlier we pick it up, the better the chances of survival.

Well, it is true to some degree. The problem is that we do not know if every detected pathology will become a real problem. Not all abnormalities develop into symptomatic diseases. We don't know which of them will. And we probably never will, as an attempt to investigate this issue would raise severe ethical issues.

Medicine today is not only about making sick people healthy. It is becoming a risk-management and quality-of-life improvement service. We need to needlessly treat hundreds of people with a mild hypertension to prevent a single death. Since not all people with hypertension die from its consequences, we have to treat a lot of people for one person to actually benefit. We don't know who this lucky person will be. It's like a lottery—lots of people have to play the game, so we can have one winner. Therefore, we treat everyone's "abnormal" findings. And this would be totally okay if there were no side effects from the treatment. If you play in a lottery you might lose just a few dollars. If you play with your life, the price to pay can be much higher.

The closer we look, the more "diseases" we find. Recently, National Health Service in the U.K. announced a nationwide "Health Check" program, where healthy people are encouraged to visit their doctors. Some lives will be saved. But how many people will be turned needlessly into patients? We don't know exactly, but the estimations are alarming.

It was easier to trust the doctors when we could see the results of their treatment immediately. But when doctors manage risks of possible (but not at all guaranteed) future problems, this undermines patients' trust in modern medicine. Treatments are often expensive and can make previously healthy people feel sick—both physically (from side effects) and psychologically (due to their changed perception of their own health).

Doctors don't give advice to their patients anymore. They give them options. We are told that this is good: it respects patients' autonomy, beliefs, and expectations. But it also takes a lot of responsibility away from doctors and leaves the decision regarding the treatment in the hands of the least qualified person. It's a part of the phenomenon called "defensive medicine." Doctors will always put their safety (and the financial safety of their families) first. This allows charlatans to thrive. Think about it: if you only prescribe sugar pills (such as homeopathy)—you can actually give any advice to your clients without putting yourself at risk, as each piece of advice is technically identical and risk-free. It's easy to actually advise a patient to take sugar pills, instead of presenting him or her with treatments, statistics, and decisions to make. If I knew enough to make a proper therapeutic decision, would I need to consult a doctor in the first place?

Don't get me wrong; I am not saying that the idea of offering a choice and providing information to patients is wrong. It's the best way we know. However, this great idea is flawed: after years of practicing medicine I would struggle to make a "good" decision myself. And if it's our life at stake, we tend to make irrational choices. There is a reason why many doctors admit that they would never consider treatments for themselves that they offer their patients. It is a complicated problem that might be impossible to solve in current legal and ethical realities.

Perhaps instead of battling homeopaths, it would be better to educate patients and doctors about the concept of medical risk-management (in the mathematical meaning). Understanding of statistics is poor among doctors and the general public—but in a world flooded with big data, basics of statistics (and its implications) should be a mandatory part of every primary school curriculum.

Are our expectations of modern medicine too high? We don't have a cure for loneliness, feeling down, lack of hope, or rejection. We don't even have a cure for most common diseases. We can "manage" certain conditions, reduce risks, prolong life. But we still cannot cure many illnesses. But neither can the "alternative medicine" shamans.

My impression is that we need to redefine our conception and definition of health and disease and introduce the concept of "risk-management of possible future health benefits." Perhaps skeptics can actually make a difference and lead the world into the changes that modern medicine needs. I invite the readers to share their ideas and opinions.

Critical Thinking

1. Why isn't it realistic or desirable to treat every symptom?
2. What are the risks of treating all abnormal findings?

Create Central

www.mhhe.com/createcentral

Internet References

American Cancer Society
   http://www.cancer.org
Centers for Disease Control and Prevention
   http://www.cdc.gov/vaccines

MACIEJ ZATONSKI, MD, PHD, is a surgeon and researcher working at BHR University Hospitals NHS Trust in the United Kingdom. He is a founder of Polish Skeptics Club and specializes in debunking unscientific therapies and claims in medicine. He is a leader of public understanding of science in Poland and is actively engaged in promoting evolution and evolutionary sciences.

Maciej Zatonski, "Problems with Modern Medicine: Too Much Emphasis on Disease, Not Enough on Managing Risk" from *Skeptical Inquirer* 30.1 (January/February 2014): 14–15.

Still Unsafe

Why the American Medical Establishment Cannot Reduce Medical Errors

PHILIP LEVITT

Learning Outcomes

After reading this article, you will be able to:

- Explain major cause of preventable deaths in American hospitals.

- Understand why there was no drop in mortality from medical errors despite implication of the systems approach.

- Describe why many incompetent doctors are able to continue to practice medicine.

Every year, there are about 138,000 preventable deaths in hospitals throughout America. At least 30 percent of those deaths are the result of the actions of doctors who by any standards are incompetent.[1,2] Because it is easier to blame a system than an individual doctor, particularly if he or she is a peer, the medical establishment has chosen to attack the problem of preventable deaths by employing what it calls a systems approach. The theory behind such an approach, which was first widely instituted at the beginning of this century, is that if you standardize the delivery of health care in a hospital, you reduce the number of errors that can be made by fallible humans. Although such an approach has worked successfully in the airline and automobile industries, it has not caused any noticeable drop in the overall number of preventable deaths in American hospitals.

In 2007, I retired from neurosurgery after 32 years. During that time I had been the chief of staff of two hospitals in South Florida over a total period of five years. In those positions, I had responsibility for overseeing the professional and ethical conduct of roughly 1,800 doctors, about a tenth of those in the state. It was nearly impossible to discipline any one of them who stepped out of line and endangered patients. A second important consideration was that I knew from daily experience that the systems methods that were put in place in my hospital and in nearly 80% of the hospitals in the country during the first decade of this century were unlikely to make a significant dent in the number of deaths due to caretakers' mistakes. Tactics such as checklists, time outs (where the nurses withhold the scalpel from the surgeon until he or she declares the name of the patient and the name and site of the operation), and labeling the correct extremity for surgery seemed merely to nibble around the edges of the identifiable hard core source of more deaths annually than automobile accidents—the inept doctors. I knew from direct experience and from sitting on numerous quality assurance committees for years and learning of their misadventures that they harmed many more patients than the occasional omission of typical systems tactics such as administering aspirin to a heart attack patient or giving preoperative antibiotics.

While researching the problem, I came upon two documents with overlapping authorship about harmful medical mistakes that contradicted each other. The first, published in the *New England Journal of Medicine*, were the Harvard Medical Practice Studies of 1991, based on data gleaned from scores of hospitals in New York State during the mid-1980s.[2,3] They are the gold standard dealing with "adverse events" a term meaning harm to patients as the result of medical management. "Adverse events" has almost completely replaced the much older term "iatrogenic mishaps" in the medical literature. "Iatrogenic" means doctor caused.

The Harvard Medical Practice Studies contained the results of screening by expert physician examiners of over

30,000 hospital charts for evidence of bad care. Nothing on that scale has been done since. The Harvard Studies analyzed, categorized, and put into easily scanned written tables the types of errors that resulted in significant harm to patients. Although follow-up studies that analyzed hospital charts have included enough patients to reach statistical significance—a venerable yardstick of scientific validity—they are still dwarfed in size and detail by the Harvard Studies.

The other document, which appeared in 1999, *To Err Is Human,* is a report written by a 19-person committee of the Institute of Medicine (IOM).[4] The IOM is a private scientific group that advises Congress and the public on matters of public health. *To Err Is Human* claimed to have as its scientific and factual basis the Harvard Medical Practice Studies. By projecting to the entire country the data from New York State in the Harvard Studies, it concluded that there were around 98,000 fatal adverse events in America's hospitals each year. Similar results have been echoed in two more recent studies published in 2010.[5,6] To Err Is Human did not contain any new facts. Its most significant and far-reaching impact was its recommendations for reducing medical errors. It concluded that the best way to do so was to apply the same general method used to reduce crashes of commercial airplanes, called the "systems approach." The authors, without scientific data arising from studies of hospitals and medicine, concluded *a priori* that most of the errors and deaths arose from faulty medical care delivery systems. It promised that if those systems were corrected that the number of deaths would drop by 50% in five years. The methods were started in 78% of American hospitals.[7] They included a variety of checklists that assured that a heterogeneous group of tasks were always carried out, such as giving aspirin and beta blockers to heart attack patients immediately upon admission to the hospital, polyvalent pneumonia vaccine to elderly patients upon discharge, and antibiotics to surgical patients within the hour before making the surgical incision.

Despite considerable change in how hospital medicine is practiced and with the vast majority of American hospitals participating, there was no drop in mortality from adverse events in the decade that followed the release of *To Err is Human.* Two research reports came out at the end of the last decade with very similar results. One of the studies was directed by the Inspector General of the U.S. Department of Health and Human Services, (HHS)[5] and the other, by a group from Harvard and Stanford medical schools.[6] The latter report was published in the November 2010 issue of the *New England Journal of Medicine,* the same time that the HHS report appeared on the Internet. In *To Err is Human,* the IOM estimated that 98,000 preventable deaths occurred based on data collected during the 1980s. During the period from the mid-1980s to mid-2000s, no other studies of a similar scope and resulting from an equally

rigorous methodology (a careful screening of hospital charts) were reported. In the Health and Human Services (HHS) report based on hospital chart review, 180,000 Medicare patients lost their lives. Its authors considered 44 percent—or 79,200 of the deaths—preventable. How does this compare with the numbers gleaned from the mid-1980s that were reported in *To Err is Human*? Given that Medicare admissions are somewhat less than half of all hospital admissions, the numbers are, sadly, comparable.

The Harvard-Stanford study looked at the inpatient charts of patients in all age groups in several hospitals in North Carolina. That state was chosen because compared to other states it "had shown a high level of engagement in efforts to improve patient safety," the authors said in their report. Those "efforts" involved the widespread use of systems tactics as championed by the authors of *To Err is Human.*[7] A typical example: every patient was given prophylactic antibiotics before surgery to prevent surgical wound infections. However, the use of these antibiotics was not only at the direction of the doctor; should he forget, a nurse was there to remind him. Another example involved the use of medication. A doctor could not prescribe penicillin to a patient without ascertaining whether the patient had any allergies to the medication. Regardless, the prescription was not filled until the pharmacist, checking with his or her pharmaceutical software, also confirmed that the patient, according to the software, had no allergies to penicillin. The system also enabled the pharmacist to double check the dose and the frequency prescribed by the physician. The nurse, a third party, also checked by asking the patient—even if the doctor already had—and double-checking the patient's chart. A system of checking and double-checking was in place, no matter how reliable or unreliable, renowned or unknown, the particular physician involved.

At the time of the scientific investigation, Dr. Christopher Landrigan, the senior author of the Harvard-Stanford study, estimated that about 96 percent of the hospitals in North Carolina and 78 percent of hospitals nationwide, were participating in the 100,000 Lives Campaign, an effort meant to save 100,000 lives a year in hospitals by putting in effect various systems approaches.[7] He and the rest of the authors of the study reasoned that if an improvement in patient outcomes were to be found, it would surely have occurred in North Carolina. Instead, the report found a much higher level of mortality from medical mishaps than expected. In doing their research, the authors of the Harvard-Stanford study continuously monitored adverse events—including deaths—and tabulated them by three-month periods over a span of six years. Their hypothesis was that the longer the systems approach was used, and the larger the number of systems methods employed, the more progressive the drop in the number of adverse events. In fact, the number of adverse events remained the same within the six-year period of the study. In 2002—the start of the study—the authors found 15 high severity harms per 100 admissions (with high severity harms defined as temporary harms requiring prolonged hospitalization, permanent harms, life-threatening harms, and death); in 2007, after the implementation of systems methods, they found exactly the same number.

Using the same method used in *To Err Is Human* and working with the data accumulated by the authors of the 2010 Harvard-Stanford article, one could project 215,000 deaths of patients in hospitals nationwide, of which 138,000 would be preventable. This number compares unfavorably to the 98,000 preventable deaths nationwide found in *To Err is Human,* a figure taken from 1984 before systems approaches were in place. If anything, the results were worse.

Dr. Landrigan, the lead author of the Harvard-Stanford paper and the director of Harvard's patient safety program, said, "We found that harms remain common, with little evidence of widespread improvement." Rather than looking for some other cause, Dr. Landrigan simply noted that the systems approach needed to be used more effectively. "Further efforts are needed to translate effective safety interventions into routine practice and to monitor health care safety over time."

A striking exception to these dismal results was the prevention of blood infections from central intravenous lines which the Centers for Disease Control and Prevention declared to be saving 3,000 to 6,000 lives a year during the same period as the Inspector General's and the Harvard-Stanford studies.[8] This occurred largely as the result of the efforts of Dr. Peter Pronovost of Johns Hopkins Medical School. However, those savings got swamped by all the other preventable deaths.

The failures of the systems approach were foreshadowed in the data of Harvard Medical Practice Studies. Table 7 of the second installment, which listed the types and numbers of adverse events shows that at least 61 percent of all adverse events could be laid at the feet of individual physicians and, according to the authors of the Harvard Medical Practice Studies, only 6 percent were attributable to systems problems.[2] The 61 percent comprised technical mishaps during surgery and other procedures and failure to order the correct diagnostic test. For verification in 2013, I asked one of the authors of *To Err is Human,* Dr. Joseph Scherger, about technical and diagnostic errors and he readily admitted that these were not amenable to systems fixes.[9] He could not reconcile for me his and his co-authors' great familiarity with the results of the Harvard Medical Practice Studies with the solution they proposed for saving lives, the systems approach. Neither could Dr. Lucian Leape of Harvard's School of Public Health, an author of both documents.[10]

The medical profession and its chief watchdogs—the state boards of licensure—had no trouble believing what was said in *To Err is Human.* In a joint statement in 2008, the medical boards of all 50 states and the provinces of Canada wrote that most medical errors were the result of faulty care delivery systems and not the fault of the individual physicians about whom they received complaints on a regular basis.[11]

The Deadly 2%

Based on information from the National Practitioner Data Bank, a federal data base which stores records of malpractice judgments, loss of licensure and hospital privilege revocations for all the doctors in the country, it is clear that a small number of doctors—about 2 percent—are responsible for half the cases in which a patient is seriously and unnecessarily harmed in the process of being treated. Dr. Robert Oshel, formerly the associate director for research and disputes at the Data Bank—he has since retired—confirms that the misdeeds of 2 percent of the physicians in practice during the last twenty years, from about 1990–2010, resulted in half of the money paid out in malpractice cases.[1] In other words, a very small number of doctors are responsible for a disproportionately large number of errors.

The distribution of error rates is not unique to hospitals in this country. Marie M. Bismark, a senior research fellow at the University of Melbourne, who is both a physician and a lawyer, found in a national sample of nearly 19,000 formal healthcare complaints lodged against doctors in Australia between 2000 and 2011, that "three percent of Australia's medical workforce accounted for 49 percent of complaints and one percent accounted for a quarter of complaints."[12]

Given such a small number of grossly incompetent doctors, it should be easy to identify and prevent them from practicing. Unfortunately, in most cases, they continue to practice. The average American hospital drops only one doctor from its staff every twenty years.[1] About 250 doctors lose their licenses each year, or 0.04 percent of the total number of practicing physicians, which is about 650,000.[1] At that rate, it would take 50 years to remove the most incompetent doctors—the 2 percent—from practice. Why do the vast majority of these doctors keep practicing? One reason is the pervasive leniency of the hospital peer review committees and state medical boards, the main institutions set up to deal with the problem.

This small number of incompetent physicians not only causes serious errors in terms of patient health; they also cost society a huge amount of money. Dr. Donald Berwick, the chief of Medicare and Medicaid from July 2010 to December 2011—he is currently a senior fellow at the Center for American Progress—estimated that $300 billion a year are spent on the waste that results from poor execution of care and on over treatment that subjects patients to care that is unsupported by science and that cannot possibly help them.[13] Giving unnecessary care is the favorite method of many less scrupulous physicians for padding their earnings.

What, then, is the solution to the large number of preventable deaths that happen each year specifically because of incompetent doctors? Combining the estimates of both Dr. Oshel and the Harvard Studies this number equals about 42,090—more than the average number of people who die from auto accidents each year.

The advocates of the systems approach try to avoid the issue of the incompetent doctor. They say we can reduce the number of preventable deaths by streamlining and routinizing the practice of medicine. However, that approach has not been successful in either reducing the number of preventable deaths or improving the practice of medicine.

Currently, hospitals do a poor job of disciplining incompetent doctors in spite of laws that exist to ferret them out. Alan Levine and Dr. Sidney Wolfe of Public Citizen, a nonprofit, lobbyist group based in Washington, D.C. and Austin, Texas, in examining the National Practitioner Data Bank, have found that although all hospitals are required by law to report serious disciplinary measures taken against a physician on their staff, 47% of American hospitals have never reported a single doctor.[14] Any practicing doctor of integrity will agree: it is highly doubtful that there are no incompetent doctors in 47% of American hospitals.

In addition, according to a separate report by the Inspector General of the Department of Health and Human Services (HHS), 26 states have laws requiring hospital administrations to report harms inflicted on patients to the state departments of health and state medical boards, but only 1 percent of adverse events are actually reported even in these states.[15] This data is critical to finding poorly performing doctors as, conservatively, 61 percent of adverse events are caused by the errors of individual physicians, not systems failures. Why don't hospitals do the required reporting? Stuart Wright, the deputy inspector general for HHS (for evaluations and inspections) wrote in his Memorandum Report to the Acting administrator of the centers of Medicare and Medicaid Services that this low rate of reporting is more likely the result of a hospital's failure to identify events rather than from its neglect to report known events.[15]

In fact, the opposite is true. Most hospital administrators know exactly who the incompetent doctors are and very rapidly learn of their mistakes. Elaborate mechanisms are set in place for reporting to the CEO on a daily basis so he or she does not get blindsided by doctors, nurses, or family members calling to complain. Once these poor outcomes are detected, however, hospitals are loath to act because both the hospital and the doctor become subject to fines, bad publicity and the loss of licenses. Until hospitals have stronger incentives to report adverse events, most will do their utmost to avoid conveying the details to state authorities.

Two Modest Proposals

One obvious solution is to impose sufficiently high penalties—a fine of at least $250,000—on hospitals that fail to report to the state board doctors who commit disabling or fatal errors. If hospitals don't report errors, then how will any agency know to levy such a fine? Even when hospitals fail to report adverse events involving negligence, the state boards can and do find out about them through other sources: the patient, his or her family, attorneys, judges, or malpractice insurance companies. If the complaints made are deemed to be legitimate, then the doctor in question may lose his or her license. Therefore, the loss of a physician's license is the one crucial and indelible marker of medical negligence and adverse events. If it is found that a hospital has failed to report the incident that caused the physician to lose his license, the fine will be imposed. No CEO of any hospital could withstand the publicity associated with such a case, let alone the fine. The existence of such a law would affect all hospitals in a state, not just the ones investigated or fined. Because no one can predict what adverse event might lead to the revocation of a doctor's license, it is likely that many more events will be reported to the state. The second proposal concerns the 2 percent who cause half the damages to medical malpractice plaintiffs in America, a special group of repeat offenders. The identities of the 2 percent are a closely held secret of the National Practitioner Data Bank. It would take congressional action to disclose them. Publicity about the money, not to mention the lives lost, because of this small hardcore group of inept doctors, could sway public opinion. And to prevent these doctors from practicing, Congress could take away their participation in Medicare and Medicaid. Currently, few doctors other than those involved in Medicare or Medicaid fraud ever lose their right to participate.

These are not by any means the only solutions, but they at least seek to address the real source of the problem—the incompetent physician. The problem of the incompetent doctor is a constant, weaving throughout the history of modern medicine. Back in 1958, David Allman, president of the American Medical Association, exhorted the association's component bodies to root out bad doctors: "Any reluctance to reprimand an erring colleague does irreparable harm to our profession. Any use of a whitewash brush to sweep dirt under the rug imperils our disciplinary system. Any compromise with personal moral convictions damages the very character which makes a man or a woman a good doctor."[16] His words, however powerful, did not result in any notable action.

The irony is that the continuing tolerance for the incompetent physician is harmful not only to the public but also to the majority of hard working, competent physicians. The inept physicians drain huge amounts of money out of a vast system that also needs to reimburse the competent ones, tarnish the reputation of the profession as a whole, and create malpractice pitfalls for those doctors who work on the same patients with them. Lawyers are often obliged by circumstances and the law to sue doctors merely because their names appear in the hospital chart before the process of legal discovery clears the field of inappropriate defendants. This often takes years.

In the meantime, the inept doctors of America are still in place, sprinkled among the 5,700 hospitals of our country. They remain almost untouched by a so-called scientific systems approach that statistically has not succeeded in lowering or even maintaining the number of preventable deaths. So the silent casualties continue. More than a million patients will die because of medical error in the next decade. Until we confront the real problem, these unnecessary deaths will continue.

References

1. Oshel, R., 2012. Personal communication.
2. Leape L.L., T. A. Brennan, et al. 1991. "The nature of adverse events in hospitalized patients. Results of the Harvard Medical Practice Study II." *New England Journal of Medicine,* 324:377–384.
3. Brennan, T.A., L.L. Leape, et al. 1991. "Incidence of adverse events and negligence in hospitalized patients. Results of the Harvard Medical Practice Study I." *New England Journal of Medicine,* 324:370–376.
4. Kohn L.T., J.M. Corrigan, M. S. Donaldson (Eds.). 1999. *To Err is Human: Building a Safer Health System.* National Academy Press, Washington, DC.
5. Department Of Health And Human Services Office Of Inspector General: Adverse events in hospitals: national incidence among Medicare beneficiaries. November, 2010.
6. Landrigan C.P., G.J. Perry, et al. 2010. "Trends in rates of patient harm resulting from medical care." *New England Journal of Medicine,* 363:2124–2134.
7. Ibid., References 19 and 20: 19. North Carolina Center for Hospital Quality and Patient Safety. About us. (http://www.nc.qualitycenter.org/about.lasso. 20. Institute for Healthcare Improvement. A network that works! The 100,000 LivesCampaign nodes. Cambridge, MA: IHI, 2006. (http://www.ihi.org/IHI/Topics/Improvement/SpreadingChanges/ImprovementStories/ANetworkThatWorks100000LivesCampaignNodes.htm.)
8. Centers for Disease Control and Prevention. 2010.
9. Scherger, J. 2013. Personal communication.
10. Leape, L.L. 2011. Personal communication.
11. Federation of Medical Regulatory Authorities of Canada, Federation of State Medical Boards and Milbank Memorial Fund. 2008. *Medical Regulatory Authorities and the Quality of Medical Services in Canada and the United States,* 4.
12. Bismark, M.M., M. J. Spittal, et al. 2013. "Identification of doctors at risk of recurrent complaints: A National Study of Healthcare Complaints in Australia." *Quality and Safety in Health Care,* 1–9.
13. Berwick, D.M. and A.D. Hackbarth. 2012. "Eliminating Waste in US Health Care," *JAMA,* 307 No. 14, 1513–1516.
14. Levine, A. and S. Wolfe. 2009. "Hospitals Drop the Ball on Physician Oversight," *Public Citizen,* May 27: www.citizen.org/hrg
15. Wright S. 2012. "Memorandum Report." *Few Adverse Events in Hospitals Were Reported to State Adverse Events Reporting Systems,* OE1-06-09-00092, July 19.
16. Ameringer, C.F. 1999. *State Medical Boards and the Politics of Public Protection.* Johns Hopkins University Press, 35.

Critical Thinking

1. What are the primary reasons hospital CEOs do not report medical errors committed by incompetent doctors?

2. Are most medical errors caused by faulty delivery systems? Discuss.

Create Central

www.mhhe.com/createcentral

Internet References

Agency for Health Care Research and Quality
  http://www.ahrq.gov
American Hospital Association
  http://www.aha.org

Philip Levitt, "Still Unsafe: Why the American Medical Establishment Cannot Reduce Medical Errors" from *Skeptic* 18.4 (2013): 44–48.

Unit 9

UNIT

Prepared by: Eileen Daniel, *SUNY College at Brockport*

Consumer Health

For many people, the term *consumer health* conjures up images of selecting health-care services and paying medical bills. While these two aspects of health care are indeed consumer health issues, the term *consumer health* encompasses all consumer products and services that influence the health and welfare of people. A definition this broad suggests that almost everything we see or do may be construed to be a consumer health issue, whether it is related to products or discussions such as the concept of getting enough sleep or what foods will keep us healthy. In many ways, consumer health is an outward expression of our health-related behaviors and decision-making processes and, as such, is based on our desire to make healthy choices, be assertive, and be in possession of accurate information on which to base our decisions.

Consumer health encompasses all aspects of the marketplace related to the purchase of health products and services. It includes such things as buying a bottle of aspirin, a cough remedy, toothpaste, or exercise equipment and selecting a doctor, dentist, health insurance policy, book, website, or other source of information. Consumer health has both positive and negative components. On the positive side, it involves the facts and understanding that enable people to make medically and economically sound choices. Negatively, it means avoiding unwise decisions based on deception, misinformation, or other factors. Health information has become increasingly large and complex. Even well-trained health professionals can have difficulty sorting out what is accurate and significant from what is not. The media have tremendous influence. A multitude of radio, cable, and television stations broadcast health-related news, commentary, and talk shows. Thousands of magazines and newspapers carry health-related items, and many health-related books and pamphlets are published each year. Many of these books recommend unscientific health practices, as do countless websites, blogs, and other computerized information sources.

Fast-breaking news should be regarded cautiously. Many reports, although accurate, tell only part of the story. Unconfirmed research findings may turn out to be insignificant. The simplest strategy for keeping up to date is to subscribe to trustworthy newsletters and other review sources that place new information in proper perspective. Advertising should also be regarded with caution. Some advertisers use puffery, "weasel words," half-truths, imagery, or celebrity endorsements to misrepresent their products. Some marketers use scare tactics to promote their wares. Some attempt to exploit common hopes, fears, and feelings of inadequacy. Cigarette ads have used images of youth, health, vigor, and social acceptance to convey the opposite of what cigarette smoking will do to smokers. Alcohol ads stress fun and sociability and say little about the dangers of excessive drinking. Many ads for cosmetics exaggerate what they can do. Food advertising tends to promote dietary imbalance by emphasizing snack foods that are high in fat and calories, especially when marketing to children. Radio and television infomercials abound with promoters of health misinformation.

Overall, consumer health encompasses all aspects of the marketplace related to the purchase of health products and services. Although health care in America is potentially the world's best, many problems exist. Health information is voluminous and complex. Many practitioners fall short of the ideal and some are completely unqualified. Quackery is widespread. The marketplace is overcrowded with products, many of which are questionable. Rising costs and lack of adequate insurance coverage have reached crisis levels. Consumer protection is limited. Only well-informed individuals can master the complexity of the health marketplace. Intelligent consumers maintain a healthy lifestyle, seek reliable sources of information and care, and avoid products and practices that are unsubstantiated and lack a scientifically plausible rationale.

Article   Prepared by: Eileen Daniel, *SUNY College at Brockport*

Consumers Should Drive Medicine

David Goldhill on America's deadly, dysfunctional **health** care system

KMELE FOSTER

Learning Outcomes

After reading this article, you will be able to:

- Understand why turning patients into customers would help solve the problems of American health care.

- Explain why the United States spends so much on health care and lags behind other developed countries in health measurements.

- Understand how most health-care purchasing power is in controlled by insurance companies and not consumers.

In 2007, David Goldhill's father was admitted to a New York City hospital with pneumonia. Five weeks later, he died there from multiple hospital-acquired infections. "I probably would have been like any other family member dealing with the grief and disbelief," says Goldhill, a self-described liberal Democrat who now serves as CEO of the Game Show Network.

But then Goldhill read a profile of a physician named Peter Provonost, "who was running around the country with fairly simple steps for cleanliness and hygiene that could significantly reduce the hospital-acquired infection rate." Provonost had been having a hard time bringing hospitals aboard, which the TV executive found surprising.

"I had helped run a movie chain," Goldhill says, "and we had a rule that if a soda spilled, it had to be cleaned up in five minutes or someone got in trouble. And I thought to myself, if we can do that to get you not to go to the theater across the street, why are hospitals having such a hard time doing simple, cost-free things to save lives?"

That's how Goldhill first became interested in the economics of the American health care system. In 2009, he published

a much-discussed feature story on the subject in the Atlantic under the provocative headline "How American Health Care Killed My Father." He has now expanded that article into a book.

In *Catastrophic Care* (Knopf), Goldhill decries a system of incentives that puts most health care purchasing power in the hands of insurance companies and bureaucrats, while cutting patients out of the equation. There's a direct link, he argues, between the way we pay for health care and the estimated 100,000 patients in the U.S. who die every year from infections they picked up in the hospital.

Reason TV contributor Kmele Foster sat down with Goldhill in October to discuss how turning patients into customers would go a long way toward solving the problems of American health care. An edited transcript of their conversation follows.

reason: In your book, the word incentives comes up a great deal.

David Goldhill: The fundamental argument I make is that removing us as the real consumer in health care and putting someone between us and providers—whether it's insurers, whether it's Medicare or Medicaid—has completely turned the incentives in the system on their head. What we see now is that the best way to make money in health care is to price high; provide excess service; be sloppy about safety; under-invest in service, which includes information technology; and lack the type of accountability we see in anything else.

reason: How did health care and health become synonymous?

Goldhill: You'll hear, "The United States spends so much on health care and lags behind other countries in health measurements." Well, we don't really measure the outcomes of health care. We measure how long we live, how vigorous we are through old age, how many of our children are born healthy. We measure those types of big things. Unfortunately, all of them have almost nothing to do with health care. The things that drive health are all lifestyle. Nutrition, exercise, stress, income, education, and public safety—all of these things drive health results far more than health care.

The most dangerous thing we do in health care policy is we imply that making sure that everyone has the maximum amount of health care is essential to health, when one could better argue that diverting 18 percent of our GDP into health care has made us significantly less healthy as a country. I always like to turn that little thing on its head and say, "You know what's amazing? No developed country's health seems to suffer, no matter how little it spends on health-care." It may be the least important factor in health, and yet it's the one we emphasize.

From there, a lot of things go wrong. From there, we have a system where much of the debate is about money: how do we pay for all the health care people? And we miss a big question: if we pay for health care in such a way that we take the individual out, are we going to subject people to excess care and excess treatment, which is a major cause of harm and injury and poor health in itself?

reason: There seems to be a real desire on the part of many Americans to not think about their health care costs.

Goldhill: The foundation of health care economics in this country is an article written by Kenneth Arrow. He said that health care can never be a normal industry because you'll buy whatever your doctor sells you. He's got all the expertise. You're desperate, you're sick, he's gonna tell you how not to be sick. You'll buy anything. There can't be any normal marketplace transaction.

So now, we never ask them what it costs, and we buy everything. It's almost what I would call Arrow's revenge, although I don't think he would take that very kindly.

There's a terrific website called the NNT.com. Every American should look at it before taking a pill or having a treatment. The NNT takes all the numbers that you see and translates it into a single number. How many people need to take this pill for one person to benefit? How many people need to have this operation? It's astonishing. I'm taking a statin for cholesterol. If you look at the NNT—admittedly, I'm contradicting my own point—it's a few people who benefit for every 100 who take it. And roughly the same number are hurt because of other risks that come from taking this pill.

It's extraordinary how removing the consumer from health care has caused us to buy everything. And because we've taken ourselves out, we've taken out the major incentive for keeping prices down. Health care should be unbelievably cheap, right? It's a capital-intensive, almost zero-marginal-cost business. Instead we've done everything we can to keep their prices high.

reason: Most of the conversation about controlling health care costs has centered around cost and not price.

Goldhill: The other day I was at a speech in which a politician said that if we could figure out a way to integrate care, we can reduce the number of MRIs performed and that will bring costs down. He and I were sitting next to each other afterward, and I said, "That doesn't bring costs down. The marginal cost of doing MRIs is zero. You already have the machine; you already have the technician. You're confusing price and cost."

In health care, we never talk about prices. We like to believe that somehow there's some force that actually determines what something costs that is independent of economics. That has been devastating to prices in health care.

There was a terrific piece in The New York Times about asthma drugs. Way into the story, toward the back, the reporter did a terrific job at looking at high prices in health care, and she recognized that these are prices, not costs. One thing that the asthma drug companies are determined to do is to avoid their drugs ever being sold over the counter. They want them sold on prescription, where the prices are high.

reason: Preventative care has been fundamental for folks who talk about controlling costs, that if we do more preventative care, that will bring down costs over time. What's your take on that? Is there much there?

Goldhill: Preventative care is an example of where the Affordable Care Act confused cost and price and visible cost. Preventative care was developing as a very competitive sector because under most people's high-deductible plans they were paying for most of their preventative care. You saw minute clinics growing all over the country—the drug stores in Walmarts and what have you. The reality is that the cost of performing most tests is almost zero. There are a lot of technologies out there that will bring it down close to zero and, more important, let you do it at home. Why? Well, they had a chance to succeed because you were paying for it.

The supporters of the Affordable Care Act think preventative care should be free. The problem with that is all that incentive to price preventative care cheaply went out the window the minute you said anybody who's insured should never have to pay a penny for preventative care. The incentive to keep prices down was gone.

It's an interesting example of what's happened in all of health care. Look at Medicare. In 1965, the average senior spent 10 percent of his or her income on health care and was paying for all of it. Fast forward almost 50 years. The average senior pays only 5 percent of their total health care costs; 95 percent is paid through Medicare. That 5 percent is now almost 20 percent of their income. They're no better off financially. The extremes are less; fewer people have extreme examples. But all you've done is you've enabled my disguise, my not knowing what something costs me, my crazy belief that someone else is really paying for it to allow the providers to push up prices.

reason: People might think that's because of all the technology in health care that technology is driving up the cost.

Goldhill: I once did a Google search seeing how many articles had been written in the previous year saying that technology had driven up the cost of health care. And then I tried to imagine how many of those articles were written on $400 laptops.

Technology does drive up the cost of anything—if you allow it to. If we said, "everybody should have a smartphone, but we know smartphones are expensive, so anything above $300 the government will pay for," well, your smartphone would be nuclear powered. It would have a can opener on it. It would do everything you can imagine. And technology will have driven up those costs in people's minds.

The issue with health care is: Do we have incentives for those technologies that bring down costs and prices? We don't. Do we have incentives for technology that seems to push up prices and costs to be adopted by providers? Yes. That's the difference. And that's what people miss.

The Reagan-era reform to bundle hospital payments had an enormous impact on hospital use in this country. Most people aren't aware of this, but the average stay per Medicare beneficiary in a hospital in terms of number of days has declined by 60 percent since then. In-patient care is totally transformed; most of it is short. What did the hospitals do in response? They cut their prices because demand declined by 60 percent? No. They invested it in things that push up their costs. So hospitals now say to Medicare, "Our costs are now seven times what they were 30 years ago. And the prices you pay us are now five times." That's not what other industries would have done.

If you go into a typical hospital, you see less information technology than you do at your Jiffy Lube. It's not because Congress pushed Jiffy Lube to adopt information technology; it's because they want to save money. Hospitals never had an incentive to save money. They had the opposite incentive. And that's why technology seems to be pushing up prices.

reason: What are the best and worst attributes of the Affordable Care Act?

Goldhill: The best part of the Affordable Care Act is basing Medicaid on income levels. One of the great dysfunctions of the Medicaid program is that it becomes the favored disease or condition program as opposed to what it needs to be, which is a safety net for those

Americans who can't afford health care. I don't like the way Medicaid functions, but I think the idea of saying, "look, this is about helping people who can't afford health care, period," is a real positive. If we're going to have a safety net, it should be structured more simply.

Unfortunately, the rest of the Affordable Care Act is the opposite of simple. It takes a system that's already way too complex, way too hard for normal consumers to navigate through, and makes it ever more complicated. I don't think there's a lot of genuine market incentives in the Affordable Care Act. I think the people who wrote it think there are. I think most of them are so constricted, so narrow, and so manipulated—I think the exchanges are a good example of this—that we are as likely to see them depress competition and all the benefits that competition brings as to enable competition.

The ACA was most interested in insurance: expanding the amount of insurance coverage in both the number of people covered and the type of coverage itself. There are obviously positives in that. Unfortunately, the American system of insurance, both public and private, is unique in that it has no brake. The principle here is that any care you need should be paid for by your private or public insurance. No other country on earth does this.

reason: You certainly don't see that in places where there's single-payer insurance policies. They have to stop at some point.

Goldhill: Somebody somewhere gets to say no. And by the way, I don't think this is fixable. It's one of the reasons I think you have to have a greater role for the consumer; in the United States, the consumer is the only one who has the recognized authority to say no.

reason: What would a system that works look like?

Goldhill: I would like to see a straightforward, simple, truly universal safety net. It would insure against what insurance can actually do well without distorting the market, which is catastrophic care. We need to protect people from health care catastrophe. You can be born with it. You can destruct suddenly at any point in life.

Beyond that, we really need to unleash in health care those forces that work in everything else. Competition, incentives for innovation, incentives for value, need to satisfy a customer, and need to be accountable to a customer. And the only way to do that is to take some of the $3 trillion we're going to spend on health care and give it back to the places it came from. Give it back to the individuals.

reason: Is that catastrophic coverage necessarily run by the government?

Goldhill: It doesn't have to be, but I think there's an argument for being single-pool. I think the more you limit it to catastrophe, the more efficiently it can be run. I think it needs to be single-pool because as we have found in insurance here, there is no way for a private insurer not to game insurance. And if you're going to make it tax-benefited, if you're going to make it the default way for people to pay for any part of health care, you are going to unfortunately incent for-profit behavior and skimming, which is really what our health care industry and insurance industry are, and we have difficulty relying on it.

I'm very attracted to what Singapore has done. Singapore has a very large environment for government health care. But it does one thing that no other developed country does. It says at every point of purchase that the individual is the customer. The effect is transformative. Not just on price, but on service and safety.

Singapore spends under 4 percent of GDP on health care, making it by far the lowest in the developed world. What's even more interesting is the average Singaporean—and this is a country with roughly the same income per person as the United States—is estimated to have enough in his health savings account after 20 years of the system to pay for 11 hospitalizations.

reason: Any good news on the horizon?

Goldhill: I think there is. I actually think we see it with our own employees here. We now have a significant percentage of our work force that really thinks about the price, the cost to them, of actually buying health care.

And we're starting to see new business models. We're starting to see new technologies take advantage of the fact that we have price-conscious consumers. This is an enormous benefit. It may end up being the biggest accidental result of the Affordable Care Act. To get subsidies on the exchanges, for companies to possibly offer insurance for less than the Cadillac tax [on high-end health plans], we're going to see more and more cost sharing.

On the island of health care, people are focused on, "Oh my God, does that mean somebody might not get health care they need?" In the real economy, what we know is going to happen is that, as you get a scale of cost- and value-motivated consumers, you then have a reason for providers and for business models to seek them out. There are tons of technologies in health care that would save cost.

You want to look at simple health care? Go to a clinic that serves the undocumented or go to a concierge practice that serves the rich. The undocumented and the rich benefit from two things. They're both the only customer. There's no one behind them. They both opted out, either voluntarily or involuntarily, of the insurance system. And what do we see there? Simple, straightforward, price-conscious care.

We're going to see that in more of our economy. People say all the time, "Where are the Bill Gateses? Where are the Steve Jobses? Where are the FedExes? Where are the Walmarts?" Well, there's never been enough scale and customers to build those business models that emphasize value, true innovation, service, and accountability. I think we're going to get to a point where enough people pay the first $2,000 or $2,500 or even $10,000 out of pocket that the Steve Jobs of health care comes along. He's soon going to have a big enough market to actually build a better product and offer better service and that's going to be great for health care.

We're already seeing hospitals advertise for safety. We're seeing cancer care centers advertise on service, convenience, and comfort. In health care, these are all seen as waste. State-of-the-art health care can be a commodity. That would be a great thing. Differentiated on service and accountability and value? We could get there. We'd get there in opposition to public policy, but it wouldn't be the first time that has happened.

"It's extraordinary how removing the consumer from health care has caused us to buy everything."

"In health care, we never talk about prices. We like to believe that somehow there's some force that actually determines what something costs that is independent of economics."

Critical Thinking

1. What are the reasons hospitals have little incentive to save money?

2. How will preventive care bring down medical costs?

Create Central

www.mhhe.com/createcentral

Internet References

Centers for Disease Control and Prevention
http://www.cdc.gov

Fair Health Consumer Costs
http://fairhealthconsumer.org

Article   Prepared by: Eileen L. Daniel, *SUNY Brockport*

Bed Bugs: The Pesticide Dilemma

REBECCA BERG

Learning Outcomes

After reading this article, you will be able to:

- Explain the risks, if any, associated with infestation with bed bugs.

- Describe why the number of bed bugs is increasing.

- Describe how bed bugs have become pesticide-resistant.

"Six different companies have now found them in movie theaters," said Michael Potter, professor of entomology at the University of Kentucky. Potter works with pest control companies and their customers all over the country. Asked where bed bugs are cropping up, he rattled off a list that included everything from single-family homes to hospitals, libraries, schools ("obviously dormitories," he noted), and modes of transportation. The problem is particularly daunting in apartment buildings since people frequently move in and out with all their belongings.

"It's bad and getting worse," he said. "It's almost like an epizootic or a pandemic where somebody coughs and six more people get it."

He is not alone in sounding the alarm.

"I don't think we've hit anywhere near the peak," observed Jack Marlowe, president of Eden Advanced Pest Technologies. Eden Commercial I.P.M. Consultant Cody Pace, who was on the same call, added that before World War II, one in three homes were infested with bed bugs. "People dealt with it, and it was part of life. . . . I hope it doesn't get to the point where we're all just living with bed bugs."

A Logistical Nightmare

They are small. They can hide in any crack or crevice. (Think furniture joints, floorboards, baseboards, box springs, picture frames, closets full of clothing, personal belongings of almost any sort.) The early stages of infestations are hard to spot.

They can spread from room to room through duct work or false ceilings. They can be transported from venue to venue on clothing and belongings.

Their eggs are even smaller and almost transparent. They are attached to surfaces by means of a sticky substance.

You can't reduce infestations the way you might with cockroaches, by cleaning up food scraps, depriving them of shelter, and putting out bait. "You *are* their meal," said Elizabeth Dykstra, public health entomologist for the Zoonotic Disease Program of the Washington State Department of Health (WDOH).

And, she said, they can survive up to 18 months without a meal.

They have a history of developing resistance to pesticides. Potter and colleagues' research has shown widespread resistance to the pyrethroid insecticides that are currently the standard treatment (Romero, Potter, & Haynes, 2007).

They have idiosyncratic tastes—they're attracted by the heat and carbon dioxide that sleeping people generate, and they will feed only through a membrane. That means significant logistical challenges for trapping and baiting. (A Rutgers University Web page provides information on devising traps out of cat food bowls and dry ice—but only for diagnostic purposes. See njaes.rutgers.edu/pubs/publication.asp?pid=FS1117.)

None of the experts *JEH* spoke with saw any prospect of the bed bug problem spontaneously lessening in coming years.

Solutions from the Last Time Around

For half a century now, most Americans haven't had to worry about bed bugs. The problem previously reached its height in the 1920s and 1930s. Bed bugs had spread from port areas to major cities and eventually reached less populated rural areas.

Through the '40s and '50s, populations of the pest declined, primarily because DDT was widely available. Consumers could, for instance, buy DDT bug bombs in grocery stores. By the time bed bugs began developing resistance to DDT—which, inevitably, they did—organophosphates like diazinon and malathion were being used to clear up remaining infestations.

Larry Treleven, whose family has been in the pest control business for 84 years, said that his father and grandfather used to fumigate used furniture in their vaults. State laws required that the furniture be tagged as fumigated before it could be resold.

It was a different way of life, according to Potter. When people traveled, they knew to check their beds. When children came back from summer camp, their clothes and bedding had

to be checked. He wondered whether people these days are prepared to exercise that kind of vigilance.

"And," he said, "people have a lot more clutter today, a lot
more *stuff*. Which makes bed bug elimination more difficult."

Today, the hazards of pesticide treatment are also more
widely recognized. Pesticide treatment options have narrowed
for other reasons. DDT, for instance, is now illegal in the United
States (U.S. Environmental Protection Agency [U.S. EPA],
1972). Besides, toward the end of the last epidemic, it had
lost much of its effectiveness because bed bugs had developed
resistance to it. Then other chemicals such as lindane and the
organophosphates diazinon and malathion were used to mop up.

The Propoxur Proposal

On October 21, 2009, Matt Beal, acting chief of the Plant Industry Division of the Ohio Department of Agriculture (ODA),
submitted a Section 18 request to the U.S. Environmental Protection Agency (U.S. EPA). The request was for an emergency
exemption that would allow a pesticide called propoxur to be
used by pest control professionals for treatment of bed bugs.

"For reasons nobody fully understands," Potter told *JEH*,
"Ohio is really getting hammered."

Mystery Pesticide

Propoxur is a carbamate pesticide with a murky regulatory
history. Currently it is used in some ant and cockroach baits,
insecticidal strips, shelf paper, and pet collars. Although it is
also labeled for use as a crack-and-crevice spray in food-han-
dling establishments, U.S. EPA does not currently permit its
use in locations where children may be present. That means no
use in residential buildings and hotels.

But there's a loophole: products that were already in the
channels of trade when current prohibitions went into effect
may still be labeled for now prohibited uses. Strictly speaking,
Beal said, use of those products is still legal. "The label is the
law," as Jennifer Sievert, public health advisor for the WDOH
Pesticide Program, put it. Indeed, because some of the labels
allow consumers to use the product indoors, the permission that
ODA is seeking (which would make propoxur available only to
pest control professionals) would actually be *more* restrictive
than the law as it now stands. That circumstance, according to
Beal, has been a factor in the choice of propoxur for the Section
18 exemption request.

Of course, legality is not synonymous with safety. In 1988,
U.S. EPA considered conducting a Special Review of propoxur
"because of the potential carcinogenic risks to pest control
operators and the general public during indoor and outdoor
applications and risks to occupants of buildings treated with
propoxur products" (U.S. EPA, 1997a, 1997b). In 1995, the
agency decided *not* to initiate the Special Review because "the
uses which posed the greatest concern had been eliminated
through voluntary cancellation or label amendment" (U.S.
EPA, 1997b). And in 2007, at the request of the registrant, it
issued a final order terminating indoor use, according to the
U.S. EPA document *Risk Management Decisions for Individual
N-methyl Carbamate Pesticides* (U.S. EPA, 2007).

Sievert interprets that history to mean that propoxur was
withdrawn because of evidence suggesting it was not safe. Potter interprets the withdrawal as a business decision; he believes
that the cost of refuting challenges to its safety would have been
more than the product was worth to its manufacturers. Either
way, there are now some gaps in the data on health effects.

U.S. EPA has placed propoxur in Toxicity Category II (the
second-highest category) for oral exposure and Toxicity Category III for dermal and inhalation exposures. Propoxur is also
classed as a "probable human carcinogen."

Why Propoxur?

A couple of years ago, Potter and colleagues at the University
of Kentucky decided to test some older insecticides and compare their efficacy to that of pyrethroids. They tested propoxur
and chlorpyrifos (an organophosphate) on five populations of
bed bugs collected from the field. Four of those populations
had proved to be highly resistant to pyrethroids. Both pesticides
killed 100% of all populations within 24 hours—"and frankly,"
Potter told *JEH*, "within an *hour*."

Ohio is not making its request in a vacuum. Beal has worked
on this issue not only with Potter, but also with the Association of Structural Pest Control Regulatory Officials (ASPCRO).
There were also some preliminary conversations with U.S.
EPA, he said, and "there's a multitude of other states awaiting
this decision."

What about the safety concerns? Beal told *JEH:* "Basically,
our role here is that we have a serious situation at hand. . . . We
feel that it's a reasonable request to ask the agency to take a
look at this. Certainly I'm not a toxicologist, I'm not a physician. I'm in the area of pesticide regulation. So we felt it was a
reasonable request."

Does that mean ODA is putting this request out as an open
question to U.S. EPA? In other words, the gist is not: We think
it's safe, and we definitely want to use it? Rather, the gist is:
Will you check this out and see if it's safe?

"Exactly," Beal said. "That's what the process is."

What if U.S. EPA says no, it's not safe? Is there a plan B?

"That is an interesting dilemma," he said. "Then we stand
back and we keep talking amongst the ASPCRO states. We talk
with the professional management folks—the pest management
professionals—and try to see if there are any other avenues for
us to go down. Fortunately, we're not at that point right now."

Contra

Early this year, Dykstra and Sievert submitted the following
comment to U.S. EPA: "We do not support the proposed health
exemption request from the Ohio Department of Agriculture to
use the pesticide propoxur . . . to treat indoor residential single
or multiple unit dwellings, apartments, hotels, motels, office
buildings, modes of transportation, and commercial industrial
buildings to control bed bugs." They cited research showing
that the pesticide "remains detectable in indoor air weeks after
initial application" and that "use of propoxur exposes the developing fetus in pregnant women to the chemical."

Carbamate pesticides, of which propoxur is one, are
neurotoxins. Like organophosphates, they inhibit cholinesterase,

Propoxur and the Regulatory Process: Information from U.S. EPA

In response to *JEH*'s request for an interview, U.S. EPA sent the following written statement about the regulatory history of propoxur and the process the agency is following in determining whether to grant ODA's Section 18 request:

Section 18 of Federal Insecticide, Fungicide, and Rodenticide Act (FIFRA) authorizes EPA to allow an unregistered use of a pesticide for a limited time if EPA determines that an emergency condition exists. EPA's review process for a Section 18 includes determining whether the use meets the applicable safety standard as well as whether the unregistered use meets the criterion of being an emergency. See www.epa.gov/opprd001/section18/for more information.

Propoxur is currently registered for use as follows:

- Indoor sprays in commercial buildings including food handling establishments to control roaches, ants, beetles, bees, etc. Labels explicitly exclude sprays in locations where children may be present (so no use in hotels, residential buildings, libraries, daycare facilities, schools). In food handling establishments, the use is restricted to crack and crevice application. Note that products in the channels of trade currently before the most recent labeling requirements may still be labeled for indoor residential use.
- Granular and gel baits for ants and cockroaches, some enclosed in bait stations.
- Impregnated insecticidal strips and shelf paper, to control cockroaches, bees, wasps, ants, etc.
- Pet collars to control fleas and ticks. Some are combination products with other active ingredients.

Information about historical use/regulation is available in the Propoxur Reregistration Eligibility Decision (1997), which can be accessed at www.epa.gov/pesticides/reregistration/propoxur/.

although poisoning with carbamates is more easily reversed with treatment, and there is a "greater span between symptom-producing and lethal doses," according to Reigart and Roberts's *Recognition and Management of Pesticide Poisonings* (Reigart & Roberts, 1999). Serious overexposure can cause death by cardiorespiratory depression. Early symptoms include malaise, sweating, muscle weakness, headache, dizziness, and gastrointestinal symptoms. Other symptoms of acute toxicity are coma, hypertension, trouble breathing, blurred vision, lack of coordination, twitching, and slurring of speech.

The biggest concern is with chronic (or acute) exposure to small children and developing fetuses, according to Wayne Clifford, who manages the Pesticide Illness and Zoonotics Disease Surveillance and Prevention program in WDOH's Office of Environmental Health. Children are not small adults, he reminded *JEH;* their neurological pathways are developing. "There's so much going on there biologically that *isn't* happening in full-grown adults, and they are much more sensitive. That's the primary population that we're trying to protect."

But the fact that propoxur is classed as a probable carcinogen is of concern for people of any age.

Dykstra and Sievert think pest control professionals should pursue alternative treatments. Such treatments might not, Dykstra acknowledged, completely eliminate the problem. But they would reduce it to tolerable levels.

"Instead of poisoning yourself or your children or whoever lives in the house," Sievert said. "That's really being played down here by propoxur proponents. In fact, there's basically no mention of it, that I can see."

Other Options

Marlowe of Eden Advanced Pest Technologies told *JEH* he is not a "fan" of the Ohio request: "From a *business* standpoint, it seems like we're headed in the wrong direction, to use a product like that around people's beds and in their bedrooms." Pesticides in sleeping quarters, he noted, are a potential liability for a company: "Even if it was made available to us, I'd probably stay with some of the other, lighter chemistries that we already have in the toolbox."

Eden uses steam heat to kill bed bugs, in combination with cedar oil and some other essential oils. Since these methods kill bed bugs only upon direct contact, Eden also applies diatomaceous earth to cracks, crevices, and any area bed bugs might be likely to crawl across. Diatomaceous earth abrades the exoskeleton, so that bodily fluids leak out and the insect eventually dries up.

Everyone agreed that diatomaceous earth is effective and that it shares an important advantage with propoxur: the ability to act residually. That is, it will act on any bugs not killed by direct-contact treatments, as well as on any bugs that get reintroduced after a treatment. A drawback, however, is that it works slowly. Potter also noted that application is tricky because it requires an extremely fine dusting, and applicators are not readily available to consumers. Pest control professionals have to be called in, and that means expense. Of course, the same would also be true of propoxur.

Another alternative, used by Treleven's company, Sprague Pest Solutions, is volumetric heating, which involves "superheating" an entire room to around 140F. Probes are used to ensure that the internal temperatures of objects in the room also reach temperatures high enough to kill the bugs. In addition, Sprague has dogs trained to sniff out any bed bugs that might remain. Unfortunately, this approach is expensive. The cost of equipping a single pest control team with a heater and generator approaches $50,000, and the setup and breakdown work make treatment an all-day, labor-intensive affair. Treleven estimated that treating a 1,700 square foot townhouse could cost a couple thousand dollars. Any conjoined units might then also have to be treated. Room-by-room treatment of multi-unit buildings could be a daunting prospect.

Treleven does recommend heat, combined with diatomaceous earth and canine detection, as a first, best treatment choice. But, he said, "If they can't afford the heating and the alternatives and things, it would be nice to have propoxur. I mean, I'm not going to lie to you. Because it is an alternative that would work."

Conclusion

In the case of bed bugs, none of the options are ideal. All can take a bite, figuratively speaking, out of someone's life.

Let's start with pesticides. Cancer risk, developmental detriments, and central nervous system effects can all subtract from longevity, fruitfulness, and life satisfaction. According to U.S. EPA's *R.E.D. Facts,* a reference dose (RfD) of 0.004 mg/kg/day is not expected to cause adverse effects over a 70-year lifetime (U.S. EPA, 1997). But as Clifford of WDOH put it, "there is not really a safe level of exposure to a carcinogen," because effects are cumulative and people may have exposures from other sources, such as residue on food. Propoxur treatments in areas where people sleep could entail extended exposures, especially since the pesticide has been demonstrated to volatilize in the air and be absorbed into the blood weeks after application (Whyatt et al., 2003).

But absent an effective pesticide, the need for relentless vigilance just as assuredly takes a bite out of life. Potter told *JEH* that he's had residents call him in tears when infestations have persisted after months of vigilant laundering and vacuuming. Added to the many stresses contemporary Americans already face, that kind of constant pressure can have a cumulative effect. Nor is money a negligible concern: the need for repeated expensive treatments can further contribute to financial insecurity—which in turn has its own, well-documented, health impacts.

Individual consumers could well come to different conclusions depending on personal circumstances, and making propoxur available could add to their choices.

But there are a couple of problems with casting this issue as a straightforward risk-benefit decision for individuals.

First, the impacts of neurotoxins on developing brains are difficult to sort out, much less document and quantify—which doesn't mean they're not happening. As Colborn writes: "Unlike obvious birth defects, most developmental effects cannot be seen at birth or even later in life. Instead, brain and nervous system disturbances are expressed in terms of how an individual behaves and functions, which can vary considerably from birth through adulthood" (2006, p.10).

Second, there's the question of whose risk and whose benefit. It's one thing for homeowners to weigh risks and benefits on their own and their families' behalf. Apartment buildings and other rental properties represent a different scenario. How many landlords, given the choice between repeated expensive heat treatments and a quick, inexpensive treatment with a U.S EPA approved pesticide, can be expected to choose the former? Perhaps a few. But it seems likely that in most cases, the decision will be a foregone conclusion. In the end, apartment dwellers could be subject, involuntarily and perhaps unknowingly, to extended exposures.

Nobody *JEH* interviewed thinks propoxur holds all the answers. ODA's exemption request is just a way of looking for something to, as Beal said, "help us through this critical time right now that we're seeing until something else further down the road can be developed to try to take care of the problem."

But will something else be developed "down the road"? Or will propoxur simply become the default treatment—at least until bed bugs develop resistance to it, too?

References

Colborn, T. (2006). A case for revisiting the safety of pesticides: A closer look at neurodevelopment. *Environmental Health Perspectives,* 114(1), 10-17.

Reigart, J.R., & Roberts, J.R. (1999). *Recognition and management of pesticide poisonings* (5th ed.). Washington, DC: U.S. EPA. Retrieved March 3, 2010, from www.epa.gov/pesticides/safety / healthcare/handbook/Chap05.pdf

Romero, A., Potter, M.F., & Haynes, K.F. (2007, July). Insecticide-resistant bed bugs: Implications for the industry. *Pest Control Technology.* Retrieved April 6, 2010, from www.pctonline.com /Article.aspx?article%5fid=37916

U.S. Environmental Protection Agency. (1972). *DDT ban takes effect.* Retrieved April 5, 2010, from www.epa.gov/history/topics /ddt/01.htm

U.S. Environmental Protection Agency. (1997a). *Reregistration eligibility decision (RED): Propoxur.* Retrieved April 5, 2010, from www.epa.gov/oppsrrd1/REDs/2555red.pdf

U.S. Environmental Protection Agency. (1997b). *R.E.D. facts: Propoxur* (U.S. EPA document # EPA-738-F-97-009). Retrieved April 5, 2010, from www.epa.gov/oppsrrd1/REDs /factsheets/2555fact.pdf

U.S. Environmental Protection Agency. (2007). *Risk management decisions for individual N-methyl carbamate pesticides.* Retrieved April 3, 2010, from epa.gov/oppsrrd1/cumulative /carbamate_ risk_mgmt.htm#propoxur

Whyatt, R.M., Barr, D.B., Camann, D.E., Kinney, P.L., Barr, J.R., Andrews, H.F., Hoepner, L.A., Garfinkel, R., Hazi, Y., Reyes, A., Ramirez, J., Cosme, Y., & Perera, F.P. (2003). Contemporary-use pesticides in personal air samples during pregnancy and blood samples at delivery among urban minority mothers and newborns. *Environmental Health Perspectives,* 111(5), 749–756.

Critical Thinking

1. What are the risks, if any, associated with bed bug bites?
2. How can bed bugs be eliminated?

Create Central

www.mhhe.com/createcentral

Internet References

Environmental Protection Agency
www.epa.gov
World Health Organization
www.who.org

Berg, Rebecca. From *Journal of Environmental Health*, June 2010, pp. 32–35. Copyright © 2010 by National Environmental Health Association. Reprinted by permission.

Article   Prepared by: Eileen Daniel, *SUNY College at Brockport*

How Not to Die

Angelo Volandes's low-tech, high-empathy plan to revolutionize end-of-life care.

JONATHAN RAUCH

Learning Outcomes

After reading this article, you will be able to:

- Understand why the U.S. medical system was built to treat anything that might be treatable, at any stage of life—even when there is no hope of a cure, and when the patient, if fully informed, might prefer quality time and relative normalcy to intervention.

- Explain why unwanted treatment seems especially common near the end of life.

- Understand why unwanted medical treatment is a by-product of two strengths of American medical culture: the system's determination to save lives and technology.

D r. Angelo Volandes is making a film that he believes will change the way you die. The studio is his living room in Newton, Massachusetts, a suburb of Boston; the control panel is his laptop; the camera crew is a 24-year-old guy named Jake; the star is his wife, Aretha Delight Davis. Volandes, a thickening mesomorph with straight brown hair that is graying at his temples, is wearing a T-shirt and shorts and looks like he belongs at a football game. Davis, a beautiful woman of Guyanese extraction with richly braided hair, is dressed in a white lab coat over a black shirt and stands before a plain gray backdrop.

"Remember: always slow," Volandes says.

"Sure, hon," Davis says, annoyed. She has done this many times.

Volandes claps to sync the sound. "Take one: Goals of Care, Dementia."

You are seeing this video because you are making medical decisions for a person with advanced dementia. Davis intones the words in a calm, uninflected voice. *I'll show you a video of a person with advanced dementia. Then you will see images to help you understand the three options for their medical care.*

Her narration will be woven into a 10-minute film. The words I'm hearing will accompany footage of an elderly woman in a wheelchair. The woman is coiffed and dressed in her Sunday finest, wearing pearls and makeup for her film appearance, but her face is vacant and her mouth is frozen in the rictus of a permanent *O*.

This woman lives in a nursing home and has advanced dementia. She's seen here with her daughters. She has the typical features of advanced dementia. . .

Young in affect and appearance, Volandes, 41, is an assistant professor at Harvard Medical School; Davis, also an MD, is doing her residency in internal medicine, also at Harvard. When I heard about Volandes's work, I suspected that he would be different from other doctors. I was not disappointed. He refuses to let me call him "Dr. Volandes," for example. Formality impedes communication, he tells me, and "there's nothing more essential to being a good doctor than your ability to communicate." More important, he believes that his videos can disrupt the way the medical system handles late-life care and that the system urgently needs disrupting.

"I think we're probably the most subversive two doctors to the health system that you will meet today," he says, a few hours before his shoot begins. "That has been told to me by other people."

"You sound proud of that," I say.

"I'm proud of that because it's being an agent of change, and the more I see poor health care, or health care being delivered that puts patients and families through—"

"We torture people before they die," Davis interjects, quietly.

Volandes chuckles at my surprise. "Remember, Jon is a reporter," he tells her, not at all unhappy with her comment.

"My father, if he were sitting here, would be saying 'Right on,'" I tell him.

Volandes nods. "Here's the sad reality," he says. "Physicians are good people. They want to do the right things. And yet all of us, behind closed doors, in the cafeteria, say, 'Do you believe what we did to that patient? Do you believe what we put that patient through?' Every single physician has stories. Not one. Lots of stories."

"In the health-care debate, we've heard a lot about useless care, wasteful care, futile care. What we"—Volandes indicates himself and Davis—"have been struggling with is unwanted care. That's far more concerning. That's not avoidable care. That's *wrongful* care. I think that the most urgent issue facing America today is people getting medical interventions that, if they were more informed, they would not want. It happens all the time."

Unwanted treatment is American medicine's dark continent. No one knows its extent, and few people want to talk about it. The U.S. medical system was built to treat anything that might be treatable, at any stage of life—even near the end, when there is no hope of a cure, and when the patient, if fully informed, might prefer quality time and relative normalcy to all-out intervention.

In 2009, my father was suffering from an advanced and untreatable neurological condition that would soon kill him. (I wrote about his decline in an article for this magazine in April 2010.) Eating, drinking, and walking were all difficult and dangerous for him. He ate, drank, and walked anyway because doing his best to lead a normal life sustained his morale and slowed his decline. "Use it or lose it," he often said. His strategy broke down calamitously when he agreed to be hospitalized for an MRI test. I can only liken his experience to an alien abduction. He was bundled into a bed, tied to tubes, and banned from walking without help or taking anything by mouth. No one asked him about what he wanted. After a few days, and a test that turned up nothing, he left the hospital no longer able to walk. Some weeks later, he managed to get back on his feet; unfortunately, by then he was only a few weeks from death. The episode had only one positive result. Disgusted and angry after his discharge from the hospital, my father turned to me and said, "I am *never* going back there." (He never did.)

What should have taken place was what is known in the medical profession as The Conversation. The momentum of medical maximalism should have slowed long enough for a doctor or a social worker to sit down with him and me to explain, patiently and in plain English, his condition and his treatment options, to learn what his goals were for the time he had left, and to establish how much and what kind of treatment he really desired. Alas, evidence shows that The Conversation happens much less regularly than it should and that, when it

does happen, information is typically presented in a brisk, jargony way that patients and families don't really understand. Many doctors don't make time for The Conversation, or aren't good at conducting it (they're not trained or rewarded for doing so), or worry their patients can't handle it.

This is a problem because the assumption that doctors know what their patients want turns out to be wrong: when doctors try to predict the goals and preferences of their patients, they are "highly inaccurate," according to one summary of the research, published by Benjamin Moulton and Jaime S. King in *The Journal of Law, Medicine & Ethics*. Patients are "routinely asked to make decisions about treatment choices in the face of what can only be described as avoidable ignorance," Moulton and King write. "In the absence of complete information, individuals frequently opt for procedures they would not otherwise choose."

Though no one knows for sure, unwanted treatment seems especially common near the end of life. A few years ago, at age 94, a friend of mine's father was hospitalized with internal bleeding and kidney failure. Instead of facing reality (he died within days), the hospital tried to get authorization to remove his colon and put him on dialysis. Even physicians tell me that they have difficulty holding back the kind of mindlessly aggressive treatment that one doctor I spoke with calls "the war on death." Matt Handley, a doctor and an executive with Group Health Cooperative, a big health system in Washington state, described his father-in-law's experience as a "classic example of overmedicalization." There was no Conversation. "He went to the ICU for no medical reason," Handley says. "No one talked to him about the fact that he was going to die, even though outside the room, clinicians, when asked, would say 'Oh, yes, he's dying.'"

"Sometimes you block the near exits, and all you've got left is a far exit, which is not a dignified and comfortable death."

"Sometimes you block the near exits, and all you've got left is a far exit, which is not a dignified and comfortable death," Albert Mulley, a physician and the director of the Dartmouth Center for Health Care Delivery Science, told me recently. As we talked, it emerged that he, too, had had to fend off the medical system when his father died at age 93. "Even though I spent my whole career doing this," he said, "when I was trying to assure as good a death as I could for my dad, I found it wasn't easy."

If it is this hard for doctors to navigate their parents' final days, imagine what many ordinary patients and their families face. "It's almost impossible for patients really to be in charge," says Joanne Lynn, a physician and the director of the nonprofit

Altarum Center for Elder Care and Advanced Illness in Washington, D.C. "We enforce a kind of learned helplessness, especially in hospitals." I asked her how much unwanted treatment gets administered. She couldn't come up with a figure—no one can—but she said, "It's huge, however you measure it. Especially when people get very, very sick."

Unwanted treatment is a particularly confounding problem because it is not a product of malevolence but a by-product of two strengths of American medical culture: the system's determination to save lives and its technological virtuosity. Change will need to be consonant with that culture. "You have to be comfortable working at the margins of the power structure within medicine, and particularly within academic medicine," Mulley told me. You need a disrupter, but one who can speak the language of medicine and meet the system on its own terms.

Angelo Volandes was born in 1971, in Brooklyn, to Greek immigrants. His father owned a diner. He and his older sister were the first in their family to go to college—Harvard, in his case. In Cambridge, he got a part-time job cooking for an elderly, childless couple, who became second parents to him. He watched as the wife got mortally sick, he listened to her labored breathing, he talked with her and her husband about pain, death, the end of life. Those conversations led him to courses in medical ethics, which he told me that he found abstract and out of touch with "the clinical reality of being short of breath; of fear; of anxiety and suffering; of medications and interventions." He decided to go to medical school, not just to cure people but also "to learn how people suffer and what the implications of dying and suffering and understanding that experience are like." Halfway through med school at Yale, on the recommendation of a doctor he met one day at the gym, he took a year off to study documentary filmmaking, another of his interests. At the time, it seemed a digression.

On the very first night of his postgraduate medical internship, when he was working the graveyard shift at a hospital in Philadelphia, he found himself examining a woman dying of cancer. She was a bright woman, a retired English professor, but she seemed bewildered when he asked whether she wanted cardiopulmonary resuscitation if her heart stopped beating. So, on an impulse, he invited her to visit the intensive-care unit. By coincidence, she witnessed a "code blue," an emergency administration of CPR. "When we got back to the room," Volandes remembered, "she said, 'I understood what you told me. I am a professor of English—I understood the words. I just didn't know what you meant. It's not what I had imagined. It's not what I saw on TV.'" She decided to go home on hospice. Volandes realized that he could make a stronger, clearer impression on patients by showing them treatments than by trying to describe them.

He spent the next few years punching all the tickets he could: mastering the technical arts of doctoring, credentialing

himself in medical ethics, learning statistical techniques to perform peer-reviewed clinical trials, joining the Harvard faculty and the clinical and research staff of Massachusetts General Hospital. He held on to his passion, though. During a fellowship at Harvard in 2004, he visited Dr. Muriel Gillick, a Harvard Medical School professor and an authority on late-life care. Volandes "was very distressed by what he saw clinically being done to people with advanced dementia," Gillick recalls. "He was interested in writing an article about how treatment of patients with advanced dementia was a form of abuse." Gillick talked him down. Some of what's done is wrong, she agreed, but raging against it would not help. The following year, with her support, Volandes began his video project.

The first film he made featured a patient with advanced dementia. It showed her inability to converse, move about, or feed herself. When Volandes finished the film, he ran a randomized clinical trial with a group of nine other doctors. All of their patients listened to a verbal description of advanced dementia, and some of them also watched the video. All were then asked whether they preferred life-prolonging care (which does everything possible to keep patients alive), limited care (an intermediate option), or comfort care (which aims to maximize comfort and relieve pain). The results were striking: patients who had seen the video were significantly more likely to choose comfort care than those who hadn't seen it (86 percent versus 64 percent). Volandes published that study in 2009, following it a year later with an even more striking trial, this one showing a video to patients dying of cancer. Of those who saw it, more than 90 percent chose comfort care—versus 22 percent of those who received only verbal descriptions. The implications, to Volandes, were clear: "Videos communicate better than just a stand-alone conversation. And when people get good communication and understand what's involved, many, if not most, tend not to want a lot of the aggressive stuff that they're getting."

Even now, after years of refinement, Volandes's finished videos look deceptively unimpressive. They're short, and they're bland. But that, it turns out, is what is most impressive about them. Other videos describing treatment options—for, say, breast cancer or heart disease—can last upwards of 30 minutes. Volandes's films, by contrast, average six or seven minutes. They are meant to be screened on iPads or laptops, amid the bustle of a clinic or hospital room.

They are also meant to be banal, a goal that requires a meticulous, if perverse, application of the filmmaker's art. "Videos are an aesthetic medium; you can manipulate people's perspective," Volandes says. "I want to provide information *without* evoking visceral emotions." Any hint that he was appealing to sentiments like revulsion or fear to nudge patients toward a certain course of treatment would discredit his whole project, so Volandes does all he can to eliminate emotional cues. That is why he films advanced-dementia patients dressed and groomed to the nines. "I give them the nicest image," Volandes told me. "If with the nicest image we show a huge effect, you can imagine what it would be like if they really saw the reality."

The typical video begins with Davis explaining what the viewer is about to see, stating plainly facts that doctors are sometimes reluctant to mention. She says, for example: *People with advanced dementia usually have had the disease for many years and have reached the last stage of dementia. They are nearing the end of life.* The video cuts to a shot of a patient. Then Davis outlines the three levels of care, starting with the most aggressive. Over footage of CPR and mechanical ventilation, she explains that in most cases of advanced dementia, CPR does not work, and that patients on breathing machines are usually not aware of their surroundings and cannot eat or talk. Then she describes limited care and comfort care, again speaking bluntly about death. *People who choose comfort care choose to avoid these procedures even though, without them, they might die.* She concludes by recommending The Conversation.

It seems a minor thing, showing a short video. As, indeed, it will be, if it happens only occasionally. I didn't get my head around the scale of Volandes's ambition until I understood that he wants to make his videos ubiquitous. His intention is not only to provide clearer information but, more important, to trigger The Conversation as a matter of medical routine. "We're saying, 'You're not doing your job if you are not having these conversations in a meaningful way with patients and their families,'" he tells me. "If every patient watched a video, there's standardization in the process. That's why I call it subversive. Very few things in medicine can change the culture like that."

Routine use, however, is far, far away. According to Volandes, only a few dozen U.S. hospitals, out of more than 5,700, are using his videos. I spoke with physicians and a social worker at three health systems that are piloting them, and all were very enthusiastic about the results. Volandes is particularly hopeful about a collaboration with the Hawaii Medical Service Association, the state's dominant health-insurance provider, which is piloting the videos in hospitals, nursing homes, and doctors' offices. Officials say that they hope to expand use statewide within three years. Right now, though, Volandes's videos have a limited reach.

The problem is not his product but the peculiar nature of the market he wants to push it into. His innovation is inexpensive and low-tech, and might avert misunderstanding, prevent suffering, improve doctor-patient relationships, and, incidentally, save the health-care system a lot of money. He goes out of

his way not to emphasize cost savings, partly because he sees himself as a patients'-rights advocate rather than a bean counter, and partly because it is so easy to demagogue the issue, as Sarah Palin did so mendaciously (and effectively) in 2009, when she denounced end-of-life-care planning as "death panels." Anyone who questions medical maximalism risks being attacked for trying to kill grandma—all the more so if he mentions saving money. For all its talk of making the health-care system more rational and less expensive, the political system is still not ready for an honest discussion. And the medical system has its own ways of fighting back.

Volandes works on his videos ceaselessly. He has curtailed his medical practice and his teaching responsibilities, both of which he misses, and last year gave more than 70 speeches evangelizing for the video project. In an effort to batter the medical establishment into submission with the sheer weight of scientific evidence, he has conducted 13 clinical trials using videos to depict different diseases and situations, and he has seven more studies in the pipeline. He says he gets by on three or four hours of sleep a night. The project has taken over his house. Davis would like her living room back; there are floodlights and a big gray backdrop where her paintings should be.

Volandes thinks he can sustain this pace for perhaps five years—by which time he hopes to have revolutionized American medicine. Davis tries to dial back his expectations, but he resists. "Not when I have nurses and doctors use words like *torture* as often as they do," he says. "In order to make a change, you've got to be ambitious. If not, then just publish and get your tenure and move on."

Volandes has entrepreneurial OCD: the gift, and curse, of unswerving faith in a potentially world-changing idea.

During my visit, I realized that I had encountered Volandes's type before, but in Silicon Valley. Volandes has entrepreneurial obsessive-compulsive disorder: the gift, and curse, of unswerving faith in a potentially world-changing idea.

It is not a huge exaggeration to say that obsessive entrepreneurs, from Cornelius Vanderbilt to Steve Jobs, made America great. It is also not a huge exaggeration to say that health care, more than any other nongovernmental sector, has made itself impervious to disruptive innovation. Medical training discourages entrepreneurship, embedded practice patterns marginalize it, bureaucrats in medical organizations and insurance companies recoil from it. And would-be disrupters are generally disconnected from patients, their ultimate customers: they have to take their innovations to physicians, who are notoriously change-averse, and then they must get the government—Medicare, first and foremost—to approve and pay for them. Imagine that Jeff Bezos, when he was starting Amazon, had needed to ask permission from bookstores and libraries.

Volandes, therefore, will fail. That is to say, he will fail if success means revolutionizing the doctor-patient relationship and making The Conversation ubiquitous within five years. Meanwhile, if the American health-care system does not learn how to harness the energy and ideas of people like Volandes, *it* will fail. Somewhere between those failures lies a path forward. We know medical culture can change for the better; it takes the treatment of pain much more seriously than it used to, for example, and it has embraced hospice care.

The best news about U.S. health care today is that a lot of reform-minded entrepreneurship is bubbling up from within. Volandes is not alone. So many patients and doctors and family members feel marginalized and bureaucratized and overwhelmed that some health systems and insurers, in spontaneous mini-rebellions, are starting to innovate, often on their own dime. I think of Dr. Brad Stuart of Sutter Health at Home, who is building a new late-life-care system that bridges the gap between hospital and hospice, allowing the very sick to receive more care at home; I think of Dr. Derek Raghavan of Carolinas HealthCare System's Levine Cancer Institute, who is building a "cancer center without walls" that uses telemedicine and other tools to make state-of-the-art treatment available to patients, regardless of where they live. I think of Dr. Woody English of Providence Health and Services, who is 67 and wants to make a difference before he retires. At his instigation, Providence has begun using Volandes's videos. "The changes will come locally," English told me, "not nationally." When I look at him and Volandes and the others, I see not only a test of whether the health-care system's medical culture can change but also a test of whether its *business* culture can change—and that change may, in the end, be even more important.

The morning after the shoot, Volandes shows me some of the footage he plans to use. We watch a patient with advanced Alzheimer's being fed through a tube that has been surgically inserted into her stomach. An attendant uses a big syringe to clear the tube and then attaches a bag of thick fluid. Over the footage, Davis's voice will say, *Often, people hope tube feeding will help the patient live longer. But tube feeding has not been shown to prolong or improve the quality of life in advanced dementia. Tube feeding also does not stop saliva or food from going down the wrong way.*

Volandes is explaining to me that tube feeding is overused in elderly dementia patients, but my mind has floated back to 2009. My father's disease, by then, had destroyed his ability to protect his airway when he swallowed; food, drink, and saliva ended up in his lungs. He coughed violently when he ate or drank. Doctors mentioned tube feeding as an option, and well-intentioned friends nudged us in that direction. But his friends had no real idea what tube feeding entailed, and neither did I, and neither did he.

"Let me ask you this," Volandes says. "Suppose I'm having a conversation with you about whether your father would want this. And I said 'feeding tube,' and you're thinking to yourself, *Food, yeah, I could give food to my mom or dad.* We just want to make sure that regardless of the way the gastroenterologist is presenting the procedure, the patient's loved ones know *this* is what we're talking about."

Not long before my father died, I asked a hospice nurse about tube feeding. He told me, with grim clarity: "I think that would be cruel." I remember that nurse with gratitude because he was right. But "that would be cruel" was not a substitute for The Conversation.

Critical Thinking

1. What are the reasons doctors treat so many terminally ill people when there is no hope of a cure?

2. Why is one of the most urgent issues facing America today that people are getting unwanted medical interventions?

Create Central

www.mhhe.com/createcentral

Internet References

American Medical Association
   http://www.ama.org
Centers for Disease Control and Prevention
   http://www.cdc.gov

Article   Prepared by: Eileen L. Daniel, *SUNY Brockport*

Antibiotics and the Meat We Eat

DAVID A. KESSLER

Learning Outcomes

After reading this article, you will be able to:

- Explain why the number of antibiotic resistant bacteria is increasing.

- Describe how meat and poultry are monitored for the presence of antibiotic-resistant bacteria.

- Describe the risks associated with consuming these bacteria.

Scientists at the Food and Drug Administration systematically monitor the meat and poultry sold in supermarkets around the country for the presence of disease-causing bacteria that are resistant to antibiotics. These food products are bellwethers that tell us how bad the crisis of antibiotic resistance is getting. And they're telling us it's getting worse.

But this is only part of the story. While the F.D.A. can see what kinds of antibiotic-resistant bacteria are coming out of livestock facilities, the agency doesn't know enough about the antibiotics that are being fed to these animals. This is a major public health problem, because giving healthy livestock these drugs breeds superbugs that can infect people. We need to know more about the use of antibiotics in the production of our meat and poultry. The results could be a matter of life and death.

In 2011, drugmakers sold nearly 30 million pounds of antibiotics for livestock—the largest amount yet recorded and about 80 percent of all reported antibiotic sales that year. The rest was for human health care. We don't know much more except that, rather than healing sick animals, these drugs are often fed to animals at low levels to make them grow faster and to suppress diseases that arise because they live in dangerously close quarters on top of one another's waste.

It may sound counterintuitive, but feeding antibiotics to livestock at low levels may do the most harm. When he accepted the Nobel Prize in 1945 for his discovery of penicillin, Alexander Fleming warned that "there is the danger that the ignorant man may easily underdose himself and by exposing his microbes to nonlethal quantities of the drug make them resistant." He probably could not have imagined that, one day, we would be doing this to billions of animals in factorylike facilities.

The F.D.A. started testing retail meat and poultry for antibiotic-resistant bacteria in 1996, shortly before my term as commissioner ended. The agency's most recent report on superbugs in our meat, released in February and covering retail purchases in 2011, was 82 pages long and broke down its results by four different kinds of meat and poultry products and dozens of species and strains of bacteria.

It was not until 2008, however, that Congress required companies to tell the F.D.A. the quantity of antibiotics they sold for use in agriculture. The agency's latest report, on 2011 sales and also released in February, was just four pages long—including the cover and two pages of boilerplate. There was no information on how these drugs were administered or to which animals and why.

We have more than enough scientific evidence to justify curbing the rampant use of antibiotics for livestock, yet the food and drug industries are not only fighting proposed legislation to reduce these practices, they also oppose collecting the data. Unfortunately, the Senate Committee on Health, Education, Labor and Pensions, as well as the F.D.A., is aiding and abetting them.

The Senate committee recently approved the Animal Drug User Fee Act, a bill that would authorize the F.D.A. to collect fees from veterinary-drug makers to finance the agency's review of their products. Public health experts had urged the committee to require drug companies to provide more detailed antibiotic sales data to the agency. Yet the F.D.A. stood by silently as the committee declined to act, rejecting a modest proposal from Senators Kirsten E. Gillibrand of New York and Dianne Feinstein of California, both Democrats, that required the agency to report data it already collects but does not disclose.

In the House, Representatives Henry A. Waxman of California and Louise M. Slaughter of New York, also Democrats, have introduced a more comprehensive measure. It would not only authorize the F.D.A. to collect more detailed data from drug companies, but would also require food producers to disclose how often they fed antibiotics to animals at low levels to make them grow faster and to offset poor conditions.

This information would be particularly valuable to the F.D.A., which asked drugmakers last April to voluntarily stop selling antibiotics for these purposes. The agency has said it would mandate such action if those practices persisted, but it has no data to determine whether the voluntary policy is working. The House bill would remedy this situation, though there are no Republican sponsors.

Combating resistance requires monitoring both the prevalence of antibiotic-resistant bacteria in our food, as well as the use of antibiotics on livestock. In human medicine, hospitals increasingly track resistance rates *and* antibiotic prescription rates to understand how the use of these drugs affects resistance. We need to cover both sides of this equation in agriculture, too.

I appreciate that not every lawmaker is as convinced as I am that feeding low-dose antibiotics to animals is a recipe for disaster. But most, if not all of them, recognize that we are facing an antibiotic resistance crisis, as evidenced by last year's bipartisan passage of a measure aimed at fighting superbugs by stimulating the development of new antibiotics that treat serious infections. Why are lawmakers so reluctant to find out how 80 percent of our antibiotics are used?

We cannot avoid tough questions because we're afraid of the answers. Lawmakers must let the public know how the drugs they need to stay well are being used to produce cheaper meat.

Critical Thinking

1. Why are the number of antibiotic resistant bacteria increasing?

2. How are meat and poultry monitored for the presence of antibiotic resistant bacteria?

Create Central

www.mhhe.com/createcentral

Internet References

Center for Science in the Public Interest (CSPI)
www.cspinet.org

Food and Drug Administration (FDA)
www.fda.gov

DAVID A. KESSLER was commissioner of the Food and Drug Administration from 1990 to 1997.

Article   Prepared by: Eileen L. Daniel, *SUNY Brockport*

The *Surprising Reason* Why Heavy Isn't Healthy

It's not just because fat ups your risk of disease. How much you weigh can keep you from getting the same health care everyone else gets. Our *special report* looks at a growing problem in women's health.

Ginny Graves

Learning Outcomes

After reading this article, you will be able to:

- Explain why overweight individuals may not get the same health care as those who are of normal weight.
- Describe why overweight men and women may have difficulty getting health insurance.
- Describe why overweight individuals are more likely to be misdiagnosed.
- Explain why overweight men and women are less likely to get cancer detected early.

It's shocking, but it's true: Being a woman who's more than 20 pounds overweight may actually hike your risk of getting poor medical treatment. In fact, weighing too much can have surprising—and devastating—health repercussions beyond the usual diabetes and heart-health concerns you've heard about for years. A startling new *Health* magazine investigation reveals that if you're an overweight woman you:

- may have a harder time getting health insurance or have to pay higher premiums;
- are at higher risk of being misdiagnosed or receiving inaccurate dosages of drugs;
- are less likely to find a fertility doctor who will help you get pregnant;
- are less likely to have cancer detected early and get effective treatment for it.

What's going on here? Fat discrimination is part of the problem. A recent Yale study suggested that weight bias can start when a woman is as little as 13 pounds over her highest healthy weight. "Our culture has enormous negativity toward overweight people, and doctors aren't immune," says Harvard

Medical School professor Jerome Groopman, MD, author of *How Doctors Think*. "If doctors have negative feelings toward patients, they're more dismissive, they're less patient, and it can cloud their judgment, making them prone to diagnostic errors." With nearly 70 million American women who are considered overweight, the implications of this new information is disturbing, to say the least. Here, what you need to know to get the top-quality health care you deserve—no matter what you weigh.

How Weight Gets in the Way

When Jen Seelaus, from Danbury, Connecticut, went to her doc's office because she was wheezing, she expected to get her asthma medication tweaked. Instead, she was told she'd feel better if she'd just lose some weight. "I didn't go to be lectured about my weight. I was there because I couldn't breathe," says the 5-foot-3, 195-pound woman. "Asthma can be dangerous if it gets out of control, and the nurse practitioner totally ignored that because of my weight."

Seelaus's nurse made a classic diagnostic error, according to Dr. Groopman. "It's called attribution, because your thinking is colored by a stereotype and you attribute the entire clinical picture to that stereotype. Because obesity can cause so many health problems, it's very easy to blame a variety of complaints, from knee pain to breathing troubles, on a patient's weight. That's why doctors—and patients—need to constantly ask, 'What else could this be?'"

There aren't statistics on how many diagnostic errors are due to weight, but the data for the general population is disturbing enough. "Doctors make mistakes in diagnosing 10 to 15 percent of all patients, and in half of those cases it causes real harm," Dr. Groopman says. Based on anecdotal evidence—patients who've told her that their doctors are often too quick to blame symptoms on weight—Rebecca Puhl, PhD, director of Research and Weight Stigma Initiatives at the Rudd Center for

Food Policy and Obesity at Yale University, suspects that being heavy could further increase the odds of being misdiagnosed.

Even if doctors are aware of the potential traps they can fall into when diagnosing an overweight patient, extra body fat can literally obscure some illnesses, including heart disease and different types of cancer. "It's more difficult to hear heart and lung sounds in heavy people," says Mary Margaret Huizinga, MD, MPH, director of the Johns Hopkins Digestive Weight Loss Center. "I use an electronic stethoscope, which works well, but I'm very aware of the issues that can crop up in overweight patients. Not all doctors have these stethoscopes—or are aware they need one."

Jeffrey C. King, MD, professor and director of maternal-and-fetal medicine at the University of Louisville School of Medicine, says that "the more tissue between the palpating hand and what you're trying to feel, the harder it is to detect a mass." That may be what happened to Karen Tang [not her real name], a 5-foot-8, 280-pound woman who went to the doctor for pelvic pain. Her doc palpated her uterus but didn't feel anything. "By the time I was referred to a gynecologist, I had a fibroid the size of a melon—so large it was putting pressure on my bladder," she recalls.

Even a routine pelvic exam can be tricky, especially if you've had children. "The vaginal walls become lax and collapse into the middle, obscuring the cervix," Dr. King says. Larger or modified speculums can help, but not all docs have them and they can make the exam more uncomfortable, says Lynda Wolf, MD, a reproductive endocrinologist at Reproductive Medicine Associates of Michigan.

That may explain the disturbing finding that obese women are less likely to get Pap smears than normal-weight women. But doctors may be partly to blame for the screening lapse, too. A University of Connecticut study of more than 1,300 physicians found that 17 percent were reluctant to do pelvic exams on obese women and that 83 percent were hesitant if the patient herself seemed reluctant.

Physical exams aren't the only things hampered by obesity. Large patients may not fit into diagnostic scanning machines—computed tomography (CT) and magnetic resonance imaging (MRI), for instance—and X-rays and ultrasounds may not be as effective, says Raul N. Uppot, MD, a radiologist in the Division of Abdominal Imaging and Intervention at Massachusetts General Hospital in Boston. "Ultrasound is the approach that's the most limited by body fat, because the beams can't penetrate the tissue if you have more than 8 centimeters of subcutaneous fat," he says.

This affects women, in particular, because ultrasound is used to diagnose uterine tumors and ovarian cysts and to evaluate the mother's and baby's health during pregnancy. Just last May, researchers at the University of Texas Southwestern Medical Center at Dallas reported a 20 percent decrease in the ability to detect problems in fetuses of obese women with ultrasound. In another study, obese women were 20 percent more likely to have false-positive results from mammograms—readings that can lead to unnecessary biopsies and anxiety.

Too much body fat can *obscure organs on scans,* giving doctors fuzzy results.

A Big, Fat Health Insurance Problem

Need to lose weight? That's not going to make your insurance company happy. If you're overweight or obese it probably costs them more. Even if you're in an employer's health insurance plan, you may all have to pay higher premiums if there are overweight people in the office filing more health claims.

But the real challenge is for those women who are trying to get private insurance—finding affordable health coverage can be difficult, if not impossible, if you're overweight. Rules vary by insurance company. But, in general, heavier women are likely to take a financial hit. For instance, a woman who is 5 feet 4 inches tall and has no other health problems will likely need a medical exam and pay higher premiums if she weighs more than around 180 or 190 pounds, says John Barrett of Health Insurance Brokers in Pasadena, California. Rates may range from 20 to 100 percent higher, depending on the carrier. And if that 5 foot 4 woman weighs more than around 220? She could be automatically declined coverage.

Women who try to lose weight don't get much help, either. "Weight counseling and early preventive treatment of obesity aren't covered by many plans," says John Wilder Baker, MD, president of the American Society for Metabolic and Bariatric Surgery. And insurance plans often won't cover bariatric surgery or other obesity treatments.

While CT scans are less affected by body fat, getting clear images in heavy patients typically requires a lot more radiation than with normal-weight patients, making it riskier, especially if numerous CT scans are required. But trying to diagnose a health problem without proper imaging is like driving blindfolded. Doctors are sometimes left with little to go on except symptoms and intuition, especially in the emergency room, where physicians make life-and-death decisions in minutes. "If we can't get the imaging because of a patient's weight, and we are concerned about a pulmonary embolism or appendicitis, for example, we have to go ahead and treat based on our clinical impression," says Archana Reddy, MD, a Chicago-area ER physician.

Being overweight can get in the way of effective cancer treatment, too, experts say. The problem: underdosing. "Oncologists usually base chemo on patients' ideal weight rather than their true weight, partly because chemo is so toxic and partly because drug trials typically include only average women, so we don't know the correct dose for bigger women," says Kellie Schneider, MD, a gynecologic oncologist at the University of Alabama at Birmingham. "But underdosing can mean the difference between life and death."

Doctors have long known that obese women are more likely to die of ovarian and breast cancers, but when Dr. Schneider and her colleagues recently gave a group of overweight ovarian cancer patients chemotherapy based on their *actual* weights, they found that the women were as likely to survive the illness as thinner patients. "Doctors aren't intentionally under-treating overweight women," Dr. Schneider says. "We're just working with limited information."

Why Heavy Patients Can't Find Help

There are no studies on how often doctors refuse to treat patients because of their weight. But Sondra Solovay, an Oakland, California, attorney and author of *Tipping the Scales of Justice: Fighting Weight-Based Discrimination,* says she hears enough anecdotes to believe it's commonplace.

Because of recent studies about various complications, A.J. Yates Jr., MD, associate professor in the Department of Orthopaedic Surgery at the University of Pittsburgh Medical Center, says there are legitimate concerns about operating on patients with a very high body mass index (BMI). But Dr. Yates also notes that some surgeons are reluctant to offer surgery to very overweight patients because the operations are more difficult and time-consuming.

And because data on surgical-complication rates is often calculated without accounting for the higher risk of an obese patient, even a few patients with complications can make the surgeon or hospital look bad to insurance companies. "If hospitals feel they're not looking good they could put subtle pressure on surgeons to avoid risky patients," Dr. Yates says. His concern is that overweight people could be increasingly discriminated against because of this.

Suzy Smith, a 5-foot-3, 400-pound woman from Colonial Beach, Virginia, believes she was one of those people. When her doctor found a large tumor on her kidney, she struggled to find a surgeon who would treat her. Her urologist said that the hospital where he practiced didn't have a table sturdy enough to hold her, and he referred her to a surgeon several hours away. "As soon as that doctor walked in the room, I could tell something was wrong by the look on his face," she says. "He told me he wouldn't operate. He wouldn't risk it," she says. Instead, he offered her cryoablation—a technique that freezes and removes tissue but is less effective than surgery for large tumors.

"I was so shocked," Smith says. "He was basically telling me he wouldn't do the thing that was the most likely to save my life." Finally, in early December 2008, a doctor removed the tumor. The surgery, after all the preceding drama, was anticlimactic. "It went fantastically well," Smith says. "My doctors were really pleased." But the overall experience, she says, was degrading and disheartening. "Here I was trying to deal with a diagnosis of cancer, worrying that the cancer might spread with every day that went by, and the medical field was closing doors on me left and right."

Infertile couples who are told they can't have in vitro fertilization (IVF) because of the woman's weight also feel doors shutting. Most fertility clinics have stringent rules. "I'd say 95 percent won't do IVF on a woman with a BMI higher than 39 [5-foot-4, weighing 228 pounds, for example], and they usually require an electrocardiogram (EKG) and blood tests if it's higher than 34, because being overweight reduces your chance of getting pregnant and having a healthy pregnancy," says Laurence Jacobs, MD, of Fertility Centers of Illinois. In most cases, he can't accept a patient with a BMI of 40, even if she has no other health issues, because IVF typically takes place

in an outpatient setting that's not set up for the higher anesthesia risks associated with obese patients. "No anesthesiologist is going to take that risk for someone who's not willing to make the effort to lose weight," Dr. Jacobs says.

Even more worrisome, a study from Duke University found that obese patients were less likely to receive procedures like cardiac catheterization that can help diagnose and treat heart disease, perhaps because doctors are concerned about potential complications, says lead author William Yancy Jr., MD, an associate professor at Duke and a staff physician at the VA Medical Center in Durham, North Carolina. Because of the high risk

How to Get the Care You Deserve

Here are ways women can speak out for better care and more respectful treatment—and get the help they need to reach a healthier weight:

- **Find a physician who isn't fatphobic.** Ask for referrals from heavier friends. Doctors who have struggled with their own weight may be more understanding.
- **Take a friend with you.** "A clinician is much less likely to treat someone badly when there's a witness," says Pat Lyons, RN, co-developer of *A Big Woman's Passport to Best Health,* a guide to overcoming barriers to health care.
- **Be your own advocate.** Have your doc run your numbers so you have all of your measures of health, from body mass index (BMI) to cholesterol and blood sugar. Ask for an assessment of your health based on the big picture.
- **Ask for tools.** Tell your doctor you're interested in sustainable health habits, like walking and eating right. Request a reasonable healthy weight and BMI range so you have goal.
- **Dig deeper.** If you've tried and tried and still can't lose weight, insist that your doc give you more help. For some people there's a medical reason for weight gain that goes beyond lifestyle choices, including medications or conditions that might cause weight gain. "We're trying to educate doctors so they provide obese women with more sensitive and in-depth care," says Keith Bachman, MD, a weight-management expert with Kaiser Permanente's Care Management Institute. The goal: to help doctors see the whole patient and look for all the possible causes of weight gain.
- **Stick to your symptoms.** During your visit say, "Here are the symptoms I'm concerned about. I know some health problems can be caused by weight, but I'd like you to focus on the symptoms I'm here to see you about."
- **Get the doctor you deserve.** If you feel your doctor isn't giving you the kind of care you deserve, find a new one. "When I asked physicians what they would do if they perceived a negative attitude from their doctor, each one said he or she would find another doctor," says Harvard's Jerome Groopman, MD. It's your right to do the same.

of heart disease in obese patients, the benefits of catheterization may outweigh the risks, he says. "But if the tests aren't performed, heavy patients may not receive appropriate therapy."

Even organ transplants may be withheld because of weight. Patients with BMIs higher than 35—if you're, say, 5 feet 4 inches tall and weigh 205 pounds—are typically less likely to be given a kidney or liver transplant because of the increased risk of postsurgery complications, including infections, blood clots, and pneumonia.

"It's a very difficult issue," says Shawn Pelletier, MD, surgical director of liver transplants at the University of Michigan Health System in Ann Arbor. "We have an obligation to use donor organs in a responsible way. But this is lifesaving surgery, and we don't want to turn people away. Obese kidney-transplant patients may not survive as long as thinner patients, but they live an average of three times longer than if they didn't get the transplant. That's a big benefit, even if there are risks."

Many experts believe the issue goes beyond the strictly medical and into the arena of ethics. "Doctors need to ask themselves, 'Is this obese person less deserving of medical care than the same person would be after weight-loss surgery?'" says Barbara Thompson, vice-chair of the Obesity Action Coalition, a nonprofit advocacy group. "How do we determine whether a person's weight somehow justifies withholding needed medical care or whether bias by providers is the reason treatment is denied?" Yale's Rebecca Puhl asks. "It's an extremely important question with significant implications."

Fat People Get No Respect

When Celina Reeder, a 5-foot-5, 185-pound woman with a torn ligament in her right knee, was told by her surgeon she needed to stop eating so much fast food before he would schedule surgery, the Woodacre, California, woman was astounded. "I left his office feeling ashamed," she recalls. "And I don't even eat fast food! The more I thought about it, the madder I got. So I switched surgeons. Anybody who thinks doctors treat heavy women the same as thin women has obviously never had a weight problem. I really felt like my doctor didn't respect me."

She may have been right. University of Pennsylvania researchers found that more than 50 percent of primary care physicians viewed obese patients as awkward, unattractive, and noncompliant; one third said they were weak-willed, sloppy, and lazy. In addition, researchers at Rice University and the University of Texas School of Public Health in Houston found that as patient BMI increased doctors reported liking their jobs less and having less patience and desire to help the patient.

Whether they know it or not, doctors' attitudes may actually encourage unhealthy behavior. Feeling dissed about their weight can make some women turn to food for comfort. "Stigma is a form of stress, and many obese women cope by eating or refusing to diet," Puhl says. "So weight bias could actually fuel obesity."

Studies have also found that overweight women are more likely to delay doctors' appointments and preventive care, including screenings for cancer, because they don't want to face criticism. "It can be frustrating to treat obese patients," admits Lee Green, MD, MPH, a professor of family medicine

at the University of Michigan in Ann Arbor. "I spend most of my time treating the consequences of unhealthy lifestyles instead of actual illnesses. People come in complaining of foot or knee pain, and I'm thinking, *Do you not see that you're in pain because you're 60 pounds overweight?* I don't say that, of course. I try to encourage them to lose weight."

Seeing heavy patients was *a waste of time,* doctors admitted in one survey.

Dr. Green seems to be in the minority when it comes to focusing on weight-loss solutions. One study found that just 11 percent of overweight patients received weight-loss counseling when they visited a family-practice doctor.

A Healthy-Weight Wakeup Call

Without a doubt, the medical community needs to take a hard look at the secret biases that may be coloring how they care for overweight women. But some progress is being made. The National Institutes of Health has been encouraging researchers to start identifying and fixing the barriers heavy people face when trying to get health care, says Susan Yanovski, MD, co-director of the Office of Obesity Research at the National Institute of Diabetes and Digestive and Kidney Diseases. And some hospitals are adding larger surgical instruments, wheelchairs, and other equipment.

There's an even bigger problem, though: when heavy women are ignored, the obesity epidemic is ignored, too—and that has to stop, experts say. "Being mistreated or dismissed by your doctor because of your weight is unacceptable. But what's just as important is that doctors are missing an opportunity to help their patients lose weight and improve their health," says Dr. Huizinga of Johns Hopkins. "Doctors and patients need to be able to speak openly about weight-related issues, whether it's the diseases caused by excess weight or the reasons why a patient overeats. That level of conversation requires a certain degree of comfort, and the basis for that is mutual respect, plain and simple," she says. "That's how we can help *all* women get healthier."

Critical Thinking

1. Why are overweight individuals treated differently by health care providers?

2. Why are overweight men and women less likely to qualify for health insurance?

Create Central

www.mhhe.com/createcentral

Internet References

American Cancer Society
www.cancer.org

MedScape: The Online Resource for Better Patient Care
www.medscape.com

Unit 10

UNIT

Prepared by: Eileen Daniel, *SUNY College at Brockport*

Contemporary Health Hazards

This unit examines a variety of health hazards that Americans face on a daily basis and includes topics ranging from environmental health issues to newly emerging or, rather, reemerging infectious illnesses. During the 1970s and 1980s, Americans became deeply concerned about environmental changes that affected the air, water, and food we take in. While some improvements have been observed in these areas, much remains to be done, as new areas of concern continue to emerge. What are the most pressing contemporary health issues? Scientists have conquered the killers of the 18th and 19th centuries: cholera, smallpox, tuberculosis, leprosy, diphtheria, and tetanus. And with the discovery of the germ theory and the advent of vaccinations and immunizations, most of the diseases that plagued humans are now history.

In the early 1970s, it was widely assumed that infectious diseases would continue to decline: sanitation, vaccines, and antibiotics were at hand. The subsequent generalized upturn in infectious diseases was unexpected. Worldwide, at least 30 new and reemerging infectious diseases have been recognized since 1975. HIV/AIDS has become a serious pandemic. Several "old" infectious diseases, including tuberculosis, malaria, cholera, and dengue fever, have proven unexpectedly problematic because of increased antimicrobial resistance, new ecological niches, weak public health services, and activation of infectious agents (e.g., tuberculosis) in people whose immune system is weakened by AIDS.

The recent upturn in the range, burden, and risk of infectious diseases reflects a general increase in opportunities for entry into the human species, transmission, and long-distance spread, including by air travel. Although specific new infectious diseases cannot be predicted, understanding of the conditions favoring disease emergence and spread is improving. Influences include increased population density, increasingly vulnerable population age distributions, and persistent poverty. Many environmental, political, and social factors contribute. These include increasing encroachment upon exotic ecosystems and disturbance of various internal biotic controls among natural ecosystems. Industrialized livestock farming also facilitates infections (such as avian influenza) emerging and spreading and perhaps increasing in virulence. Both under- and overnutrition and impaired immunity (including in people with poorly controlled diabetes—an obesity-associated disease now increasing globally) contribute to the persistence and spread of infectious diseases. Large-scale human-induced environmental change, including climate change, is of increasing importance.

In addition to the increasing threats from infectious diseases, heart disease, cancer, diabetes, mental illness, and other chronic conditions continue to impact health and longevity. While some cancers are successfully treated, others are not, including lung and pancreatic cancer. Many people have quit smoking, changed their diet, and managed stress, and heart disease rates are falling as a result. Other chronic conditions continue to affect peoples' lives and, unless cures are discovered, will continue their presence.

Article   Prepared by: Eileen L. Daniel, *SUNY Brockport*

Is PTSD Contagious?

It's rampant among returning vets—and now their spouses and kids are starting to show the same symptoms.

Mac McClelland

Learning Outcomes

After reading this article, you will be able to:

- Describe the impact post-traumatic stress syndrome among returning veterans has among family, friends, and coworkers.

- Discuss the causes and treatment for post-traumatic stress syndrome

- Describe why post-traumatic stress syndrome is currently at epidemic levels.

Brannan Vines has never been to war. But she's got a warrior's skills: hyperawareness, hypervigilance, adrenaline-sharp quick-scanning for danger, for triggers. Super stimuli-sensitive. Skills on the battlefield, crazy-person behavior in a drug store, where she was recently standing behind a sweet old lady counting out change when she suddenly became so furious her ears literally started ringing. Being too cognizant of every sound—every coin dropping an echo—she explodes inwardly, fury flash-incinerating any normal tolerance for a fellow patron with a couple of dollars in quarters and dimes. Her nose starts running she's so pissed, and there she is standing in a CVS, snotty and deaf with rage, like some kind of maniac, because a tiny elderly woman needs an extra minute to pay for her dish soap or whatever.

Brannan Vines has never been to war, but her husband, Caleb, was sent to Iraq twice, where he served in the infantry as a designated marksman. He's one of 103,200, or 228,875, or 336,000 Americans who served in Iraq or Afghanistan and came back with PTSD, depending on whom you ask, and one of 115,000 to 456,000 with traumatic brain injury. It's hard to say, with the lack of definitive tests for the former, undertesting for the latter, underreporting, under or over-misdiagnosing of both. And as slippery as all that is, even less understood is the collateral damage, to families, to schools, to society—emotional and fiscal costs borne long after the war is over.

Like Brannan's symptoms. Hypervigilance sounds innocuous, but it is in fact exhaustingly distressing, a conditioned response to life-threatening situations. Imagine there's a murderer in your house. And it is dark outside, and the electricity is out. Imagine your nervous system spiking, readying you as you feel your way along the walls, the sensitivity of your hearing, the tautness in your muscles, the alertness shooting around inside your skull. And then imagine feeling like that all the time.

Caleb has been home since 2006, way more than enough time for Brannan to catch his symptoms. The house, in a subdivision a little removed from one of many shopping centers in a small town in the southwest corner of Alabama, is often quiet as a morgue. You can hear the cat padding around. The air conditioner whooshes, a clock ticks. When a sound erupts—Caleb screaming at Brannan because she's just woken him up from a nightmare, after making sure she's at least an arm's length away in case he wakes up swinging—the ensuing silence seems even denser. Even when everyone's in the family room watching TV, it's only connected to Netflix and not to cable, since news is often a trigger. Brannan and Caleb can be tense with their own agitation, and tense about each other's. Their German shepherd, a service dog trained to help veterans with PTSD, is ready to alert Caleb to triggers by barking, or to calm him by jumping onto his chest. This PTSD picture is worse than some, but much better, Brannan knows, than those that have devolved into drug addiction and rehab stints and relapses. She has not, unlike military wives she advises, ever been beat up. Nor jumped out of her own bed when she got touched in the middle of the night for fear of being raped, again. Still.

"Sometimes I can't do the laundry," Brannan explains, reclining on her couch. "And it's not like, 'Oh, I'm too tired to do the laundry,' it's like, 'Um, I don't understand how to turn the washing machine on.' I am looking at a washing machine and a pile of laundry and my brain is literally overwhelmed by trying to figure out how to reconcile them." She sounds like she might start crying, not because she is, but because that's how she always sounds, like she's talking from the top of a clenched throat, tonally shaky and thin. She looks relaxed for the moment, though, the sun shining through the windows onto her face in this lovely leafy suburb. We raise the blinds in the afternoons, but only if we are alone. When we hear Caleb pulling back in the driveway, we jump up and grab their strings, plunging the living room back into its usual necessary darkness.

BRAIN WAVE

The VA's PTSD patient roster has tripled since the invasion of Afghanistan.

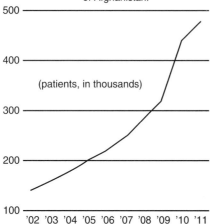

(patients, in thousands)

The Vineses' wedding album is gorgeous, leather-bound, older and dustier than you might expect given their youth. Brannan is 32 now, but in her portraits with the big white dress and lacy veil she's not even old enough to drink. There were 500 people at the ceremony. Even the mayor was there. And there's Caleb, slim, in a tux, three years older than Brannan at 22, in every single picture just about the smilingest motherfucker you've ever seen, in a shy kind of way.

Now, he's rounder, heavier, bearded, and long-haired, obviously tough even if he weren't prone to wearing a COMBAT INFANTRYMAN cap, but still not the guy you picture when you see his "Disabled Veteran" license plates. Not the old 'Nam guy with a limp, or maybe the young legless Iraq survivor, that you'd expect.

It's kind of hard to understand Caleb's injuries. Even doctors can't say for sure exactly why he has flashbacks, why he could be standing in a bookstore when all of a sudden he's sure he's in Ramadi, the pictures in his brain disorienting him among the stacks, which could turn from stacks to rows of rooftops that need to be scanned for snipers. Sometimes he starts yelling, and often he doesn't remember anything about it later. They don't know exactly why it comes to him in dreams, and why especially that time he picked up the pieces of Baghdad bombing victims and that lady who appeared to have thrown herself on top of her child to save him only to find the child dead underneath torments him when he's sleeping, and sometimes awake. They don't know why some other guys in his unit who did and saw the same stuff that Caleb did and saw are fine but Caleb is so sensitive to light, why he can't just watch the news like a regular person without feeling as if he might catch fire. Some hypotheses for why PTSD only tortures some trauma victims blame it on unhappily coded proteins, or a misbehaving amygdala. Family history, or maybe previous trauma.

Whatever is happening to Caleb, it's as old as war itself. The ancient historian Herodotus told of Greeks being honorably dismissed for being "out of heart" and "unwilling to encounter danger." Civil War doctors, who couldn't think of any other

thing that might be unpleasant about fighting the Civil War but homesickness, diagnosed thousands with "nostalgia." Later, it was deemed "irritable heart." In World War I it was called "shell shock." In World War II, "battle fatigue." It wasn't an official diagnosis until 1980, when Post Traumatic Stress Disorder made its debut in psychiatry's Diagnostic and Statistical Manual of Mental Disorders, uniting a flood of Vietnam vets suffering persistent psych issues with traumatized civilians—previously assigned labels like "accident neurosis" and "post-rape syndrome"—onto the same page of the DSM-III.

But whatever people have called it, they haven't been likely to grasp or respect it. In 1943, when Lt. General George S. Patton met an American soldier at an Italian hospital recovering from "nerves," Patton slapped him and called him a coward. In 2006, the British Ministry of Defence pardoned some 300 soldiers who had been executed for cowardice and desertion during World War I, having concluded that many were probably just crippled by PTSD.

Granted, diagnosing PTSD is a tricky thing. The result of a malfunctioning nervous system that fails to normalize after trauma and instead perpetrates memories and misfires life-or-death stress for no practical reason, it comes in a couple of varieties, various complexities, has causes ranging from one lightning-fast event to drawn-out terrors or patterns of abuse—in soldiers, the incidence of PTSD goes up with the number of tours and amount of combat experienced. As with most psychiatric diagnoses, there are no measurable objective biological characteristics to identify it. Doctors have to go on hunches and symptomology rather than definitive evidence. And the fact that the science hasn't fully caught up with the suffering, that Caleb can't point to something provably, biologically ruining his life, just makes him feel worse. It's invalidating. Even if something is certainly wrong—even if a couple of times he has inadvisably downed his medication with a lot of booze, admitting to Brannan that he doesn't care if he dies; even if he once came closer to striking her than she ever, ever, ever could have imagined before he went to war—Caleb knows that a person whose problem is essentially that he can't adapt to peacetime Alabama sounds, to many, like a pussy.

"Somebody at the VA told me, 'Kids in Congo and Uganda don't have PTSD,'" Caleb tells me angrily one day.

You can't see Caleb's other wound, either. It's called traumatic brain injury, or TBI, from multiple concussions. In two tours, he was in at least 20 explosions—IEDs, vehicle-borne IEDs, RPGs. In one of them, when a mortar or grenade hit just behind him, he was thrown headfirst through a metal gate and into a courtyard. His buddies dragged him into a corner, where he was in and out of consciousness while the firefight continued, for hours. When it was over, they gave him an IV and some Motrin, and within hours, he was back on patrol. The Army has rules about that sort of thing now. Now if you're knocked unconscious, or have double vision, or exhibit other signs of a brain injury, you have to rest for a certain period of time, but that rule didn't go into effect in theater until 2010, after Caleb was already out of the service. He wasn't diagnosed for years after he got back, despite Brannan's frantic phone calls to the VA begging for tests, since her husband, formerly a high-scoring civil-engineering major at Auburn University, was asking her to help him do simple division. When Caleb was finally screened for the severity of his TBI, Brannan says he got the second-worst score in the whole 18-county Gulf Coast VA system, which serves more than 50,000 veterans. But there's still a lot about brain damage that doctors, much less civilians, don't understand.

"I guess we're just used to dealing with people with more severe injuries," a VA nurse once told Brannan upon seeing Caleb.

Medical journals note some family members of vets exhibit symptoms "almost identical to PTSD." Except the "T" is their loved one's behavior.

Unlike PTSD, secondary traumatic stress doesn't have its own entry in the DSM, though the manual does take note of it, as do many peer-reviewed studies and the Department of Veterans Affairs. Symptoms start at depression and alienation, including the "compassion fatigue" suffered by social workers and trauma counselors. But some spouses and loved ones suffer symptoms that are, as one medical journal puts it, "almost identical to PTSD except that indirect exposure to the traumatic event through close contact with the primary victim of trauma" is the catalyst. Basically your spouse's behavior becomes the "T" in your own PTSD. If sympathy for Caleb is a little lacking, you can imagine what little understanding exists for Brannan.

Secondary traumatic stress has been documented in the spouses of veterans with PTSD from Vietnam. And the spouses of Israeli veterans with PTSD, and Dutch veterans with PTSD. In one study, the incidence of secondary trauma in wives of Croatian war vets with PTSD was 30 percent. In another study there, it was 39 percent. "Trauma is really not something that happens to an individual," says Robert Motta, a clinical psychologist and psychology professor at Hofstra University who wrote a few of the many medical-journal articles about secondary trauma in Vietnam vets' families. "Trauma is a contagious disease; it affects everyone that has close contact with a traumatized person" in some form or another, to varying degrees and for different lengths of time. "Everyone" includes children. Which is something Brannan and Caleb lose not a little sleep over, since they've got a six-year-old in the house.

Katie* Vines, the first time I meet her, is in trouble. Not that you'd know it to look at her, bounding up to the car, blondish bob flying as she sprints from her kindergarten class, nice round face like her daddy's. No one's the wiser until she cheerfully hands her mother a folder from the backseat she's hopped into. It contains notes about the day from her teacher.

"It says here," Brannan says, her eyes narrowing incredulously, "that you spit on somebody today."

"Yes ma'am," Katie admits, lowering her voice and her eyes guiltily.

"Katie Vines." Brannan was born here in Alabama, so that's drawled. "Wah did you do that?"

Her schoolmate said something mean. Maybe. Katie doesn't sound sure, or like she remembers exactly. One thing she's positive of: "She just made me . . . so. MAD." Brannan asks Katie to

name some of the alternatives. "Walk away, get the teacher, yes ma'am, no ma'am," Katie dutifully responds to the prompts. She looks disappointed in herself. Her eyebrows are heavily creased when she shakes her head and says quietly again, "I was so mad."

Caleb Vines with his service dog, Brannan, and Katie's teacher have conferenced about Katie's behavior many times. Brannan's not surprised she's picked up overreacting and yelling—you don't have to be at the Vines residence for too long to hear Caleb hollering from his room, where he sometimes hides for 18, 20 hours at a time, and certainly not if you're there during his nightmares, which Katie is. "She mirrors . . . she just mirrors" her dad's behavior, Brannan says. She can't get Katie to stop picking at the sores on her legs, sores she digs into her own skin with anxious little fingers. She is not, according to Brannan, "a normal, carefree six-year-old."

Different studies of the children of American World War II, Korea, and Vietnam vets with PTSD have turned up different results: "45 percent" of kids in one small study "reported significant PTSD signs"; "83 percent reported elevated hostility scores." Other studies have found a "higher rate of psychiatric treatment"; "more dysfunctional social and emotional behavior"; "difficulties in establishing and maintaining friendships." The symptoms were similar to what those researchers had seen before, in perhaps the most analyzed and important population in the field of secondary traumatization: the children of Holocaust survivors.

But then in 2003, a team of Dutch and Israeli researchers meta-analyzed 31 of the papers on Holocaust survivors' families, and concluded—to the fury of some clinicians—that when more rigorous controls were applied, there was no evidence for the intergenerational transmission of trauma.

I asked the lead scientist, Marinus van IJzendoorn of Leiden University, what might account for other studies' finding of secondary trauma in vets' spouses or kids. He said he's never analyzed those studies, and wonders if the results would hold up to a meta-analysis. But: "Suppose that there is a second-generation effect in veterans, there are a few differences that are quite significant" from children of Holocaust survivors that "might account for difference in coping mechanisms and resources." Holocaust survivors "had more resources and networks, wider family members and community to support them to adapt to their new circumstances after a war." They were not, in other words, expected to man up and get over it.

A veteran dies by suicide every 80 minutes.

We await the results of the 20-year, 10,000-family-strong study of impacts on Iraq and Afghanistan veterans' kin, the largest of its kind ever conducted, that just got under way. Meanwhile, René Robichaux, social-work programs manager for US Army Medical Command, concedes that "in a family system, every member of that system is going to be impacted, most often in a negative way, by mental-health issues." That was the impetus for the Marriage and Family Therapy Program, which since 2005 has added 70 therapists to military installations around the country. Mostly what the program provides is couples' counseling. Children are "usually not" treated, but when necessary referred to child psychiatrists—of which the Army has 31. Meanwhile, the Child, Adolescent and Family Behavioral Health Office has trained hundreds of counselors in schools with Army children in and around bases to try to identify and treat coping and behavioral problems early on. "We're better than we were," Robichaux says. "But we still have a ways to go."

Of course, the Army only helps families of active-duty personnel. It's the Department of Veterans Affairs that's charged with treating the problems that can persist long past discharge. But "if you asked the VA to treat your kids, they would think it was nonsense," says Hofstra's Motta.

When I asked the VA if the organization would treat kids for secondary trauma, its spokespeople stressed that it has made great strides in family services in recent years, rolling out its own program for couples' counseling and parenting training. "Our goal is to make the parents the strongest parents they can be," says Susan McCutcheon, national director for Family Services, Women's Mental Health, and Military Sexual Trauma at the VA; according to Shirley Glynn, a VA clinical research psychologist who was also on the call, "for the vast majority of people with the secondary traumatization model, the most important way to help the family deal with things is to ensure that the veteran gets effective treatment." In cases where children themselves need treatment, these VA officials recommended that parents find psychologists themselves, though they note "this is a good time [for the VA] to make partners with the community so we can make good referrals." Or basically: "You're on your own," says Brannan.

"I guess we're just used to dealing with people with more severe injuries," a VA nurse once told Brannan upon seeing Caleb.

Brannan sent Katie to the school therapist, once. She hasn't seen any other therapist, or a therapist trained to deal with PTSD—Brannan knows what a difference that makes, since the volunteer therapist she tried briefly herself spent more time asking her to explain a "bad PTSD day" than how Caleb's symptoms were affecting the family. When I visited, Katie was not covered by the VA under Caleb's disability; actually, she wasn't covered by any insurance at all half the time, since the Vineses aren't poor enough for subsidized health care and the Blue Cross gap insurance maxes out at six months a year. She's never been diagnosed with anything, and Brannan prefers it that way. "I'm not for taking her somewhere and getting her labeled. I'd rather work on it in softer ways," like lots of talks about coping skills, and an art class where she can express her feelings, "until we have to. And I'm hoping we won't have to." Certainly she seems better than some other PTSD vets' kids Brannan knows, who scream and sob and rock back and forth at the sound of a single loud noise, or who try to commit suicide even before they're out of middle school. Caleb spends enough time worrying that he's messing up his kid without a doctor saying so.

Brannan is a force of keeping her family together. She sleeps a maximum of five hours a night, keeps herself going with fast food and energy drinks, gets Katie to and from school and to tap dance and art, where Katie produces some startlingly impressive canvases, bright swirling shapes bisected by and intersected with other swaths of color, bold, intricate. That's typical parent stuff, but Brannan also keeps Caleb on his regimen of 12 pills—antidepressants, anti-anxiety, sleep aids, pain meds, nerve meds, stomach meds—plus weekly therapy, and sometimes weekly physical therapy for a cartilage-lacking knee and the several disintegrating disks in his spine, products of the degenerative joint disease lots of guys are coming back with maybe from enduring all the bomb blasts, and speech therapy for the TBI, and continuing tests for a cyst in his chest and his 48-percent-functional lungs. She used the skills she learned as an assistant to a state Supreme Court justice and running a small newspaper to navigate Caleb's maze of paperwork with the VA, and the paperwork for the bankruptcy they had to declare while they were waiting years for his disability benefits to come through. She also works for the VA now, essentially, having been—after a good deal more complicated paperwork, visits, and assessments—enrolled in its new caregiver program, which can pay spouses or other family members of disabled vets who have to take care of them full time, in Brannan's case $400 a week.

At home after school, she makes Katie a pancake snack and then, while Katie shows me the website for a summer camp that teaches military spy skills, Brannan gets back to work. Because she also helps thousands of other people—measured by website and social-media interactions—through Family of a Vet, a nonprofit created "to help you find your way, find the information you need, and find a way not only to cope with life after combat . . . but to survive and thrive!" Brannan founded the organization in 2007, after panicked Googling led her to the website of Vietnam Veteran Wives (VVW) when Caleb returned from his second tour. Life after the first tour had been pretty normal. "Things were a little . . . off," Caleb was edgy, distant, but he did not forget entire conversations minutes later, did not have to wait for a stable mental-health day and good moment between medication doses to be intimate with his wife, and then when he finally tried, pray to Christ for one of the times when it's good sex, not one of the times when a car door slams outside and triggers him, or the emotion becomes so unbearable that he freezes, gets up, and walks wordlessly out the door.

All that didn't happen until after the second tour. Brannan was in a terrible place, she says—until she talked to Danna Hughes, founder of VVW. Danna had been through much of the exact same turmoil, decades ago, and had opened a center to help get Vietnam vets benefits and educate their spouses and communities about their condition. "What choice do I have?" Brannan asks about running her own organization. "This is the only reason I am well. People care when you tell them. They just don't know. They want to help and they want to understand, so I just have to keep going and educating."

Today she's fielding phone calls from a woman whose veteran son was committed to a non-VA psychiatric facility, but he doesn't want to be at the facility because he, a severe-PTSD sufferer, was already paranoid before one of the other resident loons threatened to kill him, and anyway he fought for his fucking country and they promised they wouldn't abandon him and he swears to God he will have to kill himself if the VA doesn't put him in with the other soldiers. Another veteran's wife calls from the parking lot of a diner to which she fled when her husband looked like he was going to boil over in rage. Another woman's husband had a service dog die in the night, and the death smell in the morning triggered an episode she worries will end in him hurting himself or someone else if she doesn't get him into a VA hospital, and the closest major clinic is four hours away and she is eight and a half months pregnant and got three hours of sleep, and the clinic's website says its case manager position for veterans of Iraq or Afghanistan is currently unstaffed, anyway.

The phone never stops ringing. If it does for 14 seconds, Brannan writes an email to help get whatever someone needs, or publishes a blog post about her own struggles. Caleb was not amused the first time one of these posts went live. But now he's glad she didn't ask him his permission. "I'd have said no," he tells me on the couch one day. It's a brief emergence from his bedroom—he's been "sleeping or hiding," Brannan describes it, 20 or so hours a day for a few days. He leans forward to put his glass of orange juice on the table; it takes many, many long seconds for him to cover the few inches; today, like most days, he feels "like a damn train ran over me." "But because of the feedback she got, I know that other people were going through the same shit I was. And she's helping people." His face softens. "She's got a good heart. She's always been like that. I'm glad she's doing it," he says again, and shrugs, because that's the end of that story.

"Breathe," Brannan says to nearly every woman who calls, though when I ask her if she follows her own advice, she says no. "If I stopped, and started breathing," she says, "I would be too sad."

Kateri's eight-year-old son now counts the exits in new spaces he enters, and points them out to his loved ones until war or fire fails to break out, and everyone is safely back home.

So she doesn't. If she's not saving lives on the phone or blogging, she's offering support via Facebook, where thousands of Family of a Vet users and nearly 500 FOV volunteers congregate and commiserate. "I am now more hypervigilant than my husband," volunteer Kateri Peterson posts to her Facebook page, and people comment things like "I know that even if my husband is having a decent day I am still in that alert mode and he is asking me to please relax and for the life of me, as hard as I try, I just can't, I am still on the lookout. I know people probably think I am nuts." On a private Facebook group, Kateri tells the story of how her family was at Olive Garden when she started sobbing into her Zuppa Toscana. There was no visible reason for it. Just the general overwhelmingness of her distress, of that awful overstimulating hypervigilance, the sort of thing you develop sometimes when you live with someone who looks out the living room window for danger literally hundreds of times a day, or who goes from room to room, room to room, over and over to make sure everyone in each one is still

alive. Kateri's eight-year-old son now also counts the exits in new spaces he enters, points them out to his loved ones, keeps a mental map of them at the ready, until war or fire fails to break out, and everyone is safely back home.

It's to help kids like that that Brannan and her volunteers put together an informational packet on secondary trauma for parents to give to teachers, explaining their battle-worthy idiosyncrasies and sensory-processing sensitivities. They're common enough problems that the Department of Health and Human Services got in touch with Brannan about distributing the packet more widely.

Brannan gave the packet to Katie's kindergarten teacher, but thinks the teacher just saw it as an excuse for bad behavior. Last fall, she switched Katie to a different school, where she hopes more understanding will lead to less anxiety. Though Brannan hopes Katie will come out of childhood healthy, she still says, "She's not a normal kid. She does things, and says things. She's a grown-up in a six-year-old's body in a lot of ways."

She certainly looks like a normal kid when she comes down from her room dressed for tap class. In a black leotard, pink tights, and shiny black tap shoes, she looks sweet as pie.

"One time, a bad guy in Iraq had a knife and my dad killed him," she says, apropos of nothing.

"*Katie Vines.*" Brannan is stern but impeccably patient. She doesn't know why Katie adapted this story about confiscating a weapon from an insurgent into a story about bloodshed, but she isn't too happy about it. That kind of small talk recently ruined a birthday party one of her classmates was having at Chick-fil-A. Brannan and Katie have a talk, again, about inappropriate conversation. Katie is sorry—*God,* is she sorry, you can see it in her face and guilty shoulders, but she seems to feel like she can't help it. Sometimes, at bedtime, she asks her mom to pray with her that her teacher will like her. Once, she asked Brannan to take her to a hypnotist, so he could use his powers to turn her into a good girl.

B y this point, you might be wondering, and possibly feeling guilty about wondering, why Brannan doesn't just get divorced. And she would tell you openly that she's thought about it. "Everyone has thought about it," she says. And a lot of people do it. In the wake of Vietnam, 38 percent of marriages failed within the first six months of a veteran's return stateside; the divorce rate was twice as high for vets with PTSD as for those without. Vietnam vets with severe PTSD are 69 percent more likely to have their marriages fail than other vets. Army records also show that 65 percent of active-duty suicides, which now outpace combat deaths, are precipitated by broken relationships. And *veterans,* well, one of them dies by suicide every *80 minutes.* But even ignoring that although vets make up 7 percent of the United States, they account for 20 percent of its suicides—or that children and teenagers of a parent who's committed suicide are three times more likely to kill themselves, too—or a whole bunch of equally grim statistics, Brannan's got her reasons for sticking it out with Caleb.

"I love him," she says.

Brannan fully supports any wife—who feels that she or her children are in danger, or in an untenable mental-health environment, or for whatever reason—who decides to leave. She's here, through Family of a Vet, to help those people. But she's also there for those FOV users who, like her, have decided to stay. "I have enormous respect for Caleb," she explains if you ask her why. "He has never stopped fighting for this family. Now, we've had little *breaks* from therapy, but he never stopped going to therapy. I love him," she repeats, defensively at times.

He is her friend, and her first love, and her rock, and her lifeline, her blossoming young daughter's father, her ally, and her hero, she tells Caleb when he asks. Because the person who most often asks Brannan why she stays with her husband is her husband.

The amount of progress in Caleb's six years of therapy has been frustrating for everyone. But ultimately, says Alain Brunet, vice president of the International Society for Traumatic Stress Studies and director of the Traumatic Stress Laboratory at McGill University in Canada, "we have reason to be reasonably optimistic. Psychotherapy does work for typical PTSD." The VA tends to favor cognitive-behavioral therapy and exposure therapy—whereby traumatic events are hashed out and rehashed until they become, theoretically, less consuming. Some state VA offices also offer group therapy. For severe cases, the agency offers inpatient programs, one of which Caleb resided in for three months in 2010. The VA also endorses eye movement desensitization and reprocessing therapy (EMDR), which is based on the theory that memories of traumatic events are, in effect, improperly stored, and tries to refile them by discussing those memories while providing visual or auditory stimulus. "There's a fairly strong consensus around CBT and EMDR," Brunet says. While veterans are waiting for those to work, they're often prescribed complicated antidepressant-based pharmacological cocktails.

To stay up to date on the latest advances in PTSD treatment, the VA collaborates with outside entities through its Intramural Research Program. Currently, the agency is funding 130 PTSD-related studies, from testing whether hypertension drugs might help to examining the effectiveness of meditation therapy, or providing veterans with trauma-sensitive service dogs, like Caleb's. The Mental Health Research Portfolio manager says the organization is "highly concerned and highly supportive" of PTSD research.

But a lot of FOV members and users are impatient with the progress. Up until 2006, the VA was spending $9.9 million, just 2.5 percent of its medical and prosthetic research budget, on PTSD studies. In 2009, funding was upped to $24.5 million. But studies take a long time, and any resulting new directives take even longer to be implemented.

Meanwhile people like James Peterson, husband of Kateri of the Olive Garden breakdown, are signing up for experiments. James was so anxious and so suicidal that he couldn't even muster the self-preservation to get into inpatient treatment. With three kids, eight, five, and two, and Kateri's full-time job—as a VA nurse, actually—she could no longer manage his emotional plus physical problems: rheumatism consults, neuro consults for TBI, plus a burning rash on both feet he got in Fallujah in 2004. Chemical exposure, stress reaction, no one knows, but the skin cracks and opens up raw with lesions sometimes. Finally they enrolled him in a private clinical trial to get a needleful of

anesthetic injected into a bundle of nerves at the top of his collarbone. Kateri writes me that just moments after the injection, he "went from ballstothewall PTSD to *BOOM* chill."

That's when her symptoms got worse, precipitating another meltdown, this time at a steak house where she took him to celebrate his newfound calm. They'd "assumed the normal positions," she with her back to the restaurant, he facing it so he could monitor everyone, and suddenly, a server dropped a tray out of her periphery, setting her circulatory system off at a million miles a minute. "He just ate his steak like nothing," she says.

"When you've become hypervigilant, the place you are most functional is on the battlefield," McGill's Brunet explains. Caleb, despite his injuries and his admission that war was pretty excruciatingly awful, told me he wishes he could go back. Kateri, despite wishing her system hadn't learned to run at a heightened state, at this point is like a drug addict, needing stimulation to maintain it. For the first time since Iraq, her husband felt at peace, and was able to enjoy a steak dinner with his wife. "He just sat there," Kateri says. His normalcy "was so distressing to me that I wanted to stab him."

Researchers posit that traumatic brain injury can make the brain more vulnerable to PTSD, or that it can exacerbate its symptoms of exhaustion, agitation, confusion, headaches.

There are trials where patients take MDMA (ecstasy's active ingredient) while talking about trauma to promote more positive and less scary associations with the events. Animal trials where rats are lightly tortured and then injected with a protein that will stop the enzymes in their brains from being able to form memories of it. Some of the most interesting research involves beta-blockers, drugs that suppress the adrenaline response. In one small study, trauma victims given beta-blockers within six hours of the incident had a 40 percent less likelihood of developing PTSD. Brunet runs trials where patients take beta-blockers while talking about trauma so their reactions are weakened and then presumably lessened the next time it comes up, so far with promising results. But as of yet, "pharmacologically, there's no magic bullet," he says. And "we're much less effective at treating more complex PTSD" with traditional therapy. "Treatment offered vets might be less effective than what's offered to civilians with trauma. With veterans, there are important concomitant issues."

Like traumatic brain injury. Researchers posit that TBI can make the brain more vulnerable to PTSD, or that it can exacerbate its symptoms of exhaustion, agitation, confusion, headaches. They're not positive about that, or about whether TBI makes PTSD harder to treat. James Peterson's post-injection chill-out wore off after a month, faster than it does for other patients—maybe because of his TBI. Maybe not. Either way, as for TBI, well, "there is *no* cure," says David Hovda, director of UCLA's Brain Injury Research Center and an adviser to the Department of Defense.

In 2009, it was Hovda who delivered to the Pentagon the recommendation that because multiple concussions could cause serious long-term injury, concussions need time to heal. A fight ensued. Hovda says some of the Army's best doctors implied that if soldiers were told they needed rest after concussions, it was going to usher in an epidemic of fakers, or retired guys claiming disability way after the fact. Although, the NFL was given the same memo in the 1990s, and brain damage in boxers is even older news, so it doesn't seem like it would take a neuroscientist—or the top medical brass of an Army that builds laser cannons—to figure out that if 25 mph punches to the head cause brain damage, IED blasts that hit at 330 mph probably do too.

Eventually, Hovda's cause prevailed. These days, there are MRIs in theater, assessments after blasts, mandatory rest periods after a concussion. But those reforms came seven years into the Iraq War, after Caleb and a million other soldiers were already home. When people ask Hovda if they're gonna get better, he encourages them that they're gonna get *different*. That they will never be the same—researchers "have tried hyperbaric oxygen, hundreds of clinical trials; we're just failing miserably in trying to make a difference"—but that they should not panic. "There's good rehabilitation strategies: learn what your deficits are, learn that you're not going crazy, that you just can't do what you used to do," he says. "The human brain has an enormous amount of plasticity. New cells are born every day. New connections can be made. The good news is, teleologically speaking, if we didn't have the ability to recover from brain injury, we'd have ended up as somebody's breakfast."

He says he cannot get it out of his head, about how if he had caught that fucking sniper, that enemy sniper he'd been trying to get, then the sniper wouldn't have gotten off the shot that killed his buddy

So tonight, six years after Caleb's service ended, Brannan is cautiously optimistic but ready for anything on Lasagna Night. Early in the morning, she talked to their dog, Shilo, about it while she browned meat for Caleb's favorite dish. "Daddy will be really happy," she told the German shepherd sitting on her kitchen floor. "Of course, he's too cranky to be happy about anything, and he'll be mad because Katie won't eat it because I spent all day makin' it and the only thing she wants to eat right now is pancakes." Later, she reminds me that Lasagna Night can come apart in an instant, if Caleb has a "bad PTSD moment." These are supposed to be her easy months, she sighs, April and May and June, before the anniversaries of his worst firefights—many of them in Ramadi; a *lot* of bad things happened in Ramadi—exacerbate his flashbacks and nightmares. That's usually September through January, the "*really* bad" months, whereas in the spring, she gets a bit of "vacation," time to clean up the house and catch up on work, rest.

It's April at the moment. But: "He's processin' somethin' right now."

She used to ask Caleb what was wrong, why he was coiled so tight and poisonous, screaming and yelling at everybody. That just agitated him more. Now, she lets it go, until eventually, after a couple of days or weeks of refusing to leave the house, or refusing to stay home and just disappearing outside, he comes to her. *Haven't you noticed I'm having a bad time?* he'll ask. And then she'll just sit and listen while he says he cannot get it out of his head, about how if he had caught that fucking sniper, that enemy sniper he'd been trying to get, that'd been following them around, terrorizing their unit, if he'd have managed to kill him like he was supposed to, then the sniper wouldn't have gotten off the shot that killed his buddy.

But here we've got lasagna, and salad with an array of dressing choices, and a store-bought frosted Bundt cake with chocolate chips in it! There is no dining-room table—when they bought the house years ago, they thought they'd finish it up real nice like they did with another house, before the war, but nobody's up for that now, so we all huddle around the coffee table in the living room.

And it's lovely. Dinner lasts for hours. Brannan tries to calm Katie down despite the excitement of the visitor at dinner, while Katie shows me games and drawings as we eat. Brannan and I make fun of Caleb for being three years older than us, so *old*, and Caleb makes jokes that it does indeed feel like he and Brannan have been married for-*ever.* The plates have been cleared by then, everyone reclining, he laughs when he says this, and she laughs, and swats at him from where she's curled herself into his armpit with his arm around her.

At the front door, we all beam at each other in the warm way people do when they're separating after a nice meal. Caleb is in such a good mood that Brannan asks if he's up for putting Katie to bed so she can go lie down. Forty-five minutes later, he wakes her up screaming. Not two days after that, he tells her he's leaving her. "I'm going to get it over with and do it so you don't have to," he says, because that's just the way the scale goes that day, when he weighs the pain of being alone versus the pain of being a burden.

Way up north, and nearly as west as you can go, in Ferry County, Washington, there's a little town with no stoplights by the name of Republic. There's an abundance of parks and lakes and campgrounds—though I lose track of how many people warn me not to walk any unknown path for fear of trip wire and booby traps.

"Yeah," a county commissioner says, squinting against the afternoon sun, speaking of the high proportion of Vietnam veterans who live here, "they wanted to get away from society. And for the most part, they've blended in really well."

We're standing together on the grounds of Vietnam Veteran Wives, where Danna Hughes, founder of VVW, inspirer and savior of Brannan Vines, is holding a fundraiser and tribute for our troops. Back in the '90s, Danna served three counties and some 5,000 former soldiers via the center she founded, established nonprofit status for, and got the VA to recognize and reimburse. A 2000 VA budget crunch led to her clinic's contract being terminated—and her husband's disability pay ended when he killed himself in 2001. VVW now has more modest but no less determined facilities: a camouflage-painted mobile home planted among tree-dotted hills. Today, VVW is dedicating a new, second building, a log safe house open 24 hours a day so vets who feel themselves becoming episodic have someplace to go—it's better than just driving to VVW's parking lot and sleeping in their trucks. The closest VA hospital is 130 miles from here.

Between 200 and 300 people show up, a big turnout in a county of 7,500 spread over 2,000 square miles. Dressed in a patriotic red shirt and blue jeans, Danna smiles easy but moves pretty slow because she threw her back out again. She tells me that VVW's No. 1 priority has always been helping vets figure out how to get their benefits. "Money has to be first. You can't breathe without it." But it takes more than that. "*She,*" Danna says, meaning the wife—nearly all the vets around here are men—"NEEDS therapy." Danna used to be in beauty pageants and it shows, in the subtly flirty but no-nonsense way she addresses everyone. But she knows how it feels to have your nervous system turn against you, and that it's harder for veterans to get better if their spouses don't get treated. Danna's husband was checking into inpatient psych treatments for almost three weeks at a time, she says, only to come back to his now-crazy wife and "within three seconds" be re-exposed to someone in the emotional state that he was in when he left.

Danna Hughes set out to treat Vietnam vets and their families. But men who served in World War II show up in her office, and just cry and cry.

It may take years for the verdict to come in on whether secondary trauma will be officially acknowledged as its own unique form of hell. Meanwhile, Hofstra professor Motta says, while "a simple Google search [of the research] would tell you that the children of traumatized people have problems, the VA doesn't wanna spend the money. Even with *veterans,* they try to say, 'Well, you really had a preexisting condition.' It would cost millions upon millions to treat the people affected. They just don't want to foot the bill."

Then again, the VA already is footing some $600 million worth of PTSD treatment for veterans of Iraq and Afghanistan in 2013, via hundreds of medical centers and smaller outpatient clinics, plus 232 vet centers that offer general readjustment services. Caleb alone, just in disability checks, not even including any of his treatment or his numerous prescriptions, will cost the VA $1.7 million if he lives until he's 80.

Charles Marmar, a New York University professor who was on the team of the National Vietnam Veterans Readjustment Study, the most comprehensive study of combat stress ever conducted, points out that you really have to spend the money to treat PTSD, since the costs of *not* treating it are so much higher. "Personal tragedy, suicide, depression, alcohol and drug use, reliving terror," he rattles off as consequences. "Stress-related health problems—cardiovascular, immunologic. Heart attacks, stroke, and even dementia. Residential rehab programs, and motor vehicle accidents because people with PTSD

self-medicate and crash cars; the cost of domestic violence; the cost of children and grandchildren of combat vets witnessing domestic violence. The treatment and compensation disability programs have cost billions. And the costs of the untreated are probably in the tens of billions. They're enormous." Police time, court costs, prison time for sick vets who came home to commit soldier-style shoot-'em-ups or plain desperate crimes. Lost wages. Nonprofit assistance, outreach, social services. There are an estimated 100,000 homeless vets on the street on any given night.

Experts say it's nearly impossible to calculate what treating PTSD from Vietnam has and will cost American taxpayers, so vast are its impacts. There were 2.4 million soldiers deployed to Iraq and Afghanistan, and while no one is sure what PTSD among them will ultimately cost us, either, everyone agrees on one thing: If it's not effectively treated, it won't go away. When Caleb checked into his VA inpatient therapy in 2010, more than two-thirds of his fellow patients were veterans of Vietnam.

Vietnam vets still make up the bulk of Danna's clients—though she is assisting traumatized men who served in World War II, in the early years of which half the medical disability discharges were psychiatric, and some of those men *still* show up at Danna's office and cry, and cry, and cry. Many people at her fundraiser are saying that she saved their lives, kept them from killing themselves, kept them off the streets—or out of the woods, as it were, where she sometimes found vets living on earth floors under cardboard boxes.

"I don't just get to see the bad stuff," Danna says. "I get to see the good stuff too."

By way of example, she introduces me to Steve Holt*** and Charlene Payton Holt. Steve served in Vietnam, fought in the Tet Offensive. The chaplain assured him that he shouldn't feel bad about killing gooks, but the chaplain was paid by the Army, and who took moral advice from a chaplain carrying a .38? Back at home, Steve drank wildly. He waged war with his wife, attempted to work odd jobs where he had as little contact with humans as possible. But then he got divorced, and then he got with Charlene in 2001, and then he got in a big fight with Charlene and pulled the rifles out and sent her fleeing into the night, through the woods to the closest neighbor's house a mile away. But *then* he got inpatient psychiatric treatment in Seattle, several times, and found Jesus, and only ever has a beer or two, and now you have never seen two people so in love in any double-wide in the United States.

"I knew who he *could* be," Charlene says.

Who he is now is a handsome guy in his 60s with a white beard, big but well kept, who refers to his wife as "my bride" after nine years. Hanging around their trailer one day, I see them handle each other with immense patience, even when their computer takes forever to load and they can't find the files they're looking for because they've been crappily cataloged and it's not clear whose fault that is. Charlene has long, graying dark hair parted down the middle and super-serious eyes, which she has to lower to compose herself for a minute when I ask her, alone, if she saved Steve's life. "He loves me a *lot,*" she answers. "I've never known love like this. He is . . . awesome."

These most recent years, Steve is funnier—after all, he's not just any Carson; his dad and Johnny were first cousins—but it's not all good days. Sometimes, Charlene says, "I can feel him slipping down—it's like this . . . vortex, this hole. And I try to grab him, like, 'No! Don't go down there!' He can still get really depressed." And hypervigilant. He doesn't like living on Five Cent Ranch Road, which runs through a decidedly vulnerable valley.

> **Sometimes, Charlene says, "I can feel him slipping down—it's like this . . . vortex, this hole. And I try to grab him, like 'No! Don't go down there!' He can still get really depressed."**

"She saved my life," Steve says of Charlene, without my asking. Of the soldiers coming home with PTSD now, he says, "You need time. You need time, and perspective." Decades after his service, the VA rated Steve at 100 percent PTSD disabled, but he's found his way to his version of a joyful life. Although, he qualifies, he saw guys get thrown around in explosions the way Caleb got thrown around in explosions, but he can't say how their lives turned out in the long run because in his war, with that less-advanced gear, those guys usually died.

Finally, Steve and Charlene find what they're looking for on their computer: pictures of the land they bought nearby. Steve's building an artist's studio for Charlene on it, and eventually, hopefully, a house for the two of them. At the very top of a largely uninhabited hill, it will be hell—and sometimes impossible—to get down in winter because of the snow, but Steve doesn't care, and wants to grow old with Charlene and die up there. At that elevation, with that vantage point, it's one of the most defensible pieces of land in town.

In the vines' household in Alabama, at any unpredictable time of night, the nightmare starts in Iraq.

The desert sun is blinding, invasive; all eyes blink roughly with under-eyelid dust. It smells like blood, even before the shot slices through the Humvee and strikes Caleb in the chest. The vehicle stops, the other four guys get out, hollering, the rest of the unit firing their weapons, that awful echo at the end of an M16 round. Someone's yelling for the medic and an indiscernible string of noises seeps out of Caleb's mouth while he's dying. He's dying. He's bleeding warm and fast, and he's not going to make it.

"Our brains can do such odd things," Brannan says after she wakes up, shaky, the next morning. "Still don't get how I can so vividly dream of somewhere I've never actually been."

People around her think she needs a break, needs to rest, to take care of herself. "I know I'm not responsible for all these people," Brannan says. "But at the same time, nobody else is, either." With a half million disability cases stuck in a VA backlog, and an estimated 25 percent of Iraq/Afghanistan troops with PTSD not seeking treatment, her logic isn't entirely off. So she takes on the case of a family from Wisconsin who paid rent today, but has literally no money left. If they make an

appointment at the VA and can't get in for several weeks, how do they eat, they want to know, in the meantime? And the vet in New Jersey who didn't register for his VA benefits inside the five-year window. His life didn't fall apart until *six* years after his service, so when he walked into a VA emergency room asking for help to not kill himself, he was turned away until he could clear the requisite mountain of paperwork. And the vet who got fired from his job for being unstable and is now homeless, like 13,000 other vets under 30, who now lives with his wife and teenager in his car.

"In a perfect world, everyone would know and understand what my family is going through," Brannan says. She's convinced Caleb not to leave her, convinced him that she still wants to be married to him. Not for the first, and she doubts for the last, time. "We can reach a deeper love," she says. "When you share this sort of thing with a person, and you make it through it, it's a deeper love, really."

"They will hang in there until the last dog is dead," Danna told me of military spouses. She saw her husband through peripheral neuropathy, PTSD, prison, Agent Orange-linked disease, saw her son suffer living with a ball of anxiety and succumbing to drugs, and she doesn't regret one day.

"If you love somebody, you stick with them," she says, and there it is, naive, and beautiful, and impractically pure.

"The whole point of FOV is trying to give people hope," Brannan says. "Give people the tools to not give up." So when she finds some, she still takes to her blog and spreads it as wide as she can.

"Two nights ago," she writes in one post, "I was doing my normal nightly running around like crazy to get laundry and school bags and lunches ready for the next day, when the hubby found me in the laundry room. To the sound of the running washing machine, the 'thump, thump, thump' of tennis shoes in the dryer, and the not so romantic smell of the kitty litter box, he held me for a moment and rocked me back and forth . . . and we danced. It lasted maybe 30 seconds . . . a brief moment in the middle of a chaotic day and a difficult week . . . but a brief moment that I've stored in my heart. A light in the darkness."

Note

1. Support for this story was provided by a grant from the Puffin Foundation Investigative Journalism Project.

Critical Thinking

1. Why is post-traumatic stress syndrome currently at epidemic levels?
2. What impact does post-traumatic stress syndrome have on family, friends, and coworkers?

Create Central

www.mhhe.com/createcentral

Internet References

National Institutes of Mental Health Post-Traumatic Stress Disorder (PTSD)
www.nimh.nih.gov/health/topics/post-traumatic-stress-disorder-ptsd

National Center for PTSD
www.ptsd.va.gov

National Mental Health Association (NMHA)
www.nmha.org/index.html

Mac McClelland is *Mother Jones'* human rights reporter, writer of *The Rights Stuff,* and the author of *For Us Surrender Is Out of the Question: A Story From Burma's Never-Ending War.*

Article   Prepared by: Eileen L. Daniel, *SUNY Brockport*

Suicide, Guns, and Public Policy

E. MICHAEL LEWIECKI, MD AND SARA A. MILLER, PhD

Learning Outcomes

After reading this article, you will be able to:

- Discuss why handguns are the most common means of committing suicide in the United States.

- Describe factors associated with suicidal behavior.

- Understand the role of mental illness in suicide.

Suicide is a serious public health concern that is responsible for almost 1 million deaths each year worldwide. It is commonly an impulsive act by a vulnerable individual. The impulsivity of suicide provides opportunities to reduce the risk of suicide by restricting access to lethal means.

In the United States, firearms, particularly handguns, are the most common means of suicide. Despite strong empirical evidence that restriction of access to firearms reduces suicides, access to firearms in the United States is generally subject to few restrictions.

Implementation and evaluation of measures such as waiting periods and permit requirements that restrict access to handguns should be a top priority for reducing deaths from impulsive suicide in the United States. (*Am J Public Health.* 2013; 103:27–31. doi:10.2105/AJPH.2012.300964)

> **"Knowing is not enough; we must apply. Willing is not enough; we must do."[1a]**
>
> —Johann Wolfgang von Goethe

SUICIDE IS A COMPLEX behavior involving the intentional termination of one's own life. The prevalence, causes, means, and prevention of suicide have been extensively studied and widely reported.[1b-4] The World Health Organization (WHO) has identified suicide as a serious public health concern that is responsible for more deaths worldwide each year than homicide and war combined,[5] with almost 1 million suicides now occurring annually. In 2007, the Centers for Disease Control and Prevention (CDC) reported that 34,598 Americans died by suicide, far more than the 18,361 murders during the same period.[6] Among Americans younger than 40 years, suicide claimed more lives (n = 13,315) than any other single cause except motor vehicle accidents (n = 23,471).[6]

Psychiatric disorders are present in at least 90% of suicide victims, but untreated in more than 80% of these at the time of death.[7] Treatment of depression and other mood disorders is therefore a central component of suicide prevention. Other factors associated with suicidal behavior include physical illness, alcohol and drug abuse, access to lethal means, and impulsivity. All of these are potentially amenable to modification or treatment if recognized and addressed. It is important to distinguish between impulsivity as a personality trait and the impulsivity of the act of suicide itself. It is not generally appreciated that suicide is often an impulsive final act by a vulnerable individual[8] who may or may not exhibit the features of an impulsive personality.[9]

The impulsivity of suicide provides opportunities to reduce suicide risk by restriction of access to lethal means of suicide ("means restriction"). Numerous medical organizations and governmental agencies, including the WHO,[5] the European Union,[10] the Department of Health in England,[11] the American College of Physicians,[12] the CDC,[4,13] and the Institute of Medicine,[14] have recommended that means restriction be included in suicide prevention strategies. In the United States, firearms are the most common means of suicide,[15] with a suicide attempt with a firearm more likely to be fatal than most other means.[16] In a study of case fatality rates in the northeastern United States, it was found that 91% of suicide attempts by firearms resulted in death.[17] By comparison, the mortality rate was 84% by drowning and 82% by hanging; poisoning with drugs accounted for 74% of acts but only 14% of fatalities. Many studies have shown that the vast majority of those who survive a suicide attempt do not go on to die by suicide. A systematic review of 90 studies following patients after an event of self-harm found that only two pecent went on to die by suicide in the following year and that seven percent had died by suicide after more than nine years.[18]

The availability of guns in the community is an important determinate of suicide attempts by gun.[19] Given the public health importance of suicide and what is known about the role of guns in suicide, strategies that keep guns out of the hands of individuals who intend self-harm are worthy of careful scrutiny. Since a handgun (revolver or pistol) is far more likely to be used for suicide than a long gun (shotgun or rifle),[20] it may be particularly beneficial to focus suicide prevention efforts on this type of weapon. Only a small minority of states restrict access to handguns by methods such a waiting period, a permit requiring gun safety training, or safe storage of guns in the home. In 2010, US Department of Justice reported that only 15 states had a waiting period for purchasing a handgun.[21] Although federal law prohibits the sale of handguns to persons younger than 21 years, in the absence of federal preemption (i.e., the removal of legislative authority from a lower level of government), some states and municipalities allow the sale of handguns to younger individuals.[21]

Impulsivity of Suicide

Impulsive suicide attempts are "acts of self-harm involving little preparation or premeditation," whereas nonimpulsive suicide attempts are characterized by preparation and forethought.[22(p98)]

Impulsive suicide is a response to extreme fluctuations in an individual's psychological state, often with a triggering event that others would consider trivial.[8]

Impulsivity has been measured in different ways, including the amount of planning (measured through use of the Suicide Intent Scale[23]) and time criteria (the time between the decision to attempt suicide and the actual attempt).[22] In a study using the Suicide Intent Scale that involved 478 individuals who had attempted suicide, it was reported that 55% of the attempts were impulsive, 28% had an intermediate level of impulsivity, and 17% were nonimpulsive.[23] Examples of time criteria for defining the impulsivity of the suicide attempt in clinical studies include five minutes,[24] 10 minutes,[25] 20 minutes,[26] one hour,[27] two hours,[28] and 24 hours.[29]

Williams et al. found that 40% of suicide attempt survivors in two large consecutive series contemplated suicide for less than five minutes before the attempt.[24] In a study of 82 patients referred to a psychiatric hospital following a suicide attempt, almost half reported that the time between the first current thought of suicide and the actual attempt was 10 minutes or less.[25] Another study, based on interviews with suicide attempt survivors, found that two thirds considered suicide for less than an hour before the attempt.[27] In a study of 30 survivors of self-inflicted gunshot wounds treated at an urban trauma center, most or all of whom would have died without treatment, more than half reported having suicidal thoughts for less than 24 hours.[30] The National Violent Injury Statistics System reported that 61% of suicide victims had not previously disclosed an intent to commit suicide and that a precipitating event occurred within two weeks of the suicide for 36% of them.[31] The impulsivity of suicide is sometimes so intense and so fleeting that it has been called an "accident of the mind,"[32] one that may take a life as quickly and unexpectedly as a motor vehicle accident.

Restriction of Access to Lethal Means of Suicide

Suicidal ideation may quickly pass and remain unfulfilled if the means of suicide is not easily available. For a person in a suicidal state of mind, problem-solving skills are likely to be poor,[33] rendering it difficult to process a detailed consideration of alternative means of suicide when the initial choice is unavailable. Examples of means restriction followed by declines in suicide rates include pesticide restriction in Asian countries,[7] barbiturate restriction in Australia,[34] reduced availability of coal gas in the United Kingdom,[35] limits on access to analgesics in the United Kingdom,[36] installation of safety fences at high-risk jump sites (e.g., the Empire State Building, Eiffel Tower, and Sydney Harbor Bridge),[37] and restriction of access to firearms in many countries.[8] A systematic review of the evidence in suicide prevention studies concluded that means restriction prevented suicides.[7] A more recent review concluded that "limiting access to methods is one of the suicide prevention efforts with the most robust supporting evidence."[8(p1631)]

There appears to be a prevailing belief in the inevitability of suicide that would argue against the effectiveness of means restriction. According to this view, a person determined to commit suicide is likely to substitute one method for another ("means substitution") or delay suicide until a time when a means is readily available.[38] However, there is now a large body of evidence suggesting that means restriction not only reduces suicides by that method but also reduces overall suicide rates.[39,40]

Means substitution, when it does occur, does not seem to overwhelm the benefits of means restriction. When a highly lethal method (e.g., firearms) is not easily available, the substituted method (e.g., drug overdose) may be far less lethal, thereby increasing chances for survival.

Guns and Suicide

In a survey of 36 wealthy nations, the United States was unique in having the highest overall firearm mortality rate and the highest proportion of suicides by firearms.[41] Guns are used for more suicides in the United States each year than for homicides (17,352 vs 12,632, respectively, in 2007).[6] There is strong evidence that access to firearms, whether from household availability or a new purchase, is associated with increased risk of suicide.[8,42–45] The risk of suicide by guns is far higher in states with high rates of gun ownership than in those with low ownership rates.[46] The increased risk of suicide applies not only to the gun owner but to others living in a household with guns. One study[47] found that adults who have recently purchased a handgun are at increased risk of suicide by gun within a week of gun purchase, with the increase in risk persisting for at least six years. That study[47] and others[48] suggest that some gun purchases are made specifically with the intent of suicide.

Gun availability in the household is associated with risks and benefits. The risks include accidental or intentional injury to one's self or family members, whereas the benefits include protection against home intruders and deterrence of crime.[49] A recent review of the scientific literature concluded that in contemporary American society, the health risk of having a gun in the household outweighs the benefits, with compelling evidence linking gun availability to violent crime, accidental injury and death, and suicide.[49]

Restriction of Access to Firearms

Restriction of lethal means in the United States has focused on firearms because of their ease of access, common usage, and high mortality rate in suicide attempts. Strategies to reduce the risk of impulsive suicides by firearms have included at least two approaches: safe gun storage and regulations for purchasing guns. Storing unloaded guns in a locked place and storing ammunition separately in a locked place have been associated with a protective effect for suicide among children, adolescents, and adults.[50,51] Bans on firearm purchases for individuals at high risk for suicide, such as those with mental illness, substance abuse, or history of domestic violence, are desirable and might reduce suicides. However, criteria for identifying "prohibited persons" vary by state and are often limited to those with documented serious incidents (e.g., enforced hospitalization, felony conviction). Bans of this type, while helpful, are likely to identify only a small portion of those at risk.[45] Uniform restrictions preventing immediate access to a gun can allow time for a "cooling off" period during which the suicidal impulse may pass. A requirement for firearm safety training can delay access to a weapon for non-gun owners intending to harm themselves or others, and at the same time provide an opportunity for those who are not themselves at risk to learn about safe gun storage, thereby protecting vulnerable individuals.

Legislation restricting firearm ownership has been associated with a reduction in firearm suicide rates in many countries, including Austria,[52] Brazil,[53] Canada,[54] Australia,[55] New Zealand,[56] the United Kingdom,[57] and the United States.[58] In the United States, overall suicide rates are lower in states with restrictive firearm laws (e.g., waiting periods, safe storage requirements, minimum age of 21 years for handgun purchase) than in those with few restrictions.[59] The potential benefit of restricting access to firearms has been evaluated in models that estimate the effect on mortality rates.[60,61] In the United States, such a model predicted that 8,551 lives might have been saved from suicides avoided each year during the study period 1999 through 2004, assuming that suicide rates in each of four national regions (Northeast, South, Midwest, and West) matched that of the region (Northeast) with the lowest rate.[61] The Northeast was the region with the most restrictive firearm legislation and lowest availability of firearms. One study used a binomial regression model to empirically assess the impact of firearm regulation on male suicides in the United States, using state-level data for the years 1995 through 2004.[45] The study found that firearm regulations that reduced overall gun availability had a significant deterrent effect on male suicide, with permit requirements and bans on sales to minors being the most effective of the regulations analyzed.

There are limitations in interpreting data on means restriction. Establishing causality between an intervention and outcomes is challenging because of factors that include the complexity of suicidal behavior, heterogeneity of study designs, methodological constraints, confounder effects, variability in statistical analysis, and limited funding for large, well-designed prospective studies. There is no guarantee that measures that

work in Massachusetts (suicide rate = 11.56 per 1,00,000) will be effective in Wyoming (suicide rate = 32.29 per 1,00,000).[45] Differences in regional cultures and demographics (e.g., rural vs urban) might be important to suicidality and the choice of means. Firearm restrictions might be expected to have a greater impact on male suicides than female, since a gun is the means of suicide for more men than women.[62] A waiting period of seven days could be life-saving when an urge to commit suicide passes within one hour and a gun is not available in the household, but might not be helpful if the suicidal impulse continues for two weeks. Secure household storage of guns might be effective in preventing suicide by a child but not for the adult gun owner.

Prevention of Suicide: A Call to Action

Suicide is an extraordinarily complex and counterintuitive human behavior. Suicide prevention strategies involve the identification and modification of known risk factors. Considering the impulsive nature of many suicides, the strong association of guns and suicide in the United States, and compelling empirical evidence that restriction of access to firearms reduces suicide risk, suicide prevention strategies should include restriction of access to firearms, especially handguns.

In accordance with the medical evidence, we recommend a waiting period for purchasing handguns with a requirement for a permit or license that includes firearm safety training. For a suicidal person who does not already own a handgun, a delay in the purchase of one allows time for suicidal impulses to pass or diminish. Safe gun storage for all households delays or prevents access to a gun for a suicidal person living with a gun owner. Federal laws restricting the sale of handguns and handgun ammunition to minors should be implemented and enforced in all states. Firearms should not be sold to "prohibited persons" at high risk of harming themselves and others. Some states already mandate such measures. An opportunity to survive a transient suicidal impulse should be provided to individuals in all states.

The political, philosophical, and constitutional objections to firearm regulations, even those as modest as suggested here, cannot be minimized. Some would like to remove all firearm restrictions. We believe that reasonable people with diverse perspectives on firearm regulations have an imperative to discuss the benefits, risks, and responsibilities of firearm ownership, and to take action to minimize the risks. Different lengths of waiting periods and variations of permit or license requirements may have different levels of effectiveness depending on the locality and the population at risk. Well-designed long-term studies can evaluate these requirements so that appropriate regulatory modifications can be made in the future. However, meaningful regulations to restrict access to handguns are needed now, before more lives are unnecessarily lost. The public health benefit of preventing deaths due to impulsive suicide far outweighs the minimal inconvenience to those who do not intend to harm themselves or others.

Contributors

E. M. Lewiecki and S. A. Miller were both responsible for conceptualizing, writing, and editing this commentary.

References

1a. Stephenson RH. *Goethe's Conception of Knowledge and Science.* Edinburgh, UK: Edinburgh University Press; 1995.

1b. *The Surgeon General's Call to Action to Prevent Suicide.* Washington, DC: US Public Health Service; 1999.

2. Harvard School of Public Health. Means matter: suicide, guns, and public health. Available at: http://www.hsph.harvard.edu/means-matter/index.html. Accessed August 18, 2011.

3. Johns Hopkins Bloomberg School of Public Health. Center for Gun Policy and Research. Available at: http://www.jhsph.edu/gunpolicy. Accessed November 12, 2011.

4. Centers for Disease Control and Prevention. Suicide: risk and protective factors. Available at: http://www.cdc.gov/ViolencePrevention/suicide/riskprotectivefactors.html. Accessed April 12, 2011.

5. World Health Organization. Guns, knives and pesticides: reducing access to lethal means. Available at: http://www.who.int/mental_health/prevention/suicide/vip_pesticides.pdf. Accessed April 5, 2011.

6. Centers for Disease Control and Prevention (CDC). Web-based injury statistics query and reporting system (WISQARS). National Center for Injury Prevention and Control, CDC (producer). Available at: http://www.cdc.gov/injury/wisqars/index.html. Accessed June 7, 2011.

7. Mann JJ, Apter A, Bertolote J, et al. Suicide prevention strategies: a systematic review. *JAMA.* 2005;294(16):2064–2074.

8. Florentine JB, Crane C. Suicide prevention by limiting access to methods: a review of theory and practice. *Soc Sci Med.* 2010;70(10):1626–1632.

9. Baca-Garcia E, Diaz-Sastre C, Garcia RE, et al. Suicide attempts and impulsivity. *Eur Arch Psychiatry Clin Neurosci.* 2005;255(2):152–156.

10. Wahlbeck K, Mäkinen M. Prevention of depression and suicide. Consensus paper. European Communities. Available at: http://ec.europa.eu/health/archive/ph_determinants/life_style/mental/docs/consensus_depression_en.pdf. Accessed June 11, 2011.

11. Department of Health. National suicide prevention strategy for England. Available at: http://www.dh.gov.uk/prod_consum_dh/groups/dh_digitalassets/@dh/@en/documents/digitalasset/dh_4019548.pdf. Accessed June 10, 2011.

12. American College of Physicians. Firearm injury prevention. Position paper of the American College of Physicians. *Ann Intern Med.* 1998;128(3):236–241.

13. Centers for Disease Control and Prevention. Means restriction. In: Youth Suicide Prevention Programs: A Resource Guide. Available at: http://wonder.cdc.gov/wonder/prevguid/p0000024/p0000024.asp#head002002000000000. Accessed September 6, 2012.

14. Committee on Pathophysiology and Prevention of Adolescent and Adult Suicide. *Reducing Suicide: A National Imperative.* Washington, DC: National Academies Press; 2002.

15. Ajdacic-Gross V, Weiss MG, Ring M, et al. Methods of suicide: international suicide patterns derived from the WHO mortality database. *Bull World Health Organ.* 2008;86(9):726–732.

16. Shenassa ED, Catlin SN, Buka SL. Lethality of firearms relative to other suicide methods: a population based study. *J Epidemiol Community Health.* 2003;57(2):120–124.

17. Miller M, Azrael D, Hemenway D. The epidemiology of case fatality rates for suicide in the northeast. *Ann Emerg Med.* 2004;43(6):723–730.

18. Owens D, Horrocks J, House A. Fatal and non-fatal repetition of self-harm. Systematic review. *Br J Psychiatry.* 2002;181:193–199.

19. Shenassa E, Catlin S, Buka S. Gun availability, psychopathology, and risk of death from suicide attempt by gun. *Ann Epidemiol.* 2000;10(7):482.

20. Wintemute GJ, Teret SP, Kraus JF, Wright MW. The choice of weapons in firearm suicides. *Am J Public Health.* 1988;78(7):824–826.

21. US Dept of Justice, Bureau of Alcohol, Tobacco, Firearms and Explosives. State laws and published ordinances–firearms, 2009–2010, 30th edition. Available at: http://www.atf.gov/publications/download/p/atf-p-5300-5-2011/2009-30th-edition.pdf. Accessed March 20, 2012.

22. Gvion Y, Apter A. Aggression, impulsivity, and suicide behavior: a review of the literature. *Arch Suicide Res.* 2011;15(2):93–112.

23. Baca-Garcia E, Diaz-Sastre C, Basurte E, et al. A prospective study of the paradoxical relationship between impulsivity and lethality of suicide attempts. *J Clin Psychiatry.* 2001;62(7):560–564.

24. Williams CL, Davidson JA, Montgomery I. Impulsive suicidal behavior. *J Clin Psychol.* 1980;36(1):90–94.

25. Deisenhammer EA, Ing CM, Strauss R, Kemmler G, Hinterhuber H, Weiss EM. The duration of the suicidal process: how much time is left for intervention between consideration and accomplishment of a suicide attempt? *J Clin Psychiatry.* 2009;70(1):19–24.

26. Dorpat TL, Ripley HS. A study of suicide in the Seattle area. *Compr Psychiatry.* 1960;1:349–359.

27. Williams JMG, Wells J. Suicidal patients. In: Scott G, Williams JMG, Beck AT, eds. *Cognitive Therapy in Clinical Practice: An Illustrative Casebook.* London, UK: Routledge; 1991:206–226.

28. Li X, Philips MR, Wang YP, et al. The comparison of impulsive and nonimpulsive suicide attempts [in Chinese]. *Chin J Nerv Ment Dis.* 2003;29:27–31.

29. Brent DA. Correlates of the medical lethality of suicide attempts in children and adolescents. *J Am Acad Child Adolesc Psychiatry.* 1987;26(1):87–91.

30. Peterson LG, Peterson M, O'Shanick GJ, Swann A. Self-inflicted gunshot wounds: lethality of method versus intent. *Am J Psychiatry.* 1985;142(2):228–231.

31. Harvard Injury Control Research Center. Characteristics of victims of suicide. National Violent Injury Statistics System. Available at: http://www.hsph.harvard.edu/hicrc/nviss/documents/Suicide%20Summary%202001.pdf. Accessed November 12, 2011.

32. Missing teen believed to have jumped off bridge. Danville (CA) Weekly Online. Available at: http://danvilleexpress.com/news/show_story.php?id=5694. Accessed September 6, 2012.

33. Pollock LR, Williams JM. Problem-solving in suicide attempters. *Psychol Med.* 2004;34(1):163–167.

34. Oliver RG. Rise and fall of suicide rates in Australia: relation to sedative availability. *Med J Aust.* 1972;2(21):1208–1209.

35. Kreitman N. The coal gas story. United Kingdom suicide rates, 1960–71. *Br J Prev Soc Med.* 1976;30(2):86–93.

36. Turvill JL, Burroughs AK, Moore KP. Change in occurrence of paracetamol overdose in UK after introduction of blister packs. *Lancet.* 2000;355(9220):2048–2049.

37. Lin JJ, Lu TH. Association between the accessibility to lethal methods and method-specific suicide rates: an ecological study in Taiwan. *J Clin Psychiatry.* 2006;67(7):1074–1079.

38. Miller M, Azrael D, Hemenway D. Belief in the inevitability of suicide: results from a national survey. *Suicide Life Threat Behav.* 2006;36(1):1–11.

39. Daigle MS. Suicide prevention through means restriction: assessing the risk of substitution. A critical review and synthesis. *Accid Anal Prev.* 2005;37(4):625–632.

40. Hawton K. Restricting access to methods of suicide: rationale and evaluation of the approach to suicide prevention. *Crisis.* 2007;28(suppl 1):4–9.

41. Krug EG, Powell KE, Dahlberg LL. Firearm-related deaths in the United States and 35 other high- and upper-middle-income countries. *Int J Epidemiol.* 1998;27(2):214–221.

42. Miller M, Lippmann SJ, Azrael D, Hemenway D. Household firearm ownership and rates of suicide across the 50 United States. *J Trauma.* 2007;62(4):1029–1034.

43. Miller M, Hemenway D. The relationship between firearms and suicide: a review of the literature. *Aggress Violent Behav.* 1999;4(1):59–75.

44. Grassel KM, Wintemute GJ, Wright MA, Romero MP. Association between handgun purchase and mortality from firearm injury. *Inj Prev.* 2003;9(1):48–52.

45. Rodriguez Andres A, Hempstead K. Gun control and suicide: the impact of state firearm regulations in the United States, 1995–2004. *Health Policy.* 2011;101(1):95–103.

46. Miller M, Hemenway D. Guns and suicide in the United States. *N Engl J Med.* 2008;359(10):989–991.

47. Wintemute GJ, Parham CA, Beaumont JJ, Wright M, Drake C. Mortality among recent purchasers of handguns. *N Engl J Med.* 1999;341(21):1583–1589.

48. Cummings P, Koepsell TD, Grossman DC, Savarino J, Thompson RS. The association between the purchase of a handgun and homicide or suicide. *Am J Public Health.* 1997;87(6):974–978.

49. Hemenway D. Risks and benefits of a gun in the home. *Am J Lifestyle Med.* 2011;5:502–511. Available at: http://ajl.sagepub.com/content/5/6/502.full.pdf+html. Accessed November 12, 2011.

50. Grossman DC, Mueller BA, Riedy C, et al. Gun storage practices and risk of youth suicide and unintentional firearm injuries. *JAMA.* 2005;293(6):707–714.

51. Shenassa ED, Rogers ML, Spalding KL, Roberts MB. Safer storage of firearms at home and risk of suicide: a study of protective factors in a nationally representative sample. *J Epidemiol Community Health.* 2004;58(10):841–848.

52. Kapusta ND, Etzersdorfer E, Krall C, Sonneck G. Firearm legislation reform in the European Union: impact on firearm availability, firearm suicide and homicide rates in Austria. *Br J Psychiatry.* 2007; 191:253–257.

53. Marinho de Souza MF, Macinko J, Alencar AP, Malta DC, de Morais Neto OL. Reductions in firearm-related mortality and hospitalizations in Brazil after gun control. *Health Aff (Millwood).* 2007;26(2):575–584.

54. Rich CL, Young JG, Fowler RC, Wagner J, Black NA. Guns and suicide: possible effects of some specific legislation. *Am J Psychiatry.* 1990;147(3):342–346.

55. Goldney RD. Suicide in Australia: some good news. *Med J Aust.* 2006;185(6):304.

56. Beautrais AL, Fergusson DM, Horwood LJ. Firearms legislation and reductions in firearm-related suicide deaths in New Zealand. *Aust N Z J Psychiatry.* 2006;40(3):253–259.

57. Ajdacic-Gross V, Killias M, Hepp U, et al. Changing times: a longitudinal analysis of international firearm suicide data. *Am J Public Health.* 2006;96(10):1752–1755.

58. Ludwig J, Cook PJ. Homicide and suicide rates associated with implementation of the Brady Handgun Violence Prevention Act. *JAMA.* 2000;284 (5):585–591.

59. Conner KR, Zhong Y. State firearm laws and rates of suicide in men and women. *Am J Prev Med.* 2003;25(4):320–324.

60. Stone DH, Jeffrey S, Dessypris N, et al. Intentional injury mortality in the European Union: how many more lives could be saved? *Inj Prev.* 2006;12(5):327–332.

61. Papadopoulos FC, Skalkidou A, Sergentanis TN, Kyllekidis S, Ekselius L, Petridou ET. Preventing suicide and homicide in the United States: the potential benefit in human lives. *Psychiatry Res.* 2009;169(2):154–158.

62. Kaplan MS, McFarland BH, Huguet N. Characteristics of adult male and female firearm suicide decedents: findings from the National Violent Death Reporting System. *Inj Prev.* 2009;15(5):322–327.

Critical Thinking

1. What role does mental illness play in suicide?

2. Besides mental illness, what other risk factors increase the likelihood of suicide?

3. Why are guns a particular risk among those who attempt suicide?

Create Central

www.mhhe.com/createcentral

Internet References

Centers for Disease Control and Prevention
cdc.gov

National Mental Health Association (NMHA)
www.nmha.org/index.html

World Health Organization
www.who.org

E. MICHAEL LEWIECKI is with the Department of Internal Medicine, University of New Mexico School of Medicine, and the New Mexico Clinical Research & Osteoporosis Center, Albuquerque. Sara A. Miller is with the Richard B. Simches Research Center, Massachusetts General Hospital, Harvard University, Boston.

Acknowledgments—In memory of Kerry Adam Lewiecki.

We thank Maura Lewiecki, MLA, for her thoughtful suggestions in the development of this commentary.

Article   Prepared by: Eileen L. Daniel, *SUNY Brockport*

The New Sex Cancer

Doctors used to think this STD threatened only women. Then the men started dying.

ALYSSA GIACOBBE

Learning Outcomes

After reading this article, you will be able to:

- Discuss risk factors for oral cancer.

- Describe the relationship between oral cancers and the human papilloma virus (HPV).

- Describe why men are at increased risk for oropharyngeal cancers.

Eric Statler's wisdom teeth were impacted. Inconvenient, sure, but certainly not life threatening. As general manager of a hotel in Idaho's picturesque Clearwater County, Statler spent his 12-hour days charming and chatting up guests, which meant he couldn't afford a week of bloated cheeks and Percocet. Nor, given his myriad responsibilities at the hotel, did Statler feel he could justify time off for at-home recovery. So he procrastinated until the pain was almost unbearable and eating a turkey sandwich felt like chewing tacks.

Two months after he finally underwent the operation. Statler was still waiting for relief—his molars were gone but the pain remained. Not only did he find it excruciating to chew, but now he was losing weight and beginning to feel emotionally beat down. He decided to return to his dentist, who sent him to a local ear, nose, and throat specialist the same day. The ENT needed just minutes to solve the mystery: He took one look at Statler and said, "Son, I think you have cancer."

Statler couldn't believe it. A former college athlete, he still ran nearly every day, never smoked, and drank only a few beers a week. "My wife used to say I was the healthiest man she'd ever known," he says. The average oral cancer patient, by contrast, is a lifelong smoker or heavy drinker in his mid-60s.

But the definition of "average" has slowly been changing, as more and more oral cancer diagnoses are being handed down across the country to otherwise healthy young men. Statler soon learned that he was part of this emerging subset of oral cancer patient, a group of guys who all share one unlikely risk factor: HPV, an undetectable and untreatable STD that may act like tinder for tumors.

An Invisible Enemy

You've probably heard of human papillomavirus, or HPV, the rampant sexually transmitted disease most often associated with cervical cancer in women. How rampant? Odds are good that you once had the virus, you have it now, or you will contract it soon. In fact, the CDC estimates that half of all sexually active people become HPV positive at some time in their lives. With 6 million new infections each year. HPV is the most widely spread and overexposed STD we've ever known—the Kim Kardashian of communicable diseases, if you will.

The reason HPV moves around the way it does has to do with its stealth: In 99 percent of cases, the disease is symptom-free. (The remaining 1 percent present as bumpy, cauliflowery warts on the penis or groin area in men and in and around the vagina in women.) Most people infected with HPV have no idea they have it, who they contracted it from, or that they could be infecting others.

Cancer researchers have known about HPV's connection with cervical cancer since the 1970s, but they've only recently discovered a similar link between the virus and oral cancer. For years, the rate of new head and neck cancers had been declining in tandem with falling smoking rates. But then, after noticing a major upswing in the number of young nonsmokers being diagnosed with oropharyngeal cancer—a form of oral cancer found in the tonsils and in the base of the tongue—doctors at Johns Hopkins acted on a hunch and began testing cancerous tissue for HPV. The resulting study, published in the *New England Journal of Medicine,* revealed that exposure to HPV-16, a high-risk strain known to cause cervical cancer, made patients 32 times as likely to develop oropharyngeal cancer. By comparison, the previous top risk factors—a history of heavy smoking and a history of heavy drinking—were found to increase that risk by just 3 and 2.5 times, respectively.

"HPV is replacing alcohol and smoking as the leading cause of oropharyngeal cancer," says Ted Teknos, M.D., a professor of medicine in the head and neck oncology program at Ohio State University's comprehensive cancer center. HPV fuels cancerous growth in a man's mouth much as it does in a woman's cervix: by integrating into his DNA and hindering the function of proteins that are supposed to reduce cellular stress and suppress tumors.

Figures from the National Cancer Institute reveal that between 1998 and 2008, oropharyngeal cancer rates rose 36 percent in men—or 3.6 percent each year on average. And sometimes its victims are shockingly young, even men in their late 30s, says Robert Haddad, M.D., chief of the center for head and neck oncology at the Dana-Farber Cancer Institute. "Many of these cases are missed or diagnosed late because there are no symptoms until it's moved into the lymph nodes; plus, the patient is young and otherwise healthy," he says.

Many doctors view the increase in HPV-related oral cancer as a direct result of a change in sexual practices in the past decade—that is, our orally promiscuous ways. Because HPV is a locally invasive virus, it can spread to your mouth only through direct contact. (In other words, HPV in or around your penis won't "travel" on its own through your body to your mouth.) The most likely way to contract oral HPV is to perform oral sex on an infected partner. However, simply kissing someone who has oral HPV can also lead to infection, according to many researchers who believe that it's possible for HPV to be transmitted through saliva.

It should seem obvious, then, that oral sex is not safer sex—and that your chances of developing oral cancer increase with every type of sexual encounter. According to the same *New England Journal of Medicine* study, people who have had six or more oral sex partners over the course of their lifetime are nearly nine times as likely to develop oropharyngeal cancer.

"Many people don't think oral sex counts as sex," says Gregory Masters, M.D., an oncologist at the Helen F. Graham Cancer Center in Newark, Delaware, and a spokesman for the American Society of Clinical Oncology. "But oral sex comes with risks. And cancer may be one of them."

"Oral sex comes with risks. And cancer may be one of them."

Is Abstinence the Answer?

The day before Brian Hill was diagnosed with stage four oral cancer, he was skiing at Lake Tahoe. "I felt perfectly normal," recalls Hill, a nonsmoker then in his 40s. "I had no sores on my mouth as far as I was aware of, and no pain." He'd grown a beard for the winter, which unfortunately had camouflaged an enlarged, though painless, lymph node. "By the time I felt it, it was the size of an almond," he says.

After a course of antibiotics proved ineffective, an ear, nose, and throat doctor near Hill's home in Santa Fe performed a fine-needle biopsy and delivered the diagnosis: The lymph node contained cancerous tissue.

Hill, the owner of a medical-device company who'd sold his dental implant business a few years earlier, says he considered himself better educated in matters of oral health than the average person. And yet the tumor, which had originated in his right tonsil, had probably gone undetected for as long as 2 years.

At Houston's MD Anderson Cancer Center, Hill's doctors told him they'd been seeing a great number of nonsmokers with oral cancer, but didn't know why. Hill was treated, he recalls, with "everything but the kitchen sink," including chemo, radiation, and surgery to remove the right side of his neck. It was a brutal process during which he suffered from radiation sickness, relied on heavy-duty painkillers, ate through a tube for a year, and lost more than 50 pounds.

Hill eventually learned that his tumor tested positive for HPV-16, the subtype linked to oral cancer, although he had no idea that he had been carrying the virus. Nor would he have: Although gynecologists screen sexually active women for cervical HPV as part of routine annual exams, there is no commercially available HPV test for men and no reliable oral-HPV test for either sex.

Part of the reason no good screening options have been developed is because researchers and doctors share a "why bother?" mentality: In 90 percent of cases, a person's immune system will clear the virus naturally within 2 years, with no lasting implications. Furthermore, unlike cervical HPV—which can be managed by removing infected cells—there's no way to treat oral HPV.

But screening is also challenging because HPV is so very squirrelly: The virus can lie dormant and undetectable, yet transmissible, for years. This is why most doctors say it's pointless for people in monogamous relationships to change their sexual habits in the aftermath of an HPV-positive determination. Chances are, both partners have already been exposed.

For everyone else, however, most doctors do advise a change in sexual practice to reduce risk, including using protection when giving or receiving oral sex, and limiting your number of partners.

That said, there is one other promising preventive measure, at least for the next generation of men: vaccination. Two vaccines currently on the market—Gardasil and Cervarix—target HPV-16: they're 95 percent effective in girls and young women and 90 percent effective in boys and young men when administered before exposure to the strain. But despite the impressive percentages, vaccination is a controversial issue for many parents, in part because the possible side effects include fever, fainting, and (rarely) severe allergic reaction and blood clots. Some parents also have trouble with the idea of protecting their prepubescent kids from a virus related to sex, while other parents, mistakenly believing that HPV affects only girls (in the form of cervical cancer), assume that vaccinating boys is irrelevant. The result: Roughly 4 percent of boys have received the shot. Last year, in a move that may sway hesitant parents, the American Academy of Pediatrics included HPV in its schedule of vaccines for boys.

Got that, dads?

The Dentist Defense

Before you tick off your girlfriend and tell her you've decided to abstain from oral sex, keep in mind that several things have to go wrong for HPV to leave you DOA. First, you need to contract the dangerous HPV-16 strain of the disease (an estimated 1.5 percent of women have it). Next, your immune system has to come up short in trying to clear the virus. And then, even if these two conditions are met, you still may not develop cancer. But if you do? Doctors point out that compared with tobacco-related oral cancer, those cancers associated with HPV are much more beatable.

"The cure rates are in the 80 to 90 percent range, assuming patients are nonsmokers," says Dr. Haddad. "Part of the reason is that these patients are younger and in good shape and can tolerate aggressive treatment."

Consider Bryan Hill. He's been cancer-free for more than a decade, during which he founded the nonprofit Oral Cancer Foundation, a charity that sponsors research, patient support, and public awareness. Statler is also in remission; however, like Hill, he needed radiation, chemotherapy, and extensive surgery—doctors removed 44 cancerous lymph nodes and half his jaw.

Even though Statler's and Hill's cases are success stories, earlier diagnosis would have made their treatment and recovery less invasive and less physically taxing. In most cases, this means spotting a premalignant lesion or change in mouth tissue. While researchers are looking into the possibility of using DNA samples to detect precancerous changes in oral tissue cells, that technology is still years away. Until then, your dentist may be your best hope.

The American Dental Association recommends that dentists perform regular visual and physical exams to look for changes in and around the mouth and throat. No one else knows their way around this part of your body like they do. Ideally, the dentist will catch a tissue change before it becomes dangerous, or spot an abnormal growth in its early stages.

John C. Comisi, D.D.S., a dentist in private practice in Ithaca, New York, says he's caught dozens of precancerous lesions in the mouths of men as young as their 30s. "Anything that looks abnormal or persists over a period of a few weeks should be tested," says Dr. Comisi. "Any abnormality should be treated aggressively and removed. You can't be too sure."

Of course, no dentist will catch everything—just ask Statler, who was told his tumor pain was a toothache. That's why every

man should be aware of the possible warning signs of oral cancer: persistent sore throat, hoarseness or unexplained cough, painful sores, any swelling in your lymph nodes or neck, or a change in your voice or trouble swallowing. Your dentist or an ENT specialist should vet any suspicious condition present for longer than 2 weeks.

There's one more thing: Keep enjoying your sex life. You may never contract HPV, let alone develop cancer. But if you live in fear of either possibility, you'll be giving in to an affliction that no surgery or chemotherapy can beat. Statler certainly hasn't backed down: "For now, my wife and I haven't changed what we do in the bedroom." he says. "I just try to have as much sex with her as I can."

"The tumor in his right tonsil had probably gone undetected for 2 years."

Critical Thinking

1. What are the risk factors for oral cancers?
2. How are oral cancers and the human papilloma virus (HPV) related?

Create Central

www.mhhe.com/createcentral

Internet References

American Cancer Society
    www.cancer.org
Centers for Disease Control and Prevention
    www.cdc.gov/
Planned Parenthood
    www.plannedparenthood.org

Article   Prepared by: Eileen Daniel, *SUNY College at Brockport*

Giving ADHD a Rest: with Diagnosis Rates Exploding Wildly, Is the Disorder a Mental Health Crisis—or a Cultural One?

KATE LUNAU

Learning Outcomes

After reading this article, you will be able to:

- Discuss whether the ADHD epidemic is a mental health crisis or a cultural and/or social one.

- Explain why the rate of children diagnosed with ADHD is so much higher in North Carolina than California.

- Understand some of the causes of ADHD misdiagnoses.

Any visitor to North Carolina and California will know that the two states have their differences. The former is a typically "red state"; California is staunchly "blue." Each has certain geographic, ethnic and cultural peculiarities, different demographic makeup, family income levels, and more. Yet perhaps the most surprising divide, one many wouldn't expect, is that North Carolina appears to be a hotbed for attention deficit hyperactivity disorder, or ADHD—especially when compared to California. A child who lived in North Carolina instead of California in 2007, according to U.S. academics Stephen Hinshaw and Richard Scheffler, was 2½ times more likely to be diagnosed.

In their forthcoming book *The ADHD Explosion,* Hinshaw and Scheffler—a psychologist and health economist, respectively, at the University of California at Berkeley—examine the causes behind the startling and rapid rise in diagnosis rates

of ADHD, a neurobehavioural disorder that has somehow become epidemic. In the U.S., more than one in 10 kids has been diagnosed; more than 3.5 million are taking drugs to curb symptoms, from lack of focus to hyperactivity. While ADHD typically hits middle-class boys the hardest, rates among other groups are steadily rising, including girls, adults, and minorities. Kids are being tested and diagnosed as young as preschool. In North Carolina, as many as 30 percent of teenage boys are diagnosed. Scheffler says, "It's getting scary."

According to psychologist Enrico Gnaulati, who is based in Pasadena, California, ADHD is now "as prevalent as the common cold." Various factors seem to be driving up the numbers, factors that extend from home to school to the doctor's office and beyond. "So many kids have trouble these days," says longtime ADHD researcher L. Alan Sroufe, professor emeritus at the University of Wisconsin at Madison. "I doubt it's a change in our genetic pool. Something else is going on."

A closer look at the case of North Carolina and California may be instructive. According to Hinshaw and Scheffler, North Carolinian kids between the ages of four and 17 had an ADHD diagnosis rate of 16 percent in 2007. In California, it was just over 6 percent. Kids with a diagnosis in North Carolina also faced a 50 percent higher probability they'd get medication. After exhaustively exploring demographics, health care policies, cultural values, and other possible factors, they landed on school policy as what Scheffler calls "the closest thing to a silver bullet."

Over the past few decades, incentives have been introduced for U.S. schools to turn out better graduation rates and test scores—and they've been pushed to compete for funding. North Carolina was one of the first states with school accountability laws, disciplining schools for missing targets, and rewarding them for exceeding them. "Such laws provide a real incentive to have children diagnosed and treated," Hinshaw and Scheffler write: kids in special education classes ideally get the help they need to improve their test scores and (in some areas) aren't counted in the district's test score average.

The rate of ADHD diagnosis varies between countries; as Hinshaw and Scheffler have shown, it even varies significantly within countries. This raises an important question: is the ADHD epidemic really a mental health crisis, or a cultural and societal one?

ADHD is a "chronic and debilitating mental disorder," Gnaulati says, one that can last a lifetime. It's believed to affect between 5 and 10 percent of the population, and boys still seem especially prone. (Nearly one in five high school boys have ADHD, compared to 1 in 11 girls, according to the U.S. Centers for Disease Control and Prevention.) Kids with ADHD can have a hard time making and keeping friends. In one study of boys at summer camp, Hinshaw found that after just a few hours, those with an ADHD diagnosis were far more likely to be rejected than those without one. The disorder can persist into adulthood, raising the risk of low self-esteem, divorce, unemployment, and driving accidents; even getting arrested and going to jail, according to a report from the Centre for ADHD Awareness Canada.

In fact, the brains of people with ADHD are different. They're short on receptors for the neurotransmitter dopamine, and their brain volume looks to be slightly smaller. But no medical test or brain scan can yet give a definitive diagnosis. The gold standard comes from the *Diagnostic and Statistical Manual of Mental Disorders*, or DSM, from the American Psychiatric Association. The latest version of this "bible of psychiatry," released in May, lists nine symptoms of inattention (making careless mistakes on homework; distractibility; trouble staying organized), and nine of hyperactivity or impulsivity (interrupting others; climbing when it's inappropriate; and excessive talking, to give some examples). They'll sound familiar to anyone who's spent time with kids. "Every child is to some extent impulsive, distractible, disorganized, and has trouble following directions," says Gnaulati, author of *Back to Normal,* an investigation of why what he calls "ordinary childhood behaviour" is often mistaken for ADHD.

The DSM specifies that a child should be showing many symptoms consistently, in two or more settings (at home and at school, for example), a better indication that he isn't just acting out because of a bad teacher, or an annoying sibling. "Studies show that if you stick to the two-informant requirement, the number of cases falls by 40 percent," says Gnaulati. Surprisingly often, the diagnoses seem to be hastily given, and drugs dispensed.

It was once thought that stimulants affected people with ADHD differently—calming them down, revving up everyone else—but we now know that's not the case. Virtually everybody seems to react the same in the short term, Sroufe says. "They're attention-enhancers. We've known that since the Second World War," when they were given to radar operators to stay awake and focused. Those with true ADHD show bigger gains, partly because their brains may be "underaroused" to begin with, write Hinshaw and Scheffler. (About two-thirds of U.S. kids with a diagnosis get medication; in Canada, it's about 50 percent.) Stimulants have side effects, including suppressing appetite, speeding up the heart rate, and raising blood pressure. Kids who take them for a long time might end up an inch or so shorter, according to Hinshaw and Scheffler's book, because dopamine activity interferes with growth hormone. And those who don't need them will eventually develop a tolerance, needing a greater and greater quantity to get the effect they're after.

"Brain doping" is by now a well-known phenomenon among college and university students across North America. Many students don't see stimulant use as cheating: one 2012 study found that male college students believe it's far more unethical for an athlete to use steroids than for a student to abuse prescription stimulants to ace a test. "Some red-hot parents want to get their kid into Harvard, Berkeley or Princeton," Scheffler says. "They're going to need a perfect score, so they're going to push." With an ADHD diagnosis, students can seek special accommodations at school, like more time on tests including the SAT, a standardized college entrance exam. With parents, students, and even school boards recognizing the potential benefits that come with diagnosis, ADHD is occurring with increasing frequency among groups other than the white middle class, where rates have typically been highest: according to Hinshaw and Scheffler, African American youth are now just as likely, if not more, to be diagnosed and medicated.

Drug advertisements could also be driving rates of diagnosis upward. Hinshaw and Scheffler describe one ad from Johnson & Johnson, maker of the stimulant Concerta, which shows a happy mother and a son who's getting "better test scores at school" and doing "more chores at home," the text reads. "The message is clear: the right pill breeds family harmony," they write. Sometimes, another underlying health problem will be mistakenly diagnosed as ADHD. In his new book, *ADHD Does Not Exist,* Richard Saul documents 25 conditions that can look like ADHD; most common are vision and hearing issues. "Until you get glasses, it's very hard to understand what [the teacher] is speaking about if you can't see the board," he says.

"Same with hearing." Conditions ranging from bipolar disorder to Tourette's syndrome can also be mistaken for ADHD, Saul writes. Despite the strongly worded title of his book, he believes that 20 percent of those diagnosed are "neurochemical distractible impulsive" and have what we'd term ADHD. The rest are being misdiagnosed, and as a result, he says, "the right treatment is being delayed."

Sleep deprivation is another big cause of misdiagnosis. "It's paradoxical, but especially for kids, it does create hyperactivity and impulsivity," says Vatsal Thakkar of New York University's Langone Medical Center. Given mounting academic pressures, and the screens that populate virtually every room, many kids simply aren't getting enough downtime. A child's relative immaturity can factor in, too. In 2012, a study in the Canadian Medical Association Journal found that the youngest kids in a classroom were more likely to have an ADHD diagnosis, and to be prescribed medication. Those born in December are nearly a full year younger than some of their peers, a big difference, especially in kindergarten. (In the U.S., half of all kids with ADHD are diagnosed before age six.)

Gnaulati, who has a son, worries the deck's been stacked against boys, who are more prone to blurt out an answer, run around the classroom, or otherwise act out. "During the kindergarten years, boys are at least a year behind girls in basic self-regulation," he says. Gnaulati notes that school teachers, pediatricians, and school psychologists are all more likely be female—which he argues could be a contributing factor. "In a sense," he writes, "girl behaviour has become the standard by which we judge all kids."

In Canada, we don't track ADHD diagnosis rates as closely as in the U.S. But the rate of diagnosis does look to be picking up here, and elsewhere, too. A study by Hinshaw and Scheffler compared the use of ADHD drugs to countries' per capita gross domestic product. "Richer countries spend more [on ADHD medications]," Scheffler says. "But some countries still spend more than their income would predict." They found that Canada, the U.S., and Australia all had a greater use of these drugs than GDP suggests. A 2013 paper in the British Journal of Medicine notes that Australia saw a 73 percent increase in prescribing rates for ADHD medications between 2000 and 2011. The Netherlands had a similar spike—the prevalence of ADHD, and the rate at which ADHD drugs were prescribed to kids, doubled between 2003 and 2007.

Peter Conrad of Brandeis University, outside Boston, is studying how the DSM definition of ADHD (which we use in Canada) has been exported around the globe, leading to more kids diagnosed and treated. "Until the late '90s, most diagnosis in Europe was done under the World Health Organization's International Classification of Diseases," which is much more strict, he notes. (The ICD, for example, required symptoms of inattention, impulsivity, and hyperactivity, while an older version of the DSM required only two.)

European countries began to adopt the DSM definition, a response to the fact that so much research on ADHD comes out of the U.S.—and the DSM began to be seen as the standard. "France and Italy still have low rates," says Conrad, "partly because they don't use the DSM." A 2013 study from the University of Exeter found that U.K. kids were much less likely than those in the U.S. to be diagnosed with ADHD, which may be due to tougher criteria, or to parents' resistance to medicating their kids. Even so, other countries are catching up. According to Hinshaw and Scheffler, the use of ADHD medication is rising over five times faster around the world than in the U.S.

Many of the same pressures that motivate diagnosis in the U.S. are at play in Canada, although in different ways. Given the tight job market and increasing academic demands, students are under more pressure to succeed than ever. And while our school test results aren't tied to funding like in the U.S., "high-stakes testing" is increasingly important, says Elizabeth Dhuey, a University of Toronto economist who studies education.

For one thing, it's a point of pride for schools. Results from Ontario's EQAO standardized test are reported in the media and used to rank and compare institutions. ("EQAO: How did your school fare in Ontario's standardized tests?" reads one 2012 Toronto Star headline.) What constitutes an "exceptionality" and triggers special services also varies between provinces. In Newfoundland, ADHD has been an "exceptionality" for the past two decades; in Ontario, it isn't considered a special category, but ADHD students can access special education and other extra help on a case-by-case basis. And in B.C., school districts can get supplemental funding for students with ADHD, according to the ministry of education.

These pressures aren't abating—if anything, many are getting stronger—and so, it seems likely we haven't yet reached peak ADHD. Scheffler and Hinshaw raise the possibility that, within the decade, ADHD rates in the U.S. might reach 15 percent or higher; and that as many as four-fifths of those diagnosed could have a prescription.

The hope lies in finding better scientific markers—a definitive test that could confirm true cases of ADHD, and those who will benefit most from treatment, including medication. Otherwise, we're facing the prospect of a generation of kids living with a serious mental health diagnosis, and quite possibly taking powerful drugs long term into adulthood, with all the potential side effects they entail. Whatever is contributing to ADHD's startling rise, it's clear that this isn't a contagious disease kids are swapping on the playground. In many cases, we're giving it to them.

Giving ADHD a Rest: with Diagnosis Rates Exploding Wildly, Is the Disorder a Mental Health Crisis — or a Cultural One? by Kate Lunaue

195

Critical Thinking

1. How are the brains different between individuals with and without ADHD?
2. Why are so many ADHD diagnoses done so hastily resulting in medications dispensed?

Create Central

www.mhhe.com/createcentral

Internet References

Centers for Disease Control and Prevention
    http://www.cdc.gov/ncbddd/ADHD
National Institutes of Mental Health
    http://www.nimh.nih.gov/health/topics/attention-deficit-hyperactivity-disorder-adhd/index.shtml

Kate Lunau, "Giving ADHD a Rest: With Diagnosis Rates Exploding Wildly, Is the Disorder a Mental Health Crisis-or a Cultural One?" from *Maclean's* 127.8 (March 3, 2014).

Article Prepared by: Eileen Daniel, *SUNY College at Brockport*

Hey! Parents, Leave Those Kids Alone

In the past generation, the rising preoccupation with children's safety has transformed childhood, stripping it of independence, risk-taking, and discovery. What's been gained is unclear: rates of injury have remained fairly steady since the 1970s, and abduction by strangers was as rare then as it is now. What's been lost is creativity, passion, and courage. Now a countermovement is arising, based on mounting evidence that today's parenting norms do children more harm than good.

HANNA ROSIN

Learning Outcomes

After reading this article, you will be able to:

- Understand why today's parents are often overly concerned about their children's safety.

- Explain why today's parenting norms may do children more harm than good.

- Describe why reasonable risks may be essential for children's healthy development.

A trio of boys tramps along the length of a wooden fence, back and forth, shouting like carnival barkers. "The Land! It opens in half an hour." Down a path and across a grassy square, five-year-old Dylan can hear them through the window of his nana's front room. He tries to figure out what half an hour is and whether he can wait that long. When the heavy gate finally swings open, Dylan, the boys, and about a dozen other children race directly to their favorite spots, although it's hard to see how they navigate so expertly amid the chaos, "is this a junkyard?" asks my five-year-old son, Gideon, who has come with me to visit. "Not exactly," I tell him, although it's inspired by one. The Land is a playground that takes up nearly an acre at the far end of a quiet housing development in North Wales. It's only two years old but has no marks of newness and could just as well have been here for decades. The ground is muddy in spots and, at one end, slopes down steeply to a creek where a big, faded plastic boat that most people would have thrown away is wedged into the bank.

The center of the playground is dominated by a high pile of tires that is growing ever smaller as a redheaded girl and her friend roll them down the hill and into the creek. "Why are you rolling tires into the water?" my son asks. "Because we are," the girl replies.

It's still morning, but someone has already started a fire in the tin drum in the corner, perhaps because it's late fall and wet-cold, or more likely because the kids here love to start fires. Three boys lounge in the only unbroken chairs around it; they are the oldest ones here, so no one complains. One of them turns on the radio—Shaggy is playing (*Honey came in and she caught me red-handed, creeping with the girl next door*)—as the others feel in their pockets to make sure the candy bars and soda cans are still there. Nearby, a couple of boys are doing mad flips on a stack of filthy mattresses, which makes a fine trampoline. At the other end of the playground, a dozen or so of the younger kids dart in and out of large structures made up of wooden pallets stacked on top of one another. Occasionally a group knocks down a few pallets—just for the fun of it, or to build some new kind of slide or fort or unnamed structure. Come tomorrow and the Land might have a whole new topography.

Other than some walls lit up with graffiti, there are no bright colors, or anything else that belongs to the usual playground landscape: no shiny metal slide topped by a red steering wheel or a tic-tac-toe board; no yellow seesaw with a central ballast to make sure no one falls off; no rubber bucket swing for babies. There is, however, a frayed rope swing that carries you over the creek and deposits you on the other side, if you can make it that far (otherwise it deposits you in the creek). The actual children's toys (a tiny stuffed elephant, a soiled Winnie the Pooh) are ignored, one facedown in the mud, the other sitting behind a green plastic chair. On this day, the kids seem excited by a walker that was donated by one of the elderly neighbors and is repurposed, at different moments, as a scooter, a jail cell, and a gymnastics bar.

The Land is an "adventure playground," although that term is maybe a little too reminiscent of theme parks to capture the vibe. In the U.K., such playgrounds arose and became popular in the 1940s, as a result of the efforts of Lady Marjory Allen of Hurtwood, a landscape architect and children's advocate. Allen was disappointed by what she described in a documentary as "asphalt square" playgrounds with "a few pieces of mechanical equipment." She wanted to design playgrounds with loose parts that kids could move around and manipulate, to create their own makeshift structures. But more important, she wanted to encourage a "free and permissive atmosphere" with as little adult supervision as possible. The idea was that kids should face what to them seem like "really dangerous risks" and then conquer them alone. That, she said, is what builds self-confidence and courage.

The playgrounds were novel, but they were in tune with the cultural expectations of London in the aftermath of World War II. Children who might grow up to fight wars were not shielded from danger; they were expected to meet it with assertiveness and even bravado. Today, these playgrounds are so out of sync with affluent and middle-class parenting norms that when I showed fellow parents back home a video of kids crouched in the dark lighting fires, the most common sentence I heard from them was "This is insane." (Working-class parents hold at least some of the same ideals, but are generally less controlling—out of necessity, and maybe greater respect for toughness.) That might explain why there are so few adventure playgrounds left around the world, and why a newly established one, such as the Land, feels like an act of defiance.

If a 10-year-old lit a fire at an American playground, someone would call the police and the kid would be taken for counseling. At the Land, spontaneous fires are a frequent occurrence. The park is staffed by professionally trained "playworkers," who keep a close eye on the kids but don't intervene all that much. Claire Griffiths, the manager of the Land, describes her job as "loitering with intent." Although the playworkers almost never stop the kids from what they're doing, before the playground had even opened they'd filled binders with "risk benefits assessments" for nearly every activity. (In the two years since it opened, no one has been injured outside of the occasional scraped knee.) Here's the list of benefits for fire: "It can be a social experience to sit around with friends, make friends, to sing songs to dance around, to stare at, it can be a co-operative experience where everyone has jobs. It can be something to

experiment with, to take risks, to test its properties, its heat, its power, to re-live our evolutionary past." The risks? "Burns from fire or fire pit" and "children accidentally burning each other with flaming cardboard or wood." In this case, the benefits win, because a playworker is always nearby, watching for impending accidents but otherwise letting the children figure out lessons about fire on their own.

"I'm gonna put this cardboard box in the fire," one of the boys says.

"You know that will make a lot of smoke," says Griffiths.

"Where there's smoke, there's fire," he answers, and in goes the box. Smoke instantly fills the air and burns our eyes. The other boys sitting around the fire cough, duck their heads, and curse him out. In my playground set, we would call this "natural consequences," although we rarely have the nerve to let even much tamer scenarios than this one play out. By contrast, the custom at the Land is for parents not to intervene. In fact, it's for parents not to come at all. The dozens of kids who passed through the playground on the day I visited came and went on their own. In seven hours, aside from Griffiths and the other playworkers, I saw only two adults: Dylan's nana, who walked him over because he's only 5, and Steve Hughes, who runs a local fishing-tackle shop and came by to lend some tools.

Griffiths started selling local families on the proposed playground in 2006. She talked about the health and developmental benefits of freer outdoor play and explained that the playground would look messy but be fenced in. But mostly she made an appeal rooted in nostalgia. She explained that some of the things kids might be able to do and then asked the parents to remember their own childhoods. "Ahh, did you never used to do that?" she would ask. This is how she would win them over. Hughes moved to the neighborhood after the Land was already open, but when he stopped by, I asked how he would have answered that question. "When I was a kid, we didn't have all the rules about health and safety," he said. "I used to go swimming in the Dee, which is one of the most dangerous rivers around. If my parents had found out, they would have grounded me for life. But back then we would get up to all sorts of mischief."

Like most parents my age, I have memories of childhood so different from the way my children are growing up that sometimes I think I might be making them up or at least exaggerating them. I grew up on a block of nearly identical six-story apartment buildings in Queens, New York. In my elementary-school years, my friends and I spent a lot of afternoons playing cops and robbers in two interconnected apartment garages, after we discovered a door between them that we could pry open. Once, when I was about 9, my friend Kim and I "locked" a bunch of younger kids in an imaginary jail behind a low gate. Then Kim and I got hungry and walked over to Alba's pizzeria a few blocks away and forgot all about them. When we got back an hour later, they were still standing in the same spot. They never hopped over the gate, even though they easily could have; their parents never came looking for them, and no one expected them to. A couple of them were pretty upset, but back then, the code between kids ruled. We'd told them they were in jail, so they stayed in jail until we let them out. A parent's opinion on their term of incarceration would have been irrelevant.

I used to puzzle over a particular statistic that routinely comes up in articles about time use: even though women work vastly more hours now than they did in the 1970s, mothers—and fathers—of all income levels spend much more time with their children than they used to. This seemed impossible to me until recently, when I began to think about my own life. My mother didn't work all that much when I was younger, but she didn't spend vast amounts of time with me, either. She didn't arrange my playdates or drive me to swimming lessons or introduce me to cool music she liked. On weekdays after school, she just expected me to show up for dinner; on weekends I barely saw her at all. I, on the other hand, might easily spend every waking Saturday hour with one if not all three of my children, taking one to a soccer game, the second to a theater program, the third to a friend's house, or just hanging out with them at home. When my daughter was about 10, my husband suddenly realized that in her whole life, she had probably not spent more than 10 minutes unsupervised by an adult. Not 10 minutes in 10 years.

It's hard to absorb how much childhood norms have shifted in just one generation. Actions that would have been considered paranoid in the 1970s—walking third graders to school, forbidding your kid to play ball in the street, going down the slide with your child in your lap—are now routine. In fact, they are the markers of good, responsible parenting. One very thorough study of "children's independent mobility," conducted in urban, suburban, and rural neighborhoods in the U.K., shows that in 1971, 80 percent of third graders walked to school alone. By 1990, that measure had dropped to 9 percent, and now it's even lower. When you ask parents why they are more protective than their parents were, they might answer that the world is more dangerous than it was when they were growing up. But this isn't true, or at least not in the way that we think. For example, parents now routinely tell their children never to talk to strangers, even though all available evidence suggests that children have about the same (very slim) chance of being abducted by a stranger as they did a generation ago. Maybe the real question is, how did these fears come to have such a hold over us? And what have our children lost—and gained—as we've succumbed to them?

In 1978, a toddler named Frank Nelson made his way to the top of a 12-foot slide in Hamlin Park in Chicago, with his mother, Debra, a few steps behind him. The structure, installed three years earlier, was known as a "tornado slide" because it twisted on the way down, but the boy never made it that far. He fell through the gap between the handrail and the steps and landed on his head on the asphalt. A year later, his parents sued the Chicago Park District and the two companies that had manufactured and installed the slide. Frank had fractured his skull in the fall and suffered permanent brain damage. He was paralyzed on his left side and had speech and vision problems. His attorneys noted that he was forced to wear a helmet all the time to protect his fragile skull.

The Nelsons' was one of a number of lawsuits of that era that fueled a backlash against potentially dangerous playground equipment. Theodora Briggs Sweeney, a consumer advocate and safety consultant from John Carroll University, near Cleveland, testified at dozens of trials and became a public crusader for playground reform. "The name of the playground game will continue to be Russian roulette, with the child as unsuspecting victim," Sweeney wrote in a 1979 paper published in *Pediatrics.* She was concerned about many things—the heights of slides, the space between railings, the danger of loose S-shaped hooks holding parts together—but what she worried about most was asphalt and dirt. In her paper, Sweeney declared that lab simulations showed children could die from a fall of as little as a foot if their head hit asphalt, or three feet if their head hit dirt.

A federal-government report published around that time found that tens of thousands of children were turning up in the emergency room each year because of playground accidents. As a result, the U.S. Consumer Product Safety Commission in 1981 published the first "Handbook for Public Playground Safety," a short set of general guidelines—the word guidelines was in bold, to distinguish the contents from requirements—that should govern the equipment. For example, no component of any equipment should form angles or openings that could trap any part of a child's body, especially the head.

To turn up the pressure, Sweeney and a fellow consultant on playground safety, Joe Frost, began cataloguing the horrors that befell children at playgrounds. Between them, they had testified in almost 200 cases and could detail gruesome specifics—several kids who had gotten their heads trapped or crushed by merry-go-rounds; one who was hanged by a jump rope attached to a deck railing; one who was killed by a motorcycle that crashed into an unfenced playground; one who fell while playing football on rocky ground. In a paper they wrote together, Sweeney and Frost called for "immediate inspection" of all equipment that had been installed before 1981, and the removal of anything faulty. They also called for playgrounds nationwide to incorporate rubber flooring in crucial areas.

In January 1985, the Chicago Park District settled the suit with the Nelsons. Frank Nelson was guaranteed a minimum of $9.5 million. Maurice Thominet, the chief engineer for the Park District, told the *Chicago Tribune* that the city would have to "take a cold, hard look at all of our equipment" and likely remove all the tornado slides and some other structures. At the time, a reader wrote to the paper:

> Do accidents happen anymore? . . .
>
> Can a mother take the risk of taking her young child up to the top of a tornado slide, with every good intention, and have an accident?
>
> Who is responsible for a child in a park, the park district or the parent? . . . Swings hit one-year-old children in the head, I'm sure with dire consequences in some instances. Do we eliminate swings?

But these proved to be musings from a dying age. Around the time the Nelson settlement became public, park departments all over the country began removing equipment newly considered dangerous, partly because they could not afford to be sued, especially now that a government handbook could be used by litigants as proof of standards that parks were failing to meet. In anticipation of lawsuits, insurance premiums skyrocketed. As the *Tribune* reader had intuited, the cultural understanding of acceptable risk began to shift, such that any known risk became nearly synonymous with hazard.

Over the years, the official consumer-product handbook has gone through several revisions; it is now supplemented by a set of technical guidelines for manufacturers. More and more, the standards are set by engineers and technical experts and lawyers, with little meaningful input from "people who know anything about children's play," says William Weisz, a design consultant who has sat on several committees overseeing changes to the guidelines. The handbook includes specific prescriptions for the exact heights, slopes, and other angles of nearly every piece of equipment. Rubber flooring or wood chips are virtually required; grass and dirt are "not considered protective surfacing because wear and environmental factors can reduce their shock absorbing effectiveness."

It is no longer easy to find a playground that has an element of surprise, no matter how far you travel. Kids can find the same slides at the same heights and angles as the ones in their own neighborhood, with many of the same accessories. I live in Washington, D.C., near a section of Rock Creek Park, and during my first year in the neighborhood, a remote corner of the park dead-ended into what our neighbors called the forgotten playground. The slide had wooden steps and was at such a steep angle that kids had to practice controlling their speed so they wouldn't land too hard on the dirt. More glorious, a

freestanding tree house perched about 12 feet off the ground, where the neighborhood kids would gather and sort themselves into the pack hierarchies I remember from my childhood—little kids on the ground "cooking" while the bigger kids dominated the high shelter. But in 2003, nearly a year after I moved in, the park service tore down the tree house and replaced all the old equipment with a prefab playground set on rubber flooring. Now the playground can hold only a toddler's attention, and not for very long. The kids seem to spend most of their time in the sandbox; maybe they like it because the neighbors have turned it into a mini adventure playground, dropping off an odd mixing spoon or colander or broken-down toy car.

In recent years, Joe Frost, Sweeney's old partner in the safety crusade, has become concerned that maybe we have gone too far. In a 2006 paper, he gives the example of two parents who sued when their child fell over a stump in a small redwood forest that was part of a playground. They had a basis for the lawsuit. After all, the latest safety handbook advises designers to "look out for tripping hazards, like exposed concrete footings, tree stumps, and rocks." But adults have come to the mistaken view "that children must somehow be sheltered from all risks of injury," Frost writes. "In the real world, life is filled with risks—financial, physical, emotional, social—and reasonable risks are essential for children's healthy development."

At the core of the safety obsession is a view of children that is the exact opposite of Lady Allen's, "an idea that children are too fragile or unintelligent to assess the risk of any given situation," argues Tim Gill, the author of No Fear, a critique of our risk-averse society. "Now our working assumption is that children cannot be trusted to find their way around tricky physical or social and emotional situations."

What's lost amid all this protection? In the mid-1990s, Norway passed a law that required playgrounds to meet certain safety standards. Ellen Sandseter, a professor of early-childhood education at Queen Maud University College in Trondheim, had just had her first child, and she watched as one by one the playgrounds in her neighborhood were transformed into sterile, boring places. Sandseter had written her master's dissertation on young teens and their need for sensation and risk; she'd noticed that if they couldn't feed that desire in some socially acceptable way, some would turn to more-reckless behavior. She wondered whether a similar dynamic might take hold among younger kids as playgrounds started to become safer and less interesting.

Sandseter began observing and interviewing children on playgrounds in Norway. In 2011, she published her results in a paper called "Children's Risky Play From an Evolutionary Perspective: The Anti-Phobic Effects of Thrilling Experiences." Children, she concluded, have a sensory need to taste danger and excitement; this doesn't mean that what they do has to actually be dangerous, only that they *feel* they are taking a great risk. That scares them, but then they overcome the fear. In the paper, Sandseter identifies six kinds of risky play: (1) Exploring heights, or getting the "bird's perspective," as she calls it—"high enough to evoke the sensation of fear." (2) Handling dangerous tools—using sharp scissors or knives or heavy hammers that at first seem unmanageable but that kids learn to master. (3) Being near dangerous elements—playing near vast bodies of water, or near a fire, so kids are aware that there is danger nearby. (4) Rough-and-tumble play—wrestling, play-fighting—so kids learn to negotiate aggression and cooperation. (5) Speed—cycling or skiing at a pace that feels too fast. (6) Exploring on one's own.

This last one Sandseter describes as "the most important for the children." She told me, "When they are left alone and can take full responsibility for their actions, and the consequences of their decisions, it's a thrilling experience."

To gauge the effects of losing these experiences, Sandseter turns to evolutionary psychology. Children are born with the instinct to take risks in play because historically, learning to negotiate risk has been crucial to survival; in another era, they would have had to learn to run from some danger, defend themselves from others, be independent. Even today, growing up is a process of managing fears and learning to arrive at sound decisions. By engaging in risky play, children are effectively subjecting themselves to a form of exposure therapy, in which they force themselves to do the thing they're afraid of in order to overcome their fear. But if they never go through that process, the fear can turn into a phobia. Paradoxically, Sandseter writes, "our fear of children being harmed," mostly in minor ways, "may result in more fearful children and increased levels of psychopathology." She cites a study showing that children who injured themselves falling from heights when they were between 5 and 9 years old are less likely to be afraid of heights at age 18. "Risky play with great heights will provide a desensitizing or habituating experience," she writes.

We might accept a few more phobias in our children in exchange for fewer injuries. But the final irony is that our close attention to safety has not in fact made a tremendous difference in the number of accidents children have. According to the National Electronic Injury Surveillance System, which monitors hospital visits, the frequency of emergency-room visits related to playground equipment, including home equipment, in 1980 was 156,000, or one visit per 1,452 Americans. In 2012, it was 271,475, or one per 1,156 Americans. The number of deaths hasn't changed much either. From 2001 through 2008, the Consumer Product Safety Commission reported 100 deaths associated with playground equipment—an average of 13 a year, or 10 fewer than were reported in 1980. Head injuries, runaway motorcycles, a fatal fall onto a rock—most of the

horrors Sweeney and Frost described all those years ago turn out to be freakishly rare, unexpected tragedies that no amount of safety proofing can prevent.

Even rubber surfacing doesn't seem to have made much of a difference in the real world. David Ball, a professor of risk management at Middlesex University, analyzed U.K. injury statistics and found that as in the U.S., there was no clear trend over time. "The advent of all these special surfaces for playgrounds has contributed very little, if anything at all, to the safety of children," he told me. Ball has found some evidence that long-bone injuries, which are far more common than head injuries, are actually increasing. The best theory for that is "risk compensation"—kids don't worry as much about falling on rubber, so they're not as careful, and end up hurting themselves more often. The problem, says Ball, is that "we have come to think of accidents as preventable and not a natural part of life."

The category of risky play on Sandseter's list that likely makes this current generation of parents most nervous is the one involving children getting lost, or straying from adult supervision. "Children love to walk off alone and go exploring away from the eyes of adults," she writes. They "experience a feeling of risk and danger of getting lost" when "given the opportunity to 'cruise' on their own exploring unknown areas; still, they have an urge to do it." Here again Sandseter cites evidence showing that the number of separation experiences before age 9 correlates negatively with separation-anxiety symptoms at age 18, "suggesting an 'inoculation' effect."

But parents these days have little tolerance for children's wandering on their own, for reasons that, much like the growing fear of playground injuries, have their roots in the 1970s. In 1979, nine months after Frank Nelson fell off that slide in Chicago, six-year-old Etan Patz left his parents' downtown New York apartment to walk by himself to the school-bus stop. Etan had been begging his mother to let him walk by himself; many of his friends did and that morning was the first time she let him. But, as just about anyone who grew up in New York in that era knows, he never came home. (In 2012, a New Jersey man was arrested for Etan's murder.) I was nearly 10 at the time, and I remember watching the nightly news and seeing his school picture, with a smile almost as wide as Mick Jagger's. I also remember that, sometime during those weeks of endless coverage of the search for Etan, the parents in my neighborhood for the first time organized a walk pool to take us to the bus stop.

The Etan Patz case launched the era of the ubiquitous missing child, as Paula Fass chronicles in *Kidnapped: Child Abduction in America.* Children's faces began to appear on milk cartons, and Ronald Reagan chose the date of Etan's disappearance as National Missing Children's Day. Although no one knew what had happened to Etan, a theory developed that he had been sexually abused; soon *The New York Times* quoted a psychologist who said that the Patz case heralded an "epidemic of sexual abuse of children." In a short period, writes Fass, Americans came to think child molestations were very prevalent. Over time, the fear drove a new parenting absolute: children were never to talk to strangers.

But abduction cases like Etan Patz's were incredibly uncommon a generation ago, and remain so today. David Finkelhor is the director of the Crimes Against Children Research Center and the most reliable authority on sexual abuse and abduction statistics for children. In his research, Finkelhor singles out a category of crime called the "stereotypical abduction," by which he means the kind of abduction that's likely to make the news, during which the victim disappears overnight, or is taken more than 50 miles away, or is killed. Finkelhor says these cases remain exceedingly rare and do not appear to have increased since at least the mid-1980s, and he guesses the 1970s, although he was not keeping track then. Overall, crimes against children have been declining, in keeping with the general crime drop since the 1990s. A child from a happy, intact family who walks to the bus stop and never comes home is still a singular tragedy, not a national epidemic.

One kind of crime that *has* increased, says Finkelhor, is family abduction (which is lumped together with stereotypical abduction in FBI crime reports, accounting for the seemingly alarming numbers sometimes reported in the media). The explosion in divorce in the 1970s meant many more custody wars and many more children being smuggled away by one or the other of their parents. If a mother is afraid that her child might be abducted, her ironclad rule should not be *Don't talk to strangers*. It should be *Don't talk to your father.*

The gap between what people fear (abduction by a stranger) and what's actually happening (family turmoil and custody battles) is revealing. What has changed since the 1970s is the nature of the American family, and the broader sense of community. For a variety of reasons—divorce, more single-parent families, more mothers working—both families and neighborhoods have lost some of their cohesion. It is perhaps natural that trust in general has eroded and that parents have sought to control more closely what they can—most of all, their children.

As we parents began to see public spaces—playgrounds, streets, public ball fields, and the distance between school and home—as dangerous, other, smaller daily decisions fell into place. Ask any of my parenting peers to chronicle a typical week in their child's life and they will likely mention school, homework, after-school classes, organized playdates, sports teams coached by a fellow parent, and very little free, unsupervised time. Failure to supervise has become, in fact, synonymous with failure to parent. The result is a "continuous and ultimately dramatic decline in children's opportunities to play and explore in their own chosen ways," writes Peter Gray, a psychologist at Boston College and the author of *Free to Learn.* No more pickup games, idle walks home from school, or cops and robbers in the garage all afternoon. The child culture from my Queens days, with its own traditions and codas, its particular pleasures and distresses, is virtually extinct.

In 1972, the British-born geography student Roger Hart settled on an unusual project for his dissertation. He moved to a rural New England town and, for two years, tracked the movements of 86 children in the local elementary school, to create what he called a "geography of children," including actual maps that would show where and how far the children typically roamed away from home. Usually research on children is conducted by interviewing parents, but Hart decided he would go straight to the source. The principal of the school lent him a room, which became known as "Roger's room," and he slowly got to know the children. Hart asked them questions about where they went each day and how they felt about those places, but mostly he just wandered around with them. Even now, as a father and a settled academic, Hart has a dreamy, puckish air. Children were comfortable with him and loved to share their moments of pride, their secrets. Often they took him to places adults had never seen before—playhouses or forts the kids had made just for themselves.

Hart's methodology was novel, but he didn't think he was recording anything radical. Many of his observations must have seemed mundane at the time. For example: "I was struck by the large amount of time children spend modifying the landscape in order to make places for themselves and for their play." But reading his dissertation today feels like coming upon a lost civilization, a child culture with its own ways of playing and thinking and feeling that seems utterly foreign now. The children spent immense amounts of time on their own, creating imaginary landscapes their parents sometimes knew nothing about. The parents played no role in their coming together— "it is through cycling around that the older boys chance to fall into games with each other," Hart observed. The forts they built were not praised and cooed over by their parents because their parents almost never saw them.

Through his maps, Hart discovered broad patterns: between second and third grades, for instance, the children's "free range"—the distance they were allowed to travel away from home without checking in first—tended to expand significantly because they were permitted to ride bikes alone to a friend's house or to a ball field. By fifth grade, the boys especially gained a "dramatic new freedom" and could go pretty much wherever they wanted without checking in at all. (The girls were more restricted because they often helped their mothers with chores or errands, or stayed behind to look after younger siblings.) To the children, each little addition to their free range—being allowed to cross a paved road, or go to the center of town—was a sign of growing up. The kids took special pride, Hart noted, in "knowing how to get places," and in finding shortcuts that adults wouldn't normally use.

Hart's research became the basis for a BBC documentary, which he recently showed me in his office at the City University of New York. One long scene takes place across a river where the kids would go to build what they called "river houses," structures made from branches and odds and ends they'd snuck out from home. In one scene, Joanne and her sister Sylvia show the filmmakers the "house" they made, mostly from orange and brown sheets slung over branches. The furniture has been built with love and wit—the TV, for example, is a crate on a rock with a magazine glamour shot taped onto the front. The phone is a stone with a curled piece of wire coming out from under it.

The girls should be self-conscious because they are being filmed, but they are utterly at home, flipping their hair, sitting close to each other on crates, and drawing up plans for how to renovate. Nearby, their four-year-old brother is cutting down a small tree with a hatchet for a new addition. The girls and their siblings have logged hundreds of hours here over the years; their mother has never been here, not once, they say, because she doesn't like to get her toes wet.

In another scene, Andrew and Jenny, a brother and sister who are 6 and 4, respectively, explore a patch of woods to find the best ferns to make a bed with. Jenny walks around in her knee-high white socks, her braids swinging, looking for the biggest fronds. Her big brother tries to arrange them just so. The sun is shining through the dense trees and the camera stays on the children for a long time. When they are satisfied with their bed, they lie down next to each other. "Don't take any of my ferns," Jenny scolds, and Andrew sticks his tongue out. At this point, I could hear in my head the parent intervening: "Come on, kids, share. There's plenty to go around." But no parents are there; the kids have been out of their sight for several hours now. I teared up while watching the film, and it was only a few days later that I understood why. In all my years as a parent, I have never come upon children who are so inwardly focused, so in tune with each other, so utterly absorbed by the world they've created, and I think that's because in all my years as a parent, I've mostly met children who take it for granted that they are always being *watched.*

In 2004, Hart returned to the same town to do a follow-up study. His aim was to reconnect with any kids he had written about who still lived within 100 miles of the town and see how they were raising their own children, and also to track some of the kids who now lived in the town. But from the first day he

arrived, he knew he would never be able to do the research in the same way. Hart started at the house of a boy he'd known, now a father, and asked whether he could talk to his son outside. The mother said that they could go in the backyard, but she followed them, always staying about 200 yards behind them. Hart didn't get the sense that the parents were suspicious of him, more that they'd "gotten used to the idea of always being close to their children, and didn't like them going off." He realized that this time around, he could get to the children only through the adults; even the kids didn't seem that interested in talking to him alone; they got plenty of adult attention already. "They were so used to having their lives organized by their parents," he told me. Meanwhile, the new principal at the school said he didn't want Hart doing any research there because it was not directly related to the curriculum.

At one point Hart tracked down Sylvia, one of the girls he'd filmed at the river house. "Roger Hart! Oh my God, my childhood existed," she screamed into the phone. "It's just that I'm always telling people what we used to do, and they don't believe me!" Sylvia was now a suburban mom of two kids (ages 5 and 4), and she and her husband had moved into a new house 30 miles away. When Hart went to visit Sylvia, he filmed the exchange. Standing outside in her backyard, Sylvia tells him she bought this house because she wanted to give her own children the kinds of childhood experiences she'd had, and when she saw the little wooded area out back, her "heart leapt." But "there's no way they'd be out in the woods," she adds. "My hometown is now so diverse, with people coming in and out and lots of transients." Hart reminds her how she used to spend most of her time across the river, playing. "There's no river here," she tells him, then whispers, "and I'm really glad about that." There will soon be a fence around the yard—she mentions the fence several times—"so they'll be contained," and she'll always be able to see her kids from the kitchen window. As Sylvia is being interviewed, her son makes some halfhearted attempts to cut the hedges with a pair of scissors, but he doesn't really seem to know how to do it, and he never strays more than a few inches from his father.

When Hart shows Jenny and Andrew the film of themselves playing in the ferns, they are both deeply moved because they'd never seen a film of themselves as children and because for them, too, the memories had receded into hazy unreality. They are both parents and are still living in that New England town. Of all the people Hart caught up with, they seem to have tried the hardest to create some of the same recreational opportunities for their own children that they'd had. Jenny bought a house, with a barn, near a large patch of woods; she doesn't let her sons watch TV or play video games all that much, instead encouraging them to go the barn and play in the hay or tend the garden. She says that she wouldn't really mind if they strayed into the woods, but "they don't want to go out of sight." Anyway, they get their exercise from the various sports teams they play on. Jenny gets some of her girlish self-back when she talks about how she and the boys pile up rocks in the backyard to build a ski jump or use sticks to make a fort. But Jenny initiates these activities; the boys usually don't discover them on their own.

Among this new set of kids, the free range is fairly limited. They don't roam all that far from home, and they don't seem to want to. Hart talked with a law-enforcement officer in the area, who said that there weren't all that many transients and that over the years, crime has stayed pretty steady—steadily low. "There's a fear" among the parents, Hart told me, "an exaggeration of the dangers, a loss of trust that isn't totally clearly explainable." Hart hasn't yet published his findings from his more recent research, and he told me he's wary of running into his own nostalgia for the Rousseauean children of his memories. For example, he said that he has to be honest about the things that have improved in the new version of childhood. In the old days, when children were left on their own, child power hierarchies formed fairly quickly, and some children always remained on the bottom or were excluded entirely. Also, fathers were largely absent; now children are much closer to their dads—closer to both their parents than kids were back then. I would add that the 1970s was the decade of the divorce boom, and many children felt neglected by their parents; perhaps today's close supervision is part of a vow not to repeat that mistake. And yet despite all this, Hart can't help but wonder what disappeared with "the erosion of child culture," in which children were "inventing their own activities and building up a kind of community of their own that they knew much more about than their parents."

One common concern of parents these days is that children grow up too fast. But sometimes it seems as if children don't get the space to grow up at all; they just become adept at mimicking the habits of adulthood. As Hart's research shows, children used to gradually take on responsibilities, year by year. They crossed the road, went to the store; eventually some of them got small neighborhood jobs. Their pride was wrapped up in competence and independence, which grew as they tried and mastered activities they hadn't known how to do the previous year. But these days, middle-class children, at least, skip these milestones. They spend a lot of time in the company of adults, so they can talk and think like them, but they never build up the confidence to be truly independent and self-reliant.

Lately parents have come to think along the class lines defined by the University of Pennsylvania sociologist Annette Lareau. Middle-class parents see their children as projects: they engage in what she calls "concerted cultivation," an active pursuit of their child's enrichment. Working-class and poor parents, meanwhile, speak fewer words to their children, watch their progress less closely, and promote what Lareau calls the "accomplishment of natural growth," perhaps leaving the children less prepared to lead middle-class lives as adults. Many people interpret her findings as proof that middle-class parenting styles, in their totality, are superior. But this may be an overly simplistic and self-serving conclusion; perhaps each form of child rearing has something to recommend it to the other.

When Claire Griffiths, the Land's manager, applies for grants to fund her innovative play spaces, she often lists the concrete advantages of enticing children outside: combatting obesity, developing motor skills. She also talks about the same issue Lady Allen talked about all those years ago—encouraging children to take risks so they build their confidence. But the more nebulous benefits of a freer child culture are harder to explain in a grant application, even though experiments bear them out. For example, beginning in 2011, Swanson Primary School in New Zealand submitted itself to a university experiment and agreed to suspend all playground rules, allowing the kids to run, climb trees, slide down a muddy hill, jump off swings, and play in a "loose-parts pit" that was like a mini adventure playground. The teachers feared chaos, but in fact what they got was less naughtiness and bullying—because the kids were too busy and engaged to want to cause trouble, the principal said.

In an essay called "The Play Deficit," Peter Gray, the Boston College psychologist, chronicles the fallout from the loss of the old childhood culture, and it's a familiar list of the usual ills attributed to Millennials: depression, narcissism, and a decline in empathy. In the past decade, the percentage of college-age kids taking psychiatric medication has spiked, according to a 2012 study by the American College Counseling Association. Practicing psychologists have written (in this magazine and others) about the unique identity crisis this generation faces—a fear of growing up and, in the words of Brooke Donatone, a New York-based therapist, an inability "to think for themselves."

In his essay, Gray highlights the work of Kyung-Hee Kim, an educational psychologist at the College of William and Mary and the author of the 2011 paper "The Creativity Crisis." Kim has analyzed results from the Torrance Tests of Creative Thinking and found that American children's scores have declined steadily across the past decade or more. The data show that children have become:

less emotionally expressive, less energetic, less talkative and verbally expressive, less humorous, less imaginative, less unconventional, less lively and passionate, less perceptive, less apt to connect seemingly irrelevant things, less synthesizing, and less likely to see things from a different angle.

The largest drop, Kim noted, has been in the measure of "elaboration," or the ability to take an idea and expand on it in a novel way.

The stereotypes about Millennials have alarmed researchers and parents enough that they've started pushing back against the culture of parental control. Many recent parenting books have called for a retreat, among them *Duct Tape Parenting*, *Baby Knows Best*, and the upcoming *The Kids Will Be Fine*. In her excellent new book, *All Joy and No Fun*, Jennifer Senior takes the route that parents are making themselves miserable by believing they always have to maximize their children's happiness and success.

In the U.K., the safety paranoia is easing up. The British equivalent of the Consumer Product Safety Commission recently released a statement saying it "wants to make sure that mistaken health and safety concerns do not create sterile play environments that lack challenge and so prevent children from expanding their learning and stretching their abilities." When I was in the U.K., Tim Gill, the author of *No Fear*, took me to a newly built London playground that reminded me of the old days, with long, fast slides down a rocky hill, high drops from a climbing rock, and few fenced-in areas. Meanwhile, the Welsh government has explicitly adopted a strategy to encourage active independent play, rather than book learning, among young children, paving the way for a handful of adventure playgrounds like the Land and other play initiatives.

Whether Americans will pick up on the British vibe is hard to say, although some hopeful signs are appearing. There is rising American interest in European-style "forest kindergartens," where kids receive little formal instruction and have more freedom to explore in nature. And in Washington, D.C., not far from where I live, we finally have our first exciting playground since the "forgotten playground" was leveled. Located at a private school called Beauvoir, it has a zip line and climbing structures that kids of all ages perceive as treacherous. I recently met someone who worked on the playground and asked him why the school board wasn't put off by safety concerns, especially since it keeps the park open to the public on weekends. He said that the board was not only concerned about safety but also wanted an exciting playground; the safety guidelines are, after all these years, still just guidelines.

But the real cultural shift has to come from parents. There is a big difference between avoiding major hazards and making every decision with the primary goal of optimizing child safety (or enrichment, or happiness). We can no more create the perfect environment for our children than we can create perfect children. To believe otherwise is a delusion, and a harmful one; remind yourself of that every time the panic rises.

As the sun set over the Land, I noticed out of the corner of my eye a gray bin, like the kind you'd keep your récycling in, about to be pushed down the slope that led to the creek. A kid's head poked out of the top, and I realized it was my son's. Even by my relatively laissez-faire parenting standards, the situation seemed dicey. The light was fading, the slope was very steep, and Christian, the kid who was doing the pushing, was only 7. Also, the creek was frigid, and I had no change of clothes for Gideon.

I hadn't seen much of my son that day. Kids, unparented, take on pack habits, so as the youngest and newest player, he'd been taken care of by the veterans of the Land. I inched close enough to hear the exchange.

"You might fall in the creek," said Christian.

"I know," said Gideon.

Christian had already taught Gideon how to climb up to the highest slide and manage the rope swing. At this point, he'd earned some trust. "I'll push you gently, okay?" "Ready, steady, go!," Gideon said in response. Down he went, and landed in the creek. In my experience, Gideon is very finicky about water. He hates to have even a drop land on his sleeve while he's brushing his teeth. I hadn't rented a car on this trip, and the woman who'd been driving us around had left for a while. I started scheming how to get him new clothes. Could I knock on one of the neighbors' doors? Ask Christian to get his father? Or, failing that, persuade Gideon to sit a while with the big boys by the fire?

"I'm wet," Gideon said to Christian, and then they raced over to claim some hammers to build a new fort.

Critical Thinking

1. Why has the current close attention to safety not made a tremendous difference in the number of accidents children have?

2. Why is there a fear among parents for their children's safety and an exaggeration of the dangers that isn't based on reality?

Create Central

www.mhhe.com/createcentral

Internet References

Children's Safety Network
http://www.childrenssafetynetwork.org/about-csn

Safe Kids Worldwide
http://www.safekids.org

HANNA ROSIN is an Atlantic national correspondent.

Hanna Rosin, "Hey! Parents, Leave Those Kids Alone" from *The Atlantic* (April 2014): 75–86.